## ABOUT THE BOOK

This is no ordinary history, but one that reads like a novel. The excitement of one chapter is pyramided into the next as Idaho's pioneers struggle against the forces of nature and man. And interwoven with the drama are the touches of humor that have long characterized the writing of Rafe Gibbs.

Brought back alive are "Perpetual Motion" McKenzie, the massive trapper who broiled beaver pelts when food supplies ran out in Hells Canyon; Marie Dorion, "Indian Madonna of the Old Oregon Trail," whose wits and courage kept her children alive during a snow-locked winter in the mountains; Captain Elias Davidson Pierce, who managed to stay engaged to a girl in Indiana for 20 years while he hunted for gold in the Far West; "Diamondfield Jack" Davis, whose feuding with sheepmen led to one of the most remarkable of frontier trials; Colonel William H. Dewey, who was convinced that a flourishing city would stem from his flowery hotel amidst the sagebrush—and did; Fred Herrick, the lumber tycoon, whose "board of directors" consisted only of big-game trophies mounted on his office wall; Noah S. Kellogg, whose stubborn burro received the credit for discovering a mountain with a silver lining . . .

The unforgettable characters are many, and their stories, as told here, are never dull.

Printed by Durham and Downey, Inc., Portland, Oregon

# Beckoning the Bold

## *Story of the Dawning of Idaho*

By

**RAFE GIBBS**

Author of *Beacon For Mountain and Plain*

*Illustrated By*

**ALFRED C. DUNN**

THE UNIVERSITY PRESS OF IDAHO

1976

Copyright 1976 by Rafe Gibbs

All rights reserved

First published in the United States of America 1976

Library of Congress Catalog Card No. 76-16212

International Standard Book No. 0-89301-031-6

Printed in the United States of America
by
The University Press of Idaho
A Division of The Idaho Research Foundation, Inc.
University Station, Box 3367
University of Idaho, Moscow, Idaho 83843

Illustrated by Alfred C. Dunn

THIS BOOK IS DEDICATED TO MY WIFE, ELIZABETH,
AND CHILDREN, CHRISTOPHER, GRAYSON,
VIRGINIA, LINDA AND CONSTANCE.
THROUGHOUT THE YEARS OF MY WRITING, THEY
HAVE PROVIDED THE TWO MOST VITAL ELEMENTS
—INSPIRATION AND MOTIVATION.
R.G.

# PREFACE

"Beckoning the Bold" is not an historian's history, but a reporter's account. Idaho's past is covered as if an editor had ordered:

"Do an in-depth story of early Idaho. Get the facts . . . the color . . . the feel of the times. Places and dates are important, but give top priority to the people. There's a story in every man or woman—certainly in the bold ones who pioneered in Idaho."

So if this book doesn't read quite like a history, it was not intended to do so. It is hoped, however, that "Beckoning the Bold" will give special identity to Idaho, will provide meaning for the tourists who pass through it, and will engender pride for those who call it home.

Some will wonder why I wrote about this, and not about that. The answer is simply that I gave priority to what I thought was interesting and meaningful in the hope that it would prove to be the same to others. On this basis, a stage-coach driver got into this book for never being able to live down the accidental flicking off of "Grandma" Renfro's hat with his whip, and a Chinese packer for eating a great number of pies (up to 16 a day).

Important people? Perhaps not. But they added flair and flavor to the times. Besides, we live in an age when more humor is needed, and, if the past can provide some for the present, then stories on the lighter side are worth the telling.

This book was in preparation for quite a while—34 years. That is the amount of time I have spent in Idaho. During those years, I had the privilege of traveling over every corner of the many-cornered State, talking to people, and jotting down notes. As a result, numerous magazine articles on various facets of Idaho emerged. And now this book has come.

It came through the cooperation of Dr. Merle W. Wells, Director of the Idaho Historical Society, and Helen Miller, State Librarian, to whom special appreciation is extended. For assisting me with the research, I am also grateful to Gary M. Bettis and Ardella Morrissey of the Idaho State Library; Larry Jones and James H. Davis of the Idaho Historical Society; Charles Webbert and Rosemary Shull of the University of Idaho Library; Lloyd Howe, Executive Secretary, Idaho Department of Commerce and Development; Maude Cosho, Richard Horton, S. M. (Sam) Barton, Dick and Mary d'Easum, Camille Power, Dorothy Frost Johnson, Vicente Echevarria, John and Jan Myers, George R. Flamm, George Elliott, D. D. DuSault, and Alfred C. Dunn.

Editing of this book, as well as of all other manuscripts which I have produced in the last three decades, was done by my wife, Elizabeth. (A writer can have no greater asset than a wife who is an editor.)

In conclusion then, a lot of people made this book possible. And it is hoped that a lot of people will gain strength in meeting the challenges of the future by reading about the bold pioneers who met the challenges of the past.

Rafe Gibbs

# CONTENTS

Chapter I

# BY BOAT, HORSE AND FOOT

"We proceeded on through a butiful Countrey . . ."

—Captain William Clark on the entry
of the Lewis and Clark Expedition
into Idaho in 1805

Buckskin-clad trappers venturing in quest of beavers where Indians feared to tread, then losing their gains for the year in roistering at the Pierre's Hole spring rendezvous . . . Emigrants pushing westward over the Oregon Trail in ox-drawn covered wagons, and arrows preventing some from making it . . . Prospectors swishing gold pans beside mountain streams, and highwaymen seeking their take . . . Cattlemen and sheepmen hating the sight of each other on the open range, and guns barking . . .

Idaho's early history indeed has much of the tempest about it, but, in a way, the beginning for the state in the Far West occurred in the calm and quiet of President Thomas Jefferson's office in the White House. The only sound was the scratching of a quill pen. Jefferson was drafting a secret message to be presented to Congress on January 18, 1803, asking for an appropriation of $2,500 to send an expedition across the wilderness from St. Louis to the mouth of the Columbia River.

Scholar as well as politician, the President pondered long over the word

1

"expedition," then, no doubt with one of his wry smiles, he interposed the adjective "literary." By "literary expedition" he indicated that he was referring to geographic and scientific research, including studies of flora and fauna. Actually, he was primarily concerned with trade development, but he was not putting all his cards on the congressional table—for various reasons.

For one thing, the President had a good deal going with Napoleon Bonaparte which would double the size of the United States. This was the Louisiana Purchase, which would be concluded on April 30, 1803, and would buy from France for $15,000,000 territory including the present states of Arkansas, Missouri, Iowa, Nebraska, South Dakota, almost all of Oklahoma and Kansas, and large parts of North Dakota, Montana, Wyoming, Minnesota, Colorado and Louisiana. But not all congressmen—particularly some from New England—were happy with the idea, because they feared the voting strength of "future Western states." Certainly, they would not be interested in any expedition hastening development of the area.

The same apprehensions applied to the vast Pacific Northwest—the Oregon Country—at the time stretching from California to Alaska. This territory came with added complications, because it had been explored—mostly along the coast on a hit-or-miss basis—by Great Britain, Spain, Russia and the United States, and all four countries had claims on it. Jefferson figured that an overland expedition to the Pacific Northwest would not only help nail down the United States' claims, but would shift the bulk of fur trading from Great Britain to the United States, and, hopefully, would open a water route across the continent for trade with China.

Especially with Great Britain likely to become alarmed by an American expedition to the Pacific Northwest, "literary" became the key word in Jefferson's proposal. In today's era of probing media, the President's hidden motives would have soon been out. But what became known as the Lewis and Clark Expedition got all the way to the miles-wide mouth of the Columbia as a "literary effort." And, as a result, Idaho, that sleeping giant on the trail, would be awakened to the Nineteenth Century.

On rain-drenched May 14, 1804, the 29 men of the Lewis and Clark Expedition began to row up the Missouri River in their heavily-loaded pirogues—one boat 55 feet long with locks for 22 pairs of oars, a big square sail and a small cannon, and two lesser craft.

The party was led by two native sons of Virginia who had served together under General Anthony Wayne—Captain Meriwether Lewis, the quiet and earnest one who had been gently reared and privately tutored on a plantation next to President Jefferson's, and Captain William Clark, the rough and ready one who had learned about life dodging Indians on the Kentucky frontier.

For 1,600 miles, the men rowed that year. Well, sometimes they had to pull the pirogues over swirling rapids with ropes . . . sometimes—as on a stretch of the river they called the "Deavels race ground"—they had to swim with the boats. By November 3, 1804, they were quite ready to winter in, and began building cabins near a Mandan Indian village of earth lodges (near what is now Mandan, North Dakota). Idahoans have a particular interest in the site, because coming on the stage of the great wilderness drama here was Sacajawea, the Idaho Indian girl of 16 or 17 who was to become the most famous woman of her race, with mountains named after her and statues erected in her honor. She came with no biaring of trumpets as in later pageants depicting her debut, but shyly behind bluff Touissant Charbonneau, French-Canadian *voyageur* from Montreal, who had won her in a gambling game.

"This man wished to hire as an interpriter," wrote Clark, who promptly entered his name on the roster as "Chaubonie," but the captain had misgivings about "Chaubonie's squar" accompanying the expedition. What puzzled Clark was why Charbonneau insisted on taking this one along. She was so very pregnant!

Then it was learned that Sacajawea was a Shoshone from out Idaho way, believed to have been born in what is now the Lemhi Valley. While accompanying her band in quest of buffalo in Montana, she had been captured by warring Minnetarees, who traded her to the Mandans. She was then passed from one Mandan to another until Charbonneau was said to have bet trade goods—probably worth less than a dollar—against her, and won.

Lewis and Clark talked over the matter, and decided that Sacajawea might be of considerable value to the expedition when it got to the Idaho Country. They had been able to learn very little about that area, except that it was supposed to be rugged in parts. So Sacajawea went on the roster, too. Clark, a teasing red-head, even started calilng her "Janey."

Historians have long since downgraded Sacajawea's guiding role on the expedition—it seems that landmark memories of her childhood in Idaho turned out to be hazy—but certainly this writer does not intend to lessen her contribution to history. Even if she had never pointed out a single trail to Lewis and Clark, she would have been a tremendous asset to the expedition. Time and again, her knowledge of Indian dialects proved highly important, but most important was the fact that she was a woman. Indians met on the way to the sea felt that, if a woman was in the party, it was not bent on war.

Sacajawea, however, had difficulties with the delayed birth of her first child, and almost did not make the trip. As she lay moaning on a buffalo robe, Lewis called into consultation Rene Jessaume, a trader, who had gained favor among the Indians by practicing his own version of medicine.

"Got a rattlesnake?" asked Jessaume.

"Just the rattles of one," replied Lewis.

"That's all that is needed."

Crumpling two rings of the rattles between his fingers, Jessaume washed them down Sacajawea's throat with water. In 10 minutes, she brought forth a son.

So, on February 11, 1805, the expedition gained another member, Baptiste, who came along for the ride, strapped to the back of Sacajawea, once again lithe and agile. Just how lithe and agile was demonstrated on May 14, 1805, the first anniversary of the expedition.

The party, on April 7, had again started up the Missouri River for the Far West, and was now in six small canoes and two large pirogues. On May 14, this proud little fleet was moving through Montana when a sudden squall sprang up. Waves from the Missouri rose and roared over the most heavily loaded of the pirogues. In this boat were "our papers, Instruments, books, medicine, a great part of our merchandize and in short almost every article indispensibly necessary to . . . insure the success of the enterprize in which we are now launched to the distance of 2200 miles."

The human cargo? Unfortunately, it included at the helm Charbonneau, who could not swim, and was, according to Lewis, perhaps the most timid waterman in the world. Fortunately, it also included Sacajawea, who could swim like an otter, even with Baptiste presumably strapped in his usual position on her back.

3

With sail up, the pirogue began to twist and turn. A particularly violent gust whipped the brace of the sail out of the hand of the man trying to lower it, and the boat tipped on its side—would have gone completely over if an awning had not given resistance to the water.

Sacajawea, instinctively mindful of a woman's duty to safeguard supplies while on the trail, leaped into the water, and began to shove back to the boat packages and other objects which had spilled overboard. As she was doing this, Charbonneau, with arms raised, cried out to God for *merci* on "my sinful soul."

Private Peter Cruzatte, the bowman, grabbed his rifle, pointed it at Charbonneau, and assured him:

"If you don't take hold of the rudder and do your duty, I'll shoot you instantly."

Night after night, Charbonneau had been quick to dance to Cruzatte's fiddle. Now he responded with equal alacrity to his rifle. He took hold—both of rudder and himself.

As some of the men bailed with kettles, others rowed, and the righted pirogue was brought safely to shore. Lewis wrote:

"The loss we sustained was not so great as we had at first apprehended; our medicine sustained the greatest injury . . . the ballance of our losses consisted of some gardin seeds, a small quantity of gunpowder, and a few culinary articles which fell overboard and sunk. The Indian woman to whom I ascribe equal fortitude and resolution, with any person onboard at the time of the accedent, caught and preserved most of the light articles which were washed overboard."

After things were squared away, Lewis added that "we thought it a proper occasion to console ourselves and cheer the sperits of our men and accordingly took a drink of grog and gave each man a gill of sperits." Sacajawea was not included in the sharing of "sperits," but she received her reward a few days later when the party came to a 50-yard-wide river merging into the Missouri. Lewis and Clark decided to call this stream "Sah-ca-ger-we-ah or Bird Woman's River." Unfortunately, the name did not stick, and the stream today is known uneloquently as Crooked River. But never mind. Sacajawea would have bigger and better things named after her. Even a book would be dedicated to her. (Robert G. Bailey, pioneer printer and historian of Lewiston, dedicated his volume of Idaho historical stories, "River of No Return," to the woman "whose timely aid and assistance helped make possible the greatest nation the world has ever known.")

Near what is now Three Forks, Montana, the expedition left the Missouri River, and took to the Jefferson. The adventurers had stubbornly dragged their boats for 18 miles around the Missouri's Great Falls, but this was worse, and it finally must have begun to dawn on Lewis and Clark that there was no ready water route to the Pacific. But neither Lewis nor Clark got around to putting this discouraging thought on paper.

As the expedition approached Idaho, Lewis and Clark began looking for Indians—more specifically, Indian horses. Lewis, taking with him three men, including George Drewyer (or Drouillard), hunter and interpreter, started scouting ahead on foot, leaving Clark, who had a painful carbuncle on an ankle, struggling behind with the canoes of the main party. (The pirogues had long since been abandoned.)

Thus, on August 12, 1805, members of the party first set foot on Idaho soil

—at the continental divide site called Lewis and Clark Pass (sometimes Lemhi Pass). Unaware of the historical significance of the occasion, the advance party hurried on the next day, and came upon the Shoshone Indian band of Chief Cameahwait. The chief proved friendly—but not friendly enough to part with any horses.

He was suspicious of the strange men who came out of the East—with faces burned Indian-brown from the sun, but with stomachs that were white beneath their shirts. His main concern was that the strangers might be in league with the Blackfeet, feud-foes of the Shoshones. So the chief was neither buying the whites' story nor selling them horses.

In a gesture designed to build good will as well as to allay fears, Lewis demonstrated his rifle and presented it to Cameahwait. This did not turn the trick.

Noting the lean and hungry look of the Indians, Lewis sent out crackshot Drewyer to search for game. To be sure that was what Drewyer was doing—hunting and not getting in touch with the Blackfeet—young braves followed him, leaping and shouting. Despite this handicap, Drewyer shot a deer, and the Indians were soon feeding on it like "a parcel of famished dogs."

Confidence in the whites built up after the advance and main parties again got together. Immediately, there was mutual recognition between Sacajawea and one of the young women of Cameahwait's band. They had played together in their childhood.

Shortly, in what might be considered too much of a coincidence for fiction, Cameahwait realized that Sacajawea was his long lost sister. There was a rare, emotional reunion between brother and sister—rare for the stoical Shoshones. The chief was further softened when Sacajawea fed him a lump of sugar, and he declared he had never tasted anything finer. Not to be outdone, Lewis had his men form a "bush drag" in a creek, and with it in about two hours they caught what would make modern-day fishermen delirious and game wardens explosive—"528 very good fish, most of them large trout." A momentous and mountainous fish feast followed. In the analysis of historians, however, it was not emotion, sugar or fish that produced the horses. It was armaments.

Keeping Cameahwait's pipe well-stoked with Virginia tobacco after the feasting, Lewis explained that, if the expedition were successful, many white traders would follow, bringing many guns to the Shoshones. This would put them bullets up on the Blackfeet.

The expedition got the desperately needed horses—but only 29, allowing just enough for carrying packs and the two leaders, Lewis and Clark. The rest of the party trudged along on foot, although one story has it that Cameahwait, bursting with brotherly love, gave Sacajawea a horse—and later charged Lewis and Clark for it.

Which way to go? The swift Salmon—"River of No Return"—swirled and tumbled spasmodically westward across Idaho. But farther north over the mountains, the Shoshones pointed out, there was a pass used by the Nez Perces—and a gentler stream (the Clearwater River), which flowed into a bigger stream (the Snake River), which, in turn, merged with a still bigger one (the Columbia River). And an old member of Cameahwait's tribe, Swooping Eagle, who became better known as Toby, would be loaned to guide the party to the Clearwater.

So, with Toby leading the way, the adventurers hastened northward through Montana's Bitterroot Valley, anxious to reach trail's end at the sea before winter locked them in the mountains. Winter came early in 1805 to the high country, however. On September 11, when the party turned westward again into Idaho over what is now the Lolo Trail, the mountains were covered with snow. Traveling became hazardous—"several horses sliped and rolled down steep hills." Clark added:

"I have been wet and as cold in every part as I ever was in my life, indeed I was at one time fearful my feet would freeze in the thin Mockersons which I wore."

Some nights the travelers, nearing exhaustion, camped without water. Some days they sacrificed a badly needed horse for meat. Except for an occasional grouse, there was no food to be had with the gun . . . the game had drifted to the lower country. But, oddly enough, it was under these adverse conditions that Clark paid his tribute to the "butifull Countrey"—Idaho.

The beauty was lost on the explorers, however, when late that month they moved out of the high country, and came to a Nez Perce village at the present site of Ahsaka (Narrow) on what the Indians called the Kooskooske River (the Clearwater). Stuffing themselves with gifts of salmon and flour made from camas roots, the travelers became violently ill.

"Our men nearly all Complaining of their bowels," wrote Clark.

The Army at the time had a standard and powerful remedy for this condition —"Rush's calomel and jalap pills"—and Clark forced them down throats. Then, just to be sure, he added economy-sized doses of Glauber's salts and emetics.

On September 29, although Clark indicated that many of the men were "sick as usial," he was able to report that others were at work on the building of canoes.

The Nez Perces plied the river in dugout canoes made from the abundant yellow pine in the area (Idaho's famed white pine—still the world's largest stand—grows farther north), and the whites were anxious to follow suit. With the help of the Indians, the burning out of logs for canoes was expedited.

All the members of the expedition were greatly impressed by the Nez Perces, who had been a part of the land for more than 10,000 years—before the time of Rome, Greece, Egypt or any known civilization. The explorers found these Indians to be "industrious and jolley." The men were "excellent" horsemen as well as rivermen, and their mounts "elegant." (The Nez Perces were the only American Indian tribe which fully understood horse breeding for desired traits, and it was they who developed the spotted horse now known as the Appaloosa. The name Nez Perces—"Pierced Noses"—came from the fact that some members of the tribe pierced their noses for shell ornaments, obtained in trading with coastal Indians.)

Intrigued, Clark gave more detail in describing the Nez Perces than he did in depicting any other Indians he met:

"The Cho-pun-ish or Pierced nose Indians are Stout likely men, handsome women, and verry dressey in their way. the dress of the men are a White Buffalow robe or Elk Skin dressed with Beeds which are generally white, Sea Shells & Mother of Pirl . . . hair ceewed in two parsels hanging forward over their Sholders. . . . The women dress in a Shirt of Ibex or Goat (bighorn) Skins which reach quite down to their anckles with a girdle . . . their Shirts are ornemented with quilled Brass, Small peces of Brass Cut into different forms, Beeds, Shells & curious bones &c . . ."

The chief, whom the whites called Twisted Hair, proved to be particularly

6

friendly. He was grateful for soothing lotions given his people for eye afflictions, but was especially pleased when Lewis presented him with an American flag. To display this, he promptly had a tall flagpole carved out of the forest, inspiring Lewis to give Twisted Hair a second flag—for a war leader who was off doing battle with the Blackfeet. So it was not surprising that on October 7, as the explorers prepared to set off down the Clearwater, the chief volunteered:

"My people will keep your horses. They will be ready for the trail when you return."

With the splitting and sinking of only one canoe in rapids, the new fleet reached the juncture of the Snake River with its "greenish blue waters" flowing between bluffs of an almost treeless plain country—the present site of Lewiston. Catching up with the party at this point were Twisted Hair and another Nez Perce who had decided that Lewis and Clark might need a little help along the way.

Lewis and Clark agreed, and Twisted Hair and the other Indian accompanied the party all the way down the Snake—even to The Dalles on the Columbia. Often, Twisted Hair would go ahead to tell Indians along the rivers that the whites were friendly and were not to be shot at.

At one encampment on the Snake, however, the Indians feared trouble with the whites because they thought they "came from the clouds &c. &c. and were not men"—the first known conjecture in the area of visitors from outer space. Then the Indians spotted Sacajawea, who "confirmed those people of our friendly intentions, as no woman ever accompanies a war party . . . in this quarter."

There is a moral here: The American flag and a woman can get men a long way. But also to ponder is the fact that, when non-Army members of the expedition were finally paid off for their services by the United States government, Charbonneau received $500—his "squar" wife, not a dime.

On the evening of November 7, 1805, Clark wrote with great excitement in his diary:

"Ocian in view! O! the joy."

But Clark had been carried away by the Columbia's broad estuary. Actually, he was only at what is now known as Pillar Rock, and the Pacific was many bends in the river away. It would be almost a month later before he would carve on a giant pine beside "the Great Western Ocian" his famous postscript to 2,000 miles of struggle through the wilderness:

"William Clark December 3rd 1805. By Land from the U.States in 1804 & 1805."

The whispering pine, in a few words, said a lot, but there was no roaring of the crowd in response—only the roaring of the Pacific's winter waves. The great triumph of arrival—of mission accomplished—was witnessed merely by a few Clatsop Indians, who had no idea what it was all about, except that some white people with whom they could trade had arrived. One Clatsop, in fact, happily got the gold-braided jacket off Lewis' back in exchange for a canoe.

The explorers had hoped that a ship might be waiting for them at the mouth of the Columbia, and would take them home via the Horn. But there was none. The *Lydia,* a trading vessel, came near, but the Clatsop Indians who saw it failed to mention the fact to anyone in the Lewis and Clark party.

So America's heroes of 1805 had to spend the dreariest of winters at the crude fort they constructed near the mouth of the Columbia—Fort Clatsop. Then, in the spring, they started the long overland trek back to St. Louis, arriving there September 23, 1806, to learn that many persons thought they had become lost and were long since dead.

On September 24, Clark wrote:

"I sleped but little last night. however we rose early and commenced wrighting our letters. Capt Lewis wrote one to the presidend . . . after dinner went to store and purchase some clothes."

September 25:

"payed some visits of form, to the gentlemen of St. Louis. in the evening a dinner & Ball."

September 26:

"a fine morning. we commenced wrighting &c."

Those "wrightings" were to stir the nation—to set it in westward motion. For the first time in the minds of Americans, the Far West took shape and form. Further explorations—and settlement—could not be far away. And indeed, they were not. They came as the "wrightings" beckoned to the trapper . . . the missionary . . . the prospector . . . the homesteader . . .

All of this was highly important to Idaho as well as to the many other states which would profit from the Lewis and Clark Expedition. But Idaho owes a special debt to the daring men who came to its land in 1805, because the friendship welded between the whites and the Nez Perces by Lewis and Clark staved off war with these Indians for many years when the scattered settlers could not cope with one. The Nez Perces were pushed and pushed, but it was not until 1877, when they were pushed too far, that they waged full-scale war.

8

# Chapter II

# BEAVER IN THE TRAP

"The fur trappers . . . they were called Roaring Nor'Westers, Thunderbolts of Montreal, and Lords of the Lakes and Forests. Never in the development of North America did a small group accomplish so much in so many ways in so short a time, in two decades exploring farther than all others in two centuries."

—Robert Pinkerton as quoted in *Idaho in the Pacific Northwest* by Floyd R. Barber and Dan W. Martin

On a crisp fall day in 1809, a short, barrel-chested Welshman, with long, black hair warming his ears, sidled cautiously up to a horse tethered to a tree on an Idaho-bound, Canadian trail. Not only was the horse tied, but it was hobbled, and its movements were as limited as that of a fly in molasses. Nevertheless, the stocky man was very careful.

That is, he was careful in his carelessness, packing onto the horse—with an eye to imbalance—several kegs of whiskey. He also saw to it that one of the kegs prodded the horse in its flanks. Then, turning the animal loose, he leaned back against a tree trunk to watch developments.

No rodeo of later day ever produced a better bucking exhibition. Hind legs flailing and front legs stiff, the horse zig-zagged through a heavy stand of timber. *Crash* went a keg; *whoosh* went another. The liquor flowed freely until not a drop was left intact on the horse's pack saddle, which finally went the way of the kegs.

"And let that be a lesson to the North West Company," mused the instigator of the one-man whiskey rebellion.

His name was David Thompson, one of the original Nor'Westers, but too pious to be called a "Thunderbolt." He reached Idaho's Lake Pend Oreille on September 8, 1809, to found near what is now Hope the trading post of Kullyspell House—the first white settlement in Idaho. (A temporary trading camp had been set up by Thompson in 1808 at Bonners Ferry, which is today a picturesque river valley town on U.S. Highway 95 with a population of 1,900.)

Thompson's bosses of the British fur trading company wanted him to trade whiskey to the Indians for furs. But Thompson didn't believe in that, so let nature and the horse take care of the whiskey. He himself had sworn off both drinking and gambling in 1786—ever since, he said, he had gotten into a checker game with the devil at a lonely trading post on Canada's Saskatchewan River.

"I was sitting at a small table with the checker board before me when the devil sat down opposite me," he recalled in later years. "He had two short black horns on his forehead. His head and body down to his waist—I saw no more—were covered with glossy black curling hair. His countenance was mild and grave. We began playing . . . played several games, and the devil lost every one. He kept his temper, but looked more grave. At length he got up, or rather, disappeared."

With an experience like that, it is understandable why the Indians around Kullyspell House—Kalispels, Spokanes and Kootenais—got no "firewater" from Thompson. Also, Thompson warned the braves that they would have to give up their daily gambling sessions and get busy with traps if they were to receive in trade what they wanted most—guns.

The Indians of the area were having trouble with members of the marauding Piegan tribe to the northeast. And the Piegans had guns, obtained in coastal trading. Used to shooting buffalo from horseback at close range, the Piegans were poor riflemen when it came to long-distance targets. Nevertheless, they had quite an advantage over the Lake Pend Oreille natives, who had only lances and bows and arrows. So, although Thompson's strict rules brought no peace to the area, they did shift the balance of power. The Kalispels, Spokanes and Kootenais became crack shots with their new rifles at any distance, badly defeating the Piegans in the first gun battle with them.

Thompson's supplying of guns to the Indians also greatly alleviated their chronic hunger. The softness of the arrows they had been using were ineffective in bringing down big game, but, with the introduction of bullets, the women were happily drying meat for the winter.

Kullyspell House, built of upright logs in the French-Canadian manner, was short-lived. It served as Idaho's first commercial establishment—in fact, the first in the Pacific Northwest—for only two years. Before its abandonment in 1811, Thompson had ordered the construction of a new trading post at the junction of the Spokane and Little Spokane Rivers. This was Spokane House (near the present city of Spokane), which for 16 years flourished on the furs of Idaho as well as those of other neighboring parts.

Thompson was too much of an individualist to completely typify the early fur gatherers. For one thing, he was a strong family man, married to an Indian woman who gave him 13 children. And each night he thanked God for pulling him through another day of wilderness hazards. But he was typical as a man who was unafraid to go anywhere he thought the furs might be more abundant, thus opening up new country that the less daring might follow.

It is estimated that Thompson traveled—by canoe, horse or foot—across more than 50,000 miles of North American wilderness, and, as a trained geographer and surveyor, he marked his travels well. Certainly, he left his mark on Idaho—and on the United States at large.

And so did hundreds of other trappers. Silent and brooding, rollicking and roaring, they were a strange breed of men—often a mixture of breeds, particularly French and Indian out of Canada. The *voyageur,* whether alone in the woods, bucking the swift current of a forest stream in his canoe or challenging the ruggedness of a mountain pass on horse or foot, knew how to take care of himself. At a trading post or rendezvous site, he did not. "More money was thrown away in acts of folly and tinsel grandeur by North Westers in those days," wrote North Wester Alexander Ross, "than would have paved the streets of Montreal with the precious metal." But broke again, the *voyageur* would set out, singing—or muttering—to himself, for another year of hazards and hardship he both hated and loved. Whether he as an individual never came back was not important, but, as part of a specialized and daring group, he was highly important in providing pelts before the days of mass production of textiles and leather from cattle skins, and in blazing new trails before detailed maps were available at every highway service station.

In far-off London, a dandy named Beau Brummel set a new style in beaver hats, and the demand for beaver pelts became great. Idaho's streams in particular were natural havens for beavers, and the animals had multiplied greatly there because the Indians of the area had not used beaver flesh or skin to any extent. The word got around.

Too, as President Jefferson had hoped, the Lewis and Clark Expedition inspired Americans to enter the Pacific Northwest fur trade. In 1809, while the two big British organizations, the North West Fur Company and the Hudson's Bay Company, were vying for favor with the Indians in the area, the Missouri Fur Company was formed at St. Louis. The Battle of the Fur Barons was on.

One of the first expeditions of the Missouri Fur Company brought a small party of men, headed by Andrew Henry, to Idaho in 1810. Near the present site of St. Anthony, on the north fork (now Henry's Fork) of the Snake River, the party built Fort Henry, the first American post west of the main ridge of the Rockies. It was a failure.

The Indians of the area—mostly Shoshones—didn't take to trapping, and the winter of 1810-11 was a bitter one. Game was scarce, and, one by one, the party's horses had to be shot for food. Came spring, and the men began to desert. Henry abandoned his fort, and the site after a few years became lost until 1927 when rocks were unearthed bearing the words:

"Fort Henry, 1811 . . . Al the cook, but nothing to cook."

But what was one failure?

On June 23, 1810, another American firm—the Pacific Fur Company—had been formed in New York City by John Jacob Astor. Sometimes Astor played the flute, but mostly he dealt in furs. And he had been doing so almost since the day in 1784 when he came to New York as an immigrant from Germany. By 1810, he was the No. 1 fur merchant in the United States, but the British monopolized the known sources of supply. He tried to buy into the British companies, but they spurned him. Well, he would beat them at their own game.

When Astor did things, he did them big. Shortly after establishing the Pacific Fur Company with capital of $400,000, he sent not one but two parties to the mouth of the Columbia—one by sea and one by land. Both had trouble—big trouble.

The sea party, sailing around the Horn on the *Tonquin,* experienced violent storms, brutality, drawn guns and threats of mutiny. But the *voyageurs* finally reached the mouth of the Columbia on March 22, 1811, and, after eight sailors lost their lives sounding the channel in small boats, began the construction of Fort Astoria. Still, theirs was a tea party compared with that of the 60-odd land travelers, who experienced much greater hardships, especially in crossing Idaho.

In October of 1811, this party arrived at the abandoned cabins of Fort Henry. Included in the party was Marie, half-breed Pierre Dorion's Sioux Indian wife, pregnant and with two small sons clutching at her deerskin robes. Tall and attractive, she was a woman of dignity and courage who was to become a heroine of significance at a time when heroics were routine for men.

Near Fort Henry, the travelers cached their saddles and considerable trade goods. Then, with great misgivings, they left their horses with two young Shoshones, hacked out 15 canoes, and started on Henry's Fork to the Snake River. They got to the Snake, but not far down it. Currents and cascades were too much for them. A canoe with five men aboard whipped against a huge rock at Caldron Linn (also named Devil's Scuttle Hole), and smashed into flotsam. Four men swam to shore. The fifth, Antoine Clappine, never made it. (A gorge several miles above the site of the drowning death later became the location of Milner Dam, which brought life to arid lands with irrigation in the North Side and South Side Twin Falls projects and to a large district near Shoshone and Gooding.)

The party decided to go it by foot, splitting into three groups in the hope that at least one would get to the mouth of the Columbia before the worst of winter set in. One group was headed by giant Donald McKenzie, whom Astor had proselyted from the North West Fur Company; another by Wilson Price Hunt, a St. Louis shop owner, shrewd as a merchant but naive as an outdoorsman, and Ramsay Crooks, an energetic and bold young hunter who would eventually go far in the fur business, becoming the owner of the Northern Department of the American Fur Company.

McKenzie's party cut north, then northwest. The men struggled through some of the nation's most rugged wilderness. The strain of ascending rocky ravines was great, the pangs of hunger greater. When the food ran completely out, McKenzie said:

"We've got beaver pelts. We'll broil them in strips."

It was a big day when one of the men shot a mountain sheep. Meat—honest to goodness meat—in the pot! The men took new courage. But then there was thirst. The *voyageurs* came to Hells Canyon, and dry mouths opened as brightening eyes stared down at the Snake River flowing through it. But the bottom of the canyon, deepest cleavage in North America, was more than a mile below the tops of perpendicular lava cliffs. No one could get to the water. It was for viewing only, and Hells Canyon truly became Dante's "Inferno" for the men of McKenzie's party. They went on, throats rasping dry.

Following pretty much what today is the route of Idaho's picturesque North-South Highway, they clawed their way through dense timber and brush, over high ridges. At times, they followed Indian trails; generally, they made their own.

12

The urge to survive is rooted deep in man, and, with prodding and goading, the massive McKenzie—called "Perpetual Motion" because of his great energy—kept it that way until the party reached the Clearwater. There the men obtained canoes from Indians, and following the water route to Astoria, where they arrived on January 12, 1812, was a relative breeze.

But back on their different trails, the Hunt and Crooks parties were still struggling. Hunt, taking Marie Dorion and her two children in his party, had chosen the north side of the Snake; Crooks and his party, the south.

Off in the distance, Hunt later reported, the roaring of great waterfalls could be heard. But no one bothered to investigate. These pilgrims were not sight-seeing like tourists today on Highway 180, but were fighting for survival, so they never saw Twin Falls tumbling down 182 feet or Shoshone Falls, four miles farther on, plunging 212 feet into an abyss to form beautiful Blue Lakes. Neither did they see the Thousand Springs, with the water of underground rivers finding outlets to the Snake through cliffside cavities.

Washington Irving wrote that they crossed "a dreary desert of sand and gravel . . . treeless wastes that must ever defy cultivation." The distinguished author of the Nineteenth Century, however, reckoned without irrigation which would make the Twin Falls area bloom and bring to it the name of Magic Valley.

In the vicinity of what is now Bruneau, two events of significance occurred —the first to bring cheer; the second, anguish. The first was the acquiring of a horse in trade for a knife, tomahawk, fire steel, piece of elastic web and some beads. (Farther back on the trail, another horse to lighten the loads on human backs had been obtained for an old tea kettle.) The second event was the meeting with an ancient Indian, who advised Hunt to leave the Snake and head northwest. This route proved to be a long way between waterholes, and "we nearly died of thirst."

Life-saving water was reached at Slater Creek, and the next day, November 21, 1811, the party camped near "a beautiful little stream . . . fringed with groves of cottonwood and willow." It was the Boise River—"River of the Woods."

The site of the encampment was to become the city of Boise, capital of Idaho. But for Hunt in 1811 it was the place where he lost a horse. An Indian showed up, and claimed that the last horse for which Hunt had traded had been stolen from him, and Hunt reluctantly turned the animal over to the Indian, who threatened plenty of trouble if he didn't. However, another horse was obtained in barter, and this one was given to Marie Dorion and her children to ride, for the time of the birth of her third child was drawing near.

Moving out of the Boise Valley, the party, now bucking heavy snow, again returned to the Snake River. Then, shortly before Christmas, where the Snake enters Eastern Oregon's Blue Mountains, the weary band heard an "hello" from across the river. It came from Crooks' party, completely exhausted and starving.

Hunt, who by now had learned more than a few tricks of the wild, had a canoe fashioned from the hides of two horses recently purchased from Indians, loaded it with meat carved from the butchered animals, and sent it across the river. One of Crooks' men, wild-eyed at the sight of food, could not wait for the landing, plunged into the icy water, and drowned. Crooks came back in the frail and leaking canoe on its return trip.

"Cliffs down the river—they are impassable," he said. "Snowdrifts in the mountains—the same. We must leave the river here."

Combining the two parties under his leadership, Hunt headed northwest through the mountains to the Columbia River. On December 30, Marie's baby was born, and two days later she was cradling it in her arms as she rode on with the party, the two older children clinging to the back of the saddle. Nine days after birth, the baby died—probably from exposure to the howling winter winds. Time and again then, the men looked hungrily at Marie's horse, but it is to their credit that they left it for her and the two youngsters to ride.

On February 15, 1812, a cannon boomed at the newly-constructed Fort Astoria. The Hunt Party, including Marie Dorion and her two children, had gotten through!

In its remarkable achievement, the party was to do for Southern Idaho what the Lewis and Clark Expedition did for Northern Idaho—chart a path across it. Indeed, the Astorians opened up basically what was to become the famed Oregon Trail, traveled by thousands of settlers heading for the Far West. But an epilog to the story was to bring tragedy—to stain Idaho soil with the first blood from an Indian massacre.

In 1813, John Reed, who had made the trek to Astoria via the Clearwater with "Perpetual Motion" Donald McKenzie, set up a rough trapping post on the Boise River near where it flows into the Snake. He brought with him nine men, including Pierre Dorion, and Marie and her two children. The trapping was good, but there was continuing friction with Indians in the area.

Then, one day in January, 1814, when Marie was alone at the post except for her children, a friendly Indian came to warn her that his people were prowling the river to kill all the trappers. Marie saddled two horses, put the children on one, and started out at a gallop to sound the alarm. She was too late.

The first trapper she came upon was a Canadian named Le Clerc—dying of gunshot wounds. Marie's husband and all the others were dead, Le Clerc told her. Somehow, Marie managed to get Le Clerc on the saddle of one horse, then mounted the other with her children, and headed in the general direction of Fort Astoria, now renamed Fort George by the British North West Company. (Poorly managed, Fort Astoria lost money and Astor's partners had decided to get rid of it.)

When Le Clerc died, Marie lifted his body from the saddle, and mounted the horse herself. The farther west she and the children went, the deeper the snow became. For three days, while suffering from snowblindness, Marie could not proceed. Finally, she and the boys had to spend the rest of the winter on the banks of the Columbia near the mouth of the Walla Walla, surviving on the smoked meat of the two horses.

Weak and wan, the mother and children were discovered beside the Columbia in April, 1814, by Donald McKenzie and a brigade of North West trappers paddling canoes up the river from Astoria.

From the brush along the river, the *voyageurs* heard a woman crying out in French. Swerving their canoes to the bank, they came upon Marie Dorion and her two sons.

"We are all that remain," she said.

In 1932, the Sons and Daughters of Idaho Pioneers erected a monument to Marie just across the Boise River from Caldwell. Also, on U.S. Highway 410, where it crosses the Walla Walla River in Washington, there is now the Madame Marie Dorion Bridge. But generally, Marie has never been given the attention accorded to Sacajawea. So this writer would like to give a special salute to quite a woman—to the "Madonna of the Old Oregon Trail."

After the massacre of the Reed party, trappers usually probed the Idaho country in much larger groups. Mostly, they worked out of Astoria, but, in 1818, Donald McKenzie decided to build a fort closer to the Idaho scene. So emerged Fort Nez Perce—later Fort Walla Walla.

Once on a trek by McKenzie's trappers from Southern Idaho's Bear River Country back to Fort Nez Perce, there developed a primitive parade that the late Cecil B. de Mille would have loved to reproduce as a motion picture spectacle. First, came about a hundred singing and joshing trappers on their horses, with 154 more horses loaded with beaver pelts and other furs. Then, on the trail, they were joined by more than 500 mounted Cayuse Indians, with ornaments jangling, spears flashing. As the cavalcade strung out on a mountainside trail, it extended for miles. And only the deer and bears and coyotes were there to witness the grand exhibition.

McKenzie, who loved to lead brigades into the wilds himself, had some trouble with the Indians, but he didn't stand for much. Once, when a group of them approached him with knives ready for scalping, he stretched two out with a tent pole, and the others took off in a hurry.

Another time, McKenzie and three of his men were skinning beaver at their camp in Southwestern Idaho when a large band of Snake Indians swarmed down from the hills to wipe them out. Rolling out a keg of gunpowder, McKenzie spilled some of the contents, and lighted it. The *whoosh* of fire and smoke was impressive, but McKenzie's words were more so.

"Next time," he told the Indians, "I'll blow us all up."

He meant it, and the Indians knew he did. They did not tarry.

Thousands of beaver pelts were being taken annually from Idaho, and a bigger share was desired by the giant Hudson's Bay Company, which had been gaining strength ever since its founding on May 2, 1670. In 1821, it moved in on the North West Company, and absorbed it.

With North West out of the way, Hudson's Bay considered Idaho its exclusive trapping territory, but pesky American companies were pressing westward, and were now operating in strength as far as the Upper Missouri River. Hudson's Bay decided to start making its forays into Idaho from the east as well as from the west.

The company had constructed a new post called Flathead House on the Clark Fork River in Western Montana. From here in the spring of 1823-24, an expedition of 65 trappers was dispatched southward along the Continental Divide into Southeastern Idaho. The expedition was headed by a fiery, red-bearded mountain man named Finan McDonald, who was 6 feet 4 inches of toughness and who had once slapped an Indian chief at Spokane House, and challenged him to a duel. McDonald could take a lot of trouble, but he didn't like all that he got.

The party hadn't traveled far when it tangled briefly with some Piegans, and one of the trappers named Anderson was killed and scalped. Then, in a deep and rocky ravine several miles west of Lemhi Pass, the party camped one night beside a tumbling stream. There were no signs of Indians here, so no guard was posted.

Dawn came with two rifle cracks in rapid order from the top of the ravine. The first shot splintered the rifle stock of a sleeping man, and the second, the powder horn of another sleeper. The camp came alive, with trappers reaching for rifles, clothes and shoes.

Looking up, they saw Piegans. As if overcome by the effect of their sur-

15

prise attack, the Indians were prancing atop the ravine walls, waving guns and bows, and shouting taunts. The trappers started scrambling up a draw in pursuit. McDonald called them back. (When excited, McDonald was inclined to speak in a mixture of Gaelic, English, French and various Indian dialects, but his men usually understood him the first time.)

"May be a trap," the giant Scotchman said. "We go after them on horse-back."

Leaving 20 men to guard the camp, McDonald headed a cavalcade of 45 trappers, who sent their horses charging up the ravine. The Indians outnumbered the trappers two to one, but they were on foot.

Maybe it was the clatter of so many horses' hoofs that stampeded the Piegans. But, whatever the reason, instead of taking advantage of their high-ground position, the Indians ran. The mounted trappers raced after them.

Reaching a patch of high brush, the Indians took refuge in it, and met the charge of the trappers with a volley of rifle fire and a flight of arrows. Both riders and horses started dropping, so the trappers dismounted and found protective shields of boulders.

One Indian waved a pole above the brush. Atop the pole was the scalp of Trapper Anderson, who had been slain by the Piegans in the earlier encounter. Under the protective fire of other trappers, several men rushed the pole waver, killed him, and brought back Anderson's scalp.

As the battle reached a standoff, the Piegans offered to surrender, but the trappers were buying only vengeance.

"Who's brave enough to fire the brush?" asked McDonald. "Let it be the oldest man, and I'll guard him."

So a grizzled and wizened trapper in his seventies "volunteered." With McDonald and several others marching behind with cocked guns, the old fellow moved to the brush, flaming torch in trembling hand. Oddly, not a shot was fired nor an arrow loosed, and soon all the brush was a blazing inferno, with Indians fleeing in various directions. The trappers shot some of them down as they ran, and others, who feared to leave the brush burned to death.

What price beaver? McDonald counted the Indians' dead in the battle at 10, and the trappers' at seven.

With his ranks now depleted by a total of eight, McDonald pushed on into the Snake River tributaries of Southeastern Idaho, took several thousand beaver pelts, and returned to Flathead House. Before he got there, however, one of his own Iroquois trappers accidentally shot him, seriously wounding him and incapacitating him for some time.

"When that country (Southern Idaho) will see me again, the beaver will have a gold skin," McDonald vowed.

But there would always be somebody else. In this case, the man was Alexander Ross, who figured that, with a bigger party and with armaments including a small brass cannon, he would have less difficulty than McDonald.

So, in November, 1823, this hardy Scotchman who was a former school teacher, began a trip from Flathead House to Idaho's Snake River Country, following pretty much McDonald's route—east to what is now Missoula, Montana, south through the Bitterroot Valley, across the Continental Divide, again south, and finally back across the Divide into Southern Idaho via the Lemhi Pass.

In his narrative, which he published in London in 1855, Ross recalled:

"Looking over the party of 144, I smiled at the medley, the variety of accents of dress, habits and ideas; but above all, at the confusion of languages

16

. . . The party included two Americans, seventeen Canadians, five half-breeds from the east side of the mountains, twelve Iroquois, two Abanakee Indians from Lower Canada, two natives from Lake Nepissing, one Saultman from Lake Huron, two Crees from Athabasca, one Chinook, two Spokanes, two Kootenais, three Flatheads, two Kalispels, one Palouse, and one Snake slave! In addition to these men, there were twenty-five women and sixty-four children."

Travel was slow for this Babylonic party, which had to hunt for food on the way. Also, although everybody was mounted (horses, including pack animals, numbered 392), the time of year was not conducive to travel with unshod transportation. Today, winter travelers, in traversing many of the mountain passes, must pause to put chains on their car tires.

On March 20, 1824, deep in the Bitterroots, Ross wished he had snowshoes for the horses. The party, stretching out a mile-and-a-half through a pass, found its path blocked by heavy snowdrifts.

Ross sent a man ahead on snowshoes, leading his horse by the bridle, while another man prodded the animal from behind. When this horse became stalled with little more than head showing, another horse was sent plunging past it until this animal, too, could go no farther. And so it went until 80 pairs of ears could be seen projecting above the snow.

"The difficulty of extricating the horses proved greater than that of urging them forward," wrote Ross, "but we were partly recompensed by the novelty of the scene, and mirth and glee diffused among the people."

Laughter is a great antidote to adversity, but it was not always available when needed on that trek. In crossing the Divide, Ross reported "children calling out with hunger, women affrighted, dogs howling, a scream here and there."

While trapping on the Malad River (now called Camas Creek) west of present day Fairfield, a strange illness swept through the party. Thirty-seven persons felt cramps in the stomach, then all the nerves of the body were affected. The sufferers became almost speechless and motionless . . . began to froth at the mouth.

Mixing gunpowder with warm water, Ross poured it down throats. No effect. Next he tried fat broth well-seasoned with a couple handfuls of pepper. This concoction brought results.

Checking, Ross found that all those who had been ill had eaten beaver meat that morning, and decided that the beaver had been feeding on poisonous roots growing beside the river. So it was that the stream became known as the *Riviere aux Malades*. (McKenzie had a similar experience there in 1820.)

Indian trouble? There were some minor incidents—once the cannon had to be used as a threat—but there was no loss of human life on the entire trip, which lasted 13 months. More than 5,000 Idaho beavers, however, died in traps, and their pelts were toted back to Flathead House.

Ross was particularly pleased when he received a letter of congratulation from no less a personage than Sir George Simpson, governor of the Hudson's Bay Company in Canada. Simpson, who was accompanied on his inspections of posts by buglers and pipers, drove his men hard for the greater glory—and financial fattening—of the world's largest fur company, and he expected results without passing out too many plaudits.

The Hudson's Bay Company decided that the Flathead House approach to Southern Idaho's beaver streams was the hard way. In 1824, the company decided to close down Fort George at Astoria, to erect a huge new trading post a hundred miles up the Columbia (Fort Vancouver), and to appoint as factor Dr. John McLoughlin.

This tall (6'4") and powerfully built man, who was to become a legend even before he grew old, usually wore black clothes which contrasted strikingly with his massive head of prematurely white hair flowing over his shoulders. To many Indians, he was known as the "White-headed Eagle"; to many whites, as "the despot west of the Rockies." He was stridently stern and tenaciously tough—and equally kind and thoughtful—depending on the situation. Above all, he was capable and respected.

He avoided Idaho, but for 22 years he dominated it, controlling the fortunes of the many fur trappers he dispatched to it. Of course, those fortunes were not great. Usually, the men were so in debt to the company they never got out.

After 1824, when both England and the United States began bolstering their claims on the Pacific Northwest for a final showdown, McLoughlin—and the British government—were chagrined to learn that parties of American trappers were "poaching" in Idaho.

In 1831, there came a group headed by Captain Benjamin L. E. Bonneville, on leave from the Army. Because Bonneville knew nothing about trapping—although he had some experienced French-Canadians in his party—suspicions arose that he was actually spying for the American government. To this day, it is not known whether he was or not. But, in three years, he really got around Southern Idaho—Pierre's Hole, Upper Snake River Valley, Portneuf Valley, Upper Cache Valley, Bear Lake Valley, Salmon-Lemhi Valley, Lost River section, Wood River Valley and Boise Valley.

When his party reached the valley through which the Boise River flows, his French-Canadians are supposed to have exclaimed *"Les bois, les bois! Voyez les bois!"*—"The woods, the woods! See the woods!" This could have given the valley and river their names, except that there are references to the Boise River as early as 1825. Nevertheless, Bonneville did help greatly in putting Idaho on the map, providing the material for Washington Irving's book, "The Adventures of Captain Bonneville." Indeed, it was this book which gave a touch of glamour to the entire Far West.

Bonneville's description in the book of Idaho's Snake River Country particularly intrigued Easterners in the mid-Nineteenth Century:

"The grandeur and originality of the views presented on every side beggar both the pencil and the pen. Nothing we had ever gazed upon in any other region could for a moment compare in wild majesty and impressive sternness with the series of scenes which at every turn astonished our senses and filled us with awe and delight . . . Here, the rocks were piled in the most fantastic crags and precipices, and in another place they were succeeded by delightful valleys carpeted with greensward."

While Bonneville was still worrying the British with his wandering in Idaho, Milton G. Sublette, representing the American-owned Rocky Mountain Fur Company, showed up with a large party of trappers in the Wood River Country. More significant, however, was the arrival of Captain Nathaniel J. Wyeth.

Wyeth, who came from a distinguished Massachusetts family (he was related to John Hancock of Declaration of Independence fame and had the same aquiline profile), brought with him to Idaho a fair-sized party and a large amount of trade goods. In the summer of 1834, he erected his own trading post on the Snake River (off present Highway 91, about 12 miles west and a little

18

north of the Fort Hall Indian Agency). The post was called Fort Hall after an Eastern financial backer.

"We manufactured a magnificent flag from unbleached sheeting, a little red flannel and a few blue patches," wrote Wyeth.

At the raising of the flag, the patriotic New Englander made a speech:

"My men, when we occupy this building, we will be the only Americans engaged in business west of the Rocky Mountains. This banner is the only flag of the United States floating on the western slope of the American continent. Nearly 29 years ago, Meriwether Lewis held aloft his flag . . . as the discoverer of this country. I now raise the same starry banner in this valley in token that we still maintain, by settlement and occupation, the rights which Lewis established by discovery."

Details on the ensuing celebration—with "villainous alcohol" in profusion—were provided by John K. Townsend, a member of the party:

"We had gouging, biting, fisticuffing and stomping in the most scientific perfection; some even fired guns and pistols at each other, but the weapons were mostly harmless in the unsteady hands that employed them."

There was no celebrating at Fort Vancouver, however. Dr. McLoughlin's stepson, Thomas McKay quickly set up a competing fort in Idaho.

McKay selected a site near the twin mouths of the Boise River, where he fashioned from cottonwood poles the first Fort Boise near the present city of Parma. This makeshift structure was abandoned in 1838 with the adobe construction of a more pretentious second Fort Boise not far away on the Snake River. Still later, in the gold rush days of 1863, a third Fort Boise was established by the U.S. Army on the site now occupied by the Veterans Administration Hospital in Boise. But of major significance is the fact that, before 1834 was over, Idaho had two forts vying for its fur trade—one in the Boise Valley and the other in the Snake River Valley.

Francis Payette, a portly and genial French-Canadian, who gave his name to the city of Payette and hoped to make French the accepted language for the entire area, was placed in charge of Fort Boise. His orders from McLoughlin: Sell trade goods for less and pay more for furs than Wyeth at Fort Hall.

The contest that developed was an odd one.

Wyeth went to Fort Vancouver in a barge with 10 trappers. As the craft approached the fort, McLoughlin, peering through a telescope, noted that a man of obvious distinction headed the party. He ordered a salute fired.

Docking, Wyeth strode up a path to meet the waiting factor. He glanced with appreciation at the fine cut of McLoughlin's clothes and the shine of the silver buckles on his shoes, then thrust out his hand.

"Wyeth is my name. I am from Boston on a trading trip to the Columbia."

"Bless me!" said McLoughlin. "Welcome to Fort Vancouver."

The two gentlemen—and they were definitely such—toasted one another before a roaring fireplace (McLoughlin probably had water in his glass, for he was a teetotaler). They also exchanged tales and witticisms. But, shortly thereafter, Wyeth built a second fur trading post—Fort William—on Wapatoo Island about eight miles up the Columbia River from Fort Vancouver. McLoughlin countered by cutting the price of trade goods still further, and upping the pay for furs still more.

Then the stern factor with a soft heart began to worry that he was pushing the charming Wyeth too far. He tentatively agreed to an offer by Wyeth for the Americans to discontinue trapping within a hundred miles of any Hudson's Bay post—if hard-to-obtain trade goods could be purchased at wholesale from the company and furs obtained outside the hundred-mile limit could be sold to it at $5 minimum per beaver pelt. Governor Simpson of Hudson's Bay in Canada, however, blasted McLoughlin for even entertaining such an idea, and ordered him to get on with the business of ruining Wyeth. As it worked out, McLoughlin did not have to pursue this course too vigorously.

At Fort Hall, Wyeth's troubles mounted. Some trappers deserted; others were killed by Blackfoot Indians. The Blackfeet, too, stole horses and supplies. At Fort William, things were not much better. Indian trappers with furs or salmon to sell ignored Fort William, and went about their business as usual at Fort Vancouver.

Wyeth commented to McLoughlin, who had an Ojibway Indian wife, on his "hereditary influence" with the Indians.

Smiling, McLoughlin replied:

"I have no hereditary influence. I have made the Indians fear me. I have compelled obedience, studied justice, cultivated confidence. It takes time, Mr. Wyeth."

But time for Wyeth was running out.

On September 22, 1853, the almost-beaten Wyeth wrote to his wife in Massachusetts:

"We have lost by drowning and disease and warfare 17 persons to this date and 14 now sick with the fever. But keep up good spirits, my dear wife . . . Altho I shall be poor, we can always live."

A year later, Wyeth was beaten. He abandoned Fort William, sold what equipment he could to settlers in the Willamette Valley, and leased the property to McLoughlin, who used it for the pasturing of company cattle. Then Wyeth sold Fort Hall to the Hudson's Bay Company for $8,179.98, which, Wyeth estimated, represented a loss of more than $20,000. On the flagstaff at the fort, a London-made Union Jack replaced the Stars and Stripes the American trappers had proudly pieced together from scrap material.

Wyeth, who had worked for the Frederic Tudor Ice Company in Boston before his ill-fated Western adventure, returned to his old job. During the next 15 years, he received 14 patents for major improvements in machinery for cutting and storing ice. As he had promised his wife, "We can always live."

But life back in the Far West?

Hudson's Bay was now pretty much in control of the fur trade in Idaho—except for that in Pierre's Hole in the Teton Basin. Nobody controlled that, although the big American fur companies dominated it.

Here, in the lush-grass valley in the shadows of the spiraling Tetons, both free and company-affiliated trappers came annually in the summer for a week's rendezvous . . . to trade their furs for supplies marked up from 200 to 2,000 per cent . . . to lose their greasy black buckskin shirts in gambling . . . to get beaten up in drunken brawls . . . to make such liaisons as they might with Indian women, many of whom became wives of the trappers. The Indians trekked to the rendezvous to trade moccasins, buckskins, pemmican and horses—and to enjoy the excitement of the gathering, which was like a primitive county fair. In effect, Pierre's Hole had all the advantages and disadvantages of a fur trading post without the year-around maintenance costs.

Generally, the fighting at a rendezvous was just among the trappers. Sometimes survival at one became more difficult than in the wilderness, but usually the damage to a trapper was limited to a broken arm, a dented head, or a partly bitten-off ear. Occasionally, an Indian threatened mayhem when a white trapper stole his wife. But, if the price the trapper offered for her was right, the matter was settled amicably. Whites and reds blended as of one color.

Not so in 1832! That was the year of the Battle of Pierre's Hole.

There were hundreds of Indians at the rendezvous that year—Nez Perce, Flatheads, Shoshones and Bannocks. The Nez Perces alone had set up more than 80 tepees, with an average of five persons and two dogs per tepee. But nobody worried about the tribes represented in the camp. They were friendly to the trappers.

The Gros Ventres (Big Bellies), migrating and marauding plains allies of the Blackfeet, were not. When a large party of them (estimates of the number vary from 200 to 600) was sighted riding down a valley ridge, all activity in the huge encampment, including a horse race, ended. Both whites and friendly Indians stood ready with guns cocked. Their tenseness heightened when several of the Gros Ventres, led by a scarlet-blanketed chief, rode ahead of the others, and asked for a parley.

Antoine Godin, a French-Iroquois trapper of not much account, and another half-breed with Flathead blood, were sent out to talk. Godin could speak the Blackfoot dialect, but he was the last man who should have been given such an assignment. The Blackfeet earlier had killed his father, and he had never ceased to threaten revenge—either against the Blackfeet or the allied Gros Ventres. Not only that, strong drink at the rendezvous had added bravado to his bragging.

"While I talk to the chief," he told his companion, "you shoot him."

And that is what happened. The chief fell dead from his horse, and the other Indians who had accompanied him wheeled their mounts and raced back to the main party. Godin and his collaborator in treachery snatched up the chief's red robe, and galloped back to the encampment to await developments. The wait was brief.

Bullets and arrows began flying in two directions from behind almost every bush and rock that offered a shield. Then, at the height of the battle, a party of some 50 trappers, led by Milton Sublette, rode into the valley, and joined the fray. Executing a flanking movement, Sublette's forces drove the Gros Ventres back to a position where women had dug shallow trenches, and piled logs and branches in front of them. So, perhaps for the first time, a Western Indian battle evolved into trench warfare.

But it did not last long. During the night, the Gros Ventres faded into the hills, leaving behind 26 dead, and taking an unknown number of bodies with them. The dead on the other side totaled six white men and seven Nez Perce allies. But, in the battle, there was still one more to die.

When the dawn came, a Gros Ventres woman, refusing to leave her dead husband, stood weeping beside his body. The white trappers were for letting her go, but the Nez Perces didn't play the game that way. They tomahawked her to death.

Godin paid for his infamy that started it all on or about May 22, 1836. Picking his teeth as he leaned against a post at Fort Hall, he heard the hail of another half-breed named James Bird (also known as Jemmy Jock) from across the Snake River. Godin knew that Bird was sympathetic to the Blackfeet and Gros Ventres, and didn't trust him any farther than a real bird could soar without flapping its wings. But Bird shouted that he had some furs which he would sell cheap.

Godin paddled a canoe across the river, where a half-dozen Blackfeet emerged from the brush to join Bird. Godin became nervous, but the Blackfeet

21

calmed him by saying that they wanted to sit down and smoke a pipe of peace before the dickering started for the furs. As the pipe reached Godin's mouth, one of the Blackfeet shot him to death. Another helped with the scalping.

The raw life of the trapper in Idaho—and sometimes his raw death—did not continue much longer, for the streams were rapidly being depleted of beaver. Too, fashions changed. The silk hat replaced the beaver, and the bottom dropped out of the market for beaver pelts. The trappers, who should never be underrated either for their courage or exploratory accomplishments, turned to other endeavors.

By the 1840s, the roaring encampments at Pierre's Hole were history—good and bad. But it was not the end for either Fort Boise or Fort Hall. After the fur business faded, these frontier posts were to play important roles as emigrants sought solace at them while traveling on the Old Oregon Trail, or as the Indians called it, the Great Medicine Road of the Whites.

On June 15, 1846, the American government gave up its long-standing "54-40 or Fight" campaign, and signed a treaty with Great Britain establishing the 49th parallel as the boundary in the Pacific Northwest between Canada and the United States. The treaty stipulated, however, that possessory rights of the Hudson's Bay Company and all British subjects occupying land lawfully acquired in the Oregon Country must be respected.

The Hudson's Bay Company promptly started seeking payments for its properties, asking $650,000, and finally, in 1863, getting $450,000 from the United States. This was still a handsome profit, considering that the company had paid only eight thousand dollars to Wyeth for one of the major properties —Fort Hall. Besides, there were hardly any beaver left by that time.

As for all those hundreds of thousands of beavers which had been taken out of Idaho, their tailcraft in building dams on remote mountain streams would be sorely missed. In fact, the beavers' process of slowing spring runoffs in the high country would be missed so much that a century later the Idaho Fish and Game Department decided it had to put beavers back where the trappers had taken them out. So airplanes were engaged to fly over the State's most rugged areas, and beavers were dropped in pairs by parachute. Who, in this day and age, would want to paddle a canoe, ride a horse or trudge on foot where the early trappers had?

# Chapter III

# BRINGING OF THE MESSAGE

"Let the Church awake from her slumber and go forth in her strength to the salvation of these wandering sons of our native forests."

—William Walker in a letter published
in the *Christian Advocate* in 1833

Although the trappers blazed many trails, the missionaries were the ones who marked them with milestones—Idaho's first school, printing press, sawmill and gristmill. Missionaries, too, introduced agriculture—indeed, even awakened the sleeping desert with irrigation. By fostering livestock raising, they demonstrated that life need not depend on a wild hare in a snare. Pioneers in stability—these generally were the missionaries as they went about their gospel chores. And they were pioneers of special courage—courage without a gun on the hip.

Sunday afternoon, July 27, 1834, at Fort Hall . . . a hot sun beating down . . . puffs of dust rising up as about 60 whites and Indians converged on a grove of cottonwoods . . . The shade seekers were about to make religious history by attending the first church service held in Idaho.

As the one-day parishioners sat down in a circle, some munching pemmican, one cleaning a rifle and another whittling with a knife bigger than the stick he was attacking, the Reverend Jason Lee, Bible in hand, stepped forward. The six-foot-four, black-bearded Methodist minister, who looked a little like the latter-day Abraham Lincoln, was destined to establish a mission in Oregon's Willamette Valley. But, pausing at Fort Hall, he had been persuaded by Captain Nathaniel J. Wyeth to conduct a service there.

Lee read the Fifteenth Psalm, and sang a hymn, beginning, "The Lord of sabbath let us praise . . ." He sang alone, because nobody else knew the words. Then he took for the text of his brief sermon Paul's message to the Corinthians:

"Whether, therefore, ye eat or drink, or whatsoever ye do, do all to the glory of God."

The Indians in the crowd didn't understand a word, but none of the whites listened with more rapt attention than they. Under any circumstances, the tall stature and deep voice of the Reverend Lee would have commanded respect, but the Indians had learned from Catholic French-Canadian and Iroquois trappers about the men who brought the word of God. This word, to the red man, was strong medicine which might help him defeat his enemies, and he was ready to listen even if he couldn't understand.

As soon as Lee finished, however, everybody quickly arose, and moved to an open area where the regular Sunday horse racing, with earnest betting, was held. While riding a horse in a race that day, a French-Canadian named Kanseau was thrown by his mount in a collision with another horse, and killed.

Next morning, Lee conducted the first formal funeral service held in Idaho. A little worried, French-Canadian friends of the deceased followed up the Methodist service with an improvised version of the Catholic rites. Then, because Kanseau had been married to an Indian woman, her fellow tribesmen chanted and danced in their own primitive ceremony.

Wrote Wyeth in his journal:

"Kanseau was at least well buried."


Lee's calling to the Far West has been traced back to the visit to St. Louis in 1831 of four Nez Perce Indians (one was part Flathead). Seeking someone to interpret for them the powerful "White Man's Book of Heaven"—the Bible —the Indians came to St. Louis, because they knew that it was now the home of Captain William Clark. The co-leader of the Lewis and Clark Expedition had become a folk hero among the Nez Perces, and the Indians figured that, if anybody could help them, Clark could.

The retired trail-blazer put the lost-looking travelers in touch with Catholic priests, who took them in. But the hot and humid climate of St. Louis and the strange foods served in the city quickly proved the undoing of two of the Indians. They became ill, and died. The other two were impressed by the fact that the priests were able to baptize the sick men just before they died.

Catholic Bishop Joseph Rosati of St. Louis was greatly taken by the Indians' plea from the wilderness, which was to be likened to the cry of the ancient Macedonians to the Christians to "come over into Macedonia and help us." The bishop approved the sending of missionaries to the Far West, but St. Louis was burgeoning, and priests were in short supply. Father Mathew Condamine of the cathedral clergy volunteered his services, but for some reason he did not make the trip west.

So, without the benefit of Black Robes, the remaining two Indians started the long trek homeward. One died on the way. The other reached a Nez Perce buffalo hunting camp on the Missouri River, where he was slain in a battle with the Blackfeet.

The "Macedonian cry" of the Indians might have been forgotten, except for

William Walker, a half-breed Christian from Ohio. He came to St. Louis on business, heard the story, and took action in 1833 by writing a letter which was published in the *Christian Advocate*. In it, he appealed for missionaries to save the souls of the "wandering sons of our native forests." Jason Lee, financed by the Methodists, responded. Others followed.

In 1834, the Presbyterian and Congregational churches' American Board of Commissioners for Foreign Missions sent Congregationalist Samuel Parker, a 56-year-old preacher who had been the headmaster of a girls' boarding school, to St. Louis with two other ministers. They were to catch a fur trader's caravan there, but arrived too late to join one that year. Parker's associates decided to devote their services to the Pawnees in Kansas, and Parker returned to New York State where he met Dr. Marcus Whitman, a devout Presbyterian.

A hardy and stocky man who had a country medical practice, Whitman was anxious to do missionary work among the Western Indians. So, in May of 1835, he and Parker sought and obtained permission from the American Fur Company to join one of its wagon trains heading westward from St. Louis.

The trappers generally did not think much of the permission granted by their bosses. Fearing that the missionaries might try to tighten the loose lives they led, the more belligerent members of the caravan began a program of continuing harassment. They hooted and jeered at the missionaries . . . splattered them with rotten prairie chicken eggs . . . cut loose their raft in a river crossing, almost costing their lives. To get any sleep at night, Parker and Whitman had to pitch their camp on the outer fringes of the caravan—wide open to Indian attack.

Then tragedy gave the missionaries a break. Cholera swept through the caravan, the sick trappers came pleading to Dr. Whitman for help. With Parker's assistance, Whitman treated the stricken men with calomel, and was able to save the lives of all but three. After that, the missionaries had no more trouble with the bullying trappers. If one so much as leered at Parker or Whitman, another would threaten to do a carving job on him.

At Fort Laramie in Wyoming, where the wagons of the party were put in storage, came a big decision. Whitman would return to the East to get more supplies and to bring back as his wife the golden-haired, beautiful and buxom Narcissa Prentiss. (Narcissa had agreed to be Whitman's bride—only if she could go to the Oregon Country with him as a missionary.) Parker would continue on in search of mission sites.

Before Whitman started back, however, he had some surgery to perform. A grizzled mountain man came up to him, and announced:

"My name's Jim Bridger. I've been carryin' an Injun arrow in my back for a long time, and it's mighty painful. Suppose you could get it out, Doc?"

With an audience of 30 or 40 trappers and traders, including Kit Carson, Whitman extracted the arrow—three inches long. In the eyes of the watchers was three-dimensional admiration—for Whitman, for Bridger, and for the Indian who had fashioned the arrow.

The grateful Bridger, who, at 18, had answered an advertisement in a St. Louis newspaper by Andrew Henry for "enterprising young men" to come west as trappers, offered the protection of his brigade to Parker as far as Pierre's Hole in Idaho. Also offering protection and guide service were Nez Perces headed by Chief Tackensuatis, pleased that a spiritual leader was coming their way. Parker never had it so good as he did on the trip to Pierre's Hole.

The Indians, he wrote in his journal, "vied with each other to see which could do the most for my comfort." Little girls dug among bushes to find for him the choicest of wild strawberries. When he rested, women formed shade over his head with woven tree branches. Tackensuatis' wife strewed mint leaves in his tent.

Like trappers before him, however, Parker found the going rough from Pierre's Hole to the joining of the Snake and Clearwater rivers—site of present-day Lewiston. Ascending and descending high mountain ridges, he became very ill, and bled himself. This, of course, only weakened him further, and he was barely able to walk. But he could still preach.

At the funeral for an Indian boy, he awed the elders with a sermon on the resurrection and the judgment. Chief Tackensuatis said it was "tois"—good, adding that he now knew more about God.

At what is now Lewiston, Parker looked about appreciatively, and observed that the area "combines many advantages for a missionary station." (He also accurately described the soil of the Palouse Country, and predicted its present fame as a bountiful wheat region.) But the missionary pressed on, finally deciding that Whitman might better establish a mission in the Walla Walla area. As for himself, he was bone-weary. Going to Fort Vancouver, he took a ship home to New York via the Sandwich (Hawaiian) Islands. The Macedonian cry was still unanswered for the natives of the Idaho wilderness.

On a cold February day in 1836, a lone rider prodded his horse along a snow-crusted road in Western New York. Sometimes he sent the horse into a trot, sometimes into a gallop.

"Darn fool's sure in a hurry," a farmer along the way muttered.

And indeed the rider, Dr. Marcus Whitman, was. He was trying to overtake the Reverend Henry H. Spalding and his wife, Eliza, who had a two-day start on him.

Whitman had a problem. The glamorous Narcissa had agreed to marry him on February 18, but she still stipulated that they must both journey to the Oregon Country as missionaries or there would be no wedding. The American Board for Foreign Missions liked the idea of a husband and wife team going to the Far West so well that it had decided there must be two such teams in the party. It was left up to Whitman to find the second couple.

Spalding and his wife had been passed over earlier by the Board because Eliza was pregnant, but her child had been born dead, and now the couple was headed for a Presbyterian mission in Missouri to serve among the Osage Indians. Spalding was determined to do missionary work one place or another, because, being an illegitimate son, he figured that he had to work twice as hard for the Lord as the average person. A brooding man, he rarely saw the bright side of life. His wife, Eliza, was not exactly an exuberant person either.

Somewhere along the road, Whitman, on his lathered horse, caught up with the Spaldings in their wagon which was to make history. At this roadside meeting, Spalding is reported to have told Whitman:

"I will not go into the same mission with Narcissa, for I question her judgment."

It is doubtful that Spalding explained why he questioned Narcissa's judgment because, if he had, Whitman might have called the whole thing off. Two years earlier, Spalding had proposed to Narcissa, and she had turned him down. On the rebound, Spalding married Eliza Hart, a highly intelligent woman, but otherwise no match for Narcissa.

Whitman, who was persuasive enough to finally get Narcissa to set a wedding date, now convinced the rejected suitor to come along to the Oregon Country on the honeymoon.

On February 18, 1836, Whitman and Narcissa were married in Angelica, New York. It was quite a wedding—but the Spaldings did not attend. Those who did wept copiously when Narcissa, who had an exceptional voice, sang the hymn, "Yes, My Native Land," which goes "In the deserts let me labor, on the mountains let me tell how He died—the Blessed Savior—to redeem a world from hell. Let me hasten, far in heathen lands to dwell."

At St. Louis, the American Fur Company again agreed to provide the protection of one of its wagon trains across the plains. And here Whitman and Spalding made the mistake that many early emigrants to the Far West did. They let the women decide what household goods and furnishings should go into a covered wagon, and Narcissa and Eliza tried to outdo each other in bringing along the comforts of home. From time to time, in river crossings and canyon ascents, the load had to be lightened, with choice furnishings left beside the trail for Indians to wonder how they would fit into a tepee.

(This writer remembers viewing with his mother the silent motion picture version of Emerson Hough's "Covered Wagon." In one scene of the movie, a man pitches a trunk off a wagon at a river crossing. In the trunk are his wife's prized possessions, including table linens and silver service. As the husband starts to drive the wagon across the river, the wife picks up the trunk and returns it to the back end of the wagon. And, with this, the mother of this writer whispered loudly enough to be heard five theatre rows away, "Good for her!")

Another mistake made by the missionaries was taking the Spaldings' wagon, which they had shipped to St. Louis. A small, springless Dearborn with gay yellow wheels, it had originally been purchased for use on Missouri roads out of the Osage Indian mission. Now the men decided that the women could ride on it, but the catch was that on most of the westward trek there were no roads.

Narcissa soon deserted the wagon for the side-saddle of a horse, but Eliza grimly and joltingly clung to the Dearborn for about a thousand miles. Thin and wiry, Eliza was quite capable of riding a horse, but it is conjectured that she preferred the bouncing wagon, because, if she rode horseback, it would naturally be with Narcissa.

The trappers were delighted with the novelty of having two white women in their party, and treated both with courtesy, although Narcissa drew the greater attention. The mountain men continually jockeyed for position to ride a spell with Narcissa, and tell her lurid tales of the wild, some of which Narcissa wished she had never heard. Only on rare occasions, however, did a trapper pull his horse up beside Eliza in the wagon.

At Fort Laramie, the trappers shifted their loads from wagons to pack saddles, and Jim Bridger told the missionaries to "git rid of the Dearborn." Spalding was agreeable, but Whitman was not. It did not occur to Whitman that significant history would be made when Narcissa and Eliza became the first white women to cross the Continental Divide. He was determined to do something truly epochal—to take that badly battered little wagon, with its bright yellow wheels now faded, all the way to the Columbia. The Dearborn rolled on.

As the caravan neared the site of a trappers' rendezvous in Wyoming's

27

Green River Valley, a rider was dispatched ahead to give word of the party's coming. When the trappers at the rendezvous learned that two white women—one a "real looker"—were in the approaching caravan, they mounted their horses, and raced to meet it. Nearing the caravan, they started to whoop and holler, jumping their horses over clumps of sagebrush or zig-zagging them in fancy patterns—like little boys showing off before little girls.

Lanky Joe Meek, who years later claimed that he first came to the Pacific Northwest "when Mount Hood was only a hole in the ground," was among them. For the next few days until the rendezvous ended, Meek, who already had an Indian wife (a Shoshone named Mountain Lamb), followed Narcissa's movements with a smitten look. Watching this "disgusting performance," Eliza did so with smoldering eyes and tightly-pursed lips.

By this time, Eliza had traded the wagon seat for a side-saddle, and it was just as well. Enroute to Idaho's Fort Hall, an axletree snapped in two as the front wheels groaned over rocky terrain. Narcissa, whose pen kept a running flow of words going for future delivery to her mother, wrote that she thought this was good riddance of the wagon, but "no—they are making a cart of the hind wheels, and lashing the forward wheels to it, intending to take it through in some shape or another."

Past Fort Hall, along the Snake River, the wagon got a real shakedown test. Spring rains had been heavy that year, leaving a webwork of gullies. The wheels bounced about as much as they rolled. Deciding to lessen the strain on them, Whitman ripped off the wagon box. The rear wheels were then placed crosswise over the front axle to ride piggyback.

As Whitman drove off with only two wheels and an axle, the trappers who continued to accompany the missionaries spat in disgust. And the mules pulling the abbreviated cart were thought to be stubborn!

In fording the Snake at one point, it took two men swimming beside the contraption to get it across. The real showdown, however, came at Fort Boise. There everyone assured Whitman that it was impossible to get wheels across the Blue Mountains.

Dejectedly, Whitman gave in. The missionaries had not been able to take a wagon from St. Louis to the Columbia, but they were the first persons to get one across Idaho—well, at least part of one. And Whitman was confident that some day wheels would roll from coast to coast. (In 1934, the Sons and Daughters of Idaho Pioneers erected a monument to Whitman on Highway 30 near Hagerman, commemorating the memory of the man "who brought the first wagon over the trappers' path that afterward became the Old Oregon Trail.")

From Fort Boise, the party went to Fort Walla Walla, then rode in a fur-bearing bateaux to Fort Vancouver. The missionaries were disappointed to learn that Parker had already sailed for home, so any decisions on a mission site were entirely up to Whitman and Spalding. The first decision they reached was that any single mission was not big enough to hold both Narcissa and Eliza, nor, for that matter, the outgoing Whitman and the withdrawn Spalding, who had words from time to time on the long trek across the plains and mountains.

Whitman selected a site on the right bank of the Walla Walla River, at Waiilatpu ("The Place of Rye Grass"), near the mouth of Mill Creek (reached now by driving on U.S. Highway 410 about six miles west of Walla Walla). Spalding pushed on 125 miles farther northeast to Lapwai ("Butterfly Valley") where a meandering stream flows into the Clearwater (at the junction of U.S. Highways 95 and 12, about 12 miles from Lewiston). At last, a mission had come to Idaho, and the reason was probably due more to the incompatibility of four courageous missionaries than to the Macedonian cry of four Indians.

While the missions were abuilding, Narcissa and Eliza remained at Fort Vancouver as guests of Dr. McLoughlin and his Indian wife, and loved every minute of it. The civilized luxuries of the fort were sheer delight after the arduous trip through the wilds during which the women had gone hungry at times rather than eat the flyblown jerky relished by the trappers. Narcissa called Fort Vancouver "the New York City of the Pacific Ocean."

Now that the women knew they would not have to live together at the same mission they got along fine. They visited a Hudson's Bay sailing ship, and took horseback rides together through the vineyards and orchards surrounding the fort, pausing to watch workers at a sawmill, gristmill and dairy. But soon their life would be much more primitive—at least for a time. In November of 1836, declining the gracious McLoughlin's invitation to stay the winter at Fort Vancouver, they took off for their respective missions.

At Lapwai, the Spaldings lived for the first three weeks in a buffalo hide tepee. Chief Tackensuatis of the Nez Perces, grateful that the Spaldings would take up where the Reverend Parker had left off, rounded up as many Indians as possible to assist in the building of a 42 by 18-foot cabin. Not all the braves responded, because manual labor had long been considered women's business.

To set an example, Tackensuatis took an axe into the woods, but he proved to be clumsy with it, and shortly turned it over to his wife. He did help, however, with the hauling of logs to the cabin site.

Two days before Christmas, the Spaldings moved into their mission home, which had two parts—one for living quarters, and one for the holding of services and the teaching of classes. The Nez Perces were proud. No other tribe in the entire Idaho Country had teachers who could instruct them in the ways of the white man, especially the spiritual ways.

Spalding and Eliza worked well as a team. Eliza did paintings of biblical scenes, and Spalding held them up for the Indians to study as he explained them. An interpreter—Spalding called him a "crier"—translated the words. Particularly impressive to the Indians were the painting and story depicting the parting of the Red Sea to permit passage of Moses and his people through it. The Nez Perces were keenly aware of occasions on Idaho lakes and rivers when they could have used such a miracle.

Spalding himself worked "little miracles" in providing shelter and food by constructing at Lapwai Idaho's first sawmill and gristmill, and by raising crops with a primitive irrigation system to augment wild game. He planted Idaho's first potatoes. The initial crop was a failure, as Spalding barely got back his seed, but it was still the beginning for a product that was to gain much fame for Idaho.

Many times Spalding, who had a couple of weeks of medical study to his credit, wished that he had pursued the subject at greater length. Much of his time was spent in the practice of medicine, for the Indians were sorely in need of healing of the body as well as of the spirit. Game was plentiful in the area at the time, and disorders from gluttony occurred frequently.

When in doubt about an ailment, Spalding resorted to bleeding, reporting that he often went "by lot, opening five or six Indians at a time, then going about more pressing business, leaving them to stop the blood when they pleased." Actually, Spalding probably saved some lives this way. At least, he used a sterile knife, and, when the Indians did a blood-letting job on themselves, they did not. Their carelessness with the knife sometimes led to fatal infections.

Spalding took greatest pride in Eliza's school—Idaho's first—which opened at the mission January 27, 1837, to about 100 Indians.

"Here a scene commenced," Spalding wrote, "more interesting, if possible, than any we had before witnessed. Nothing but actual observation can give an idea of the indefatigable application of old and young, mothers with babes in their arms, Grand-parents & Grand-children. Having no books, Mrs. S. . . . is obliged to supply the deficiency with her pen, & print her own books."

This problem was alleviated somewhat in 1839 when a small printing press arrived at the mission—the gift of a native church in Honolulu. On May 16 that year, Spalding started operating the Pacific Northwest's first printing press. Books and pamphlets turned out on this press included a primer, hymnbook, code of laws for the Nez Perces, and a translation of the Gospel of Matthew. Most of the printing was done in the Nez Perce language.

Spalding was grateful for help he received in this regard from a young missionary, Congregationalist Asa B. Smith, who, with his wife, Sarah, was sent out by the Mission Board in 1838 to help Whitman and Spalding. Smith, who was of a scholarly bent, in short order reduced the Nez Perce language to writing, and compiled the first Nez Perce dictionary and grammar.

Smith, however, spelled more trouble than he did Indian words. In the first place, he and his wife had thought they would be sent to Siam, where life would be cultured and easy. Instead, they landed at Kamiah on Idaho's Clearwater River, about 60 miles above Lapwai. Trying to figure a way to get reassigned to Siam, Smith proceeded to downgrade the entire mission in the Pacific Northwest, particularly that of Spalding.

In his reports to the Board, Smith deplored, among other things, Spalding's practice of supplying such material goods as cattle, garden seeds and hoes to the Nez Perces to get them started in agriculture.

"The more we do to encourage their selfish desires, the more difficult it will be to bring them under the influence of the gospel," Smith assured the Board. "The only hope is in giving them the pure unadulterated word of God & enabling them to understand it."

Actually, the Nez Perces didn't have any selfish desires in developing agriculture. To the contrary, they began to rebel against Spalding's efforts to get them off the hunting trails and into the fields, although there would come a day when they would greatly appreciate what the missionary had taught them, particularly in livestock raising.

The Nez Perces also began to rebel against Spalding's strict rules. With nothing more than spiritual power over the Indians, Spalding nevertheless would mete out severe punishments for various crimes—mostly involving stealing by one Indian from another. Attendance at church services and the school began to drop off.

Then French-Canadian priests started working out of the Hudson's Bay post at Fort Walla Walla, drawing many followers among the Indians. Spalding became bitter, but persisted in his work. For a while, he let up on holding "court" for crimes, but, as the Indians became more unruly, he returned to it. Most of the older Indians remained loyal to him, but the younger ones began committing acts of vandalism on the mission. One morning, Spalding went out to the pasture to find two of his cows poisoned. Another day, he discovered that Indians had demolished his mill dam.

On April 2, 1847, he wrote to the Mission Board in Boston:

"Perhaps one fourth of this tribe have turned Papists, and are very bitter against the Protestant religion. Villages, lodges, and even families have been separated."

Of some comfort to the Spaldings in their trials at Lapwai were the four children they now had. These included a daughter named Eliza after her mother. Born November 15, 1837, Eliza was Idaho's first white child.

At Waiilatpu, Whitman and Narcissa were also having their problems. And they had no children to comfort them. A daughter, Alice Clarissa, had been born March 14, 1837—the first white child in the Pacific Northwest—but she died eighteen months later.

The Whitmans had gotten off on the wrong foot by building their mission on land claimed by Chief Umtippe of the Cayuses. The Hudson's Bay Company people at Fort Walla Walla had been scrupulous about reimbursing the Indians for their property. They didn't pay much, but they did pay. More important, Umtippe had heard that American government people were quite generous about handing out money. But the Whitmans hadn't paid a dime! What Umtippe didn't understand was that the Whitmans were not American government people. They were poor missionaries. Fortunately for the Whitmans, Umtippe died about a year after the whites built their mission, and the matter of land ownership was no longer pressing.

There were other sore spots, however. Where Eliza had great compassion for the Indians, Narcissa had only the necessary minimum. Then there were the emigrants who were beginning to move into the Oregon Country. Many of them were virtually destitute when they reached Waiilatpu, and the Whitmans would offer them shelter and food. At times, they had as many as 60 or 70 people staying with them. This influx of whites worried the Cayuses.

But it was a halfbreed Indian from Maine named Joe Lewis who brought the walls of Waiilatpu tumbling down. He passed the false word among the Cayuses that he had heard Whitman and Spalding plotting to poison the Indians so the missionaries could make a quick land grab.

On November 27, 1847, Spalding rode with his daughter, Eliza, now 10 years old, to Waiilatpu to enroll her in the English school run by the Whitmans. After getting Eliza settled, Spalding was about to return to Lapwai when Whitman asked if he would like to accompany him the next day to Umatilla, 25 miles away.

As a physician, Whitman was on call among the Indians—at no pay—over a wide area. Measles had swept through the lodge of Chief Hezekiah of the Cayuses on the Umatilla River, and, although Whitman was becoming alarmed by the warlike attitude of the Cayuses, he could not refuse the plea for medical help.

Enroute to Umatilla, Spalding's horse stumbled in a gopher hole and threw him, injuring the missionary's leg—an accident that probably saved his life. While Whitman looked to the measles victims in Hezekiah's lodge, Spalding rested in the lodge of another Indian, an old friend named Stickus. Finishing his mission of mercy, Whitman went to Stickus' lodge to pick up Spalding, but the leg was giving too much pain for him to travel.

Whitman decided to ride back to Waiilatpu alone. Arriving there, he found Narcissa greatly worried about mounting rumors of Cayuse intentions to destroy the mission. The two talked far into the night, but they took no action to protect either themselves or the 72 persons then residing in various structures of the mission. The Whitmans were, after all, disciples of peace.

The next afternoon—November 29—Cayuse Chief Tilokaikt and another Indian named Tomahas rapped on the Whitman's door. Saying they needed medicine, Tilokaikt and Tomahas were admitted into the living room. Then, as Whitman turned his back to get the medicine from a drawer, Tomahas withdrew a tomahawk from beneath his blanket, and struck the doctor-missionary on the back of the head.

Whirling to defend himself, Whitman now faced a knife in the hand of Tilokaikt as well as Tomahas' tomahawk. The two Indians hacked at him until he fell dying. Narcissa, who had been in the kitchen, came screaming into the room, which was beginning to fill with other Indians. One of them shot her in the arm. Then the frenzied Cayuses carried her outside, dumped her in the mud, and began beating her with a quirt. And so died the beautiful woman who had sung at her own wedding a plea to "let me hasten, far in heathen lands to dwell," and had caused trappers to jump their horses crazily over clumps of sagebrush upon her arrival.

The blood-letting at the mission did not stop with the slaying of the Whitmans. Eleven other whites were killed outright, and three more persons, including Helen Mar, young daughter of Joe Meek by his second Indian wife (a Nez Perce), died of injuries later. Fifty-one persons were taken captive—among them, little Eliza, Spalding's daughter. The rest escaped. Now the hunt was on for Spalding.

The day following the massacre, Father John Baptiste Brouillet, who had established a Catholic mission on the Umatilla, set out for Waiilatpu, unaware of the tragic happenings there. His relations with Whitman were strained, but he felt he should pay a courtesy call while administering to Indians in the area. He made the call on the morning of December 1.

"What a sight did I then behold!" he wrote.

Bodies still lay where they had fallen amidst now burned buildings. The captives, mostly women and children, huddled together, staring at the dead with terror-stricken eyes. Enlisting the aid of Joseph Stanfield, who had been spared because he was a French-Canadian and not an American, Father Brouillet buried the victims of the massacre in a wagon box. He said that he had to conceal his tears at the price of his own life. And he had a mission to perform—to find Spalding, and warn him.

Brouillet knew that Spalding had delayed his departure from Umatilla because of his injured leg, but he might now be approaching Waiilatpu, riding to certain death. Taking his Indian interpreter with him, Brouillet hurried by horse toward Umatilla. The Cayuses had let him go without difficulty, but he had not gone far when complications developed.

The priest and his interpreter were joined by another horseman—Edward, son of Cayuse Chief Tilokait. His father, Edward explained, wanted him to go to Umatilla to tell the Cayuses there of the great victory over the missionaries.

Then the priest got a break. Edward and Brouillet's interpreter stopped their horses on the trail to light their pipes. Brouillet rode on, and, around a bend, came upon Spalding on his horse, headed for Waiilatpu.

Hurriedly, the priest told him what had happened, and urged him to ride for his life. But Spalding was too stunned to move—until Edward and the interpreter trotted up on their horses. Brouillet pleaded with Edward to say nothing about seeing Spalding. But Edward shook his head.

"My father must know that Spalding is found," he said, and began racing his horse back to Waiilatpu.

Brouillet then gave what food he had to Spalding, who spurred his horse toward Lapwai, fearing the worst. A heavy fog settled over the mountain valleys, and this afforded Spalding concealment during the afternoon. He continued to ride throughout the night, hid in the timber during the day, and set off again the next night.

Hearing the sounds of mounted Indians, he rode into a patch of brush, and crouched in silence until the warriors passed. Later that night, when he again dismounted to rest the horse, the animal bolted at a strange sound, and he could not catch it. He was now afoot, wearing shoes that were far too tight.

But, in two nights of torture augmented by his injured leg, Spalding walked 60 miles, and reached the Snake River at Alpowa. Here was the camp of his friend, Chief Timothy, whom he had baptized. But, playing it safe, Spalding waited until nightfall again before creeping up on the camp.

From one of the lodges, he heard the singing of the evening Methodist service. Spalding smiled, but the smile did not last long. From another lodge came proud talk of the Whitman massacre. Spalding stole down to the Snake, found a canoe, and silently guided it across the river. The next day he located another canoe to cross the Clearwater near Lapwai Creek.

He was home, but the sight he saw as he peered through tall grass from a hillside chilled his heart. The mission was crowded with Indians, some of them looting and shouting war cries. Not knowing what to do next, Spalding had the matter settled for him by a woman riding by on a horse.

When she recognized Spalding, she wheeled her mount, and raced down the hill to announce his presence. This was it, thought Spalding, who knew that he could flee no further on his injured leg, which by this time was an inferno of pain. But, when a group of Indians climbed up the hill to where he lay, he saw that they were all friendly Nez Perces, led by Luke, one of his early converts.

The Indians carried him down to the mission, bathed and bandaged his swollen feet and injured leg, fed him cornmeal pudding and milk, and put him to bed.

"Sleep," they said. "Your wife and the three small children are safe."

So they were. When Eliza had learned of the massacre, she had sought and obtained refuge at the nearby home of William Craig, a mountain man who had married a daughter of an old Nez Perce shaman, James, and was a power among the tribesmen.

The crisis was still not over, however. There was the matter of the 51 hostages held by the Cayuses. The Indians wanted ransom in the form of Spalding or trade goods.

Learning of the situation, James Douglas, who had recently succeeded Dr. McLoughlin as chief factor at Fort Vancouver, sent Peter Skene Ogden, a stocky fur trader, and 16 other Hudson's Bay men to Waiilatpu to deal with the Cayuses. (The town of Ogden, Utah, was named for Trader Ogden, who led six Snake Country expeditions.)

On December 23, Ogden met in council with the Indians, and told them that, if trade with Hudson's Bay for furs were to continue, a settlement would have to be made. For the release of the 51 prisoners, Ogden said that Hudson's Bay would pay 12 guns, 12 flints, 600 loads of ammunition, 62 three-point blankets, 63 cotton shirts and 37 pounds of tobacco. The Cayuses agreed to the trade.

When the Spaldings at last were able to embrace their daughter, Eliza, they found her "too weak to stand, a mere skeleton, and her mind as much impaired as her health by the experiences she had been through." The experiences also had a great effect on the parents. Nevertheless, the Spaldings wanted to continue their work at Lapwai. But the Mission Board ruled otherwise, and they moved to the Willamette Valley, then to the Walla Walla Country.

Twenty-four years later, in 1871, the Lapwai Mission was reopened in accordance with President Ulysses S. Grant's so-called "Peace Policy" with the American Indians. The missionary again in charge at Lapwai was the Reverend Henry H. Spalding, but his second period of tenure was brief, for he died August 3, 1874. The funeral was a big one, and most of those attending were Nez Perces, silent and somber. In their hearts they knew that Spalding in his own, unbending way had tried to do right by them.

In 1821, at a Catholic seminary in Mechlin, Belgium, Father Charles Nerinckx, famed for his missionary work among the American Indians of Kentucky, addressed a class of young men studying for the priesthood. He asked:

"How can it be that Napoleon found millions of men ready to sacrifice their lives to ravage a nation and to aid him to conquer the world while I cannot find a handful of devoted men to save an entire people and extend the reign of God?"

The question hung heavy over the head of one young man in the audience. His name was Pierre Jean De Smet. Within a few years, he was in the United States, serving as a Jesuit missionary among the plains Indians.

Then, in the summer of 1840, he rode to the trappers' rendezvous at Pierre's Hole with Jim Bridger's brigade. Now 39, rotund and racked with malaria, he nevertheless appeared a commanding figure as he sat his horse, with black robe flowing over the saddle.

Sixteen hundred Nez Perces and Flatheads, who had been awaiting De Smet's coming, shouted welcomes, and waved rifles and spears and bows. The priest beamed. Even Napoleon, he thought, never received a greeting such as was being given to him, a simple soldier of Christ. What he did not know until later was that several days earlier the Indians, after chanting Catholic prayers taught them by the Iroquois, had slain 50 Blackfeet in battle without loss to themselves.

Now, as the Indians knelt, De Smet said the first mass offered in Idaho, with the place becoming known as "The Prairie of the Mass." Because the service was such a success, the missionary decided to return immediately to St. Louis to raise funds to establish missions in the Pacific Northwest.

Coming back the following year with Fathers Nicholas Point and Gregory Mengarini, De Smet stopped off at Fort Hall before proceeding northward, and was greeted by trader Francis Ermatinger. Although a staunch Episcopalian, Ermatinger not only treated the Catholic priests as honored guests, but sold them supplies at one-third the usual cost. Then, as they were leaving, he shoved many gifts in their pack saddles. Having dealt with loose-living trappers for years, he believed that the country could do with some religion—any kind.

Father DeSmet's first mission, called St. Mary's, was established in Montana's Bitterroot Valley near what is now Stevensville. Racing against winter, the priests managed to construct before the end of 1841 a mud-daubed cabin with scraped deerskin windows.

"At night," Father Mengarini wrote, "we rolled ourselves in several blankets, and then in a buffalo robe; yet in the morning we awoke to find robe and blankets frozen into one piece. We crept out of our frozen shell and set it before the fire to thaw; and this we did daily throughout the long months of winter."

The next year De Smet traveled widely from St. Mary's throughout Idaho's Coeur d'Alenes, where he received many pleas from the Indians to establish a mission in their area. So he designated Father Point to construct Idaho's first Catholic mission on the St. Joe River, not far from the present town of St. Maries. Here, on the first Friday of December, 1842, Point planted a cross, and dedicated the mission to the Sacred Heart. In the spring of 1843, "a new village was laid out; trees were felled, roads opened, a church erected and the public fields sown. By October, 1844, the little village contained one hundred Christian families."

There was a major problem, however. Each spring the site was inundated by river floods. So, in 1846, the mission was abandoned, and a new site was sought. Thus, the Sacred Heart Mission, which a century later would be designated a National Historical Landmark, came to be located on the Coeur d'Alene River between the present cities of Coeur d'Alene and Kellogg.

The mission church, on which construction was completed in 1853, stands today off U.S. Highway 10 at Cataldo as one of the most remarkable historical buildings in Idaho. There were no nails available when it was built, so wooden pins were substituted.

When Father Anthony Ravalli, S.J., and two lay brothers rode into the valley with orders to build the church, the major tools they had were a broadaxe, augur, pulleys, and a whipsaw, which the priest had fashioned from the steel rim of a wagon wheel by flattening it, then toothing it with a chisel and file. Where would they get wood for walls and beams and columns of the building that was to be 90 by 40 feet? Tall Father Ravalli turned in the saddle to gaze at a forest. Paints? The missionary noted the clay colors daubed on tepees and faces, and chuckled. But artisans?

Born in Ferrara, Italy, Ravalli had studied painting and architecture in Rome. He knew how to construct a fine building, but his Indian workmen had only a desire to serve the white man's God. And, unless they served Him well, Ravalli warned, they would not be permitted to work on the building.

Early in the construction, as tribesmen kneed plunging ponies to raise two-foot thick pillars with grass-woven ropes, a giant among the Coeur d'Alenes showed up for work. Ravalli shook his head.

"You beat your wife with a willow branch this morning. No work today."

In silent penitence, the big fellow sat out the day on the river bank . . . and his wife knew no more beatings.

But Ravalli's kindliness actually generated more work than his strictness. Then there was the time he "breathed life" back into an Indian squaw, and the red men who observed this "miracle" could not do enough for the priest after that.

The woman, who had had trouble with her husband, became despondent, and hanged herself with buckskin thongs to a tree in the forest. When Ravalli, who was called to the scene, cut her down, he could detect no beating of her pulse. But her neck was unbroken.

Ahead of his time, the priest, who had studied some medicine in Rome as well as architecture and painting, began to give the squaw mouth-to-mouth resuscitation. Repeatedly, he also raised and lowered her arms. This went on for almost an hour. Then, slowly, the glow of life started to return to the woman's face. Ravalli knew that he had won. And not only against death. He

35

had also won the hearts of the Indians who had been watching the whole procedure.

Today, as one approaches the old church built with the aid of the appreciative Indians, he is first impressed by the six great white columns which grace the front. How were they turned out? That is a secret which died with Father Ravalli.

The mission served not only as a house of worship in the wilderness but as an important stopping point for travelers until 1877, when the Federal government moved the Coeur d'Alene Indians to Hangman Valley, where the town of De Smet is now located. In 1853, Isaac I. Stephens, governor of Washington Territory, paused at Sacred Heart Mission, and later wrote a glowing tribute to the architectural beauty of the building. Captain John Mullan, who built a road across Northern Idaho bearing his name, called the church the "St. Bernard of the Coeur d'Alene Mountains." And, as a church should be, it was a place of peace. There Colonel George Wright, with the help of the missionary priests, concluded a treaty with the Coeur d'Alenes, ending the Indian War of 1858.

The mission became commonly known as the "Cataldo Mission" after Father Joseph Cataldo, S.J., and the nearby town of Cataldo also bears his name. A man of great energy and purpose, Father Cataldo was the priest who, in 1881, purchased a half-section of land on the Spokane River at $3.50 an acre, and founded on it in 1887 Gonzaga University—initially a one-room building.

In 1830, Joseph Smith, a young farmer at Fayette, New York, after revealing the discovery of some long-buried "golden plates" with writings in an ancient language (which later became the basis for the "Book of Mormon"), founded the Church of Jesus Christ of Latter-Day Saints. With every Saint or Mormon in effect a missionary, the church grew rapidly in numbers despite persecution by those who scorned it.

Headquarters of the church moved to Independence, Missouri—and to more persecution. So Smith took a look at some unwanted swamplands in Illinois on the Mississippi River, and there the Mormons founded the city of Nauvoo, which within four years grew into the largest city in Illinois with a population of about 20,000. (Chicago was just beginning to spread out its roots.) But to thriving Nauvoo there had also come people of other faiths and some of no faith—certainly with no faith in the Mormons. Mostly immigrants from Europe, the non-Mormons looked down on the religion spawned in the new country, and took umbrage particularly at the tenet of the church allowing plural wives.

Torches were put to Mormon homes, and leaders thrown in jail at Carthage, Illinois. Then, on June 27, 1844, Smith, who had been mayor of Nauvoo, and his brother, Hyrum, were slain when a mob stormed the jail. It was again time to move on.

This new movement of a determined people, continuing over a period of years, became one of the world's most remarkable exhibitions of faith and endurance. With some having only handcarts to push or pull, the freedom seekers headed across the plains and mountains for "Upper California"—Utah.

The first of the emigrating Mormons reached the Great Basin of the Salt Lake on July 24, 1847. (The date is now celebrated annually by the Mormons as Pioneer Day.) Upon arrival in the valley, the Mormons' new leader, Brigham

Young, who had been stricken by mountain fever, raised up from his bed in a wagon, gazed across the vast mountain-circled amphitheatre, and said:

"This is the place."

He was not necessarily implying that it was the most desirable place spotted on the long journey. Actually, he sought the reverse—a place like the swamplands on the Mississippi River which nobody else seemed to want. The Great Basin of the Salt Lake was far from swampy, but, as desert country, it was harsh and forbidding. It was, as Young said, the place.

The small but powerfully-built man, with sweeping beard and all-encompassing eyes, had no intention, however, of limiting the new Zion to the basin. In 1855, he sent 28 missionaries under the leadership of Thomas B. Smith to the Lemhi Valley in Southeastern Idaho. Young's instructions to the group were to take along enough supplies to last a year "so that you will not be a burden to the Indians. Be able rather to help them if they need it, so they will be friendly to us . . . It is cheaper to feed the Indians than to fight them."

On June 15, after a tortuous trek of 379 miles from Utah, the missionaries began the building of a mission, which, in view of the time and place, took the form of a fort. It was called Fort Limhi (later changed to Lemhi) after a Nephite king mentioned in the "Book of Mormon."

At Fort Lemhi, the missionaries preached a new way of life by example with communal farming on irrigated land, and gristmill operations that followed the harvest. And, from time to time, they shared food with the Shoshones and Bannocks in the area. But the Indians did not like what they saw—or liked it so well they wanted to steal it. In brief, Young's idea of casting bread upon the troubled waters to smooth the way through Indian country did not work—at least not in the Lemhi Valley.

On February 25, 1858, the Indians started driving off a herd of cattle grazing on a hillside near the fort. Several men went out to stop them, but, discovering that the red men numbered more than 150, the Mormons hastily retreated to the fort. The Indians then attacked the fort, killing two of the missionaries and wounding five. The word was received from Salt Lake City—"come home"—and, on March 28, 1858, the fort was abandoned.

Two years later, however, the Mormons were back in Idaho, founding on April 14, 1860, the Territory's first permanent settlement, just over the border from Utah. This was the town of Franklin, which also gained historical fame as the site of Idaho's first school to serve white children (only Indians were taught at the Reverend Spalding's school in Lapwai). The school building of log construction had both a dirt roof and floor, with a fireplace to ward off the chill of winter. Slates and pencils came from the rock which was plentiful on a hillside near Franklin. Seats or benches were made from rough-hewn log slabs, and the 20 pupils studying under Hannah Comish squirmed from slivers until adults, using the school as a meeting place, did some squirming, too, and corrected the situation with a planing session.

While the Mormons were building homes in Franklin, they lived in the boxes of their wagons, formed in a huge circle. The running gears had been pulled from beneath the boxes for the hauling of logs. The first permanent homes were log cabins, followed by structures of frame and stone construction. Builders of the latter were Mormons heeding Brigham Young's words:

"Why not quarry rock, and build stone houses, and make stone fences? Stone makes a good fence, and it will not winter kill. Build good fences, have good gardens, and make yourselves comfortable and happy serving God."

Actually, the Mormons who pioneered Idaho's first permanent settlement, named after Franklin D. Richards, thought they were in Utah, and did not learn otherwise until the survey of 1872. But, most important to Idaho, was the fact that the Mormons, despite the attack in the Lemhi Valley, were still pushing out from the Great Basin of the Salt Lake. Otherwise, settlement of much of Southern Idaho would no doubt have been long delayed.

Within 10 years, the Mormons had towns scattered all over the Upper Cache Valley—Weston, Dayton, Clifton, Preston, Oxford . . . Members of the Church of Latter-Day Saints also were responsible for the early development along the Bear River, the largest stream in the United States which does not flow into an ocean—its destination the Great Salt Lake in Utah.

In Bear Lake Valley, a new Paris bloomed in the fall of 1863. (The story goes that the town was supposed to have been named after settler Fred Perris, but the early residents liked the postal department's misspelling because it made them feel as if their town were a cultural, religious and political center. And, to a degree, it was.) Paris was quickly followed by such neighboring communities as Montpelier, Bloomington and St. Charles.

Then just a few miles north of Paris the town of Ovid sprang up. It never did grow very big (present population, 145), but it did produce a man with a big idea. On March 25, 1867, Gutzon Borglum was born at Ovid, a genius member of a Danish family of nine children.

As a young man, Borglum went off to Paris, France, to pursue an art career, but his Western heritage was strong enough to bring him back to America's wide open spaces. And, on a 700-foot granite face of Mount Rushmore in the Black Hills of South Dakota, he carved the gargantuan images of four great United States presidents—Washington, Jefferson, Lincoln and Theodore Roosevelt.

First attempts at colonization of the Malad Valley in 1864 failed, but, in 1866, there came more Mormons to establish Malad City. A stagecoach junction point, Malad City rose rapidly in significance, and was able to take the seat of Oneida County away from Soda Springs, a settlement started as a military post in 1863 by General Patrick E. Conner.

All, however, was not smooth going for the Mormons in coming to the new land. There was that matter of polygamy—not practiced by all the Mormons— but by many of the church leaders.

In 1882, the United States Congress passed the Edmunds Act, outlawing polygamy, and, three years later, Idaho's Territorial Legislature went a step further. It passed the Mormon Test Oath Law, forbidding anyone to vote, hold public office or serve on juries if he belonged to an organization allowing the practice of polygamy. That meant all Mormons, not just those involved in plural wife situations. As for those actually practicing polygamy, they were subject to arrest. And hundreds of arrests were made.

Fred T. Dubois, who later served as both a Territorial Delegate to Congress and a United States Senator, was a U.S. marshal at the time when the arrests were at their peak. He wrote in his memoirs:

"I recall the case of a Franklin blacksmith named Nash, who, after conviction for illegal cohabitation, asked me if he could go home and arrange his affairs before being taken to the penitentiary. The term of court seemed certain to last at least three weeks longer, so I told him that he could go, but that he must be back within that time. On the appointed day, he turned up. The same thing took place in a number of other instances."

But the situation was not long in changing. In 1890, leaders of the Church of Latter-Day Saints issued a proclamation declaring that all members should cease to practice polygamy. That led, in 1893, to Idaho, now a state, restoring full citizenship to all Mormons within its borders. And there were many, particularly in Southeastern Idaho.

Roots of the Mormons had grown deep and strong. At Idaho Falls in 1939, construction was started on a Mormon temple, a beautiful edifice of white marble. (Although today the flourishing city of 35,776 population has 60 different churches, it remains a major Mormon center.) At Rexburg (a misspelled honoring of the name of pioneer Mormon settler Thomas Ricks), the Mormons established Ricks College in 1888 as the Bannock State Academy. Starting out with elementary education, the school worked up to college studies in 1915. And, at the University of Idaho in Moscow, the church established in 1928 its first Institute for Mormon religion studies at a public institution of higher learning.

The success of the Jesuits at Sacred Heart Mission in Northern Idaho, and —more significantly—the discovery of gold in the Boise Basin in 1862, led Catholic Archbishop Francis N. Blanchet of Oregon to send two French priests, Fathers A. Z. Poulin and Toussaint Mesplie, to the basin in 1863 to build the area's first Catholic church. (Idaho did not get its own Catholic bishop—the Most Reverend Alphonsus J. Glorieux—until some years later.)

Caught up in the spirit of the various boom mining camps, the missionaries, within a year, supervised the building of not one but four churches—St. Thomas' at Placerville, St. Dominic's at Centerville, St. Joseph's at Idaho City and St. Andrew's at Silver City—plus a small chapel at Boise City. Poulin set up his parsonage at Silver City, and Mesplie at Idaho City.

A big man, weighing close to 300 pounds, Poulin was further identifiable by the large sombrero he wore and the heavy cane he twirled. He couldn't get within a hundred yards of a swearing miner or teamster without the language being toned down.

Mesplie, on the other hand, was a little man, with keen black eyes and short-cropped hair. While Poulin loved to rough it with the miners, helping them hoist a heavy timber and, incidentally, demonstrating his great strength, Mesplie liked to sit at his desk poring over his diaries. He had served 20 dangerous years among the Indians in the Far West, and he was writing a book about his experiences. Then, in 1871, fire swept through Idaho City, and he lost everything—diaries and manuscript.

Gifted in consoling families who had lost a loved one, Mesplie could not be consoled in his own loss.

"Zey is all gone, all burned up!" he mourned to a friend. "My love, my life's labor! All, all, all! But, oh, why?"

The Catholics, like those of various other denominations, established a college in Idaho—the College of St. Gertrude at Cottonwood—which grew out of a boarding and day school opened in 1927. The college has long been of special interest to this writer, because it gave to Idaho from its faculty one of the State's outstanding historians—Sister M. Alfreda Elsensohn.

Methodism came to the Boise Basin soon after Catholicism. The Reverend C. S. Kingsley, former editor of the *Pacific Christian Advocate* of Portland, preached his first sermon in Union Hall at Idaho City on November 22, 1863. Announcing that the hall would be "made warm and comfortable for ladies and children," he drew a large crowd.

It was bitterly cold in Idaho City that winter, but Kingsley nevertheless started immediately on the construction of a church. Freezing his feet in the process, he was laid up for a couple of weeks, but managed to finish the job early in 1864. Later, this building was sold to the county for a courthouse. Kingsley then erected a substantial brick church, and this also in time became the county courthouse.

A self-made botanist, Kingsley was a great lover of flowers. He thought that everybody else in Idaho City should be, too—and, as a sideline, he sold flowers among other things. The *Idaho World* of April 22, 1869, reported:

"Kingsley got up a lot of flowers in the shrub from San Francisco a few days ago, and, in an hour after he opened the lot for sale, he found purchasers for them all. Among them were roses, dahlias, fuchsias and other choice flowers."

A kindly man, Kingsley was a friend to everyone he met, but when lawlessness ran rampant in the basin, he became a leader of the Vigilantes—in fact, presided over the first secret meeting of the Vigilantes held in Idaho City. In those days, a person had to be adaptable. Reverend Kingsley was.

On October 12, 1867, a stagecoach, six horses pulling, careened into Boise City, and rolled to a stop in a swirl of dust. From the door stepped an imposing figure. He was six feet tall, wore a heavy beard which the British called "Piccadilly Weepers," had a generally dignified look about him—but an engaging twinkle in his eyes. This man, a distinguished graduate of Columbia University in New York City, was Idaho's first bishop—the Right Reverend Daniel Sylvester Tuttle, Episcopalian Missionary Bishop of Montana, Utah and Idaho.

"When I got off that stage from Salt Lake City I had a broken neck, bruised head, aching bones and disturbed temper," he recalled. "But, otherwise, I was fine."

He also chuckled about the vast territory he had come to serve. In it, at the time, there was only one established Episcopal church. This was at Boise City.

Three years earlier, in 1864, Reverend Michael Fackler had arrived in Boise City, and had constructed on the corner of Bannock and Seventh Streets a church. In 1867, he departed for the East by ship from San Francisco to bring his invalid wife back to Boise. But he never got there. Cholera swept the ship, and Fackler was among the many who succumbed to the disease, dying as the ship approached Key West, Florida. St. Michael's Cathedral in Boise is named for both the saint and the man who built the city's first Episcopal church—in fact, the first Protestant church in all of Idaho, Montana and Utah.

(The white-towered church, now known as Christ Chapel and looking like a bit of transplanted New England, can be seen today on the Broadway side of the Boise State University campus. When the church was located on the new site, Dr. Eugene B. Chaffee, retired president of Boise State, who did so much to build up that university, was appointed official greeter to welcome the historically-minded each Sunday between 2 and 4 p.m. But the church, which was erected more than a century ago with funds obtained through bazaars, ice cream socials and home talent shows, has more purpose than providing a glimpse of the past. It opens its doors to the future by being the scene of about 50 weddings annually.)

In 1870, Bishop Tuttle got a bell for the church. It became the custom to ring it when someone in Boise died—one stroke for a male; two for a female; then a pause followed by the number of strokes necessary to enumerate the age of the deceased. The practice was discontinued, however, because the sports in the town got to betting on how many times the bell would toll.

As bishop, Tuttle might have been expected to spend most of his time at his headquarters in Boise, but instead he was usually on the road—bouncing in a stagecoach or riding a horse to scattered mining camps. His eloquence was great. Saloon keepers hated to see him coming, because business dropped sharply when he was speaking in camp. To the gamblers, he was the "Star Gospel Sharp."

Although he spent most of his time in Idaho, the bishop did not neglect other parts of his far-flung diocese. In 1872, he established St. Mark's Hospital at Salt Lake City.

Gradually, Easterner Tuttle got used to his new Western setting, but he never ceased to marvel at its paradoxes. In a letter to a New Yorker, he wrote that he had spent an unusual afternoon in Idaho City. While he was discussing the philosophy of Herbert Spencer in the law offices of Colonel Samuel A. Merritt and Major R. E. Foote, the bishop said that he could hear outside the sounds of frenzied betting on a horse race.

One stagecoach driver who had Tuttle often as a passenger was quoted in the *Portland Oregonian:*

"The boys all love him. He is as quiet and modest as he is learned and scholarly. He can have my overcoat any night the snow flies."

After 19 years in Idaho, Tuttle went on to bigger things in St. Louis, becoming the presiding bishop of the Protestant Episcopal Church in the United States, with authority extending over all foreign missions. He lived to celebrate in 1916 his Golden Jubilee as a bishop.

A lasting—and steadily growing—monument to the early endeavors of the Episcopal Church in Idaho is Boise State University. The university, now state-supported, was organized in 1932 under church sponsorship.

Many of Idaho's first settlers could not speak English, which meant that a minister who knew their language was one of the most welcome persons to ride into a settlement. Definitely this was true of the Northern Idaho community of Genesee, settled largely by German Lutherans.

By 1887, Genesee had a doctor and a dentist, but no minister. A circuit-riding German preacher had passed through the community in 1885, but he had paused to preach only a couple of sermons. Late in 1887, however, the Reverend Henry Rieke, another German minister, came to town from Wisconsin. The exchange of greetings in the old country language was most warm. Deciding that he was once again among his people, Rieke began holding services wherever space was available.

On November 30, 1890, St. John's Evangelical Church was dedicated to become a familiar landmark of Genesee. When the church celebrated its golden anniversary, the minister who preached the sermon was the Reverend Marcus Rieke, grandson of the first pastor.

The Jews who came to early Idaho were not missionaries. They were simply Jews who quietly, but determinedly, brought their religion with them. Not great in number, they were mostly merchants, pleased to learn that there was little prejudice against them out in the wide open spaces.

Indeed, the Mormons, beginning to filter north more and more from Utah, held the Jews in great esteem. The Saints linked their own flight from persecution to the Biblical travails of the Jews, and sometimes even referred to them as "brother Jews."

The rapidly growing Jewish communities in America's East and Midwest

41

had their discomfort from crowding, but there was comfort in numbers, too. It took a strong Jew to pull up stakes, and head for the Far West. Such a Jew was Moses Alexander.

Youngest of a family of eight children, he was born in Bavaria November 13, 1853. The father died shortly thereafter, and the children had to hustle to support an invalid mother. There was little opportunity for schooling, but somehow Alexander learned Latin well, because his most treasured possession was a prize received for scholarly achievement in the language—a Latin book inscribed by the King of Bavaria.

At 14, Alexander came to America, living for a while with two sisters in New York City, then moving to Chillicothe, Missouri, to work as a janitor in a clothing store operated by a cousin. In time, Alexander started his own store in Chillicothe, acquired a wife, Helena, and four children, and became mayor of Chillicothe.

Things were going well in Chillicothe, but the Far West held more promise. On July 14, 1891, Alexander opened a store in Boise.

His business prospered, but the same could not be said for his religion. There were then perhaps a hundred Jews in the Boise Basin, and Alexander decided to do something about them. On February 17, 1895, he called a meeting in his home, and the congregation of Beth Israel was formed. The Minute Book of the temple lists leading businessmen of Boise as the officers: President, David Falk; vice-president, M. Alexander; secretary, Charles Stolz; treasurer, D. Spegel, and trustees, Nathan Falk, L. Weil and E. Shainwold.

Ambitious plans were made by these well-to-do merchants, and they were achieved in 1896 with the erection of Temple Beth Israel at 1102 State Street. Beautifully designed in the Moorish manner, it was built to serve a congregation of 500. Well kept, it still serves today (now only four times a year on the major Jewish holidays), but never for 500.

Alexander was disappointed in attendance at the temple, but not in the role he played as an Idaho political leader. In 1897, he was elected mayor of Boise by a big majority. Choosing not to succeed himself, he did not run in the next election, but, in 1901, he again became mayor.

In 1902, President Theodore Roosevelt came to town. This caused some concern. The "boys in the know" said that Roosevelt would have nothing to do with the mayor because he was not only a Democrat but a Jew. The tall, handsome Alexander, however, was not perturbed. He put on his best "bib and tucker," engaged the fanciest rig in Boise, and met Roosevelt at the edge of town. Then the two rode together in a parade through Boise, waving and smiling in tandem to the crowds.

Roosevelt stated in a speech:

"I wish to say what pleasure it has given me to come here and to witness with my own eyes what you are doing in this state with irrigation. Idaho will, I firmly believe, grow with peculiar rapidity and with peculiar stability during the years now immediately opening. While a great part of the growth will surely be due to the development of the State's unexplored mineral resources, I think the most permanent and useful part of growth will be the development of her irrigated agriculture."

Roosevelt, who covered the situation very well except for failing to mention the potentials of lumbering, manufacturing and tourism, made some political hay in Idaho, but Alexander baled it. In fact, he became gubernatorial material.

In 1908, he was nominated as a candidate for governor, but inter-party feuding cost him the nomination. Capturing the nomination four years later, he campaigned hard, making some speeches from street corners, some in farm fields. He spoke of "useless boards and slow-motion commissions," declaring that he had not realized how badly the people of Idaho had been stung until he found in the State House an office labeled "Bee Inspector."

Idahoans loved Alexander's style, and elected him Governor—the first Jewish governor in the history of the United States. More important, he proved to be a good governor, both in his first and second terms.

Alexander was ahead of the times. So, too, was the State of Idaho.

Chapter IV

# A LONG, LONG TRAIL A-WINDING

"No other race of men with means at their command would undertake so great a journey—none save those could successfully perform it with no previous preparation, relying only on the fertility of their invention to devise the means to overcome each danger and difficulty as it arose . . . They have undertaken to perform, with slow-moving oxen, a journey of two thousand miles. The way lies over trackless wastes, wide and deep rivers, rugged and lofty mountains, and is beset with hostile savages. Yet . . . they are always found ready and equal to the occasion, and always conquerors. May we not call them men of destiny?"

—Jesse Applegate, who traversed the Oregon Trail in 1843, and became an early Oregon legislator

A woman seated in a covered wagon behind plodding oxen, part of a train winding along the Platte River in 1846, glanced at a man-formed mound of rocks beside the trail. Stuck into the rocks was a small cross fashioned of aspen boughs, and tied to the top of the cross was an infant's blue bonnet, trimmed with white lace. Tears started to form in the woman's eyes, but they did not reach the surface, for, like so many other pioneer women, she had learned to cry inside.

"Git along!" she shouted at the oxen.

The bonnet over the grave symbolized the new era of the Oregon Trail. Those who had traveled it before were mostly mountain men going west in quest of furs, and hoping to return with their own hides intact. Now, the trail knew entire families planning to settle permanently in the Far West, particularly in the Oregon Country around which an aura of magic had been spun.

Starting on the Missouri River at Independence, the trail cut northwest to the Platte River at Fort Kearney. The route then followed the south bank of the Platte, a river once described as "a thousand miles long and six inches deep." Stretching past Scotts Bluff and Fort Laramie to the Sweetwater River, the trail crossed the Wind River Range at South Pass, dropped down to Fort Bridger, then entered Idaho at its southeastern corner. Before starting across Idaho, the trappers of the past had abandoned their wagons. But a new era had dawned.

In 1840, Joe Meek and a mountain man friend, Bob Newell, decided to chuck the fur business, and make permanent homes for themselves in Oregon. Rounding up some dilapidated wagons which had been abandoned at Fort Hall, they cannibalized them for parts and put together three vehicles which would at least roll. Then they trained Indian ponies to pull them.

When this uncertain caravan was ready, Meek and Newell loaded on their Indian wives and children, and started across Southern Idaho for Oregon. Not only did they get across Idaho, but they made it intact over the Blue Mountains. When they arrived at Waiilatpu, Dr. Marcus Whitman was ecstatic.

"I knew it could be done, and you did it!" he cried. "Oh, you will never regret it! You have broken the ice, and when others see that wagons have passed, they, too, will pass, and in a few years the valley will be full of our people."

To Dr. Whitman, "our people" were whites from settled America. The missionary was beginning to have the feeling that until they came in numbers and spread their influence—and way of life—there would be little Christianizing of the natives of the wilderness. And numbers were vital to safety from Indian attack.

Meek left his daughter, Helen Mar, with Narcissa Whitman for schooling—it would be the last time he would see her or the Whitmans alive—then drove on to Fort Walla Walla. There the party—the first to take wagons to the Columbia—left the vehicles and ponies, and proceeded down the river in boats to the Willamette Valley, where Meek settled down to the relative tameness of being the first United States Marshal of Oregon Territory and an envoy of the Oregon Provisional Government to Washington.

His roaring years—1829 to 1840—as a trapper, operating mostly out of Fort Hall, were over. Books have been written on his hair-raising exploits, but it is hard to beat his own words. For example:

"I'd been over on Prior's Fork to set traps and found old Ben Johnson's boys (the Blackfeet) over there, just a walkin' up and down them 'ar streams with their hands on their hips a gatherin' plums. They gave me a tilt, shot my horse in the neck, and sent us head over heels in a pile together, but we raised a-runnin'. I could see the blanket wads comin' out of their muzzles, but I just sat on my horse's back with the savages squattin' and' grabbin' at me, an' raised a fog for about half a mile until I was out of their reach."

But Meek's main contribution in opening the West was not in daring to trap for beaver where the Indians didn't want him to trap. It was in daring to make that wagon trek to the Columbia. The way to a new life in the promised land was now clear—via the Oregon Trail. Jesse Applegate, who led a train across the trail from Independence, Missouri, in 1843, told how it was done:

"Sentinels fired their rifles at four o'clock in the morning to wake the camp.

Fires were lighted and the herders drove the oxen into the circle of wagons to be yoked for the day's journey . . . Promptly at seven, the bugle sounded, and the wagon train was on its way. Women and children often walked beside the trail, gathering wild flowers and odd-looking stones. Boys and young men on horseback kept the loose stock from straying . . .

"At noon, the emigrants stopped to eat . . . Sometimes the officers of the train got together at noon to consider the case of someone who had violated the rules or had committed a crime. He was given a fair trial, and, if found guilty, was sentenced according to the nature of his offense. (In one case of murder, the condemned man was given a choice of hanging or shooting. He took the rifle bullet.)

"All through the afternoon the oxen plodded, and when the wagons arrived at the spot chosen by the guide as a camping place, preparations were made to spend the night. Livestock were driven out to pasture, tents were pitched, fires built, and supper was on its way . . .

"After supper, the children played their favorite games; the elders gathered in groups and talked . . . Some of the young folk danced to the music of fiddle or accordion . . .

"Guard duty commenced at eight o'clock. Fires were dimmed at an early hour, and everyone retired to rest for tomorrow's march. Usually the sleep was undisturbed save perhaps by the sharp yelp of a coyote on a nearby hill, and the challenging bark of the camp dogs."

Applegate's idyllic description was accurate enough—when there was no trouble. Often there was, in the form of treacherous terrain, dreaded disease or warring Indians.

"All is smooth sailing until we reach a spongy crossing at a point which was once a creek," wrote Lewis Bissell Dougherty in 1848. "It may be two wagons are driven across safely. Then, when the third one is driven in or on, down it goes to its hubs. You either double the team or unload and haul the empty wagon out. Now it will not do to try another wagon, so every one takes his butcher knife and a blanket, cuts as much grass as he can carry in the blanket, piles it on the marshy draw and tramples it down. Then a wagon is driven on and nearly always over. Sometimes before all the train is over the grass has to be replenished."

But there was little that could be done when cholera swept through a train. More often than not in that period the disease was fatal.

"Five of our comrades had previously become the prey of cholera, and yet, like a sleuth-hound, it was still pursuing us," Reuben Cole Shaw wrote in his diary on June 22, 1849. "We were congratulating ourselves on being done with the dread disease, but here again was the prospect of losing two or more of our esteemed members . . . and of another long delay. Owing to this disease we were already 40 or 50 days behind, and, as the game had been driven from the road by earlier hunters, our supplies were being rapidly consumed, and we were liable to be caught in the early snows on the mountains, making the outlook very discouraging."

In 1844, tragedy began stalking the Sager family in a wagon train on the trail—after the Sagers had known the joy of the birth of a child in Kansas, the seventh in the family. Near Fort Laramie, Wyoming, nine-year-old Catherine, trotting beside the Sager wagon with an eye out for wild flowers, stumbled and fell. One of the wagon's wheels rolled over a leg, crushing it. Without benefit of physician, the leg was patched up.

47

*The wagons rolled on.*

After a long, dry spell, the train came to the Green River. The hot and weary travelers plunged into its cool waters, and were as renewed as if they had found the Fountain of Youth. But then the father of the Sager family caught mountain fever, and, in a few days, died, whispering, "What will become of the children?" The oldest son of another family took over the driving of the Sager wagon, with the children and mother clustered behind—Catherine feeling pain in her injured leg from every jolt of the vehicle, and the new baby fussing in its mother's arms.

*The wagons rolled on.*

At Rock Creek, near the present site of Twin Falls, the mother followed the father in death. Cause? Understanding women on the train said that "she was just plumb wore out."

*The wagons rolled on.*

Later, Catherine Sager lamented:

"We wanted so much to bury Mother in her best dress. But she had hidden her treasured satin one so well in the bottom of the wagon that we could not find it in time. A calico dress had to do."

*The wagons had to roll on.*

At first, the Indians gave no trouble, but, when the whites started coming in ever-greater numbers, the Indians became alarmed, and began their harassing attacks. When a man stooped down at a spring to take a drink, he kept his eyes raised to the horizon for fear of what might emerge on it.

Most keenly felt by the emigrants, however, was the fear of the unknown. Little wonder it was that John East, a Missouri farmer heading for Oregon in 1843 with the Applegate train, paused with his oxen at the Missouri line. Looking back with watering eyes, he doffed his battered hat, and waved it.

"Farewell to America!" he said.

But nothing stopped a new train from forming. The prize was great. Bills in the United States Congress in 1843 promised to give to every male settler in the Pacific Northwest 640 acres, another 160 to his wife, and 160 to each child. The bills did not pass, because ownership of the land was still in dispute with Great Britain, but the emigrants were sure the matter would be settled in favor of the United States. Until then, they would assume squatters' rights. So it was "Oregon or bust."

Upon entering Idaho, the early Oregon Trailers never ceased to be amazed by Soda Springs. Wrote Wakeman Bryarly in 1849:

"We arrived on July 11 at Soda Springs—by some called Bear Springs . . . The whole valley is the most interesting spot of earth that I ever beheld. Here is a grand field for the geologist, mineralogist, naturalist & any other kind of 'ist' that you can conceive . . . The greatest curiosity of all is 'The Steamboat Spring.' This is situated upon the edge of the Bear River, half a mile from the first spring. Out of solid rock, with a hole 1 foot in diameter, gushes forth the water, foaming, whizzing, sizzling, blowing, splashing & spraying."

But it was at Soda Springs that the emigrants began to check most carefully the "Bone Express." This was the system of leaving messages on the bleached bones of buffalo or oxen which had died on the trail. Sometimes a message merely said that "John and Mary are all right," but other times the message was in the form of a warning: "Watch Out for Indian Attack."

In Idaho, the attacks were becoming more and more frequent. What was

48

generally not understood by the travelers was that the Indians, more than protecting their property, were seeking to ease the pangs of hunger. The buffalo were still plentiful on the plains, but for the most part they had faded from Idaho, and many Indians, particularly in Southern Idaho's desert areas, sometimes went for days on a diet which featured grasshoppers as the main dish, topped off by roots or berries. The stock accompanying the wagon trains made the Indians drool.

The first warning of attacks in Idaho was at Soda Springs, telling of the Little Spring Creek Massacre. A wagon train, which had camped on the creek one night, pulled out in the morning, leaving behind a wagon with a father and mother and their five children. The father had insisted on staying at the creek until he found his horses, which had either strayed during the night or been stolen by Indians.

A party of trappers, headed by George W. Goodheart, came upon the scene several days later.

"I think the Indian murderers came up when the emigrants were sound asleep around the wagon, and killed the father," said Goodheart. "It looked like the mother had grabbed the baby, and started to run. I think her screams woke the children. She was found dead with her baby in her arms. The oldest boy was about a rod from the wagon. The next oldest boy was around behind the wagon . . . with a broken arrow in his back . . . The girl was lying about three feet from her mother. The boy next to the baby was in bed with his throat cut."

Goodheart and his men buried the family in the wagon box which had brought the seven across the plains, and today a large stone monument in the city cemetery at Soda Springs marks the "Wagon Box Grave."

One of the most hazardous obstacle courses the emigrants had to run through Idaho was near American Falls. The formation of huge boulders in the area became known as the Gate of Death, Devil's Gate or, most commonly, Massacre Rocks.

Some of the Indian attacks reported in the Massacre Rocks area cannot be authenticated, but certainly the story of the attack on the train of George W. Adams, August 9-10, 1862, has a factual ring to it. Not only were the names of all nine emigrants who were slain in the fighting listed with their home towns (mostly in Iowa), but it was stated that "90 head of stock were lost, $17,500 in cash, and $30,000 in wagons, provisions, clothing, etc."

The attack began with about 75 mounted Indians swooping upon the Adams train, and firing rifles. Forming the wagons in a circle, the emigrants returned the fire, but the Indian force was too much for them. Time and again, the shrieking raiders broke through the wagon-formed corral, looting, and killing two persons and wounding many.

Some of the defenders, thinking that the Indians were more interested in booty than in scalps, tried to escape by running back down the trail. But the red men gave quick pursuit, killing three men, and wounding a woman.

About that time, the Newman & Kennedy train came along, picked up the survivors among those who had fled, and joined the defense of the Adams train. The attackers let up during the night, so the next morning a party of 40 men under Captain John K. Kennedy went looking for stolen stock. They did not encounter any—but about 300 Indians.

In the battle which followed, three men were killed. But fortunately another train—of John Walker—came along to bolster the forces of the outnumbered whites. The Indians took off, and the emigrants buried their dead.

H. F. Swasley, a member of the Adams train, wrote in a report for his home town newspaper in Iowa:

"Beneath the shadow of the inhospitable Snake River Mountains, we laid them down in their final resting place. On Tuesday morning, Miss Elizabeth Adams (sister of the wagon train master), a highly accomplished and beautiful young lady, who was wounded in the retreat while assisting her mother to escape, died, and was buried amid the sobs of strong hearted men. The quivering lips and moistened eyes of the company showed that she had endeared herself to all by her gentleness and self-sacrificing bravery."

Another major point for Indian attacks was in the City of Rocks area near the present town of Almo. Among the attacks reported in the area was one chronicled in the *Territorial Enterprise* of Virginia City, October 1, 1862 (now in Montana, Virginia City was then part of Idaho Territory):

"A party of emigrants numbering 40 persons was attacked near the City of Rocks . . . Five young ladies were carried off, and, it is thought, women and children in all to the number of 15. All the men were killed except one who made his escape and arrival at Humboldt about the 20th of September . . .

"Every train which has passed over that portion of the route in the vicinity of the City of Rocks since the 1st of August has had trouble with the Indians. When our informant left Humboldt, several wagons had just arrived whose sides and covers were transformed into magnified nutmeg graters by Indian bullets."

Some emigrants passing through Idaho on the Oregon Trail found the Indians friendly—in one case, at least, too friendly.

In 1852, Cincinatus H. Miller journeyed across Idaho with his parents in a wagon train enroute from Indiana to Oregon. Thoroughly disliking the name of Cincinatus and admiring a courtly Mexican outlaw of early California called Joaquin, Miller later adopted the outlaw's name. As Joaquin Miller, he became the renowned "Poet of the Sierras." And, in his autobiographical "Crossing the Plains," he told the story of a very friendly Idaho Indian chief.

Heading west out of Fort Hall, the wagon train bearing the Millers also had in it the Wagoner family of many children—eight or nine. One of the children, a teen-age girl, was about the prettiest creature ever known in Indiana—or Idaho.

An Indian chief, riding a fine spotted horse, came upon the wagon train near the Snake River. During the exchange of greetings, the chief spotted the Wagoner beauty. This was the squaw of squaws, and the chief wanted her.

"What you take for girl?" he asked the father.

In jest, Mr. Wagoner replied:

"No less than 10 beautiful spotted horses like the one you're riding."

Galloping off, the chief again approached the train before the day was over with 10 spotted horses—and all his warriors. He was ready to trade, but Mr. Wagoner, of course, was not.

"The bargain was made, and the girl will be taken by force," said the chief.

Thus, a jest had become a very serious matter. Wrote Miller:

"The chief was an honest man and meant exactly what he said, and had a right to the girl. The majority (of the people in the train) agreed, and thought the best way out of it was to let papa (Miller's father) marry them. This seems

50

strange now, but it was the Indian custom to buy wives, and as we were in the heart óf a warlike people, we could not safely trifle with the chief.

"The girl was about to throw herself in the river from the steep bluff where we were, at which the chief, seeing her terror, relented, and led his warriors off, scornfully refusing what presents were offered him for his forbearance."

This writer regrets that Miller never mentioned the chief's name, because it deserves a place in Idaho history.

Unfortunately no such mercy as related by Miller was shown to the people of a wagon train which passed through the City of Rocks in 1863. Every man, woman and child was tomahawked to death by Chief Pocatello and his band of Bannocks. The number of dead is not known.

The City of Rocks, a weird conglomeration of cathedrals, mosques and turrets formed of eroded granite, became familiar to many Oregon Trailers deciding to take the Hudspeth Cut-off to California. (The City of Rocks, comprising 18,500 acres, was designated a Natural Landmark by the Federal government on September 24, 1974.) At this point, it became a big decision for many Oregon Trailers—whether to continue on across Idaho to Oregon or to cut down through Utah to California.

A Swiss adventurer by the name of John August Sutter was beckoning in California. In 1839, Sutter, calling himself "captain" and wearing a French officer's uniform he had acquired in trade for a beaver pelt in the Pacific Northwest, presented himself to the governor of the Mexican province in his capital at Monterey. Displaying letters of introduction from important personages, Sutter talked the governor into giving him a huge grant of land above San Francisco Bay to found a colony. Then, at what is now Sacramento, he built a big adobe fort, and proceeded to use schemes far ahead of his time to induce emigrants to settle on his land.

One of the things he did was to hire an old mountain man, Caleb Greenwood, and his three sons, to sit around Fort Hall, and spit and whittle—and convince Oregon-bound emigrants that the Sacramento Valley was really the place. The Greenwoods spit and whittled slowly, but talked up a storm.

"You ain't got a chance with the Injuns here on to Oregon," Greenwood would tell the emigrants. "But the road to California—no trouble."

"Pa's right," a son would chime in. "And, if it ain't Injuns, it's the Snake River. Got to cross it twice. You may make it once. But the second crossin' . . . ."

Then came the clincher from the old man:

"When you git to Sacramento, you will be met by 10 *caballeros* ridin' fine horses. They will present you with potatoes, coffee and dried beef. Then each head of a family will be given six sections of land from Captain Sutter's Spanish grant."

The Greenwoods talked almost too good a story. Typical of what happened as a result was related by Benjamin Franklin Bonney, who as a young man was in a train which came under the spell of the Greenwoods at Fort Hall in 1846:

"After the Greenwoods had spoken, the men of our party held a pow-wow which lasted nearly all night. Some wanted to go to California, while others were against it. Samuel Barlow, who was in charge of our train, said that he would forbid any man leaving the train and going to California. He told us we did not know what we were going into, and that there was a great uncertainty about the land titles in California, that we were Americans and should not want to go to a country under another flag. Some argued that California would become American territory in time, others thought that Mexico would fight to hold it and that the Americans who went there would get into a mixup and probably be killed. Barlow said we should go to Oregon, and make Oregon an American territory and not waste our time going to California to help promote Sutter's land schemes."

To counteract such talk, Greenwood and his sons were up early next morning. The old man gave a speech, pointing out that "California's climate is better than Oregon's, there is plenty of hunting and fishing, and the rivers are full of salmon."

Eight wagons, including the one of the Bonney family, pulled out for California. As they rolled away in the dust, someone from the main train was heard shouting:

"Good-bye! We will never see you again. Your bones will whiten in the desert or be gnawed by wild animals in the mountains."

What actually happened, Bonney said, was that his family got to Sutter's Fort with the others, but became disillusioned with the idea of becoming "Spanish subjects," and the next spring headed back north for Oregon.

There was no one along the trail selling Idaho. It was either Oregon or California.

What was needed more than a tout like Greenwood was a prophet predicting that, with the coming of irrigation, the grim, gray land of Southern Idaho would know both beauty and profit. But it would have taken a pretty convincing prophet to have sold E. S. McComas on casting his lot in the desert when he was passing through in 1862. He wrote:

"The country all the way down the Snake River is one of the most desolate and dreary wastes in the world. Light soft ground with no soil on top, looking like an ash heap, dust six inches deep and as light as flour. When a man travels all day in it he looks like a miller. You can see nothing but his eyes and them look red. The dust is here so light that it sometimes raises 300 feet above the train. The ground is covered with two of the most detestable shrubs that grows, grease would (wood) and artemesia or wild sage."

(Some early and enterprising Idaho settlers at Shoshone tried to make sagebrush pay by organizing on February 14, 1907, the Sage Brush Tonic Company. From the "most detestable shrub," the firm brewed tonic water for men's shining domes, and heralded its merits under the slogan: "Did you ever hear of a baldheaded Indian?" The tonic, of course, never did grow the lush hair of an Indian on a white man's scalp. But it did no harm either, and that was something in those days, for as Rudyard Kipling wrote: "Wonderful little our fathers knew. Half of their remedies cured you dead.")

While Greenwood at Fort Hall was plugging for California, G. W. Bush, who worked at the fort, was warning the travelers that they would find little food in crossing Southern Idaho, because, where there was some, Indians had probably beaten them to it.

"Take my advice," he would say. "Anything you see as big as a blackbird, kill it and eat it."

When the Oregon Trailers reached the Boise Valley, with grass belly-high on the oxen, they must have thought that they had entered paradise. Basil Nelson Longsworth reported in 1853:

"There is very good soil along the Boise River, the bottoms being from two to four miles wide and mostly covered with a heavy growth of grass. There might be thousands of tons of pretty fine hay made here."

52

By this time, however, the travelers were only a couple of hundred miles from their planned destination in Oregon. They kept on going—unless death intervened.

On August 20, 1854, five covered wagons, with Alexander Ward in command, pulled off the trail to have lunch beside the Boise River, about 25 miles west of the present city of Boise. The Ward party, for some reason that is not clear, had gotten a day behind the main train with which it was traveling to Oregon. In the party, besides Ward, were his wife, four sons and four daughters, a sister of Mrs. Ward named Mrs. White, and nine men, including Dr. Adams and a Dr. B. Babcock.

While the emigrants were resting in the shade of willows, one of the Ward boys shouted that Indians were making off with a pony which had strayed from the riverside encampment. Four of the men leaped on their horses, and raced in pursuit.

Meanwhile, Ward, not knowing how many Indians might be in the area, became uneasy, and decided he had better get the wagons rolling. The party had no more than wheeled back on the trail, however, when a great cloud of dust swirled toward the little train. The dust was kicked up by Snake Indians, riding at a fast gallop. Accounts of the number vary from 60 to 200, but, under any circumstances, the Indians represented a formidable force.

As the four men who had ridden after the stolen horse returned at the sight of the charging red men, the wagons were quickly formed into a circle. Reaching the train, the Indians started firing rifles and loosing arrows. Ward was the first to die with a bullet in his head as he thrust out his rifle from behind a wagon wheel.

The other men continued to repulse the attack, with the women and children reloading guns. They held out until sundown when the last man died with an arrow in his chest. Then the Indians swept over the wagons.

Mrs. Ward was clubbed to death, but not before she was tortured with a hot iron, and forced to watch three of her children die screaming at a flaming stake. Mrs. White's body was found a quarter-mile from the wagons, where she apparently had managed to flee before Indians caught her and tomahawked her to death.

Two of the Ward boys, Newton and William, although shot with arrows, managed to escape by hiding in the sagebrush. Newton became unconscious. He was found the next day by members of the main train who had ridden back to learn what had happened to the Ward party. William, like his brother, also became unconscious, glimpsing, before he passed out, Indians unwittingly "riding their horses over me." After coming to, he managed to make his way to Fort Boise, each step sending pain shooting through his chest, which had been pierced by an arrow.

A U.S. cavalry troop, under Major Granville O. Haller, was dispatched to the Boise Valley from The Dalles, Oregon, with orders to round up the culprits and punish them, but all the Indians who were found claimed that they were nowhere near the massacre scene. That did not end the matter.

The *Portland Oregonian* reported that "feeling ran high. Many persons advocated annihilation of the Indians and seizure of the Hudson's Bay Company posts still remaining upon United States soil since the Indians had obtained guns and ammunition from these posts." As the pressure mounted, Major Haller was sent back to the Boise Valley the following summer, and told not to return with his troops "until justice had been done."

About 200 Indians were rounded up by the cavalrymen for a council, at which Major Haller threatened punishment for all if the massacre participants were not revealed. This drew only stony looks at first, but, as the council continued, the interpreter whom the major had engaged, whispered to him that he saw four of the killers in the crowd—Nambigud, Warbe, Pambouya and Beesheet.

Promptly ending the council, Haller placed the four under arrest. Beesheet "sang." He not only admitted his part in the massacre, but agreed that the other three had also been participants, and offered to take the cavalrymen to a distant camp, and point out more participants. Beesheet, however, was stalling for an escape opportunity. As soldiers accompanied him to horses to ride to the camp, he darted from them, and started zig-zagging through the sagebrush. A cavalryman's rifle dropped him dead in his tracks.

Major Haller then held a quick trial for Nambigud, Warbe and Pambouya. When all three were found guilty, a scaffold was built, and the Indians were driven in a horse-drawn wagon under dangling ropes. As soon as the ropes were knotted around their necks, the driver of the wagon slapped reins across the horses' rumps. Death came quickly.

Some of the Indians did not understand why the convicted men were not tortured before they were hung, but all understood that the warpath could lead to the gallows. Just as a reminder, this particular gallows was left standing for several years. And all during the period there were no more Indian uprisings in the Boise Valley.

The tranquility, however, did not attract settlers in any number. They would come only with the cry of "Gold!"

The early Idaho Indian grew fearful of what he saw from a mountain top—
—University of Idaho Historical Archives

Covered wagons coming in ever-increasing numbers over the Oregon Trail.
—University of Idaho Historical Archives

Many battles were fought, but in the end the Indian was no match for the U.S. Cavalry trooper, well-mounted, well-armed and well-disciplined. —Haynes Photo

Earlier, the Indians had welcomed white missionaries with their "gospel medicine." In 1836, the Reverend Henry H. Spalding constructed this mission building —first in Idaho—near Lapwai. In later years, it served as a stable for Indian ponies.

—Eastern Washington Historical Society

In the Coeur d'Alenes in 1848, Father Anthony Ravalli, S.J., erected this church which has become known as the Cataldo Mission. Still intact, it is now a National Historic Landmark.

The first big push of white settlers came in 1860 when three cents worth of gold was discovered glimmering in a pan in North-Central Idaho. Prospectors—of all ages—poured into the Territory by the thousands.

Ore of Idaho assayed rich—in silver as well as in gold. And it became highly important to the Union in the Civil War.

In the gold camps, men built sluice boxes—some miles long—for washing out the precious metal with greater efficiency.

—Eastern Washington Historical Society

Mining towns mushroomed in various parts of Idaho. In the north, for instance, there was Wardner, with Jerome Day, and Sam and Frank Poteet riding Noah Kellogg's burro, the most famous jackass in mining history.
—University of Idaho Historical Archives

In the Owyhee Country of the South, Silver City took root on the slopes of War Eagle Mountain, becoming known throughout the world for the rich mines surrounding it.
—Idaho Historical Society

Boise emerged as the metropolis of Southern Idaho's booming mining activities. In the Overland Hotel (built in 1863), there was much "wheeling and dealing" over claims.
—University of Idaho Historical Archives

Life on the frontier was generally hard—and lonesome—for women, and in many ways they were the bravest of the brave.

As the land gave up more and more of its wealth, however, the plush decor of the East began to appear in the West.

A woman could even shop for the latest in footwear at the general mercantile store of a mining camp.

Then gradually the gold and silver of Idaho began to run out—with the deep-bedded ore of the Coeur d'Alenes a notable exception. Most of early Pierce, scene of Idaho's first gold strike, disappeared, but not the old courthouse.

Today, fabulous Silver City has only ghostly reminders of its glory days.

And once roaring Placerville is a right peaceful little community with a robin finding restful solitude in the town's cemetery.

Chapter V

# GOLD—JUST AROUND THE NEXT MOUNTAIN

"I knew I had the shaping of the destiny of that country."

—Captain Elias Davidson Pierce,
discoverer of gold in Idaho

A roving, black-bearded adventurer from Ireland, a young carpenter from Connecticut, a trail-wise Indian girl, and three cents worth of gold glinting in a pan—these were among the alloys from which the State of Idaho was forged. To blend them, it took a lot of doing—indeed, some hair-raising experiences —but little was accomplished easily when the West was young.

The catalytic process really began on the moonless night of August 12, 1860, when the Irishman, Captain Elias Davidson Pierce, and 10 other defiant gold seekers, including the Yankee carpenter, rode secretly out of Walla Walla at the "many waters" of Southeastern Washington. They were spurless, lest the jangle of rowels add to the clop of horses' hoofs, and sound the alarm of their leaving.

Pierce had let it be known around town and fort that "Indians or no Indians, I'm aiming to go there to look for gold." "There" was what is now north-central Idaho—at the time, "taboo land" for the white man. By the Treaty of 1855, it was the reservation of the Nez Perce Indians, and the more warlike chiefs of the tribe had warned that they would kill any white man entering their primitive

55

domain. The 1,500,000 sprawling acres of the reservation contained rugged mountains, deep canyons and fast streams, which could also spell trouble.

As Pierce, tall both in and out of the saddle, rode silently through the night, however, he did not look so much ahead as behind. He was confident he could cope with Indians and wilderness, but Indian Agent Andrew J. Cain at Fort Walla Walla had threatened to send cavalry after Pierce's party if it dared to enter the reservation. For Pierce to be thwarted by U.S. troops at this critical point in his long quest for fortune would be too much.

Ever since 1839, when Pierce at 15 had fled potato blight and looming famine in Ireland, he had been seeking riches—great riches. He had been galled by the meager financial prospects of "reading" for the law in West Virginia and fighting in the Mexican War. After the war, a pretty girl, Rebecca Jones, caused him to pause in little Pennville, Indiana, drowsing beside the Salamonie River—but not for long. In 1848, James W. Marshall had discovered gold at Sutter's mill in California, and, in '49, the big talk in Pennville was of fortunes that could be made overnight in the Far West.

"Wait for me," Pierce told Rebecca to whom he had become engaged. And then he promptly headed for California with a wagon train rumbling out of St. Joseph, Missouri.

For 11 years now Rebecca had been faithfully waiting, Pierce reflected that August night in 1860 as he jogged his horse across barren, rolling hills in quest of the forbidden fruit of the Nez Perce Nation. But the bonanza was now near—perhaps only a little more than a couple of hundred miles away—and Rebecca would not have to wait much longer.

It will be difficult, especially for women readers, to understand the patient Rebecca. This can be done by understanding Pierce. He was handsome in a square-jawed way, but most important were the leprechaunish twinkle in his eyes and the convincing manner in which he told tales of the fortune he would make. A luxurious life, he continually assured the ever-loving and ever-believing Rebecca in letters, was just around the next mountain.

Pierce had known many mountains in trading with the Indians and in seeking gold from California to British Columbia, but always the stories filtering out of the Idaho mountain country gnawed deepest at his vitals—especially the tale of a Nez Perce Indian (just which Indian and when and where nobody seems to know):

"One night three of us camped in a canyon. The moon came up over the Bitterroots, and, as its beams struck the western wall of the canyon, we saw something like a star gleaming in the rocky cliff. We were frightened—it looked to us like the eye of the Great Spirit. We ran away. Next morning we went back there. But we have forgotten the place."

The Shoshone Indians disclaim any such word as *E-dah-how,* meaning "Light on the Mountains," and referring to the rising sun, with its light coming down from the mountains at the dawn of each new day. Still, that is the widely-accepted legend of how the Territory got its name. To Pierce, however, Idaho was the shining light of gold reported to have been seen by the three Indians. "Will o' the wisp," some called the story. Not Pierce.

Three different times, between 1852 and 1860, Pierce penetrated deep into the Nez Perce Nation. Ostensibly, he was trading for horses with the Indians (buying for about $10 in Idaho and selling for about $100 in California), but actually he was seeking the elusive big gold strike. Finding promising traces in the summer of 1860, Pierce returned to Walla Walla to interest a party of "some strength" in further exploration. But Indian Agent Cain warned:

"The moment you or any others enter the Nez Perce Nation it will create war between the Indians and whites. A hundred well-armed men could not go in there with any degree of safety. The moment you undertake such an expedition you will be entering the jaws of death."

Many of the men who had planned to accompany Pierce into the Nez Perce Nation abandoned the idea. Ten did not. On August 12, 1860, deciding that they could wait no longer, they had packed and saddled up, and were now on their way.

Here it becomes difficult to fill the gaps of omission, to sift fact from legend.

The Pierce party was not pursued by cavalry—not that time. But Indians? Pierce, in his 669 pages of memoirs, made no mention of encountering any. But Historians Merle W. Wells and Merrill D. Beal, in writing their well-documented "History of Idaho," found that the party spent more than a month at least "ducking Indians." Pierce, it should be added, had contended for years that the Nez Perces were happy to have him prowling their rivers and streams, and a man normally does not change his story when he dictates his memoirs in later life.

Then there is the matter of Jane, the Indian girl, who is reported to have served as a guide for the party. Pierce mentioned the acquiring of "a guide who knew the country"—no more. He failed to indicate whether the guide was Indian or not, whether male or female. Considering the times, Pierce may have been chauvinistically inclined, but Byron Defenbach in his book, "Red Heroines of the Northwest," was not. He gave Jane most of the credit for getting the Pierce party to where it wanted to go.

Jane is supposed to have come into the picture this way:

At the merging of the Alpowa and Snake Rivers, Pierce and his men were still glancing behind for cavalry when they should have been maintaining "eyes front" for signs of Indians. Before they realized what was happening, they came upon a large band of Nez Perces, mounted and armed. As the gold seekers reined their horses, the leader of the Nez Perces raised his right arm, but said nothing. Just pointed—west.

Outnumbered and outgunned, the Pierce party got the message. Wheeling their horses, the men headed back for Walla Walla, but they had not retraced many miles of their trail when they stubbornly cut back northeast.

Again they were stopped by an Indian party. This time the Indians spoke. The tones were angry, and the gestures that went with the words menacing. Most of the men in the Pierce party were then quite willing to hurry back to Walla Walla. Not Pierce, however.

He had an ace in the hole—Chief Timothy (Tamootsin), a friendly Indian who had become a Christian under the teaching of Missionary Henry H. Spalding at Lapwai. Timothy felt it was his duty to help fellow Christians, and Pierce, seeking help, guided his party to Timothy's camp.

Timothy agreed at a campfire council that there was a way around the main reservation to the country where Pierce wanted to go, but he would have to obtain a guide. Then Jane, Timothy's 18-year-old daughter who had been taught English by the Reverend Spalding, stepped before the council fire, and said:

"I will go with the white men."

A woman's voice in an Indian council, according to Historian Defenbach, "is like a pistol shot in church." There was consternation and confusion. Chief Timothy shook his head, but Jane protested that she knew every rock and bush of the way. With the high and sharply-etched cheekbones of her father, she was not pretty, but what she lacked in looks she made up in spunk. Finally, the chief gave in. And, as Jane rode off with the gold seekers, her father was still telling Pierce what a smart girl she was, and what a fine guide she would be.

To avoid running into a wandering Indian who might sound the alarm, much of the traveling was done by night. That meant a horse stumbling into a gopher hole or brushing too close to a tree and scraping a rider's leg . . . a low branch searing and numbing a man's face . . . restless sleep in the daytime that was abandoned to pan for gold in a half-stupor. But all this was better than Indian bullets.

The party pushed northward along what is now the border-line between Washington and Idaho. The terrain became more rugged. In places, the timber was heavy, and the undergrowth as thick and tangled as a trapper's beard.

"What do we do now, Cap'n?" the men would ask.

Pierce would reply: "Cut a trail."

It is indicated that, although Pierce was a strong man, he was averse to expending his strength on hard labor, and did little of the cutting himself. After all, he was a captain—or had been one.

Just south of the present city of Moscow, the travelers turned east—by daylight. The Indians in this area were friendly—as long as no one disturbed their camas root grounds where the women dug winter supplies of the potato-like plants.

Fording the rippling Potlatch River at what is now Kendrick, the party moved —slowly and arduously—toward the North Fork of the Clearwater River. Pierce said:

"I had been in some rough places, but that was the crookedest I ever went through, owing to the dense forest and fallen timber. Some days we didn't make over a mile . . .

"About sundown (the day is uncertain), we could see the North Fork, a clear sparkling stream; could see it meandering through deep-walled canyons. We had to make a heavy descent of about one mile to look ahead. It seemed impossible to make it with our pack animals. Night came on, and it was so dark we could not see to travel—not only that, we were in great danger of dashing our animals headlong over a perpendicular precipice. I was in the lead when we came to a place I thought we might possibly find a footing for our animals to stand on. There we then halted for night, without water, all hungry and tired, and no way to prepare supper. In the morning, we rolled, slipped and slid our animals to the river."

In their trail panning, the men found traces of gold, but no followup to quicken the heartbeat, and it was a badly discouraged crew that camped the evening of September 30, 1860, in a meadow where Canal Gulch and Oro Fino Creek wander out of the timber to join forces. That is, everybody was discouraged except 24-year-old Wilbur Bassett, the Yankee carpenter in the party. Taking pick, shovel and pan, he ambled up the creek.

Dig, shovel and pan . . . dig, shovel and pan. Nothing. One more time . . . still another. Then, as mud swirled from the pan down the creek, Bassett spotted tiny flecks of gold in the gravel residue . . . about three cents worth. Not much, but the most important three cents worth of gold in the history of Idaho. Bassett didn't know this, but he had a feeling there was more gold, and, with a wide grin, hurried back to camp.

58

The response was a big letdown for Bassett. Some of the men, reclining against saddles, didn't even raise their heads. Three cents worth of gold . . .

But the next morning all the men arose at dawn, quickly washed down beans and salt pork with scalding coffee, and began to explore Bassett's discovery. Some pans produced as much as 30 cents in fine-grained gold. Then the men formed a crude sluice box of cedar bark, and, before the day was done, they had gleaned $80 worth of gold. This was it!

"I never saw a party of men so much excited," recalled Pierce. "They made the hills and mountains ring with shouts of joy."

After several more days of exploratory work and mining, the successful gold seekers hurried back to Walla Walla to get more supplies and equipment, and to return before the winter set in. On the way back to Walla Walla, they met various groups of Indians, but were not bothered, because they were headed in the right direction.

The gold findings were displayed at Walla Walla "in old Preston & Merrill yeast powder cans," but Pierce was disappointed to find only a few backers for the return trip to the strike. There was still strong opposition from those who feared that an influx of miners in the Nez Perce Nation might set off Indian war cries. Nevertheless, Pierce managed to get a "flour stake" from a pioneer mill (one of the operators was F. T. Dent, brother-in-law of General Ulysses S. Grant). He also obtained prospecting and mining equipment from the Walla Walla firm of Kyger & Reese.

At first, about a hundred men were set to make the second trip to the Clearwater Country, but word came that warring Chief Kamiaken of the Yakimas had made a mysterious—and perhaps ominous—visit to the Nez Perce area. By twos—threes—and tens, the party dwindled.

Finally, on November 15, 1860, with snow squalls already in the air, 33 men and 120 horses departed from Walla Walla. The Indians met by this group at the Snake River were friendly, and willing to ferry gear across the river in dugout canoes for a price. But, just as the dickering was completed, a lone man on a well-lathered horse rode up—Indian Agent Cain. Ignoring Pierce, Cain tried to persuade the Indians not to ferry the white men's equipment. The Indians, however, preferred to deal with Pierce. Trade goods came with his conversation.

The ferrying started, and Cain engaged an Indian to race to Fort Walla Walla, and bring the cavalry. The cavalry arrived in a swirl of dust—after Pierce's party was long gone. The commander of the troops talked with the Indians, who said there had been no trouble—just some ferrying business. Snorting, the commander signaled his bugler to sound off, and the troops jogged back to Fort Walla Walla.

On bleak December 3, 1860, 33 men and 119 horses (one flour-laden horse injured itself in a kicking spree on a mountain trail and had to be shot) moved into the valley of discovery. It was covered with about eight inches of snow, with more on the way.

No hibernating for the men, however. They immediately began clearing land, whipsawing lumber to build cabins. The mountain cold became bitter, but the men were warmed by their work as well as by gold fever, sometimes sawing in driving snow while wearing only underwear above the waist.

The town of Pierce was aborning. So was a state. There was no stopping. With the completion of crude but serviceable shelters, the men turned to the building of sluices to be ready for the spring thaw when placer gold operations would really start. One sluice built that first winter ran for three miles. This sluice and the many others constructed as new discoveries were made all pointed urgently in one direction—to settlement leading to statehood.

With the coming of spring, the population of the new town of Pierce began to swell like a mountain stream. Then the prospectors fanned out, and new mining camps sprang up. By 1862, there were some 20,000 miners in the area, and the government of Washington Territory (once part of vast Oregon Territory) was way off across the mountains in Olympia. Congress heeded the pleas of the miners, who wanted such basic things as roads and law and order, and, on March 3, 1863, carved out of Washington Territory the new Territory of Idaho, with Lewiston, an emerging freighting center, as the temporary capital.

The new territory encompassed the present states of Idaho, Montana and most of Wyoming. Covering more than 325,000 square miles, it exceeded the size of the State of Texas by about 60,000 square miles. Montana Territory was cut off in 1864, and Wyoming in 1868. Still, with all the trimmings, Idaho boasted 83,557 square miles of land with great and varied potential, and, on July 3, 1890, after the capital had been shifted to Boise, the Territory became a state, the 43rd in the Union.

Idaho had long had everything a settler could want—fertile soil for raising crops, lush grass for grazing stock, good water for drinking (and for irrigating if need be), fine timber for building a home and warming it. But emigrants had generally been inclined to pass the land by—until the discovery of gold. Indeed, it was this discovery that speeded up the process of settlement in the entire Pacific Northwest.

And what happened to the persons credited with playing leading roles in Idaho's gold-plated drama of development back in 1860?

Whether her role as guide was fact or legend, Jane herself was very real. Eventually, she married John Silcott, pioneer government contractor at Lapwai (later a ferryman), and became well known in Lewiston as well as Lapwai. When she died January 17, 1895, Silcott had her buried at the confluence of the Clearwater and Snake rivers, and a substantial monument was erected over her grave.

Neither Bassett, who discovered the gold, nor Pierce, the leader of the party whose burning passion for the bonanza made the discovery possible, ever became rich. Both Bassett and Pierce sold their claims at Pierce for pittances.

Bassett went back to carpentering at Cheney, Washington, but often wandered into the hills seeking a new strike. He died at 72, almost a half-century after Discovery Day in Idaho, and was buried at Wilbur, Washington.

For years, Pierce kept on roving. In the spring of 1861, he went to Olympia to lobby the Washington Territorial Legislature for a wagon road from Walla Walla to the mines. Discouraged with his lack of success, he drifted, looking for new ore strikes in Southern Idaho, Montana, Wyoming, Oregon and California.

Then, in 1869, it finally happened. Pierce received a letter from an old friend in Pennville, Indiana, advising that a fellow named Isaac Underwood was "paying an unreasonable amount of attention to Miss Rebecca Jones." So, after stalling for 20 years, Pierce hurried back to Pennville, and married Rebecca on November 1, 1869.

The triumphant bride, who at long last had learned the advisability of competition, was not allowed to linger long in Pennville after the wedding. Pierce took her with him back to the Far West, and, for 14 years, the two of them engaged in trading and gold seeking in California and Nevada.

Returning to Pennville in 1883 for retirement, they lived off what Pierce made from raising chickens and from his pension as a veteran of the Mexican War—$15 a month, boosted in later years to $34. Like Bassett, Pierce died at 72—on February 15, 1897. A brother-in-law paid the funeral expenses.

Pierce now rests in a hillside cemetery of the little Indiana community, his grave marked simply by a metal star placed there by the Grand Army of the Republic. And perhaps a star is the most fitting symbol for that man of destiny who did so much to brighten the prospects for the wilderness that was Idaho in 1860. Ironically, however, it was Jane of the Nez Perces who rated the much more pretentious grave marker. And some historians say she wasn't even there.

# Chapter VI

# THE HAND THAT ROCKED THE GOLD CRADLE

"A frenzy seized my soul; houses were too small for me to stay in; I was soon in the street in search of necessary outfits; piles of gold rose up before me at every step; castles of marble, dazzling the eye with their rich appliances; thousands of slaves bowing to my beck and call . . . were among the fancies of my fevered imagination. The Rothschilds and Astors appeared to me but poor people; in short, I had a very violent attack of gold fever."

—Memoirs of a Gold Seeker

In the icebox winter of 1861-62, a bearded prospector sat in his windowless cabin at the new Idaho mining camp of Florence, eating his supper beside a flickering candle, and finishing off the meal with hot tea. The meal was a thick paste made from flour, and the tea was a bitter-tasting innovation steeped from pine needles.

Outside, the snow lay in 12-foot drifts. Inside, only one piece of wet wood burned feebly in a crude fireplace. (In the deep snow, wood was almost as hard to come by as food.) The prospector shivered, and clutched both hands to the cup of pine-needle tea to thaw his numbed fingers. A man would suffer much to fill a baking powder can with gold dust, and the suffering might as well be at Florence in the Northern Idaho mountains on Slate Creek, a tributary of the Salmon. The promise of wealth at Florence was good—far better than at Pierce.

The strike at Florence had been made in 1861 by a party led by little (5'5"),

21-year-old John Healy, who, like Captain Pierce, had left Ireland as a boy to parlay native determination and shrewdness into a fortune in America. Healy, however, almost did not make it to Florence.

He was digging for gold-bearing gravel in a 10-foot hole at Pierce when he heard a tree-felling companion cry, "Timb-er-r!" With no time to scramble out of the hole as he saw the big pine toppling toward him, Healy crouched against the side. The tree crashed across the hole, with a large branch gouging his right leg and pinning it against the wall of the hole.

A makeshift pump, powered by a flutter wheel in Oro Fino Creek, had been rigged to keep water from seeping into the hole. But now the pump was broken, and the hole began to fill rapidly. Healy had only his head clear of the water when a half-dozen men managed to move the fallen tree, and free him.

No bones were broken, but, for quite a spell thereafter, the injured leg had little feeling, and Healy dragged it along with the aid of a cane carved from a willow branch. That is what inspired him to look for a new gold field.

With his dragging leg, Healy could no longer work his claim, but he could ride. Many good strikes had been made in areas fingering out from Pierce—the richest at Elk City—and Healy decided that he might as well be searching in Idaho's big beyond for still greater hordes of gold. With nine other prospectors, he started heading south.

One of the nine, George Grigsby, had reported:

"An Injun showed me a nugget he'd found in the Salmon River. I swear it was worth at least $24."

So it was to the Salmon River Country that the men hurried. The fifth evening out they were slowed down by Nez Perce Indians.

The mounted band was headed by Chief Looking Glass, who was to play a major role in the Nez Perce Indian War of 1877. Two men rode ahead to learn the chief's intentions. He made them clear by grabbing a horse's bridle, and motioning that the white men must ride back where they came from. The prospectors argued. Looking Glass put his hands over his ears, and shook his head. Riding back to the main party, the worried pair of whites explained they were in for trouble.

"They're bluffing," said Healy. "We keep going."

As the prospectors rode on, with rifles held across their saddles, the Indians swooped down upon them, screeching like banshees. They leaned from their horses to snatch at bridles of the prospectors' mounts, or to jab the riders with rifles. Some of the Indians had quirts, and they lashed out with these. Grigsby raised his rifle to fire, but another prospector shouted for him to lower it.

"That's just what the devils want."

The harassing went on for miles until finally the Indians tired of the game, and rode off. The prospectors pushed their weary horses hard, not stopping until midnight when they came to Lawyer's Canyon (named after Nez Perce Chief Lawyer, who was given his name by whites because of his speechmaking ability, and who in later life enhanced his courtly role by wearing a silk top hat). Here the prospectors climbed from saddles, and fell into the sleep of the exhausted.

The next morning, with the sounds of approaching horsemen, they grabbed for their rifles. The riders turned out to be five other prospectors, who had been turned back from the Salmon by another band of Nez Perces.

"Just when I got a chance at a good thing, the Injuns got to spoil it," growled one of the five, fresh from California. (Later, a prospector was to complain that he "found more Indians in Idaho than gold.")

To get reinforcements, Healy and two others decided to ride back to Oro Fino, a couple of miles from Pierce. They convinced nine others that the Salmon River Country was worth fighting for. Now the whites numbered 24.

But Looking Glass had been rounding up his own reinforcements, and had been joined by bands of Chief White Bird and Chief Eagle of the Light. The Indians outnumbered the prospectors five to one.

When the two forces again met, there was more conversation—mostly a long speech by Looking Glass. The prospectors did not understand much of it, but they did understand:

"You must either go back or fight."

"Fight it is," cried a prospector, and others echoed his determination.

Then, adopting the tactics of the Indians, the whites rode through the lines of the Nez Perces, screaming and waving rifles. Startled and confused, the Indians made no move to pursue the invaders. And so the Salmon River Country was opened to prospecting, with the Indians losing more ground.

At first, the prospectors were greatly discouraged by only meager shows of color. Hunger stalked the camp. One of the men looked at a mule belonging to Prospector Jack Reynolds, and opined that "mule meat is just the juiciest thing you ever put in your mouth."

Reynolds threatened to shoot any man who killed his mule "which has been so faithful to me." The next day the hunger situation was eased with the slaying of two elk, but that night Indians ran off half the horses in the camp—and the faithful mule. Reynolds grieved for days.

The color in gold pans, however, began to pick up. Then Healy and a man named Snixter made a big strike in what they called Dragoon Gulch (the two prospectors had served together in the U.S. Dragoons). When Snixter looked at the residue in a pan he had been swirling, he saw about $10 in gold dust and nuggets. Walking over to a tree, he banged his head against the trunk, then turned to Healy.

"No," he said, "I'm not dreamin'."

The new stampede to the Salmon River Country was on. The town of Florence, named after the adopted daughter of "Doc" Ferber, who helped lay out the townsite, began to rise in a high basin north of the Salmon River. The first building of consequence was a saloon.

Florence—for a time—was Idaho's richest gold camp. In the first year, it is estimated, 3,500 miners averaged $4,000 each, about $50,000,000 in today's values.

An old Dutchman named Jacob Weiser, who had barely managed to keep body and soul together in Southwestern Idaho trapping for the Hudson's Bay Company, drifted up to the new camp with thousands of others. One day at dawn he started panning for gold in a gulch out of Florence. The color in the first pan made him whistle. He had not done that since the time he discovered two beavers in a single trap.

The old man rigged a makeshift sluice, and went to work in earnest, pausing only once to fumble in his pack for some jerky. When it became too dark for him to see what he was doing, he stopped. In the single day, he garnered more than $6,000 in gold.

Weiser was not exactly handsome, and some say that he was nicknamed "Baboon" and that the site of his strike—Baboon Gulch—was named after him. Most historians, however, give that honor to a man named Peter Bablaine or Baboin, who did better than Weiser at Baboon Gulch. With the swirling of

65

one pan, Bablaine took $800 from it, and eventually departed from the gulch with his horse balking at carrying 75 pounds of gold dust in addition to the rider. (Another Weiser, Peter, who had been with the Lewis and Clark party, did leave his name in Idaho—to the city of Weiser and the Weiser River.)

Although highly profitable, some of the mining in the area was hard—mighty hard. But Yankee ingenuity made possible the impossible, and Southern sagacity helped, too, for many of the miners came from below the Mason-Dixon line.

In some of the ravines, there was insufficient stream water to utilize sluice boxes. So a miner would dig a shallow well, and let it fill with water seepage. Then he would dip the water from the well with a container—even a hat would do in a pinch—and pour the water over a cradle-like, wooden rocker with one hand while he agitated it with the other. The water, running back into the well, would be used over and over again. When mud thickened it to a molasses texture, the miner would bale it from the well, and wait for a new supply of fresh water to seep into the hole. That was a difficult way to make a living, but, when the process produced $100 a day in gold dust, it held promise that the living would be high.

(Dunham Wright, a prospector in Southern Idaho's Placerville area, told of using part of a boot to do his mining. "A dipper to dip water with to rock the rocker was the worst difficulty we had to contend with, for none could be bought. I cut a leg off of my leather boots, fitted a piece of board in one end, tacked it there, fastened a piece of wood diagonally from the bottom of the dipper to the top for a handle, and I was heeled for my work.")

As the news of the wealth to be found in the Salmon River Country filtered to the outside world via Walla Walla, Florence began to boom still more. Some estimates place the area's peak population as high as 20,000.

Not everybody, of course, was a hard-working prospector. In fact, because of their remoteness, the early Idaho mining camps such as Florence got some of the West's roughest characters, fleeing from a sheriff in more settled parts. There was, for instance, Henry J. Talbotte, best known as "Cherokee Bob."

A Georgian with Indian blood, he was about as belligerent a maverick as had drifted to the Pacific Northwest. His favorite declaration when drunk in a saloon was:

"Just gimme a slave totin' a basket of loaded pistols, and I kin lick a whole regiment of Union soldiers."

At a theatre in Walla Walla, he and some of his friends got into an argument with a group of soldiers. As dancing girls kicked their way across the stage, the shooting started. When it ended, two of the soldiers lay dead. Several more were wounded. Cherokee Bob scrambled on his horse, and rode out of town at a fast gallop.

He came to Florence. Enroute, he picked up a new friend named Bill Mayfield, and Mayfield's love of the moment, a shady lady known only as Cynthia or "Red-Headed Cynth." Like Cherokee Bob, Mayfield was on the run. He had killed his man in Nevada.

In Florence, Cherokee Bob and Mayfield did some fast reconnoitering. Learning that one of two partners operating a saloon had just died, the gunmen paid a call on the surviving partner. Cherokee Bob did the talking as he toyed with the hammer of his pistol.

"I loaned your late partner some money—more than this business is worth," he said. "But I'll be generous. You kin take a couple hundred dollars to git out of town. Otherwise . . ."

The surviving partner, who wanted to continue as a survivor, got out of town. Next to go was Mayfield. It happened this way:

Cherokee Bob took a shine to Red-Headed Cynth. Mayfield objected, so Cherokee Bob said that the lady should decide. The one on whom she turned thumbs down would have to leave. Grinning with confidence, Mayfield agreed. The grin faded, however, when Red-Headed Cynth flew into the arms of Cherokee Bob.

Feeling sorry for his short-term partner, Cherokee Bob tossed him a poke of gold dust as he mounted a horse to ride out of town. Mayfield drifted to Placerville, a new mining camp in Southwestern Idaho, but he didn't last long there, either. A card sharp named "Slicker" Evans shot him to death in an altercation during a poker game.

In Florence, Cherokee Bob, now the sole owner of the saloon, prospered. He was too fast with a gun for the citizens of Florence not to respect him. But many—especially the women who had started to arrive—had no respect for the red-head. That bothered Cherokee Bob.

Came a New Year's Eve ball in a dance hall to mark the arrival of 1863. Red-Headed Cynth wanted to attend the affair, but the night was too big a one in the saloon for Cherokee Bob to take his eyes off the cash registers. So he asked a newly-acquired friend, Bob Willoughby, to escort the red-head.

Willoughby, with Red-Headed Cynth decked out like a Christmas tree, had no more than entered the dance hall with its whining fiddles when the crowd threatened to leave—demanding their money back, of course. The worried manager had whispered words with Willoughby and Red-Headed Cynth, and they departed quietly.

Cherokee Bob was not so quiet the next day when he learned what had happened. He roared:

"I'll kill him!"

He was referring in this lethal manner to "Jakey" Williams, operator of a competing saloon, who had led the opposition to Red-Headed Cynth's attendance at the dance. When Jakey learned that he was the main target of Cherokee Bob's wrath, he slipped out of his saloon, and sought refuge in one house and another. Cherokee Bob and Willoughby were never far behind.

Finally deciding that the matter had to come to a decisive conclusion, Jakey re-entered his saloon, grabbed a shotgun from behind the bar, and went looking for his stalkers. Sighting Willoughby coming around the corner of a building, Jakey dropped him with 16 slugs in his body.

By this time, Jakey's friends had entered the fray, and, as Cherokee Bob was about to fire his pistol at Jakey, a man with a rifle shot the badman from Georgia. He died several days later.

One version of the story has it that Cherokee Bob never had a chance. According to this version, Red-Headed Cynth, trying to prevent Cherokee Bob from committing murder (or tiring of him and wanting to see him killed), had taken the caps from each chamber of his cap and ball pistol.

And what happened to Red-Headed Cynth? Her last known address was Placerville, where she went to again join Mayfield—before he, too, was gunned down.

Not everybody struck it rich at Florence. Leaving Florence, a group of disgruntled prospectors, headed by James Warren, a college graduate who preferred to use his sharpened mind in gambling and prospecting, moved down the south side of Salmon Canyon. About 40 miles southeast of Florence at a site which at first glance had seemed unlikely for ore producing, the prospectors opened up the Warrens gold district. It was not as lucrative per square foot as the Florence area, but it did manage to produce $6,000,000 in gold in five years.

The boom town of Warren's Diggings—later, Warrens or Warren—also produced something unique in the way of theatrical organizations—a club dedicated to deadpans among the gold pans. Various early Western mining towns such as Idaho City, Idaho, Virginia City, Nevada, and Central City, Colorado, managed from time to time to import whole troupes of top-flight entertainers—even opera companies—from New York City. But the North-Central Idaho bonanza camps were a little remote for that. So, at Warren, a group of miners and businessmen formed Hocum Felta, and put on their own entertainment. Because they felt it wouldn't be very good, the rule was that neither the entertainer nor the audience could smile. Deadpan comics, who outdid themselves and managed to draw a few snickers, became celebrities in the town.

Warren had another special claim to fame—because of "Three-Fingered" Smith's hundred-night stand in its barrooms.

Bad luck seemed to follow Smith, a tall and stringy fellow, like a shadow through Idaho's early mining camps. He never bothered to correct assorted tales as to how he got his nickname, but a son, Henry, who died in St. Alphonsus Hospital in Boise in 1942, finally revealed the true story of the unfortunate circumstance.

It seems that the father's muzzle-loading shotgun accidentally fired while he was talking to a friend. He happened to have both hands cupped over the barrel, and the shot blew off the middle two fingers of each hand. Three-Fingered Smith always shied from admitting the facts, because he believed that no man should be careless with a gun.

But the loss of the fingers was only the start of his troubles. He also lost his wife. She ran away with another man, and left him with several children to look after. The children grew up all right, but one son was frozen to death while delivering mail to a mining camp. Some Indians stole Smith's horses, and, while he was chasing the red rustlers, they shot him. Badly wounded, he managed to crawl for 35 miles to the cabin of an old friend, "Jews-Harp Jack," who pulled him through the crisis.

Then his luck changed. At Florence, he made a rich strike, and decided to spend his good fortune quickly at Warren. Entering a saloon, he would buy it, and declare that "drinks are on the house," imbibing more than a few himself. It is not known how many saloons he bought, but it is alleged that in a hundred nights he went through a hundred thousand dollars, winding up broke.

People with surprising talents showed up in the mining camps. Near Florence, in the winter of 1861-62, miners found on a trail an unconscious, starving and half-frozen prospector, who had become lost from his party and who had wandered in the wilds for 30 days. The miners carried the man to Florence, and gradually during the winter he regained his health.

When he was able to walk about, he announced that he wanted to do something for the town. But what, he wondered, as he trudged through the snow. Ah, yes, snow—that was it. He would carve an ice statue. After all, he was Charles Leopold Ostner, who had been an honor art student at the University of Heidelburg. With piercing eyes and a Vandyke beard, he looked every inch the artist, but he was not a fussy one. It mattered not in what medium he worked.

He had his friends form a huge pile of snow on the street, then water was slowly poured over it, and the mound became ice. Screening this with canvas, Ostner went inside with hammer and chisel, and started to work. When the canvas was finally pulled away, Florence had an ice statue of General George Washington astride his horse, looking very much as he must have felt while riding through Valley Forge on a winter's day. In a way, it was a tribute to one man who had suffered from the cold to another.

Miners came from many miles around to admire the statue—while it lasted. Even Southerners thought it was a good likeness of the father of their country from which they wanted to be separated.

With his debt paid, Ostner did not linger long in Florence. He drifted south, buying an interest in a toll bridge for pack trains on the South Fork of the Payette River at Garden Valley. Prospering (toll charge per pack horse was $5), he decided that he wanted to do something for the Territory of Idaho. He would recreate Washington on his horse, but this version would remain intact in June as well as in January.

So, for the next four years, Ostner chipped away in his spare time on a huge Ponderosa pine log. Working mostly at night, he carved the fine features of Washington's face beneath the light of burning pitch-pine from the forest.

The presentation of the finished statue at an elaborate outdoor ceremony, attended by Governor David W. Ballard and other dignitaries, was held in a snowstorm on January 8, 1869, at Boise, for by this time the territorial capital had been moved from Lewiston. The press was generally very laudatory of the work, although a reporter on *The Owyhee Avalanche* of Silver City took a "left-handed" jab at the statue:

"*The Tidal Wave* (an opposition newspaper) has found an artist in Chas. Ostner, but Jo Barry exhibited at his room on New Year's Day, a picture which 'knocks the socks off' Chas. Ostner, 'or any other man.' A table loaded with champagne, punch, wines, brandies, whiskies, cake and red apples, with a bland invitation to 'help yourself,' is rather a nice picture. Much obliged, Jo."

Obviously, the Territorial Legislature paid no attention to *The Owyhee Avalanche,* for, in a burst of enthusiasm, it voted a return gift to Ostner of $7,000. Before the session was over, however, the Legislature got to thinking that it had been a little too generous for the time and place, and cut the amount down to $2,500.

For years, Washington rode high on a stone base on the capitol lawn. Other capitols might have statues of bronze or stone on their grounds, but Idaho's capitol had one of native wood. Weather deterioration was heavy and repairs costly, however, so, since 1934, Washington and his horse have been viewed by thousands inside the capitol. Wearing a coat of gold paint, the statue resides in a glass case, waiting to be photographed by tourists. As century-old art, the statue is of incalculable value. And it might never have been created if some miners had not happened to be following a trail near Florence in the winter of 1861-62, and picked up an almost dead prospector-artist.

As Ostner had moved on, so did others. In H. H. Bancroft's history, the North-Central Idaho miners were "like quicksilver, running after any atom of gold in their vicinity." But, at the time, the miners were in a good neighborhood for finding more than atoms of gold. With all that was being discovered—some of it just stumbled over—two things of major significance happened.

First, many of the Nez Perce Indians—those whose lands were not at stake —got carried away by the spin-off of prosperity through trading with the whites, and generally made no objections when leaders sold off more than 6,000,000 acres of reservation to the U.S. government for $325,000. This came to about 5 cents an acre for land which, within five years, would produce about $25,000,000 in gold. Still, the Nez Perces had 785,000 acres left, and that was a lot of property, they decided. Besides, the Indians were already becoming somewhat resigned to the idea of giving up their land. (Later, Idaho's U.S. Senator Fred T. Dubois spoke lengthily to a council of the Indians at Fort Hall, explaining that the government desired to acquire more land. When he finished, there was silence—also lengthy. Finally, an Indian spoke in excellent English: "You say the Great White Father in Washington wants more of our land?" Dubois nodded. "Well," continued the Indian, "what's the use of talking about it? He'll take it anyway.")

Second, the town of Lewiston began to emerge as one of the Pacific Northwest's most important inland shipping and trading centers. The first seeds planted there were of a business variety, and they flourished.

A trader named Seth Slater had fathered a trading post in the area, calling it Slaterville. The settlement consisted of five tents, two for storing supplies, two for providing housing, and one for serving liquid refreshment. So that no one could miss the latter, one half of the top was covered with a blue blanket and the other half with a red blanket. Further enhancing the outside was a sign scrawled with charcoal, reading "WHISKEY." The interior of the tent, however, was quite simple. It was furnished only with a whiskey barrel and two tin drinking cups.

Although quite satisfactory for the needs of the time, Slaterville did not last long. The Clearwater there was too swift and shallow for easy access by boat, so Slater moved his little "community" down to the confluence of the Snake and Clearwater. This site had been picked more prudently by an enterprising Nez Perce Indian chief, with the unlikely name of Reuben, for the construction of a crude warehouse to handle trading with the whites. He got a lot of competition as more tent stores were hastily pitched, giving to the site at first the name of Ragtown.

Then, on May 19, 1861, several of the early businessmen were sitting beside the Clearwater—a sort of Chamber of Commerce meeting on a log— when someone observed that Ragtown could do with a new name.

"How about Lewiston . . . to honor Meriwether Lewis of the Lewis and Clark Expedition which passed through here?" asked Victor Trevitt, operator of a tent mercantile store.

The others thought that was a great idea. The name not only had class, but a solid historical foundation. And so Ragtown became Lewiston.

Trevitt chuckled. He had a secret which he did not reveal for some time afterward. He came from Lewiston, Maine.

Soon, under the new name, the town was operating on a big scale. Mining equipment and supplies were shipped to it up the Columbia and Snake, and gold dust was sent back down the rivers.

In 1863, when Idaho Territory was established, with William H. Wallace appointed by President Abraham Lincoln as the first governor, Lewiston became the first capital. Progress—and culture—were on the march, with the river town even acquiring a college before the turn of the century.

(A major cultural step was taken at Lewiston in 1893 with the establishment there of Lewiston State Normal School. The college has undergone various name changes and a period of closure (1951-1955), but operates healthily today as Lewis-Clark State College.)

A reporter, reminiscing in 1878 in the *Lewiston Teller,* told of an early Christmas dinner given by pioneer settler John M. Silcott, who later married Indian Jane of Pierce gold discovery fame:

"The cuisine was elaborate, although a little irregular. There was no turkey, but a wild goose, which filled the place very acceptably; there was no roast pig, but a stuffed cub bear stood upon the platter; there was no pumpkin pie, a dish for which the old pioneer always felt a longing that was hard to satisfy; there was no great variety of confections, nor were there any fashionable wines, for which every one of the guests had perhaps a desire inspired by past association; but they did have pure alcohol. The government had supplied Dr. Thebodo's dispensary (at Fort Lapwai) with a five-gallon can of this potent drug, and the seal was intact till that Christmas morn.

"There was perhaps not a guest under this hospitable roof who could not have appreciated the most delicate bouquet of the best wines of an aristocrat's cellar, but they were equal to the occasion of enjoying raw alcohol with water in no extravagant portions, and each and every guest did the contents of that sealed can justice. And further, none ever complained that the alcohol did not do its expected work."

(In the same period, the mining camp of Dixie, southeast of Lewiston, had a Christmas party, and, even though it was held in a saloon, no liquor flowed, because some children were at the party. The fat bartender, who played Santa Claus, discreetly covered the displays of liquor with blankets. For his reindeer, he had a burro wearing deer antlers.)

On August 2, 1862, Idaho's first newspaper—*The Golden Age*—was introduced at Lewiston. One of several predecessors to the more permanent *Teller* or *Tribune, The Golden Age* lasted only three years, but they were lively years. At the time of the paper's founding, America's far-off Civil War in which General Robert E. Lee of the Confederate Army was then doing right well, was the burning issue, and Southern sympathizers in Lewiston gave warning that fair treatment of the war news filtering to the Far West was expected. When the American flag was raised over *The Golden Age's* little frame building, the friends of the South put 20 bullet holes through it.

Fortunately, Lewiston had a newspaper when the Great Zamlock showed up there, because it was part of the most baffling trick of this noted man of magic. Folding up a copy of the latest local newspaper wherever he appeared, he would place it inside a book. Then he would proceed to "read" any item in the folded paper through the cover and pages of the book. The trick was relatively simple for Zamlock, as he had a phenomenal memory, and would simply memorize every line of type in the paper upon his arrival in town.

When he asked members of the audience to name items for him to read, a livery stable operator bobbed up, and wanted the details of his advertisement. Zamlock was letter perfect. Next, a small boy asked for "the story of the big fish."

Zamlock started to recite:

71

"The Clearwater River had receded rapidly and left a big sturgeon impounded between Holbrook Island and the City of Lewiston . . ."

Just then a black woman arose, and started hurrying from the auditorium.

"Wait, madam," called Zamlock. "The show has just begun."

"Don't care," came the over-the-shoulder reply. "The way you see through things, this is no place for a decent lady with only a calico slip on."

Up the trail from Lewiston, the mining town of Oro Fino not only had culture in the form of the Oro Fino Lyceum and Debating Club, but a little store which had on its dusty shelves almost a complete set of Sir Walter Scott's novels. These books caught the eye of a scholarly prospector named William A. Goulder, who later taught school in Lewiston, and served as a territorial Legislator and as assistant editor of the *Idaho Statesman* in Boise. Lacking funds to buy the books, Goulder agreed to read them aloud to his comrades who shared a dingy cabin with him—if they would all chip in and make the purchase. This was agreed to, and, in the winter of 1863, the nightly reading started, with Goulder giving to his voice the best possible mellifluous tones and soporific effects.

"Very soon all my friends would be snoring in perfect rhythm and harmony with the voice of the reader," Goulder wrote in his memoirs. "Then I would cease reading aloud and enjoy for an hour or two a season of delight and profitable reading. At the first sign of my friends' awakening, I would resume my sleep-compelling style of reading, which would soon again produce the desired effect . . .

"I thus read all of Scott's stories, except 'The Fair Maid of Perth,' whose delicate constitution and refined superstructure had thus far kept her away from the rude scenes of a wild mining camp."

Indeed, "The Fair Maid of Perth" would have had difficulty coping with the hazards of the time and place. Even Lewiston, Northern Idaho's most civilized town at the time, involved dangerous living. The *Portland Oregonian* advised that "if you have a mule in Lewiston, you should take it to bed with you to prevent it being stolen." Lewiston, however, was a relatively safe place compared with the trails leading to it.

The men who packed gold over the mountains for shipment from Lewiston to West Coast cities rode not only tall in the saddle, but precariously. One of the packers who defied highwaymen in carrying the dust from mines in the Florence area to Lewiston was "Doc" Noble. Fast with a gun, he feared no man, and had a crew who felt likewise.

On one trip, however, while winding along a trail on the Salmon River south of White Bird, Doc's outfit was fired upon by highwaymen hiding behind rocks. The horses stampeded, and a running gun fight followed. The robbers got the better of it, and about $75,000 in gold.

Later, the fleeing bandits were overtaken in the Seven Devils area, and all were killed. But, on their bodies and in their pack saddles, was not more than $100 in gold dust. It was decided that they had hidden their loot somewhere near the site of the robbery, and, for all that anybody knows, it is still there.

The most famous of all robberies in the area was "The Lloyd Magruder Case," which doubles in spades some of the Western thrillers on television today. By rights, however, it should be called "The Hill Beachy Case" or "The Case of Beachy's Extra Sensory Perception."

The balding and bearded Beachy with apparent ESP operated the Luna House in Lewiston besides serving on the town council. In its day, the long, two-story hotel served the best and worst people who paused in the river town on their way to one mining camp or another.

In the middle of an October night in 1863, Beachy sprang out of his hotel bed, screaming and sweating.

"I just saw my friend, Lloyd Magruder, being murdered by a man with an axe," he told his startled wife.

"Go back to sleep, Hill," she said. "You've been dreaming."

Indeed, he had—but a very real dream.

The discovery of gold in Idaho had lured Magruder, the victim in the dream, west from Maryland, but he soon found that, to support a wife and four children, he could make money faster by trading than by digging. Setting up a store at Elk City, he began to freight supplies to other mining camps with horse and mule pack trains.

At the time of Beachy's dream, Magruder was returning with a train of 60 animals from Virginia City, Montana, where he had traded supplies for $30,000 in gold dust. He was accompanied by four wranglers—Charley Allen, William Phillips, and the brothers, Horace and Robert Chalmers.

Sixty horses and mules are a lot of livestock to handle, so Magruder was delighted when three more men asked to join the party. They were D. C. Lowry, David Howard and James Romaine. Then still another, a grizzled old mountain man named William Page, fell in with the caravan. Page was harmless. Not so the other three. They were members of the Montana bandit gang of suave Henry Plummer, who used his position as sheriff to learn who was carrying large amounts of gold dust out of Virginia City.

For some reason, the three desperadoes took a liking to old Page, who told tall tales all day and chewed tobacco continuously—even in his sleep. They confided in him that they planned to kill Magruder and his crew, and take the $30,000, warning Page that, if he breathed a word, he would also die. Page shakily assured them that he was not "the talkin' kind."

Came night on the Little Clearwater, between the Salmon and Clearwater rivers, where the caravan had camped. It was a beautiful wooded spot with lush patches of grass where the Nez Perces traditionally camped on their way to buffalo hunting grounds. Overlooking the site were the peaks of what is now known as Magruder Mountain.

With snow starting to swirl down, Magruder and Lowry, on the first guard duty shift, huddled beside a campfire, rifles across their laps. Saying that he had better get some more wood for the fire, Lowry laid down his rifle, picked up an axe, and stalked off into the darkness. When he returned, he came up behind Magruder, who was bending over to light his pipe with a glowing twig. Viciously, Lowry drove the axe blade into Magruder's head. Howard, waiting in bushes for the attack, sprang into the firelight, grabbed the axe from Lowry, and proceeded to strike Magruder again and again—just to be sure.

Then Howard hurried to the sleeping Chalmers brothers, and killed them the same way. Phillips, also asleep, was slain by Romaine with a Bowie knife, but managed to cry out before he died. Aroused by the sound, Allen sat up on his bed of cedar boughs. As he did so, Howard fired both barrels of a shotgun into him. Horrified, Page watched the slaughter.

"Now," said Lowry, "we hide the bodies, and get rid of the pack train."

The bodies were pushed over a precipice into thick brush. Disposing of 60 horses and mules was not so easy. But the killers managed by driving them into a box canyon, and shooting them.

Several days later, a man, with his face half-hidden by his upturned mackinaw collar, came into the Luna House at Lewiston, and asked for four tickets on the stage about to depart for Walla Walla. Beachy, seated in his office, happened to glance at the stranger through an open door. He puzzled. Where had he seen that man before? As the stranger walked outside and climbed into the stagecoach, Beachy remembered. He had seen him in his dream, attacking his friend, Magruder, with an axe.

Hurrying outside, Beachy pretended to be checking that everybody was all right in the stagecoach. He peered into the vehicle. Yes, there was no doubt about it. The ticket buyer was the man he had seen in his dream. And two of the men were trying to hide cantinas. Beachy was sure the cantinas contained gold dust.

He thought about going back into the Luna House, and getting a gun. But who would believe the evidence of a dream?

Three days later, a pack train from Bannack, Montana, pulled up beside the board walk fronting the Luna House. Beachy came running out.

"Seen anything of Magruder's outfit?" he asked one of the packers.

"Several days ahead of us. Should have been here by now."

Beachy went into action. He began asking all around Lewiston if anyone had seen the strangers come into town, and found a ranch on the outskirts where they had left their horses and gear. Beachy recognized some of the gear as belonging to Magruder.

Having himself made a deputy sheriff and obtaining warrants for the arrest of the departed four, Beachy started on the trail. With little more than the dream to go on, he agreed to assume full responsibility if proven wrong. He was a determined man.

By horseback, stage and boat, Beachy raced to Walla Walla and then to Portland. At Portland, he learned that the four he was seeking had just taken a ship for San Francisco, and another ship would not be leaving for nine days. The nearest telegraph office was in Yreka, California, 400 miles away, and Beachy knew that he had to get to Yreka before the ship docked in San Francisco. Traveling overland by day and night, he made it, and telegraphed the warrants for arrest to the police in San Francisco.

When he arrived there, the police were holding his men. With an executive warrant from Governor Leland Stanford of California, "Sheriff" Beachy claimed the four as his prisoners.

"We'll fix you for this when we get out of it," Howard told Beachy.

"You're not getting out of it," replied Beachy.

Bringing the prisoners back to Lewiston in chains, he placed them under heavy guard in the Luna House. Now all that was needed was a confession, and the old man, tobacco-chewing Page, seemed the most likely prospect for producing one.

With town authorities cooperating, Beachy set the stage for Page's "singing" in the Luna House. One room was made up to look like a trial court. An adjoining room was left vacant except for four ropes with nooses hanging from the ceiling over four boxes.

As Page was led into the "trial room," he passed the open door of the adjoining room, and saw the dangling ropes. One look was enough. Page told all, stressing that he had had no part in the actual killings.

When Lowry and Romaine were confronted with Page's story, they admitted that what the old man had said was true. Howard contended to the last that the story was fabrication. But the three confessions were enough for conviction at the first legal court trial held in the new Territory of Idaho.

Judge Samuel Parks declared:

"The punishment of the law will be visited upon you . . . The robber and the murderer may learn from your fate that there is no safety for them, and that the way of the transgressor is indeed hard."

On March 4, 1864, before most of the population of Lewiston and a goodly number of Nez Perce Indians from Lapwai, Lowry, Romaine and Howard were led to a scaffold in a little ravine southeast of town, a place now known as Vollmer Park.

Romaine closed his eyes.

"All ready," nodded Howard.

"Launch the boat—she's nothing but a mud scow anyhow," said Lowry.

The trap was sprung, and three bodies dropped through the platform.

Page was given his freedom for turning state's evidence. Feeling sorry for him because most of the townspeople held him in contempt, Beachy gave him a job as a handyman at the Luna House. But Page was not long in following the three desperadoes to the grave. He was killed in a drunken brawl by a man named Albert Ingo.

Only $17,000 of the $30,000 in gold stolen from Magruder was recovered. This was given to Mrs. Magruder at Elk City. Beachy was awarded $6,244 by the Territorial Legislature for "services and money expended in the pursuit of the killers."

It was never proven that Plummer, the Montana sheriff, master-minded the robbery and killings, but this made little difference. He and his chief cohorts had been hanged on January 10, 1864, by the Virginia Vigilantes for other assorted crimes, including 102 known murders. Plummer's last request was to "give me a good drop," and this request was honored.

The hangings in Lewiston and Virginia City slowed down activities of highwaymen—for a while. Some mines started using the mailman for toting their gold to safe haven. The mailman was delighted to do this "moonlighting," because, with the pay he received for carrying the mail, he barely made expenses. For delivering gold dust, he pocketed a fee of 4 per cent of its value.

One of the early mailmen on the hundred-mile route from Florence to Lewiston, who profited handsomely this way, was Warren P. Hunt. He was never robbed of any gold, but he came close.

Robbers had an effective grapevine to alert them to big shipments of gold leaving Florence, so, when Hunt was about to start out one day with $40,000 in gold dust on his pack horses, it was not surprising that two strangers showed up in Florence. Some miners, becoming suspicious, passed the word to the mailman.

Hunt looked up a miner friend he could trust, gave him the $40,000 in gold dust in an old gunnysack, and told him to take off for Lewiston. Then Hunt found an excuse to delay his own start until the next day. When, as expected, he was held up on the trail by the two strangers, he had no gold. It was in the gunnysack ahead.

The precarious life of Idaho's gold boom days did not go unnoticed in the garrets of New York's Greenwich Village. In these garrets writers were turning out dime novels by the bushel basket to meet the demand of avid readers who longed for more excitement than their own lives afforded. There was adventure to spare in Idaho, and the novelists seized—and enlarged—upon it.

In 1908, Arthur L. Meserve began "The Hunter's Secret; or, Gamblers Among the Redskins" with this bit of stilted but alluring conversation:

" 'And this, I suppose, Phil, is Bannock City, and yonder are the "Shining Mountains," which give Idaho its name?' "

" 'I suppose you are right, Dalt. At last we have reached this new El Dorado, where our fortunes are to be made and where any quantity of thrilling adventures and hairbreadth escapes are to be our fortune.' "

Meserve's novel was toned down somewhat from "Tornado Tom; or, Injun Jack From Red Core," penned in 1880 by T. C. Harbaugh, who chose North-Central Idaho as the setting. Harbaugh declared that his daring characters roamed "that wild part of Idaho which some geographers have called the *terra Incognito* of the Far West, and others 'the land of death.' "

Then there was the 1886 thriller by Frank Dumont—"Blue-Blazes; or, The Break o' Day Boys of Rocky Bar." Dumont stated:

"At the period of which we write the silver regions bordering upon the Salmon River and its chain of mountains in Idaho were infested with all the lawless element of the States. Here the criminal sought a haven among kindred spirits and struck terror to the honest miner's heart, and the traveler compelled to journey in coaches considered himself fortunate if he escaped these 'chevaliers.' "

The demand for more and more Idaho stories led some writers to turn to tales about steamboating in the Territory. In "Diamond Dick Jr.'s Dash for Life; or, The Tragedy of the Rawhide Trail" (1900), W. B. Lawson gave his conception of the Idaho steamboat scene by starting off with some rapid-fire patter:

" 'Two fer one, ten fer five, twenty fer ten—this way, gents, an' do yer bettin' on the little ball. Hocus, pocus, presto, chango—now you see it an' now you don't. Come up, Rube, an' try yer luck.' "

" 'Name ain't Rube!' "

" 'Then Josh.' "

" 'Ye can't josh me. I'm Hiram Hornet, of Hornetsville, mister, an' I allers wear my stinger where it's easy tu git at. I'm six foot three in my yarn socks, an' I'm a dreffle bad man to meet.' "

"This conversation took place on the *Spread Eagle,* a little steamer that plied on the Kootenai River between Bonners Ferry, Idaho, and Kaslo, on Kootenai Lake."

While most of the dime novels were not conducive to encouraging settlement in Idaho, some painted pictures which no doubt inspired many an Easterner to take the next train west. "Yreka Jim's Joker; or, The Rivals of Red Nose," authored in 1884 by Edward L. Wheeler, had this enticing introduction:

"A beautiful autumn day was drawing to a close, over a magnificent Idaho landscape, which, though mountainous and rugged in the extreme, was pleasing to the eye, and such as an artist would go into ecstacies over.

"Gigantic mountains soared heavenward, met on their tapering descent by heavily timbered foothills; here wide canyons pierced the mighty range; deep and fathomless abysses prevailed; crystal cascades, leaping from ledge to ledge, sparkled like sheets of diamonds, only to swell into fiercer torrents as they surged on toward a running level."

Altogether, the early pulp productions with Idaho settings probably left the reader a little confused and uncertain about the big land. But then, Idaho still is a place which must actually be seen to be believed.

Chapter VII

# COLOR OF GOLD ON THE SOUTHERN HORIZON

"The Boise Basin of Idaho alone did better in the production of gold than all of Colorado between 1863 and 1866."
                                                    —Historian Ralph H. Gabriel

Many people today look upon Idaho's early mining era as just "a rough period which contributed little more than wealth from the earth and grave mounds for persons shot while trying to extract it." Not so!

Spawned in the era were businesses, banks, churches, theatres, newspapers . . . to serve the needs of the burgeoning population attracted by the cry of "Gold!" Roads and rails—they came to Idaho because they were vital to its mining population. Homes were needed, and, to provide them, Idaho's lumbering industry was given impetus. Thus, much of the wealth that was taken from beneath the earth was spent in developments on the surface.

Color the roughness of the era golden, but for more reasons than one.

Legend has it that somewhere along the Old Oregon Trail in the 1840s small boys from a wagon train found "a blue bucket full of shiny golden pebbles." Now, a blue bucket in those days was pretty common stuff. It was a popular type of water pail that swung from the side of many a covered wagon headed west. The pebbles, however, were uncommon. They were heavy. So the boys, for a while, used them as sinkers on their fishing lines. Then they found them good for throwing, and tossed most of them away before someone on the train, who knew gold when he saw it, spotted one of the "pebbles."

77

Where had they been found? No one was sure. So the "Lost Blue Bucket Mine" became a part of Western lore. Lost? Today, some historians, probing various versions of the story, doubt it in its entirety, contending that it was only a tale dreamed up to titillate a pioneer group around a campfire. But, in the 1860s the story seemed real enough to have men looking for the Lost Blue Bucket Mine over hundreds of miles of the Old Oregon Trail, including off-shoots to California. (The Moscow area in Northern Idaho also has a Lost Blue Bucket Mine on Paradise Creek, which inspired early University of Idaho students to name their literary and humor magazine *The Blue Bucket*.)

In 1862, Captain Tom Turner and 50 men from the Willamette Valley were seeking the Oregon Trail's Lost Blue Bucket Mine. They had backtracked to the area around Auburn, Oregon, when they were joined by Moses Splawn, who had been told by a Bannock Indian at Elk City that there were "chunks of yellow metal to be found far to the south." Maybe, thought Splawn, the Indian had stumbled upon the Lost Blue Bucket Mine, and didn't know it.

Splawn searched for a while with the Turner party, then wanted to go on farther east. All except seven demurred. These seven accompanied Splawn, and were soon met by a party of eight under George Grimes, bringing the total to 16.

It was this group which discovered gold in the Boise Basin. About where Centerville now stands in Boise County, exciting traces of color were found, with Dave Fogus of the party turning the first shovel of pay gravel. Mining had barely started, however, when Indians began shooting at the white invaders. A bullet clipped the hair over the ear of a man named Joseph Branstetter.

Grabbing a shotgun, Grimes started creeping through the brush, but the enemy was nearer than he thought. A rifle bullet tore into his chest.

The day before, while looking at a picture of his daughter, Grimes said that he had dreamed of an Indian killing him, and that he would never see his daughter again. As in the case of Hill Beachy dreaming about Lloyd Magruder's death, there seemed to be extrasensory perception. But perhaps in those days, with the possibility of death always around the next bend in the trail, people dreamed about it more.

As he lay dying now, Grimes, only about 27, left a message with Splawn for his wife and daughter. Then he looked up at Splawn, and pleaded:

"Mose, don't let them scalp me."

To be sure that this did not happen, the miners buried Grimes deep in one of the mine holes beside a creek, and the creek today bears his name.

Fearing that its number was too small to continue to work the area, the party left for Walla Walla where about 50 more men were recruited. Then, returning in October, 1862, with a pack train of supplies and equipment, the reinforced party began digging in earnest in the Boise Basin, which, in the next 10 years, would produce gold estimated in value from $100,000,000 to $200,000,000.

Camps, which quickly emerged into towns, began to spring up like wild flowers, with emphasis for quite a while on the wild. Pioneer City or Pioneerville or plain Pioneer evolved in 1862, after at first being called Hog'em by disgruntled prospectors who found all the good claims taken by a few "early birds." Some folks ignored all the above assorted names, referring to the place as "New Dublin" in recognition of all the Irishmen who flocked there. Next came Placerville, Buena Vista (many Californians took the first ship north to

Portland after the discovery of gold in the Boise Basin, then hurried overland to the area), Centerville, and Bannock (Bannack) City, which was later renamed Idaho City, because a lot of its mail was being sidetracked to Bannack, Montana, then in Idaho Territory.

Feuding developed between Placerville and Idaho City as to which would become the metropolis of Southwest Idaho (fledgling Boise was ignored). Placerville had a bit of a head start. It not only got in 1864 the Boise Basin's first ore mill, a 10-stamp unit, but it had early in its life good stage and mail service from Umatilla (the basin's first post office was established at Placerville on January 4, 1864). By the end of 1864, the town claimed a floating population of 15,000 men. (The women, largely at first of shady character, apparently were not counted.)

Idaho City, however, gradually forged ahead of Placerville. The floating population of Idaho City in its prime was estimated as high as 25,000, making this mountain mecca for miners the largest city in Idaho in the Golden Decade —in fact, the entire Pacific Northwest. Stable populations of Placerville and Idaho City at their peaks, however, probably ran only about 5,000 and 7,000 respectively.

Still, by 1865, there were 249 business places in Idaho City alone. These included 41 saloons, 4 breweries, 15 restaurants, 36 grocery stores, 23 dry goods and clothing stores (silk, lace, merino and tarleton were the favored fancy dress fabrics), 12 blacksmith shops, 23 law offices, 3 tailor shops, 10 Chinese wash houses, 6 hotels, and 6 barber shops, complete with bathtubs in the rear. (Significant of the thinking in Idaho City at the time was the naming of two main, intersecting streets. They were called Montgomery and Wall after the famous financial thoroughfares of San Francisco and New York City.)

Giving Idaho City a special edge over Placerville was its sturdy jail of hand-hewn timbers and hand-wrought nails. One of the first buildings constructed in the town, the jail was used by the Federal government to confine its prisoners in the area until the territorial penitentiary was built at Boise in 1869.

A drawback at Idaho City was the fact that much of the wealth lay beneath the townsite. A well digger, hired to find water, struck gold instead at 18 feet, and the townspeople then began knocking down houses and tearing up streets in quest of more. Even in modern days, traces of gold have been found by panning street gravel.

When some prospectors found rich gold in a gulch near the end of Main Street, they kept the discovery a secret for a while by reporting that the gulch was a haven for bears. Today, the gulch is still known as Bear Run.

Meanwhile, south of Boise, in the Owyhee desert country (Owyhee is an early form of the spelling of Hawaii), came the booming of new bonanzas. Late in 1862, Captain Turner, still doggedly looking for the Lost Blue Bucket Mine, drifted with remnants of his party into the Owyhee Country—a harsh yet beautiful land of yawning canyons, flat-iron and anvil and saddle-shaped rock formations, dusty sagebrush, quaking aspen, and shy desert flowers. The men found some gold and staked some claims, then moved on. The place, they decided, was definitely not the site of the Lost Blue Bucket Mine.

In May of 1863, however, a party of 29 men, headed by Michael M. Jordan, started following up Turner's trail, and began prospecting on a creek flowing into the Owyhee River. Turning up good placer prospects on the little stream, which became known as Jordan Creek, the party ushered in Idaho's famous "48-hour gold rush."

The 29 men, soon dubbed the "Twenty-niners," went to Placerville to record their claims and obtain supplies and equipment. They were followed back to Jordan Creek by about 2,000 other prospectors. Most of these, deciding that the only good prospects had already been staked out by the original party, returned to Placerville at the end of two days or just kept on moving. That was one of the biggest mistakes made in Idaho mining history. Many more strikes would be made, not only of gold but of silver, and the Owyhee County town of Silver City would become internationally famous as their center.

As for little Boise, it was delighted to be caught in the middle of two great mining booms—to have Idaho City as its father and Silver City as its mother. Naturally situated as a trading center, the youngster was certain to grow big and strong.

To look over Boise in those days was to see dust clouds continually swirling to or from it. These were stirred up not only by emigrant trains, but by pack and wagon trains hauling freight destined for the mining camps.

When major wagon roads to Boise were completed—after a fashion—many small packers went broke. Two or three freight wagons, linked together and pulled by six or twelve horses or mules (oxen were still used in a few instances), became the "in" thing. The driver sometimes rode a lead animal, but usually he sat high on the seat of the No. 1 wagon. In his hand he held a long whip to step up the hoof draggers. With more than four horses or mules pulling, the whip was not long enough, so the driver kept a sack of pebbles on the seat beside him.

At first, most of the freight to Boise came via Walla Walla or Umatilla on the Columbia, with some moved up from Salt Lake City. Then, in 1869, the tracks of the Union Pacific Railroad were pushed to Kelton, Utah, and Boise began to look more and more to Utah for supplies. The new link became strong and long-lasting.

Although the mining camps were largely dependent on Boise for the supplies routed through it, the camps gained some self-sufficiency. Kegs of alcohol shipped from Boise were processed locally by adding water, burnt sugar and different chemicals, depending on whether the end product desired was Kentucky (?) bourbon or French (?) cognac.

A newcomer to Placerville, beaming after rolling some whiskey around his tongue, asked the bartender of the Magnolia Saloon (now a home-spun museum) where he got it. The bartender pointed to a town well outside the saloon. Looking a little uncertain, the newcomer nevertheless ordered another shot.

The mining camps had their own doctors, needed frequently for making repairs after saloon and street fights. An item in Idaho City's *Boise News* (first newspaper in Southern Idaho) for November 28, 1863, under "BROKEN HEADS," stated:

"Several parties were found in the streets Tuesday morning, some with fractured skulls, bunged eyes and swollen faces, indicating there had been a fuss somewhere during the night, blood being freely sprinkled on woodpiles and sidewalks. Many of the restaurants and saloons closed their doors when the fuss began. Three parties were roughly handled. Maloy's wound was a dangerous one—the skull in the forehead fractured, perhaps by having the cock of a pistol driven through it. Dr. Raymond operated on Tuesday, and Maloy is now recovering."

No other details were provided, for, in Idaho City at the time, that would have been gilding the lily.

The doctors were not always as successful as Raymond in the case of Maloy. Indeed, they often arrived at a scene of violence to find no pulse beating.

On a slope at the end of a winding road leading west out of Idaho City, there are today 40 acres of timber never to be cut. Once part of the fabulously wealthy J. Marion More mining claim, the west forty was Idaho City's first cemetery. In it are more than 200 graves, and only 28 of those who lie there are said to have died of natural causes.

One of those who passed away "unnaturally" was Herman C. St. Clair, who was hanged in Idaho City on January 1, 1898, for the kiling of John Decker. St. Clair's last words were on the philosophical side:

"Whiskey, cards, and fast women are a combination that will bring almost anyone down. A man may get along all right with one or two of these vices, but, with all three mixed, hell is the final windup."

The burial places of St. Clair and the others who rest in the Idaho City Cemetery are particularly impressive, because, instead of following orderly rows, they stretch out under the shade of giant evergreens, dotting the hillside here and there.

But perhaps even more impressive is the old cemetery at Placerville. Either Placerville had an unusually large number of wealthy families in its boom mining days, or an especially fine stone cutter, or both. Many of the grave markers are not only costly-large, but beautifully done.

Looking for the last resting place of the "Fiddlers Three," this writer found the grave inside a square formed by four towering pine trees. A bronze plaque cast in concrete has long since replaced the wooden marker first allotted to the "fiddlers," but the original inscription has been carefully preserved. it reads:

"Fiddelers [Fiddlers] Murdered in Orphit [Ophir] Creek."

The story of the three men buried in the common grave has various versions, with the best known one telling of three fiddlers being murdered and robbed while on their way to play for a dance at Centerville. But that was not what really happened, according to Mrs. Edna Gallup, who came with her father, Henry Ashcroft, to Placerville on June 21, 1893. Before she died in Placerville at 95 in 1967, she firmly declared that three fiddlers do not lie beneath the "Fiddlers Three" marker—just one. The others are a banjo plucker and a miner who couldn't play any instrument.

The way Mrs. Gallup told it, there was a prospector named George Wilson who struck rich, gold-bearing ore on Ophir Creek. Handcrushing the ore, he picked out the gold with a pocketknife—more than $10,000 worth. Then, in the winter of 1863-64, Ashcroft, Mrs. Gallup's father, suggested that Wilson take the raw gold to Boise City, and exchange it for $20 gold pieces.

"With the cash, you can finance new equipment for your claim, and hire workers as well as guards," Ashcroft explained.

So, riding to Boise City, Wilson made the exchange without any trouble. On the way back, however, he was ambushed. His bullet-riddled body was found beside empty saddle bags on Ophir Creek. And nearby were the bodies of two more gun-shot victims, Fred Cursons, a fiddler, and Larry Moulton, a good man on a banjo and a fair one on a guitar. It was surmised that the musicians, on their way to play for a dance, had happened to witness the murder and robbery of Wilson, and were slain for knowing too much. All three men were buried together in the pine-bordered grave which somehow became known as the last resting place of the "Fiddlers Three."

Two other graves in the Placerville Cemetery also caught the eye of this writer. One was that of a three-month-old baby. This grave was marked by a large granite tombstone completely surrounded by a netting of heavy wire in the form of a bassinet. For many years each spring, it is said, the parents carefully covered the bassinet with wild flowers.

On another grave was a large stone cross. When it was placed at the site many years ago, there was nothing unusual about it. But, as this writer came upon it, he noted in an arm of the cross a nesting robin. As many humans for many centuries have looked to the cross as something to cling to, so did the robin, providing a peaceful postscript to Idaho's turbulent mining history.

Today, in fact, the whole town of Placerville—what there is left of it—is about as peaceful a looking place as you can find. Set in a gentle valley among evergreen-covered mountains, it now beckons to city folk who want to get away from it all, and who are refurbishing old homes or building rustic new ones—trying to recapture the time that was.

Editorially, the press in the early days strove for uplift. The *Boise News* of September 29, 1863, commented:

"Sam Houston and Co. are opening a circulating library in this place (Idaho City) and Placerville. They have a library of some 2,000 volumes. The reading portion of the community will be glad to hear this announcement. Books and newspapers are much cheaper and better companions during the long winter evenings than any likely to be met with in the streets or bar-rooms of the city. Patronize the library." (At the time, it cost 50 cents to a dollar to get a newspaper delivered to Idaho City, depending on the packer, but even such foreign imports were much cheaper than the local saloon entertainment.)

The people of Idaho City did some uplifting by their boot straps. They built churches and theatres, started a dancing school, and organized debating and sledding clubs.

Too, Idaho City claimed the Territory's second Masonic Lodge, established July 7, 1863. (Masonry was first introduced in Idaho at Lewiston, December 23, 1862, after a lodge proposed earlier in the year at Oro Fino failed to materialize.) Even before a lodge was formally established in the Boise Basin, however, a Masonic funeral was held in the winter of 1862-63 at the basin mining camp of Centerville.

The funeral of William Slade, believed to be the first conducted by Masons in Idaho, drew some 80 of the brothers. Because there was not a single ritual apron around, white pocket handkerchiefs were substituted, according to Colonel George Hunter in his "Reminiscences of an Old Timer."

When the services were over, the brothers adjourned to a hall—the back room of a saloon—with a table placed in the center. On the table were a gold scales and a large leather pouch, labeled "For the Widow and Her Children." Around this table, the brothers marched, each pausing to select a weight and balance it with gold dust, which was poured into the pouch.

As one old fellow, his mustache wet with tears, came up to the scales, he said:

"We can do something to atone for our cussedness, can't we?"

Then, without bothering to select a weight, he poured all the dust he had into the pouch. Others began to follow suit. When the pouch was presented to Widow Slade, it contained more than $3,000 in gold. Indeed, "cussedness" was not the only trait prevalent in those days.

In the same winter, 1862-63, saws started whining day and night at a lumber mill on Grimes Creek. Sometimes the lumber was stacked directly from a saw on a buyer's wagon—at $100 to $200 per thousand feet. In Idaho City, where the inclination was to do things in a big way, a steam sawmill started up in July, 1863, turning out 10,000 to 15,000 feet of lumber per day. The mill was also important in keeping time, because people set their watches and clocks by the steam whistle, which tooted at 6 a.m., 12 noon and 6 p.m.

Buena Vista had a brick-making plant, but bricks ran much higher than lumber, and only those who had struck it really rich could afford a brick house. Most of the buildings in the mining camps were of log or frame construction, strung together without any thought of fire hazard. This was most unfortunate when flames started sweeping through Idaho City on May 19, 1865.

The alarm for Idaho City's biggest fire was sounded at about 9 p.m. on that spring day in 1865 when miners and dance hall girls and bartenders shoved their way through the front door of a saloon onto Montgomery Street, screaming, "Fire!" No cry was more dreaded in the early-day mining towns.

A strong wind, blowing from the south, carried flames from building to building, with the popping of pitch in pine boards sounding like pistol shots. Wells, Fargo & Co.'s office went. Then the Idaho Saloon, offices of the sheriff and probate judge, the City Hotel, Magnolia Hall, Harris' Drugstore . . .

"The whole town's going!" exclaimed a satin-frocked dance hall girl. clutching at the sleeve of a miner. "Do something!"

But generally there was little to be done.

Not so in Craft's Store, whose huge safe served as a bank for many miners. Entering the establishment, George Dwight was met by the very calm owner and operator.

"George, I've got a job for you," Craft said.

"I'm at your service."

Craft pulled open the doors of his safe to reveal neat rows of buckskin pouches of gold dust, each pouch tagged with the owner's name.

"Altogether there's about a hundred pounds of gold," Craft calculated. "Can you carry it, George?"

"Like a baby."

Tossing the pouches into a gunnysack, Craft then hoisted the sack onto Dwight's shoulder.

"All right, George. Get out of town—but not too far."

(It was not until 1867 that Idaho City got a branch of the First National Bank of Idaho. Up to that time, miners customarily stored their wealth with store operators or saloon keepers—both considered honest professions. Then Christopher W. Moore, after operating a trading post at Ruby City in Owyhee County, opened a store in Boise, where a bank was established as a sideline. On March 11, 1867, this became the First National Bank of Idaho, with headquarters at Boise, and branches in Silver City and Idaho City. The First Security Bank of Idaho, with headquarters in Boise, evolved the same way—from the Anderson Brothers Bank at Eagle Rock (Idaho Falls), which was established in 1865 on a trading post foundation.)

When the 1865 fire started in Idaho City, the theatrical company starring

83

Julia Dean Hayne was performing Shakespeare's "Romeo and Juliet" in the Forrest Theatre. The Forrest had opened the year before with the announcement that "smoking is prohibited in the theatre so that ladies can come and enjoy the performance without any apprehension of having their lungs inflated and inflamed with the fumes of tobacco." But now the entire building was about to be filled with smoke.

Came Scene 3, Act I, and Romeo strode into a hall of the House of Capulet, announcing that "I ne'er saw true beauty till this night." Tybalt, nephew of Lady Capulet and bitter foe of Romeo and all his kin, declared:

"This, by his voice, should be a Montague. Fetch me my rapier, boy. Now . . ."

But Tybalt never got to finish the speech—not that night. Someone at the rear of the theatre shouted, "Fire!" The stampede was on.

With sword clanking, Romeo leaped off the stage, and started scrambling with the cash customers for the nearest exit. All his belongings were in a nearby hotel, and he was not about to lose them. His beloved Juliet—"the true beauty?" She was left to shift for herself.

In the smoky dawn, Romeo and Tybalt were observed chummily eating breakfast of canned oysters, warmed over the hot ashes of the Forrest Theatre. They were seated on Romeo's precious suitcases.

The Magic Palace Theatre, operated by James Pinney (who would later become "Mr. Theatre" in Boise), also burned to the ground. Pinney could have used a stage hand who worked for the Jenny Lind Theatre.

Named after the famous Swedish singer, the 800-seat Jenny Lind Theatre was Idaho City's most plush entertainment palace—even the newer Forrest Theatre had failed to outdo it. Claiming "all the appurtenances of a San Francisco theatre," the Jenny Lind had red-plush box seats tabbed up to $15, a dress circle, orchestra pit, gallery, bar and parquet.

Handling scenery at the Jenny Lind was a former fireman from New Orleans, who had fought some first-class fires in the Southern city. Determined to save both the theatre and his job, the ex-fireman braved almost unendurable heat to extinguish each blaze that flared up at the Jenny Lind. He literally lost his shirt, but kept the theatre intact.

Around it, the new Idaho City would be built, and, with it, funds would be raised to aid the destitute, numbering in the thousands. The very next night a benefit performance was held at the Jenny Lind. Some persons stood outside the jammed theatre to hear the singing through open doors. After the fire (believed to have been started by a disgruntled saloon patron), there were few homes to go to, but the people were not about to leave. Not yet.

Eventually, when the gold gave out, most of the residents had to take off for other parts, but those who stayed remained fiercely loyal to their town. When this writer visited Idaho City in 1974, the sign on Highway 21 listed the population at 180, but an old-timer pointed out that the sign was "20 years out of date."

"Why, the population now is at least 200," he said.

And the 200 in 1974 successfully rounded up enough support to keep Horseshoe Bend, booming with a lumber mill-fostered population of 500, from taking the county seat away from Idaho City. They figured that their town was too historically significant for that to happen.

Indeed, just to drop into Idaho City's old Miners Exchange Saloon today is to take a long step back into the past. You drape your coat on elk horns, and your elbow on a vintage bar. The Miners Exchange first opened its swinging doors in 1865, but the bartender says apologetically that the bar dates back only to 1880. Off in the corner, some young musicians start tuning up for a session of "good old Western music." In the style of the day, they are wearing beards and long hair. As you gaze at their reflections in the bar's polished mirror which was shipped precariously to Idaho City by wagon train, you smile. A century might not have passed at all.

Silver City in the 1860s became the metropolis of Owyhee County, but it was a Johnny-come-lately among the area's mining camps. The first boom camp to spring up with the discovery of gold by the Jordan party was Booneville, named after one of the men in the party—a kinsman of Daniel Boone. Unfortunately, however, Booneville was tucked in the narrow mouth of a canyon, leaving little elbow room for all the miners who flocked to it. So another town took root farther up the canyon. This was Ruby City, first seat of Owyhee County. Then Ruby City also developed growing pains, and this gave impetus to the forming of a third town—Silver City—nesting 6,179 feet high on the slopes of War Eagle Mountain.

Among the founders of Silver City was Colonel William H. Dewey, one of the most flamboyantly colorful figures in all of Idaho's early history. (He acquired his title at a miners' meeting in Kentucky where almost any impressive-looking man was assumed to be a colonel.)

This writer first became intrigued by the colonel some years ago while visiting with Mrs. William E. Borah, widow of Idaho's famous U.S. Senator. Mrs. Borah, a woman of distinctive wit and charm who was known as "Little Borah," was recalling the official grand opening on February 20, 1903, of the Dewey Palace Hotel in Nampa. After commenting that Borah, then a promising young attorney, was the principal speaker at the affair, Little Borah turned her remarks to her impression of Colonel Dewey.

"Greeting guests at the door," she said, "was this massive figure of a man (although not tall, he weighed 285 pounds), wearing a bush of a beard and a stickpin that had a diamond as big as a marble—and the diamond was splattered with yesterday's egg."

Colonel Dewey, however, could not always afford diamond stickpins—not even eggs for breakfast.

Born the son of poor parents in Massachusetts on August 1, 1823, Dewey ran away from home at 11, figuring that he could do better on his own. Tugboating on the Erie Canal, which linked Lake Erie at Buffalo with the Hudson River at Albany, had started as a highly profitable enterprise in 1825, and young Dewey decided to get in on the action. He obtained a job driving a mule beside the canal. By his 18th birthday, he owned two tug boats, and was worth more than $20,000.

Branching out into the contracting business, Dewey built an arcade building at Tonawanda, New York—the first in the United States. But the most booming city in the nation at the time was San Francisco, so Dewey went there in 1852, and formed a contracting firm with Mike Jordan.

The contracting business prospered, but Dewey and Jordan were not happy. Bigger fortunes than theirs were being made overnight in Nevada's Comstock Lode. The partners took off for Virginia City, plunged heavily in the mining business, and promptly went broke.

Jordan left for Southern Idaho. Dewey, recovering from an attack of malaria, lingered in Virginia City. Then, one day in 1863, Dewey got a letter from

Jordan, who said that he had found some gold in the Owyhee Country, and that "there is plenty more around."

Not having enough money to buy a horse, with or without a saddle, Dewey put all his possessions in a pack on his back, and walked from Virginia City to what is now Silver City in Idaho. Dewey went into mining operations with Jordan, and the money began to pile up.

There would be financial downs as well as ups, however, and there would be tragedies. Dewey would flip a $20 gold piece with Jordan to determine who would get to go off and fight some Indians. Jordan would win the toss, then would lose his life in the encounter with the red men. Three of Dewey's wives died, two in childbirth. Only the fourth, a young Irish girl from San Francisco, Isobel (Belle) Hagen, would eventually survive him.

Then, in 1884, there was the feuding in Silver City between Dewey and a man named Joseph Koenig. On the afternoon of August 2, the two men were seen arguing as they walked into the Sommercamp Brewery. The sound of pistol shots followed. Then one man walked out—Dewey.

The colonel was arrested, tried and convicted of second degree murder, and sentenced to eight years in the territorial prison at Fort Boise. But, in May, 1885, a new trial was obtained when a reluctant witness came forth. This was Maggie Brady, who said she had not wanted to "get mixed up in that court business." She now testified that Dewey had killed Koenig in self-defense. Without waiting to hear any more of the defense testimony that had been lined up, the jury declared Dewey "not guilty."

During most of his personal troubles, however, Dewey was making money. In 1871, he bought the Black Jack Mine from W. B. Knott, extracted a fortune from it, and sold it. Then he purchased the Trade Dollar from Frank St. Clair and James Douglas. This mine brought Dewey 12 million dollars before he sold it in 1900.

Now he was ready to take on Thunder Mountain, thrusting skyward in the wilds of Valley County to the north of Boise. The stampede to Thunder Mountain, where the towns of Thunder City and Roosevelt were spawned to live short lives, was likened to the Klondike gold rush.

Not only was the going rough to Thunder City and Roosevelt in their heyday, but the coming back was rougher—at least for most of the gold seekers, with their dragging steps telling the story of their failure to strike it rich. Dewey, who built his own stamp mill at Thunder Mountain, was a big exception. Of course, he had plenty of financing—and determination.

(In 1909, Monumental Creek was dammed by an earth slide, and a lake formed over the town of Roosevelt, submerging some 50 business buildings and homes, and giving Idaho its own version of the lost continent of Atlantis.)

Dewey undoubtedly got a lot of satisfaction out of finding the treasures hidden in the earth millions of years ago, but his real love was developing and building. This could be profitable, too.

In those days, you did not ask the government to build a road. You asked it to grant you a franchise to build one yourself. This is what Dewey, with Jordan and Silas Skinner as partners, had asked of the Idaho Territorial Legislature in 1864. The franchise was granted to build a toll road from Boise to the Owyhee mines, and for some years the franchise paid off handsomely—at $3 per team and wagon, $1 per horse and buggy, and $.25 per saddle horse.

To speed things up further, Dewey joined with U.S. Senator George L. Shoup (who had previously served as Idaho's last Territorial Governor and first State Governor) and A. H. Bommer to form the California, Oregon, Idaho Stage Company. Next, Dewey built the Boise, Nampa, Owyhee Railroad from Nampa to Emmett, then from Nampa to Murphy in Owyhee County. These lines eventually became part of the Oregon Short Line Railroad. Later, Dewey built the railroad from Emmett to McCall, which, in 1913, was absorbed by the Union Pacific.

Warmed up, Dewey decided in 1896 to take on a town. The town was the deceased mining camp of Booneville. Dewey bought it, lock, stock and barrel, and proceeded to bring it back alive under the new name of Dewey.

Nothing was too good for a town with a name like that. To make it one of the finest communities in Idaho, the colonel built deluxe stores, a steam laundry, an elaborate house for his superintendent of mines, a water system with fire hydrants which were declared to secure for the town an "almost perfect immunity from fire," and a livery stable more impressively prosperous than most hotels of the period. But the *piece de resistance* was the Dewey Hotel. With its steam heat and electric lights, and with its cupolas and double portico, it made the fancy livery stable look shoddy.

For a while, Dewey was the place to be if you fancied plush Victorian living on the frontier. But it was too good to last. Despite the town's modern fire hydrants, fire swept through it in 1905. Among other structures burned to the ground was the Dewey Hotel. The curtain, for the second time, came down on Booneville-Dewey.

Greater recognition for Colonel Dewey came with his role in the development of the city of Nampa (home of Northwest Nazarene College, which was started as an elementary school in 1913). Dewey didn't build Nampa—it was really started when he got there—but he did build its Dewey Palace Hotel, and the spin-off from this building was what made early Nampa.

The colonel figured that, if he built a truly magnificent hotel (bigger and better than the one he had constructed at Dewey), it would be like an Aladdin's lamp in the desert, with new city developments spiraling from it. And he was so right.

In 1886, he bought 2,450 acres of sagebrush and jackrabbits—the homestead site of Alexander Duffes. Then, in 1900, Dewey had the sagebrush and jackrabbits cleared from the property, and, finally, at the start of 1903, *the* hotel was ready for service—the finest hostelry between Omaha, Nebraska, and Portland, Oregon.

Three stories high (getting water to the third floor was a bit of a problem), the hotel had wide verandas with circular steps, huge white pillars, gingerbread cupolas, lighted towers, and 81 sleeping rooms. Two huge domes, covered with sheet copper, were enviously visible from Caldwell. The hotel was the first structure in Idaho to use steel lath, and the paneling throughout it was of solid oak. Dewey had the furniture specially made in Grand Rapids, Michigan. Marshall-Field of Chicago was pleased to be selected to furnish the carpets, linen and silver. All of the original dishes—any surviving plate today would be a collector's item—had the picture of the hotel stamped upon them. There was even a bowling alley, with one afternoon a week devoted exclusively to the ladies.

Travelers, including such celebrities of the day as Lillian Russell and "Diamond Jim" Brady, went out of their way just to stop at the Dewey Palace Hotel. More important, many of the persons who came to the hotel bought acres and lots.

87

Dewey got to see a flourishing city stemming from his flowery hotel—just barely. In 1903, he died at 80 in a room of the Dewey Palace—the first death to occur in the hotel. The Dewey Palace itself survived for a half-century until tourists more and more began choosing the easy in-and-out of modern motels springing up in Nampa (now grown into a city of more than 20,000 population). The colonel's hotel was shattered by wrecking crews—a most regrettable erasure on the slate of history—but his dream of a greater Nampa and Idaho remained intact.

For years, the hotel was operated by Dewey's son, Cornelius (Con), who once, in a reminiscing mood, recalled that dream. On a hot summer day in 1886, Con said that as a boy of 12 he was riding with his father in a buggy across Deer Flats. The colonel had just left a meeting, after being presented with some fat cigars and a jug, also on the fat side.

"Turning the reins of the team over to me, my father settled back in the buggy for a smoke, and sat studying the desert," said Con. "Occasionally, he flung the jug over his arm, and took a swig from it. After a time he started talking to me, more as though he were thinking out loud.

" 'Son,' he mused, 'this is great country. The soil is deep and rich, and, with irrigation it will grow anything from oranges to squash. I can see this vast desert turned into an oasis, thousands of acres of fruit . . . farm acres dotted with homes. Located as it is, it will be a tributary to all that is great in Idaho. Yes, sir, son, I can see this country as a paradise.'

"Lad that I was, all I could see was Deer Flats covered with sagebrush and jackrabbits scuttling along. I looked at Dad, and only thought that he had had several nips too many out of the jug. Now I know that it was the day he bought those 2,450 acres."

The colonel's dream came true—in the grand manner—but, prior to the turn of the century, the area was still mostly mining country—and still a bit untamed. Back in Silver City, on March 25, 1868, with America's Civil War over, a miners' civil war, generally referred to as the Owyhee War, broke out.

The opposing factions were the miners of two adjoining mines—the Ida Elmore and the Golden Chariot. The Ida Elmore was the richer of the two mines, producing $270 in gold per ton of ore even with crude refining methods, and the Golden Chariot miners kept pushing their underground shafts toward those of the Ida Elmore. Finally, they broke through, and the shooting started, with bullets ricocheting from one tunnel wall to another.

While the fighting continued below ground, with about a hundred men involved, more fighting developed topside. Both sides quickly engaged expert gunslingers—there were always some around at a price. The miners of the Ida Elmore then threw up timber fortifications at the entrance to their mine, and the Golden Chariot men retaliated by obtaining an old cannon and threatening to blow the whole Ida Elmore to hotter regions. The cannon was never touched off—it was feared that it might blow up in the faces of the gun crew —but the firing of smaller arms kept up all day and throughout the night. Two men were killed—John C. Holgate, owner of the Golden Chariot, and Meyer Frank of the Ida Elmore. Perhaps a dozen miners were wounded, several critically.

The sheriff closed all saloons in Silver City, but refused to go near the combat zone, contending he would be a dead man before he could say "Stop the fighting!" He sent word to David W. Ballard, Idaho's third Territorial Governor, and Ballard dispatched troops from Fort Boise.

About the time the cavalry galloped up, however, a truce had been reached. Governor Ballard then hastened to Silver City, serving as arbitrator in the drawing up of a formal agreement on the property rights of the two mines. With this agreement signed, and with saloon doors once more swinging open to miners of both camps, the troops returned to Boise.

On April 1, the peace was shattered. J. Marion More, one of the chief owners of the Ida Elmore, who also had rich holdings in Idaho City and was known as the "father" of that town, was strolling with four or five companions down Silver City's main street. Seated on a bench in front of the stage office was Sam Lockhart of the Golden Chariot. More tossed a comment, and Lockhart pitched one back. More words, growing hotter and hotter, were exchanged. Then a pistol began firing. The smoking weapon was held in the hand of Lockhart.

Hit in the chest, More started staggering down the street, pushed open the door of the Oriental Restaurant, and collapsed on the floor between two tables, crockery showering down upon him. The Chinese proprietor lifted up More's head, looked into his eyes, and said:

"Big boss dead."

The war was almost on again. The *Owyhee Avalanche,* which had gotten out several extras during the major conflict, described the new situation as "tense." But no more shooting broke out. Lockhart was arrested, but the charges were dropped. After all, More had started the argument, and Lockhart was greatly outnumbered.

The rise and fall of Silver City is reflected in the story of the *Owyhee Avalanche.* Started as a weekly (50 cents a copy) at Ruby City, August 19, 1865, the *Avalanche* was moved the following year to Silver City, which by then greatly overshadowed Ruby City. Competition developed with the establishment at Silver City of another weekly named the *Tidal Wave,* but this folded in 1870, leaving the *Avalanche* unchallenged on War Eagle Mountain.

This encouraged the *Avalanche* in 1874 to become the first daily newspaper in Idaho, with William J. Hill—"Old Hill"—as publisher and editor. Even before he reached 30, he was known as Old Hill because, as a ferry operator and volunteer with the cavalry, he had managed to survive so many encounters with Indians (he was wounded five different times).

In publishing his paper, Old Hill was assisted by his wife whom he referred to as "Mrs. Avalanche." Shortly after his marriage to her in 1872, he wrote in the *Avalanche*:

"We have been thinking of drowning Mrs. Avalanche, but, if some one will offer us fifty dollars, we will give him a quit claim deed to the interesting creature."

Old Hill wouldn't have sold her at any price in 1875, however, when she and Judge W. C. Whitson saved his life.

Six miners, contending that Old Hill was continually taking the side of the "monied corporations against the working classes," stormed into the newspaper office. Both well-lubricated and well-armed, the miners advised the editor that "we're gonna spill your blood here and now."

Old Hill picked up two defense weapons from his desk—a Bowie knife and a paste pot (San Francisco newspapers were clipped extensively to augment the telegraph service to the *Avalanche,* and a paste pot was always handy). The knife and pot were little defense against the pistols being drawn, but just then the long barrel of a musket was thrust through the office's back door, which led to the press room. On the other end of the musket was Mrs. Avalanche. Also, at that critical time, the front door opened, and in walked Judge Whitson with his cane. As a lever was pressed, the cane became a sword. Lowering their pistols, the miners made a hasty exit.

Old Hill's greatest battles, however, were fought with the pen. And his main opponent was Milton Kelly of the *Idaho Statesman* in Boise.

Kelly, following up the fracas in the *Avalanche* office, made similar charges to those of the miners against Old Hill. The Boise editor wrote:

"From first to last the *Avalanche* has defamed the laborers and upheld their oppressors. The Miner's Union, the Grange, and every other movement on the part of the laboring people have been denounced by the *Avalanche,* while corporations have been sustained. When the miners refuse to work and want their pay, the *Avalanche* denounces them as outlaws and tells them they are not entitled to their wages."

Old Hill replied in the *Avalanche*:

"You are a gratuitous, black-hearted liar, Milty. The *Avalanche* never defamed laboring men, nor the Miner's Union, nor the Grange, nor any other movement for the benefit of the laboring class; on the contrary, we have always been a friend to the honest laboring men, and have complimented and supported the Miner's Union through thick and thin so long as it confined itself to the objects for which it was instituted and pursued a lawful and proper course."

And so the battle of words continued between Milty and Old Hill until the *Avalanche* folded as a daily on April 26, 1876. Sold to J. S. Hay, the newspaper returned to weekly status.

The decline of the *Daily Avalanche* began with the collapse of the Owyhee mining boom in the fall of 1875. Ore deposits began to wear thin—even for the fabulous Poorman Mine, whose ores produced in the first flush six days of operation $500,000 in gold and silver. Then the San Francisco Stock Exchange collapsed, and the Bank of California failed. Obtaining financing for Owyhee operations became extremely difficult.

Old Hill, whose departure from Idaho was described by one writer as a "public calamity," went to California, and purchased the *Salinas Index*. Besides publishing this newspaper, he served as mayor of Salinas for six terms, and also as a state senator. He died in Salinas in 1918, and his funeral was one of the best attended in that city.

Meanwhile, for some years, the *Owyhee Avalanche*—and Silver City— struggled to keep alive. Early in the game, the county seat had been moved from Ruby City to Silver City, but, in 1934, with only a few stragglers left in the "Queen City" of Owyhee County, the county seat was again moved—to Murphy. At the time, Murphy had no greater population than Silver City, but it did have nearby a camp of the Civilian Conservation Corps—the make-work program for young men in the great Depression. In the Owyhee election to determine where the county seat should go, it was ruled that the CCC men should be allowed to vote. They did, and Murphy won in a landslide over such bigger towns as Homedale, Grand View and Bruneau.

With a population still no more than 75, Murphy remains the seat for Owyhee County—7,648 square miles of beautiful and rugged remoteness. But that is not Murphy's main claim to fame. It is the only town of its size in the United States with a parking meter.

Silver City today is mostly a ghost of its old self, although it comes very much alive once a year. Traditionally, the annual meeting of the Owyhee Cattlemen's Association is held there in the summer, drawing about 600 high-hatted and high-booted delegates for palaver in the shadows of a golden history.

The Boise Basin and Owyhee Country produced most of Southern Idaho's mineral wealth before the big decline, but there were other areas of significance.

In 1863, in the sphere of the Sawtooths northeast of Mountain Home, gold was discovered on high bars around Atlanta and Rocky Bar. A great wealth of ore was extracted from placer operations within the first three years. Then the pickings quickly became slim, although many of the miners were slow to admit it.

Besides the gold of their heyday, Atlanta and Rocky Bar were noted for "Peg-Leg Annie" Marrow, who lived in both mining camps. An unpolished gem of the mountains, she would never fit in a Tiffany showcase, but she did fit in the rough settings of the mining camps.

One winter, while enroute to Rocky Bar with a woman companion from Atlanta, where Peg-Leg Annie then operated a restaurant, she froze her feet as she remained beside the body of her friend who had died of exposure. For years, legend had it that her feet were amputated above the ankles by a miner named "Tug" Wilson while she was sedated with a quart of whiskey. Apparently, however, the truth of the matter is that a Mountain Home doctor named Wicker rode over more than 50 miles of trail in bitter cold to perform the operation.

For quite a while, Peg-Leg Annie talked about getting artificial limbs, but she never did anything about it. Another story has it that friends did do something, and bought her artificial limbs, but she did not bother to wear them. Whatever the case, artificial limbs did not seem necessary. After all, skirts in those days reached almost to the floor, discreetly hiding the peg legs, although not muffling the sound.

The mere tapping of those peg legs across her restaurant floor could stop a fight that was likely to endanger the furnishings, for Peg-Leg Annie "took nothing from nobody." She had both a voice and pistol which could roar.

Once, outside her restaurant, a town bully was making a young tenderfoot dance to the tune of his exploding gun. Whether or not the fact that the tenderfoot was a good customer of the restaurant had anyhing to do with it, Peg-Leg Annie barged out the door, her pistol blazing.

The bullets were all well-placed, spurting dust at the feet of the bully.

"Now you dance," Peg-Leg Annie said.

The bully did.

For years after the gold gave out, Peg-Leg Annie lived on in the mountain country. She couldn't afford to leave. The story is told that she made a lot of money in the roaring days of Atlanta and Rocky Bar, and entrusted it one day to her lover, a smooth-talking Italian, to deposit or invest for her in San Francisco. She never heard from him again, but she never lost confidence that she would.

Father Pierre-Jean De Smet, the first Catholic missionary in Idaho, wrote in 1844 of his travels in Southeastern Idaho:

"Here Indians roam over wealth that would make nations rich. Where I now sit, I can see gold in the rocks."

91

But the priest never did anything about the gold. Like Peter of the Apostles, he was fishing for men, and this kind of fishing left him no time for prospecting in the area. But later there would be men with time on their hands—such as men with military discharge papers in their pockets.

The Civil War got as far west as Arizona and New Mexico, where minor skirmishes developed, but generally the Far West, except for serving by providing badly-needed gold for the Union to exchange for equipment and supplies, sat out the war on the sidelines. After the fighting ended in 1865, however, many of the soldiers, shucking either blue or gray uniforms and keeping their pistols, headed west, hoping to find both gold and a new life.

Among those who came to Idaho in 1866 was a group of former Confederate soldiers, who started prospecting on Napias Creek (Napias is the Indian word for gold) where it flows into Panther Creek, a tributary of the Salmon. There, in a high basin of Idaho batholith, the men from Virginia and Georgia and the Carolinas discovered traces of gold on July 16. Sinking a shaft to bedrock, they started panning out gold at the rate of $1 to $5 a pan.

General Robert E. Lee of the South had been forced to surrender his sword to General Ulysses S. Grant of the North, but, to the happy Southern prospectors in Idaho, Lee was still the greatest general who ever lived. So they named the site of their discovery Leesburg.

Within a few months, the population of Leesburg swelled to 3,000, and the miners desperately needed supplies. As a result, 15 miles to the southeast, in one of the West's most beautiful mountain valleys, there arose the trading center of Salmon City (at the junction of U.S. Highway 93 and State Highway 28).

Supplies were brought to Salmon City by wagon train from Utah, Washington and Montana, then were loaded onto pack mules for carting up the steep mountainside to Leesburg. Flour toted thus to Leesburg cost $30 a hundred pounds, and sugar, 80 cents a pound. Kerosene sometimes sold for a staggering $25 a gallon. Whiskey was much cheaper, because, if it spilled in a freight wagon, it flavored the food supplies. Spilled kerosene ruined them.

Miners at Leesburg did well, but many traders at Salmon City did better, especially as new mining camps sprang up around Leesburg, bringing more than 7,000 persons to the area. One of the new camps, just a "whoop and holler" up the canyon from Leesburg, was started by former Union soldiers and sympathizers. They called it Grantsville.

From time to time, naturally, fighting broke out between the two camps. But no one was ever killed except for a stranger passing through. Eventually, the two camps quietly merged, and became just Leesburg. The Southerners always did figure they would win.

One of the strangest mining developments in Idaho's history was in the Yankee Fork Country—strange because, although prospectors kept discovering gold in the area, stampedes failed to materialize until high-grade ore was simply being shoveled off the surface of the land.

About half-way between Challis and Stanley (north of Sun Valley), there is a 30-mile-long stream, wild and frothing and bouncing like a mad cougar. This is the Yankee Fork, skirting the great granite outcroppings of Idaho's batholith on the way to the Salmon River. Millions of years ago gold as well as silver was deposited in the area adjacent to the rushing waters, but the land beckoned only to the few—at first.

Indians called the Yankee Fork Country "The Land of Deep Snows," and limited their treks there to the summer months for the hunting of game and picking of berries. (In modern times, those deep snows, which extend into Sun Valley, would lure thousands of skiers annually.)

In 1870, a small party of prospectors headed by D. B. Varney and Sylvester Jordan got around to checking on the gold possibilities of the Yankee Fork Country. Some gold was discovered, but nothing exciting.

Then, in 1873, John G. Morrison wandered into the valley, and made a very promising discovery—the Morrison Placer. Morrison hired 45 men to work his claim—and live in tents. They nearly froze to death, but made a handsome profit for Morrison.

Stampede? Not yet.

Next, in 1875, William A. Norton, using only a hand mortar, pounded out $11,500 worth of gold in a month at a mine he named the Charles Dickens after his favorite author. But still no stampede.

Came the memorable day of August 17, 1876, for James Baxter, Morgan McKeim and E. M. Dodge. On the morning of that day they stumbled on an open vein of gold, which became the fabulous Custer Mine. A mountainside had slid down—or been washed away—to expose the vein. It was just a matter of breaking the ore loose, sacking it, and toting it by pack mules to a Salt Lake City mill. Sixty thousand dollars worth of gold was acquired in short order this way.

It was not until a year later, however, that miners finally took the Yankee Fork Country seriously, with the Salt Lake Tribune reporting the paths to Yankee Fork "lined with stampeders . . . They are afoot or on horseback, in bull teams and shaky wagons. To old timers it looks like a Pike's Peak rush."

The towns of Bonanza City and Custer sprang up two miles apart on the Yankee Fork, and by 1879 boomed with a combined population of 5,000. Off to the northeast in the shadows of the Salmon River Mountains, Challis developed as a freighting center. It would later become significant as a headquarters for cattlemen and sheepmen, but as long as the Yankee Fork gold rush lasted—and it was great while it did—the conversation in Challis revolved around the richness of each new ore strike.

At first, Bonanza City and Custer were served by little more than trails, but, in 1879, a toll road was built from Challis. Although the road was narrow and rough, stagecoaches as well as freight wagons rattled over it. The two towns also soon had newspapers—the *Yankee Fork Herald* and the *Custer Prospector.*

The big triumph, however, was the construction at Custer of a giant ore refinery—the General Custer Mill. In that post-Civil War period, patriotism ran high, so the American flag was flown on a pole rising from the roof of the mill. Daily it was raised and lowered with a rope until one day the rope became tangled at the top of the flagstaff.

A young man volunteered to climb the pole and untangle the rope. Agile as a bobcat, he moved up quickly, but, as he neared the top, a rush of wind caused the pole to sway. Then, with a crack like a rifle shot, the pole snapped in two, and the young man crashed to his death. His grave is one of the unmarked mounds in the cemetery at Custer, which today, like its sister community of Bonanza City, is crowded only with memories.

Ketchum and Hailey and Bellevue became important mining centers with the discovery of rich quartz ledges in the Wood River Country in 1879. (At one time it was predicted that Hailey would become "the Denver of Idaho.") As well as gold, there were impressive deposits of silver and lead. Biggest of the area's silver and lead producers in the Eighties was the Minnie Moore.

Those were roaring days in the Wood River Country, but they did not roar quite as much as those of Idaho's earlier mining camps. T. E. Picotte, a roving journalist from Canada who became editor and publisher of Hailey's *Wood River Times* made up for that with his inventive mind.

In 1882, he printed a series of entirely fictitious reports about a wild man seen stalking game on the Camas Prairie. This very large figment of Picotte's imagination was described as "thickly covered with hair, a tusk protruding from each side of his mouth, sharp claws for nails, and presenting a most horrible appearance."

The stories of the wild man were widely picked up by the press of the nation, particularly in the East. New Yorkers were delighted with the accounts, but were equally delighted to have Idaho so far away. Or was it Iowa?

Over in Bellevue, the *Daily Sun* got fed up on Picotte's perfidy, and, in February, 1883, printed a banner story giving a detailed account of the death of the wild man, slain, according to the *Sun,* by a duck hunter. Enraged at the obituary—also widely reported—Picotte lashed back in the *Wood River Times:*

"This smart Aleck who edits the *Bellevue Sun* has killed the wild man of Camas, and thus idiotically robbed the press of this section of a prolific source of items and Wood River of a great deal of free advertising by the copying of such items by the Eastern and foreign press. The next sensation imagined by the *Times'* numerous and brilliant staff of contributors will be copyrighted, trademarked, patented, and protected in every way possible."

Whether the "free advertising" caught the eye of Financier Jay Gould in New York is not known, but he did take an interest in the Wood River Country. When gold mining was at its peak in Idaho in the 1860s, Gould was busy cornering the world's gold market, which precipitated the "Black Friday Panic" of 1869. But, in the Eighties, Gould had a little more time, and came out to Idaho to try to corner the mining output of the Wood River Country. He didn't quite corner it, but he did take a sizable chunk of profits back to New York. And he also found that fishing in Silver Creek was good. (It is still good—if you know the right holes.)

Then the flourishing mining days of Southern Idaho ended. But Idaho's role as one of the world's leading mineral producers was just beginning. Its biggest of all strikes—in the Coeur d'Alenes of Northern Idaho—was made in 1884.

Meanwhile, the Chinese still had some cleanup work to do.

# Chapter VIII

# ERA OF THE DRAGON AND FIRECRACKERS

"The greater portion of Idaho's mining claims have been turned over to Chinamen, who are content with small earnings and who will maintain, no doubt for many years to come, a moderately productive industry in these abandoned fields."

—U.S. Commissioner of Mining
Statistics in March, 1871

On May 10, 1869, with a strong wind rustling the sagebrush at Promontory Summit, Utah, chugging engines of the Central Pacific and Union Pacific railroads rubbed pointed noses. Western and Eastern America had been linked by long, thin lines of rails at a cost of $165,000,000 and many lives.

Between the two engines lay a special tie of polished California laurel. Into this tie would be driven spikes from different Western states, including a silver and gold one from Idaho. The first spike to be driven—from California—would be golden.

Leland Stanford, president of the Central Pacific (after whose son Stanford University was named), and Thomas C. Durant, dubbed "the promoter of the century" for getting the Union Pacific on its way, had been given the honor of sinking the first spike. The two men, however, graciously beckoned to a woman who was standing in the forefront of the crowd at the tracks, and handed her a sledge hammer.

95

Raising it shakily, she lowered it with a boom on the tie, missing entirely the golden spike. Her name was lost to history, because, dropping the hammer, she retreated blushingly to the anonymity of the crowd, and forever afterwards apparently kept mum about her miserable demonstration.

Taking over the hammer, Stanford and Durant proved their ability as "spikers," but not necessarily the superiority of the male. Not only had both executives done some practicing, but holes had been drilled into the laurel tie so that the spikes would go in effortlessly. While the regimental band from Camp Douglas played the most appropriate music it could muster, the drinking of champagne amidst the sagebrush followed.

The ceremony meant much to the Territory of Idaho. True, the transcontinental line was south of the border (because of this, some Idahoans would agitate for the annexation of Northern Utah). But the *Idaho Statesman* of Boise had predicted that the nearness of the railroad would bring a great increase in population to Idaho farmlands, and that cheap labor would be transported to the Territory to "unlock the rocks" of dormant mines. In regard to the mines, the *Statesman,* which had declared in 1867 that "there is no place for John Chinaman here—he won't mix well with our people," was not thinking in terms of Chinese, but the Chinese were thinking in terms of Idaho.

Beckoned by the California gold rush of '49, Chinese had come to the Pacific Coast by the shipload from Canton and Peking and Hong Kong. Their hope generally was to strike it rich in America, return to China to live in luxury, and be buried extravagantly among ancestors in native soil. And this hope was more important than the degree of realization. Although the Chinese were shoved around, winding up mostly as cheap labor—in the mines and elsewhere—they continued to dream.

By the late 1860s, half the factory workers in San Francisco were Chinese, and agitation in California against them began to mount. Eventually, the people of California would vote 154,638 to 883 against further immigration from China, and, shortly thereafter on March 20, 1879, the national Congress would pass an exclusion bill, killed by the veto of President Rutherford B. Hayes. Two years later, however, a treaty with China giving the United States the power to "regulate, limit, or suspend" Chinese immigration would be ratified by the Senate.

Meanwhile, thousands of Chinese had been given jobs at $30 a month working on the construction of the Central Pacific and Union Pacific railroads, for, as Charles W. Crocker, a contractor, said, "The Chinese did pretty well building the Great Wall of China, so they can sure build a railroad." When the two lines were joined at Promontory Summit in 1869, however, the Orientals were out of work. With the prejudicial heat on in California, they began flocking to the mines of Idaho. They would soon encounter more prejudice in that territory, but they had been advised by Chinese who had gone north earlier that Idahoans, in their feelings toward Orientals, "weren't half bad," although the Territorial Legislature in 1864 had passed an act taxing Chinese miners four dollars a month.

At first, the people of Idaho were simply amazed by the new invasion of Chinese which followed the driving of the golden spike. The *Owyhee Avalanche* of Silver City reported:

"They come like crickets on the march, on jackasses and on foot, over ditches, woodpiles and fences and everything else."

At one time, it is said, there were more than 10,000 Chinese in the Boise

Basin alone. And not only were they "over everything," but into everything.

Some of the Orientals did odd jobs, from toting water to becoming servants in white homes. Many went into business for themselves—restaurants, "nuts and bolts" stores (lichee nuts and silk cloth), medicinal herb dispensaries, laundries offering to turn out "polished shirts," loan offices, and gambling houses.

In the barber trade, the Chinese provided particularly tough competition. Calling at places of business, they needed no barber shop, and thus had no overhead. Too, with a shave and a haircut, the Chinese threw in a facial massage, even working on the eyelids. This made them highly popular among the tired businessmen.

But mining was the big thing. Organizing many of the Chinese into tongs, for the raising of funds as well as for the protection and security of the individuals, leaders leased "played out" mining properties, and put their countrymen to work in them at "six-bitty" (seventy-five cents) to a dollar a day. The mines again became profitable. Thus, there were Chinese exploiting Chinese as well as whites exploiting Chinese.

Some Chinese prospected and mined on their own, although, at first, this was strictly taboo in various mining camps. The early mining laws for the Nez Perce and Salmon River mines stated:

"Chinese or Tartars are hereby prohibited from working these mines, under any or all circumstances."

An act of the Territorial Legislature of 1864, however, gave the Chinese the right to work in the mines—by paying a tax of $4.00 a month. The 1866 Legislature raised this tax to $5.00 a month. But it was not always collected, because sometimes when the tax collector came around—usually a sheriff or his deputy—the Orientals headed for the woods.

There was some jumping of Chinese claims by whites, who contended that federal laws forbade the owning of mines by Orientals. But the flexible Chinese came up with an answer for that. They paid other white men to "jump" their claims, then to sit beside the workings with weapons handy, warning off anybody with designs on the claims. "China herders," these guardians were called.

The Chinese—those who ran laundries—also garnered a fair amount of gold, without mining, from the dust that sifted from pockets into the wash. And Chinese merchants could pick up extra dust by running their long fingernails through it after it had been weighed, then cleaning their nails.

A very able merchant at Idaho City was a Chinese named Pon Yam. Prosperous, he lived unostentatiously except that he sported the second largest diamond in the Territory—surpassed only by that of Silver City's Colonel William E. Dewey.

In the Tong War of 1872, this able merchant demonstrated that he was not only wealthy but wise by settling the war before the wielding of hatchets and knives and the firing of pistols actually started. The war was declared in Idaho City between the See Yup and Yung Wah tongs over a killing on Mores Creek. The See Yups and Yung Wahs did not get along anyway, because the See Yups were largely common laborers, and the Yung Wahs mostly businessmen, whom the See Yups continually charged with gouging.

Then one day an old Yung Wah, who ran a small store on Mores Creek, was fatally struck on the head, and his store robbed. Some See Yups had been seen earlier loitering about the place. This was too much for the Yung Wahs.

They threatened to clear Idaho City of all See Yup vermin, and the See Yups indicated that they were similarly inclined toward the Yung Wahs. Chinese miners did not go to work, and Chinese stores closed. Rarely was an Oriental seen on the street. When one did scuttle from house to house for food or "talk-talk," he kept a hand inside robe or coat, no doubt clutching a pistol or hatchet or knife. And thus the situation continued for days.

George Ainslee, editor of the *Idaho World,* came up with a suggestion: As the sheriff looked the other way, members of both tongs should march to open sagebrush country outside of Idaho City, and fight it out to the last man.

Obviously, Ainslee did not understand the Oriental mind, because the suggestion was scorned. Merchant Pon Yam, however, did understand. For business reasons, he had never become affiliated with either tong, and was in an excellent position to serve as a mediator. So he called a conference with white pillars of the Idaho City community, and it was agreed that each faction owed indemnities to the other. When the tong leaders were advised of this decision, they did not hesitate to provide itemized bills, but each tong refused to turn over an ounce of gold dust to the other.

Even Solomon might have had trouble with such a development, but for Pon Yam it was no problem. He had been losing quite a bit of business by the stalemate, so he personally paid the bills presented by both sides, and the war was over—on November 11, 1872, way ahead of another armistice on November 11.

As wars go, the Tong War of 1872 wasn't much, but it did provide something to think about. In its wars, the United States usually winds up paying for the damages incurred by both sides. So why not pay off before the shooting starts?

The Chinese loved gambling even more than the travelers on the early Mississippi River boats. They might be shelved in sleeping quarters like bolts of cloth in a store, and their diet might be 90 per cent rice, but they had money to bet.

At Pierce, one of the first buildings the Chinese constructed was a two-story, log joss house. Worship, however, was confined to the second floor, and gambling was wide open on the first. At dusk, a Chinese crier would go about the town calling, "Mei hanna!"—"The game is open!"

Fan-tan games went on nightly in the Chinese gambling houses of the various mining camps, and, when a player lost heavily, he adjourned to the street to set off firecrackers. This was to drive away the "devil who made him do it"—play badly, that is.

During the Chinese New Year, there was more shooting of firecrackers—and the prancing of dragons and the tossing of candies to the sidewalk spectators. This was a period of atonement for the Chinese, and white boys, who had teased the Orientals for their pigtails and shuffling walk, did some atoning of their own. They came bearing gifts of cakes and cookies, and got in return much more elaborate gifts.

Adult whites who called upon Chinese leaders in the community fared even better. They were not only presented with gifts of silk and jade, but were warmed with the finest American whiskey and French champagne. The Chinese sipped their own whiskey, a white and sticky concoction, but still an improvement over some Indian whiskey, which utilized, among other things, tobacco and gunpowder.

The *Idaho Statesman* of February 13, 1896, reported:

"The Chinese of Boise devoted themselves yesterday to the celebration of their New Year day . . . Mayor Pierce gave the Chinese 24 hours in which to celebrate, and during that time they were privileged to make as much noise as they pleased. That they availed themselves of the opportunity can be testified to by many people who were awakened early yesterday morning by the firecracker bombardment."

The rest of the year, the Chinese stayed pretty much to themselves. In such mining towns as Idaho City, Silver City and Pierce, they not only had their own joss houses, but their own Masonic lodges. Masonry had long been established in China, and the Chinese who came to Idaho brought their rituals with them, although their lodges were not affiliated with the Grand Lodge of Idaho —nor with any other American grand lodge. (A leading organization of Ketchum was the Grand Order of the Orient, but it was for Occidentals only.)

A Chinese Masonic funeral in Silver City in the winter of 1897-98 was something special. The deceased was Song Lee, prominent merchant and Mason of a high order.

Ordinarily a Chinese of Song Lee's wealth and standing would have been cremated, and his ashes shipped to China for burial without previous interment in an American cemetery. (Poorer Chinese were often buried in shallow graves with the hope that rains would wash away the earth, exposing the coffin to the elements so that soon nothing would be left in it except bones. Then, when funds became available, the bones or their ashes would be shipped back to China. It was believed that the devils departed with the flesh, and it was undesirable to send devils to China. The kinfolk there were already plagued by too many.) Song Lee, however, had come to love the hills of Idaho, and he had left word that he would be pleased to rest forever in Silver City's cemetery on one of those hills—after a first-class American funeral. (In the Idaho City cemetery, it was noted that the Chinese were buried at the bottom of the hill, but, in the Silver City cemetery, Song Lee rated a higher spot.)

The Chinese Masons took charge of the funeral. They had a band which featured a beer-keg drum, piccolo and cymbals, but they felt that, in keeping with Song Lee's wishes, an American band should be engaged, too. So they hired one. The only catch was that this band had never played for either a Chinese or American funeral. Thus, it was that the band had to improvise. For the procession to the cemetery, it played—over and over again—"There'll Be a Hot Time in the Old Town Tonight," the hit tune of 1896. For Song Lee's "swan song," as he was lowered into Idaho earth, the band struck up "Down Went McGinty."

The Chinese Masons were so pleased that they paid the bandsmen a hundred dollars in gold dust—much more than they had asked.

A Chinese who took a particular liking to American food—as long as the food was pie—packed for Grostein and Bernard out of Lewiston from 1878 to 1889. In fact, the Oriental was so addicted to pie, especially huckleberry in season, that he was known only as Pie Biter.

Unusually big and tall, Pie Biter possessed great capacity for tucking away his favorite dessert. On his better days he consumed as many as 16 pies. Whenever he was in town, he left a standing order at the Skookum Bakery for a dozen pies daily, then he often selected several additional ones upon picking up his order.

In freighting to Idaho County mines, Pie Biter rode the bell horse. The animal was always selected for its gentleness, because, besides Pie Biter, it had to carry a specially built wooden box full of pies. The box was fastened on the side of the saddle so that the Chinese could reach into it from time to time without dismounting.

When Pie Biter retired in 1889, he had a small fortune of $10,000. In China this would be a lot of money, so Pie Biter decided to return there even if his homeland was not known for its pie production.

Came the day of departure on a steamboat from the Lewiston dock, and all the bystanders were impressed when a Skookum Bakery wagon pulled up with 50 pies—all for delivery to Pie Biter's stateroom. The Oriental pie addict was last seen sticking his head out of a porthole as he sadly munched one of his last pieces of American culinary art.

The labor of the Chinese contributed greatly to the wealth of the Territory. Too, the imports of goods from China swelled the national treasury through import duties besides boosting the take of freighters.

Except for an inclination to smoke opium—if they could afford it—the Chinese were generally law-abiding "citizens." If one dared to step out of line, tong or family was quick to provide discipline. On various occasions, however, whites, as they became more and more antagonistic toward the Chinese, were quicker with a rope.

The classic tale of a larcenous Chinese who successfully evaded the wrath of both Orientals and Occidentals is that of Ah Kee of Boise. Ah Kee, a very fat fellow with a pleasant smile continually showing through a fierce, horseshoe-shaped mustache, was a businessman of assorted interests. He dispensed both medical and legal advice, sold herbs, and operated a sort of savings and loan association.

Rarely did the Chinese spend beyond their income (under any circumstances, all debts were to be settled during the Chinese New Year period), but Ah Kee was an exception. He got way overdrawn on the money deposited with him, and that made it necessary in 1869 for him to round up all the unspent gold dust in his shop, saddle his horse, and ride into the night.

The word that "Ah Kee has skipped" quickly got around Boise, and soon a racially-mixed posse, armed with writs for the fleeing Oriental's arrest, was in galloping pursuit. With the posse steadily gaining—Ah Kee's horse had a lot of weight to carry—the fugitive pulled up his lathered mount at Olds Ferry, which took passengers across the Snake River to Oregon and vice versa.

Urging the ferryman to hurry, Ah Kee got aboard the ferry, and studied the situation as the river craft pulled out. Glancing first at the block and cable which operated the ferry, and then at his pursuers who were pulling up on the Idaho shore, Ah Kee knew what he had to do.

As the ferry docked on the Oregon shore, he paid the ferryman in gold dust both for his fare and the cost of a new cable, withdrew a hatchet from a bag he carried, and cut the cable. Then, unsheathing a rifle from a case on the saddle of his horse, he ordered the terrified ferryman to start walking down the river bank. Before taking off himself, he turned to wave his rifle and shout across the river:

"You all go to hellee!"

Not all Chinese in trouble were as fortunate—or as slick—as Ah Kee. There were, for instance, the five Orientals who were hanged from tree limbs beside a road winding out of Pierce.

D. M. Fraser, a lean man with firm jaw and piercing eyes, had operated a store at Pierce ever since its first boom mining days. On the morning of September 10, 1885, he was found in his store, shot and hatcheted to death. There was no pistol around, but, beside his body, lay a hatchet of the type favored by the Chinese who had come to Pierce in considerable number to work over old mines.

There had been more popular men in town than Fraser (he had to limit amounts of credit), but, on the other hand, his ancestors were not buried in China. Rising up in wrath, the whites of Pierce pointed the finger of suspicion at Lee Kee Nam and his partner, Chinese merchants who had been the No. 1 competitors of Fraser. But there was no evidence against them. A confession would have to be obtained.

Organizing as vigilantes, the whites marched into the Chinese store, and yanked out the protesting Lee Kee Nam. Then, led by a man carrying a rope, they escorted Lee Kee Nam down the street to the nearest pine tree. When he refused to confess, the vigilantes strung him by the neck to the tree, raising and lowering him until he became unconscious.

Then they went back to the store, and dragged out the terrified partner. Brought to the tree to view the apparently dead Lee Kee Nam, the partner babbled that the "dead" man alone had been responsible for Fraser's murder. When Lee Kee Nam revived and heard what his partner had said, he wrathfully turned on him, declaring that it was really the other way around.

Both were guilty, decided the vigilantes.

Further remarks by the partners, each striving to clear himself, implicated three other Chinese—not the most savory characters in town. One was a barber with a tongue as sharp as his razor, the second a fast-shuffling gambler, and the third was the kept-man of a Chinese prostitute.

As far as the vigilantes were concerned, the case was neatly wrapped up. But several of the leaders thought that maybe the Chinese were entitled to a bonafide trial.

Pierce was then part of Shoshone County, and the county seat was at Murray. That was where the trial would have to be held. So the deputy sheriff at Pierce, who had previously been "too busy" to take any part in the affair, swore in six men to help him get the prisoners to Murray, a five-day trip across the mountains.

On September 18, the party pulled out of Pierce, with the prisoners roped together in a wagon, and the posse, except for the driver, on horseback. The little caravan did not get far before it was stopped by a large group of armed and masked horsemen.

Relieving all members of the posse of their weapons, the masked men ordered them to "high tail it back to Pierce," leaving the wagon with its load of prisoners. When an expanded posse returned later to the scene, it found all five Chinese hanging dead from a pole lashed between two pines. Nearby stood the empty wagon. It had obviously been driven from under the prisoners.

When word of the hangings reached Portland, Chinese merchants there organized a committee to go to Pierce and conduct an investigation. After several days of interrogations in Pierce, this committee returned to Portland, and, during a stopover at Lewiston, reported that it had found that the five hanging victims were indeed guilty of killing Fraser, and that they well deserved what they got.

The Chinese Consul at San Francisco, however, received a contrary report, and promptly fired off a strong letter to the Chinese Minister in Washington,

D.C., who contacted the U.S. Secretary of State, who, in turn, contacted Edward A. Stevenson, newly appointed Governor of Idaho Territory. Stevenson was directed to conduct a thorough investigation. It is still open to debate how extensive an investigation was carried out, but the Governor's reply to the Secretary of State was a lengthy one.

He first pointed out that the deputy and his posse "were so badly frightened on being suddenly surrounded by a large number of blackened, disguised, masked, armed men . . . they were unable to recognize any of the party." He regretted that some people had seen fit to "take justice into their own hands." However, he assured the Secretary of State that there was "no doubt that the Chinese hanged were the identical parties, who so cruelly, shockingly and brutally murdered, without the least provocation (except jealousy), one of the best citizens of Idaho."

Further, Stevenson declared, "many such devilish acts have been perpetrated by Chinese; and their . . . highbinder piratical societies, together with their low dens of infamy, prostitution and opium smoking, have disgusted our people . . ." The Governor promised the Secretary of State that, as long as the Chinese remained in Idaho, they would be given the full protection of the law, but he sorely hoped that "the day is not far distant when Congress will relieve us of their presence."

Let it be said for Governor Stevenson that, although he may have let his prejudices show in every other line of his report, he was not merely practicing penmanship when he wrote about "protection of the law" for the Chinese. It was his firm action that quelled the general threat of violence to the Chinese, who, by now, were scattered all over Idaho. The Boise Anti-Chinese League had been gaining wide support for setting May 1, 1886, as a deadline for all Chinese to leave the territory peaceably—or else. But the league backed down when Stevenson issued a strong proclamation warning all such movements to preserve law and order, and directing law officers "to use every precaution to prevent all riotous demonstrations."

All Idahoans did not think of the Chinese in as derogatory terms as Governor Stevenson indicated they did. There were, for instance, the people of Warren, and the way they looked upon "China Sam." They thought he was the greatest man in town. Of course, China Sam leaned over backwards to cultivate that feeling.

The late Vardis Fisher, Idaho's most famous native-son writer, paid special tribute to China Sam in "Idaho" of the American Guide Series. He wrote:

"For many decades, this gentle and whimsical Chinese gentleman was custodian of the town's property and morals, and came to be known, indeed, as the Mayor of Warren and the most honest man in Idaho. He was not only watchman-in-chief, the alert guardian of residence and mine; he was also tender of babies and chopper of wood for overworked housewives, mail carrier to prospectors and trappers in outlying canyons, and nurse to the sick and distressed."

Also at Warren was China Sam's good friend, "China Can." An herb doctor, China Can was highly popular with the white children he treated. With his herb prescriptions, there always came Chinese candy.

And then there was pretty little (not much more than 4 feet tall) Polly—Polly, the legend, and Polly, the fact. The legend was that Polly was won in a poker game by Charlie Bemis, a Warren saloon keeper and fiddler for square dances. But the fact was that Bemis, son of a prominent physician, won only

102

her heart while she treated him for wounds suffered in a fight growing out of a poker game.

A native of Hong Kong, Polly related to Countess Gizycka in 1921 the story of her coming to Warren in the 1870s. In an interview for a magazine article, Polly told the countess:

"My folluks in Hong Kong had no grub. Day selle me . . . slave girl. Old woman, she shmuggle me into Portland. I cost $2,500. Don't looka it now, hmmm! Old Chinee-man, he took me along to Warren in a pack train. I never seen a railroad."

The "old Chinee-man" to whom Polly referred was a wealthy resident of San Francisco, who, for reasons that are not clear, drifted to Portland and then to Warren. For years, the story circulated that at Warren Polly's owner got in a no-limit poker game with Bemis, and, when the Chinese ran out of chips, he put up Polly. Holding a full house, Bemis, according to the tale, cleared the table of chips and the Chinese of his chattel.

Old-timers at Warren, however, could not remember such a poker game. They did remember that Bemis got into a fight with a white man over a poker game, and was badly beaten up, suffering the loss of one eye. Then Polly nursed him back to health, and became "his woman." Later, on August 13, 1894, the two were married by Justice of the Peace A. D. Smead.

This is apparently the fact of the matter. But, if Bemis did not win Polly in a poker game, how did she become free from her Chinese owner? Neither Bemis nor Polly ever explained that.

Shortly after they were married, they left Warren, and took up a small and lonesome homestead on the Salmon River at the mouth of Crooked Creek. There, in a deep canyon, they lived for years off the land—vegetables from a little garden, fish from the river and creek, and deer and elk from the forest. Bemis, who in earlier days had been able to keep a can rolling with a six-shooter, now had trouble seeing at long distance, so Polly spotted game for him, and crept with him near it, enabling him to bring it down with one shot. (Bullets were hard to come by.)

After 1922, when Bemis died, Polly lived alone in the little canyon cabin her husband had built. In the cabin, she heard her first battery-powered radio, a gift from old friends at Warren. In 1923, she got to Grangeville, and saw the wonders of a railroad, automobiles, and motion pictures. Then, in 1924, came the big trip to the big city—Boise—where Polly stayed at the Idanha Hotel, and took a streetcar ride.

Boise had had streetcar service since 1891, although it was on the way out by the time Polly got there. (For many persons, June 22, 1926, when motor buses came to Boise, was a sad day. It had been considered worth a nickel, a *Statesman* reporter wrote, just to have the streetcar conductor, the most important person in town, waddle up to you, and stick out his stomach decorated with fascinatingly efficient change dispensers. If he said, "Hello, Johnnie. I understand you can now swim two laps at the Natatorium," your day was made.)

As for Polly, she, too, got a big thrill out of being greeted by the streetcar conductor—and waved to a seat without charge—but, when her visit was over, she was happy to return to her mountain retreat. Her summing up of Boise:

"Lots of people. I like it, but it makes me tired to look so much."

As old age crept upon her, Polly deeded her land to Charles Shepp and Peter Klinkhammer, with the agreement that they would look after her until she died. Rigging a telephone line across the river, they called daily to ask Polly, "How are you doing?" One day in 1933, after she had reached 81, she replied, "No good."

Putting her on a horse, Shepp and Klinkhammer rode with her over rugged mountain trails to War Eagle Mine, where they had requested that an ambulance be waiting to take her to Grangeville. On November 3, 1933, she died, and was buried in Prairie View Cemetery at Grangeville.

Among the most popular Chinese in Lewiston was one who went by the very non-Oriental name of George Morey. Coming to the river port as a cook in 1883, Morey went into business for himself, establishing a central buying agency for restaurants.

This agency greatly improved food service profits for his customers, making them very happy, and the enterprising Chinese became a leader in Lewiston's Chinatown. If a problem arose, the word went out: "Seek the worthy advice of George Morey."

The old Catholic Dormitory in Lewiston served not only as Morey's office, but as a meeting place for both Orientals and Occidentals. Whites respected him, and Chinese held him in awe. In matters of both Oriental religion and business, the word of Morey was law.

For the last two decades of his life, he was an advisor to the tongs—not just in Lewiston, but throughout the United States. This resulted in Morey being concerned with many litigation cases, and handling much correspondence.

Never too certain of his English, he would contact one of his friends on the *Lewiston Tribune* editorial staff when he had an important telegram to dispatch. The newspaperman would carefully phrase the dispatch for Morey, and, although such a message frequently had the makings of a good story, the trust was never betrayed.

When Morey died in 1927, there were more whites than Chinese at his funeral. Wallace B. Stanton, city editor of the *Lewiston Tribune,* wrote:

"He was only a Chinaman, but he lived a life worthy of being emulated by everyone. Morey was an honorable man."

Throughout early Idaho, there were many China Sams, China Cans, Pollys and George Moreys who were among the favorite people.

And then, there were the Chinese at Elk City who fell into great disfavor in the winter of 1893 by inadvertently fouling up the mail. In the early mining camps, mail was highly treasured, and some of Elk City's Orientals were responsible for ruining a whole batch of it. The catastrophe developed this way:

Mail to Elk City in the winter had to be toted 60 miles over the Old Nez Perce Trail from Mount Idaho by a carrier on snowshoes. The carrier in 1893 was Jack Anderson, and on one trip he was having a rough time. Not only was the snow wet and inclined to stick to his snowshoes, but the pack of mail on his back was giving him trouble. More than the heaviness of the pack was the fact that some cans in it, labeled tobacco and addressed to Chinese at Elk City, kept prodding him like spurs.

As Anderson camped for the night at Ten Mile Cabin, he decided to correct the situation. Picking up a piece of wood, he began to pound on the locked mail bag, smoothing the surface by flattening the cans inside.

What Anderson did not realize was that the cans contained opium instead

104

of tobacco. Now, opium is a sticky substance, somewhat like molasses. And, when the cans were flattened, they began to leak, oozing their contents throughout the mail.

Came the opening at Elk City of the long-awaited bag which Anderson was left holding, and the people were horrified. Their precious mail was all glued together in one solid chunk. For a long time afterwards in Elk City, it would have paid anybody wearing a pigtail to get a haircut—except perhaps the highly popular Lee Mann. His standing in the community was exemplified by an Elk City correspondent's report in the *Idaho County Free Press* on April 5, 1889:

"Lee Mann, our enterprising merchant, has his splendid store finished which is a great improvement to the town."

The cold war against the Chinese in early Idaho—indeed, throughout the Far West—was real enough. Down in Texas, in the court of Judge Roy Bean, it was more than a cold war. Bean, who was known as "the law west of the Pecos," had an Irishman brought before him for murdering a Chinese. Turning the killer loose, Bean opined:

"I just can't find any place where it says it is against the law to kill a Chinaman."

Generally, however, the war against the Chinese was more of a war of the press than of the people. Fortunately, most of the Chinese could not read English. If they had been able to do so, they would not have appreciated, for instance, the fine sense of the illogical expressed in an *Owyhee Avalanche* editorial, urging the Chinese and Indians to do combat. The editorial pointed out:

"While our sympathies in such a contest would incline to the side of the Celestial on account of his being the least of the two evils, people generally, we think, could bear the loss on either side with a certain degree of composure. Neither the Indian nor the Chinaman should have been allowed to live in the same country with white people."

The *Boise City Republican* declared:

"We do not want him (the Chinaman) here, and when he finds it out he will go, and in his stead will come a class of laborers of our own kindred, of our own religious faith, who will be subject to our laws, and pay tax towards the support of the government."

(The *Republican* forgot about Idaho's tax on Chinese miners.)

The *Ketchum Keystone* heartily endorsed the Anti-Chinese League (George Lewis, editor of the *Keystone*, was president of the chapter in Ketchum), but urged a certain amount of restraint for fear of a break between the governments of China and the United States. It suggested the "no job" approach:

"P. P. Baxter of this place has received a letter from J. M. Rice, immigration agent located at Omaha, asking the probability of importing to our territory a large number of Swedish and Bohemian girls for cooks and laundresses . . . The only true means of expelling the heathen is to close employment for him. This cannot be done easily and immediately unless there is some provision for the vacancies thus ensued. There are few girls within the territory who want such employment, but there are thousands throughout the East who only want the promise of employment and some assistance in securing traveling rates to induce them to come West. An organized action in this matter would probably be more expedient and effective than to wait until such girls come one by one . . . This is the only legitimate way of expelling the Chinese labor, and we trust the people of Ketchum will countenance no other means."

Women had not yet been given the vote when the *Hailey Times* sought their aid in making a clean sweep of the Chinese:

"No great social reform has ever been accomplished without active sympathy and cooperation of the women; and, if we can succeed in enlisting the good women and pure girls of Hailey in the Anti-Chinese cause, the hated Mongolian will have to go—and quickly, too!"

Later, however, the *Times* turned around, and criticized the Anti-Chinese League for boycotting Chinese businesses. And the people did some criticizing of their own. At Atlanta, a movement was started to cancel subscriptions to the *News* for advocating the running of all Chinese out of town.

The *Idaho County Free Press* of April 27, 1888, published a warning note:

"The Chinese government has made a demand upon the United States to indemnify it for the loss of all the Chinamen who have been killed in this country by mobs and vigilantes and it assesses the life of each Chinaman at $2,250."

But generally little room was found for John Chinaman in the wide open spaces of the Far West. If he filled a niche, he was tolerated—even liked and appreciated—but, as the niches closed with the coming of more whites, as the ore pickings became slimmer and slimmer, the Oriental had little choice other than to fold his tent and steal silently away.

Dick d'Easum, in his book "Fragments of Villainy," put it this way:

"They were invited in to work on the railroad and in the mines. No tickee to come. Pretty soon everybody mad at John. You buy tickee and go home. Chop chop."

True, some did go home to China. But for most that was too far, too expensive. A few, particularly the very popular ones such as Pon Yam of Idaho City, stayed on until death. And the thousands of others? They left the clean mountain air and broad expanses of Idaho and other parts of the Far West to crowd into the already congested Chinatowns of San Francisco, Denver, Chicago, New York . . .

Chapter IX

# SOUND OF WAR DRUMS

"Father, help us.
  You are close by in the dark.
  Hear us and help us.
  Take away the white men.
  Send back the buffalo . . ."

—From the "Ghost Dance Prayer" by
an unknown Indian poet

General Ulysses S. Grant once suggested that the best way to control the Western Indians would be to cut off their natural source of food by killing all the buffalo. Colonel George H. Wright, however, had another idea—to kill off the horses of the Indians who were now used to doing their fighting as well as hunting of big game from the saddle. This the man of rawhide in a blue uniform proceeded to do in a campaign in 1858 which brought the Indians of Northern Idaho and Eastern Washington to stringent terms.

It all started in the spring of that year when Lieutenant Colonel Edward J. Steptoe, a handsome dark-haired and broad-mustached man, set off from Fort Walla Walla with a cavalry detachment of 159 men for the Colville Country. Several years before Captain Pierce made his big gold strike in Northern Idaho, some miners had started placer operations in the Eastern Washington area.

107

Two of them were brutally murdered by Palouse Indians, who objected to white men trespassing on their lands, and Colonel Steptoe was ordered by General Newman S. Clarke, commanding officer of the Department of the Pacific, to investigate.

Reaching the Palouse River, Steptoe encountered a band of Spokanes.

"Why are you here with cannon and many men?" asked the leader.

Steptoe explained his Colville mission, stating that he wished to clear up the matter of the killings so that there would be peace. The Spokanes didn't believe a word of this—for good reason. Steptoe wasn't headed in the right direction. Why this was so was never explained. The Spokanes indicated their displeasure, but did nothing—not on that day.

Then, on May 16, 1858, Steptoe's forces pushed on to the vicinity of what is now Rosalia, southeast of Spokane. They got no further. War drums had been throbbing in the night, and the cavalrymen found themselves confronted by an estimated 1,200 painted warriors—Spokanes, Coeur d'Alenes, Palouses and Yakimas. The long-feared uniting of Indian tribes had been achieved.

Steptoe had a couple of cannon along, but he knew that he was so vastly outnumbered that his command faced possible annihilation in a pitched battle. He turned to his bugler:

"Sound retreat."

The cavalrymen started riding back to Fort Walla Walla. Tagging along, the Indians dared the whites to start fighting. The troopers, with necks reddening, held their fire, but the Indians did not. A bullet struck a cavalryman in the back, and he toppled from his horse. The battle was on.

All day in the heat of a blazing sun, the cavalrymen, fortunately positioned on an advantageous hill, fought off the sporadic charges of the Indians. Some of the red men had only bows and arrows and tomahawks, but many had even better guns than the cavalrymen—except for those two cannon. Their booming kept the Indians from doing to Steptoe what their Sioux brethren would do to Custer in the Battle of the Little Bighorn in 1876.

Realizing, however, that the situation was hopeless, especially with ammunition running low, Steptoe decided to take off in the night. Leaving cannon and other equipment and supplies behind, the cavalrymen raced their horses for the Snake River. Most of them made it. Not all. A total of 25 cavalrymen lost their lives in the fixed and running encounters.

At the Snake, the troopers were met by a large band of Nez Perces, headed by Chief Lawyer, who told Steptoe:

"We will ride back with your men and destroy the Spokanes, Coeur d'Alenes, Palouses and Yakimas."

But Steptoe knew that his battered force, with many of the survivors still carrying bullets or arrowheads, was in no shape for another fight at this time. And ammunition was almost depleted. The colonel shook his head.

Disappointed, the Nez Perces helped ferry the cavalrymen across the river. Then they watched the badly shrunken detachment head back to Fort Walla Walla.

Steptoe's report of the affair did not set well with General Clarke—nor with many of the settlers in the Pacific Northwest, who feared a general Indian uprising.

George H. Wright, a no-nonsense colonel with the shine still on his eagles, came from San Francisco to Fort Walla Walla. A man of stern jaw and intense eyes, he had relatively short hair for the period. The hair was unruly, and

Wright was careless about combing it—but that was the only thing about which he was ever known to be careless. He was just the man, General Clarke figured, to be given the assignment of punishing the Indians. So, in August, 1858, Wright was ordered to depart from Fort Walla Walla with a sizable cavalry force—about 700 men—to do just that.

Smoke signals and tom-toms carried the word of Wright's coming, and Coeur d'Alenes, Spokanes and Palouses were waiting on a hill near Four Lakes, 15 miles southwest of the present city of Spokane. If the Indians had studied at West Point as Colonel Wright had, they would have known that their best bet was to hold the hill, but they started riding out to meet the cavalry. Soon they were in full flight, leaving behind 17 dead and many wounded. Wright lost not a man.

But he was not through. Pursuing the Indians, he chased them all the way to Idaho's Cataldo Mission in the Coeur d'Alenes. Enroute, about 20 miles east of Spokane, he carried out his theory of stopping war by getting rid of as many as possible of the Indians' horses. About 800 of the animals were rounded up and shot to death. For years, their bones lay bleaching in the sun and rain and snow.

The slaying of the horses long bothered Colonel Wright, who spent a big share of his life in the saddle. He wrote:

"I deeply regretted killing those poor creatures, but dire necessity drove me to it."

Both awed and angered at the devastating power of Wright, the Indians surrendered. At the mission, the colonel laid out his terms: "You must turn over for punishment (hanging) the men who began the attack on Colonel Steptoe, must return all property taken from the whites, must permit white men to travel freely through their country, and must designate five men, including a chief, as hostages for one year."

Awe won over anger, and the Indians mumbled their acceptance of the terms.

Altogether, before he was finished with his campaign, Colonel Wright had 11 Indians hung for assorted crimes. Included was a young Yakima warrior named Qualchian, accused of murdering an Indian agent. Wright had trouble snaring Qualchian, so he took his father, Owhi, into custody, and sent out word that the father would be hanged if Qualchian did not show up promptly at the cavalry camp. What happened next was covered in one sentence by Wright in his official report:

"Qualchian came to me at 9 o'clock, and at 9 1/4 a.m. he was hung."

Peace came to both Northern Idaho and Eastern Washington. But there would continue to be other Indian trouble in other parts of Idaho Territory.

Back in 1833, Captain Benjamin Louis Eulalie Bonneville, whose colorful adventures were chronicled by Washington Irving, watched a small band of Bannocks (Bannacks) outbluff a much larger band of Blackfeet on the Snake River in Southern Idaho. Instead of characterizing the Bannocks as fearless fighters, however, Bonneville intimated that the Blackfeet were poor ones. He should have given more credit to both tribes.

The Bannocks operated in relatively small bands both in peace and war. In peace, if numbers were not great, there was more food to go around when it was found. In war, a limited force was more mobile. So for some time small bands had been swooping down on wagon trains traveling the Oregon Trail, killing many of the emigrants and bringing back to the Bannock camps cattle "as good to eat as the buffalo." Leaders of these attacks varied from time to time, but one of the most colorful—and hostile—was Chief Pocatello, after whom the city of Pocatello was named.

Then, in December of 1862, a band which was larger than usual attacked a group of whites moving south from the Salmon River Country to Utah. One man was killed and another wounded. The rest of the party made it to Richmond, Utah, where they reported the attack. A posse was sent out after the Indians, but withering fire from the Bannocks caused a quick retreat.

This brought Colonel Patrick E. Connor with 200 troopers from Salt Lake City. They arrived at Franklin, the new Mormon settlement in Idaho, on January 29, 1863, just in time to prevent a possible massacre. Waving weapons, Cache Valley Shoshones, aided and abetted by Bannocks, had been doing a war dance around the home of Preston Thomas, the Mormon bishop, threatening death and destruction to the settlement if more grain were not forthcoming for flour.

In the ensuing Battle of Battle Creek or Bear River, almost 400 Indians were killed. As far as is known, this was the greatest Indian loss in a single battle with the United States Army. Those who survived were assigned to the Fort Hall Reservation. For quite a while, the whites believed that the raiding tribes had been completely tamed. They were wrong, because the Indians, like the Phoenix bird, would rise again with their feathered war bonnets once more streaming in the wind.


In the Pacific Northwest, as this is written, stories keep cropping up of a legendary man-beast called Bigfoot (or Sasquatch in Indian tales). These stories have intrigued the public as much as those of the Cardiff Giant did in the 19th Century—before he was exposed as a two-ton hoax. To back up the legend of Bigfoot-Sasquatch, many unexplained footprints have been found, but footprints need the maker to go with them to really be believed.

Idaho history provides not one but three giants to go along with its imprints of big feet. There were the Indians Howluck (alias Bigfoot) and Nambe (also alias Bigfoot), with the city of Nampa deriving its name from the latter. This writer, however, is particularly intrigued by the third Bigfoot, a character who ran heavily on the legendary side. According to the stories, which if mostly fiction were mostly good fiction, this Bigfoot engaged in a personal war in the 1860s of no little consequence.

His real name was said to have been Starr Wilkinson—an appropriate label adopted from that of an infamous desperado of the period who left a trail of terrorized victims behind him. Son of a white father, Archer Wilkinson, who died by hanging, and a Cherokee-Negro mother, Bigfoot had only a quarter of Indian blood in him, but he proudly considered himself an Indian.

As such, he was unquestionably one of the biggest red men ever to stalk the North American continent. He was 6'8" or 6'9" tall, and weighed about 275 pounds (mostly muscle and bone—no fat). His hands were huge, but his feet were more so. They were 18 inches from heels to big toes.

Altogether quite a man, Bigfoot could bend a horseshoe with ease, outrun a horse for anything over a half-mile, or put the latter-day, fictional Tarzan to shame as a river swimmer. Nevertheless, he was shy—around women. His bigness bothered him.

Surprisingly then, while traveling on an Oregon-bound wagon train churning dust out of his native Oklahoma, Bigfoot took a shine to a petite girl on the train. The girl reciprocated—until she became attracted to an artist on the train named Hart.

By the time the train started winding along the Snake River in Idaho, Bigfoot had had enough interference with the romance of his life. There were words with Hart. The artist drew his gun and fired, shooting Bigfoot in the shoulder, which, to him, was like suffering a mosquito bite.

Bigfoot's powerful hands reached for Hart's neck, closed, and did not open until the artist was dead. Then Bigfoot picked up Hart's body as if it were a sack of weevily meal, and tossed it into the Snake.

Now, although Bigfoot had intended to go all the way to Oregon, he decided that he had better leave the train, and devote his great energy to Idaho. The young territory could have done without his kind of energy. He began attacking and robbing miners and settlers in their homes, travelers in stagecoaches and wagon trains. He did not always kill them, but never hesitated to do so when he felt it necessary. Generous in sharing his loot, the giant in buckskin was looked upon by Indians in the Owyhee Country and the Boise Basin as a sort of Robin Hood.

Ambling along the Boise River, Bigfoot, it is said, came upon some stock with a brand he recognized as belonging to the wagon master of the train from which he had taken his hasty departure. For some reason—probably involving weather—the train had wintered in the Boise Basin. The jilting by the girl who was part of the train still rankled, so enlisting the aid of about 30 Indians, Bigfoot attacked the circled wagons, killing all in them, including the girl. Later, he is reported to have lamented this action, but, if he did, he failed to soften his attitude toward whites in general.

Bigfoot did a lot of horse stealing. He wanted the animals mostly for their trade value, because he seldom rode one. Not only could he travel faster than a horse in the long run, but he could go into places from which a horse shied away. Consequently, he preferred to stalk his prey on foot.

So it was that at dawn one day, Bigfoot, with two other unmounted Indians, crept up on a freight train of about 20 wagons camped just north of New Plymouth on the Payette River. The red men were making off with a goodly number of horses when barking dogs alarmed the camp.

Mounting five horses left by the raiders, freighters from the train rode in pursuit. North of Weiser, the posse came upon the stolen horses and the Indians. In the ensuing gun battle, two of the Indians were killed, but the third —a giant of a fellow—started running, herding six horses ahead of him. The freighters, who had dismounted during the gun fight, got back on their horses, and galloped after Bigfoot.

Both Bigfoot and the six riderless horses got to the Snake River well ahead of the freighters. Starting the horses swimming across the stream, Bigfoot then jumped in himself. He was waiting for the horses when they reached the other side, and was last seen herding the animals on the run.

Dismounting, one of the freighters placed a booted foot in a track left by Bigfoot in the riverside mud.

"Gawdamighty!" he said. "His feet are twice as big as mine!"

Fame and fear of Bigfoot spread. The total of robberies and killings for which he was responsible is any historian's surmise, but it all came to an end in July, 1868. The man who finally terminated Bigfoot's crime career was John W. Wheeler, an imported gunman who had first come to Silver City during the battle between miners of the Golden Chariot and Ida Elmore. Wheeler was out to get Bigfoot, because the giant had stolen some particularly fine horses from him.

Somehow, according to Wheeler's version of the story, the gunman had learned that Bigfoot and two Indian companions intended to hold up a stagecoach on the Boise-Silver City Road, south of the Snake River. Wheeler was waiting in the brush with a rifle when the armed red men came walking toward the spot selected for the holdup. Firing, Wheeler dropped one Indian dead, and a second fled. This left Bigfoot to fight it out in the desert with Wheeler.

As the giant started to crawl through the sage, Wheeler called:

"Stand up and fight like a man."

This was too much of a challenge for Bigfoot not to take, and he got to his feet, clutching a double-barreled rifle and daring Wheeler to come out into the open himself.

Wheeler sprang from behind his hiding place. Two rifles cracked. Staggering, Bigfoot fired again, then tried to run to the dead Indian, apparently to get the fallen one's rifle. But Wheeler shot him twice more before he could reach the body.

Drawing a knife from his belt, Bigfoot started for Wheeler with his weapon. Wheeler emptied his rifle into Bigfoot's barrel-like chest, but that did not keep him from coming. Drawing his pistol, Wheeler fired at the giant's legs, breaking one. That stopped Bigfoot.

The Indian's right arm had also been broken by a bullet, but, as he lay dying, he reached out with his left for a canteen at Wheeler's belt. Not trusting Bigfoot even with death hovering over him. Wheeler put a bullet into the second arm before he pressed the canteen to the lips of the big fellow. Then, feeling compassion for the man who had been so hard to bring to earth, Wheeler pulled out a pint of whiskey. Bigfoot was able to finish it off before he died.

Years later, Wheeler wrote the account of Bigfoot's demise for the *Idaho Statesman*. He included all the details of the gun fight, but he failed to explain why he had not tried to collect a thousand dollar reward for Bigfoot—dead or alive.

Some say that Wheeler did not reveal at the time of Bigfoot's killing that he was at the holdup site for fear of being suspected of trying to rob the stage himself. This thought has merit as Wheeler's name had come up in other stagecoach robberies. After Bigfoot's death, he was convicted and sent to the Oregon penitentiary for an attempted stagecoach holdup in the Blue Mountains. On the other hand, Wheeler may have skipped the reward money because of an old superstition among thieves—that to collect the reward for a dead man who had been a fellow criminal was to invite haunting by him. And who would want to be haunted by Bigfoot?

This thought would have ended this writer's chronicling of the story of Bigfoot, except that as this book was being written a monument was dedicated to him—on August 22, 1974—at the site of Old Fort Boise near Parma. Officially recognizing that the giant left a big stamp on Idaho history, Governor Cecil D. Andrus presided at the dedication ceremonies. After all, among the Idaho Indians of his time, Bigfoot was thought of as a Robin Hood, and there are markers in Sherwood Forest where the English raider roamed.

Oregon's Wallowa Mountains were the homeland of Chief Joseph of the Nez Perces. Besides the Wallowas, the Nez Perces, of course, claimed much other territory—all the land between the Bitterroot and Blue Mountains, bordered on the north by the Palouse River and on the south by the Salmon. This was a rather loose claim as the somewhat nomadic Indians had never carved out boundaries with the exactness of whites. But the Wallowa Country, with ancient trails leading through lush green valleys and over high-rimmed canyons to jewel-like lakes in pine-crested settings, was what "Old Joseph," before he died in 1872, had told his son, "Young Joseph," he should never barter away.

The country is mostly too rugged for farming, but it is excellent for raising livestock, and for just living where there are thousands of natural sights to delight the eye—and plenty of elbow room. This land, specially prized by the Nez Perces, was what the U.S. Government had decided to take from them. That was basically why the peace-minded Chief Joesph eventually went to war in 1877.

Ever since the coming of Lewis and Clark, the Nez Perces had been generally friendly with the whites. They had even fought against fellow red men to help the palefaces out.

But now the Nez Perces who lived in the Wallowas as well as those in the Upper Salmon River Country were told that they must leave for resettlement with other Nez Perces on the Lapwai Reservation in North-Central Idaho. The Indians objected. The new country might be fine—after all, the Reverend Henry H. Spalding had selected it for his mission when he had a lot of sites to choose from—but it would not be home.

Toohoolhoolzote, tribal orator, spoke the feelings of his fellow men when he told a council headed by General Oliver Otis Howard:

"You white people get together, measure the earth, and then divide it . . . Part of the Indians gave up their land. I never did. The earth is part of my body, and I never gave up my body."

General Howard, of Civil War fame, had lost his right arm in the Battle of Fair Oaks, and then had gone on to serve with distinction in the battles of Antietam, Fredericksburg, Chancellorsville and Gettysburg. Brought up in a religious family, he believed in the brotherhood of man—in fact, was known as the "Christian or Praying General." But he was a soldier first, and he had his orders. He replied:

"I stand here for the President, and there is no spirit good or bad that will hinder me. My orders are plain, and will be executed."

When the council ended, Howard's will prevailed. Chief Joseph agreed to join Looking Glass and White Bird in moving onto the reservation in North-Central Idaho, but Joseph was dismayed when he learned that he had only 30 days in which to make the move. He protested. Howard was adamant.

So the big trek began for hundreds of men, women and children, and thousands of horses, cattle and dogs. The great Texas cattle drives were small-time stuff compared with this. The clinging mountain trails had to be traversed and the turbulent rivers and creeks to be forded made a plains crossing seem like a picnic.

The farther the Indians got from their homeland, the unhappier they became —especially the young men. With two days to go before they reached their new home—or prison, as some figured—three youthful members of White Bird's band—Shore Crossing, Red Moccasin Tops and Swan Necklace— decided to do some revenge killing.

The three Indians started out after Larry Ott, who had slain Shore Crossing's father. They did not find him that day, but there were other marked men

113

around, and, before the sun set, blood red became the dominant color in the scattered white settlements.

At Slate Creek, the Indians came upon the home of Richard Devine, an old man who had a habit of setting his vicious dogs on any Indian who came around. Devine died with a bullet through his head. Next, the mini-war party moved to John Day Creek, killing Henry Elfers, who also had a hostile attitude toward Indians. Then followed the murders of two more Indian-hating whites, Henry Beckroge and Robert Bland. Whiskey Merchant Samuel Benedict, who had once shot to death a drunken Indian who was bothering him, was hit with a rifle bullet, but managed to escape in the brush.

Then proudly the avengers rode back to camp, throwing it into an uproar, with some Indians for and some against what had been done. When Chief Joseph, camped with his Wallowa band at Tolo Lake, heard the news, he was dismayed. He raced to White Bird's camp. But, by this time, more young Indians had left for the warpath. This party was larger, killing and burning whatever was white, including women and children. The Nez Perce Indian war was on.

General Howard at Lapwai received a desperate plea for help from settlers at Mount Idaho. The general, who had already called for reinforcements from Walla Walla, dispatched Captain David Perry with 99 men to Mount Idaho. On June 17, Perry's unit met 80 or more warriors led by Chief White Bird in what is now known as Whitebird Canyon.

Deftly, the red men outmaneuvered the whites up and down and around the rugged terrain. They split Perry's forces into two detachments, virtually wiping out one of them. With the remnants of the two units once more united, however, Perry made a surprisingly strong stand about four miles from Mount Idaho.

Chief White Bird was master of the battle, and, in time, could have annihilated the government forces, now down to fewer than 70 men. But, apparently fearing reinforcements would be coming from Lapwai, he chose to retreat up the canyon. Before he did, he rode out upon a projecting boulder, and defiantly waved a pole from which fluttered a collection of white scalps.

On July 3, two scouts, Charles Blewett and William Foster, were fired upon by Nez Perces near the head of Lawyers Canyon, about 10 miles from Cottonwood. Escaping, they raced back on their horses to Cottonwood. Quickly, 10 cavalrymen under Second Lieutenant Sevier M. Rains, with Foster as guide, were sent out after the Indians. None came back. All were found dead beside the bodies of their horses, with saddles and rifles gone.

General Howard, who had sent a message to his superiors in San Francisco, concluded with the statement that "I think we will make short work of the situation," now took personal charge of the fighting. On the Indian side, Chief Joseph, a gentle and kind man with handsome and serene features, emerged as the war leader, justifying well, before the end came, his Indian name of Thunder in the Mountains, and earning a new one—the "Indian Napoleon."

Some say that he was only a spiritual leader, and that many historians have given him too much credit for the Indians' brilliant war tactics. But this writer is inclined to take the word of the late, unforgettable General Edward R. Chrisman in ROTC lectures at the University of Idaho:

"Chief Joseph led what is perhaps the most masterful fighting retreat in the history of warfare. The U.S. Armed Forces don't believe in retreating, but, in case you ever have to do so, remember Chief Joseph."

Before Joseph's retreat began, another major battle would be fought on the Clearwater River in timber country southeast of Kamiah. For two days, July 11 and 12, the fighting raged, but finally the Indians had to give way to a howitzer and Gatling guns of General Howard.

A hero of this battle was a young surgeon—Dr. George M. Sternberg. He not only treated the wounded under fire, but, by hopping from wagon to wagon, managed to keep 25 of the casualty victims alive on the rough trip to Grangeville.

The big retreat—up the Lolo Trail—started, with the goal of joining the Crows in the Yellowstone area, and ended with trying to reach freedom in Canada. In the march were about 300 men, 600 women and children, and more than 2,000 horses. The women and children, not really a drag as some have indicated, helped with cooking, scouting and rounding up the stock. And rabbits caught in snares set by small boys brought meat to the pot.

Meanwhile, General Howard was reforming his forces, getting reinforcements from various posts, including Fort Boise. He also acquired some Bannock Indian scouts. (The Bannocks still hated the Nez Perces, and vice-versa.) When Howard started after Joseph, only 150 miles separated them.

Choosing to take a dodging, roundabout route to Canada, swinging south along the Bitterroot River to Lemhi or Lewis and Clark Pass, the Indians greatly alarmed settlers in the river's valley. But the Nez Perces did them no harm, paying for food in gold dust.

Then, on August 9, came the Battle of Big Hole River. General Howard's forces had still not been able to catch up with Joseph, but Colonel John Gibbon, in command of the 7th Infantry at Fort Shaw on the Sun River in Montana, took on the moving Nez Perces. And he was badly whipped, with 29 men killed, and 40 (including the colonel) wounded. But the Indians, too, suffered many casualties.

*The trek continued.*

On August 15, in Birch Creek Valley, the Nez Perces came upon a freight wagon train hauling whiskey and other supplies to Salmon City. Some young Indians, smarting from the losses at the Big Hole River despite victory and looking to the liquor in the wagons, shot to death five of the teamsters. They also confiscated whiskey and whatever else took their fancy. Joseph and the other chiefs were angry. But what was done was done.

*The trek continued.*

When the Indians reached Camas Meadows on the night of August 20, they learned that General Howard's forces were camped only 15 miles behind them. Some of the Nez Perces, taking a page from Colonel Wright's book of warfare, slipped back to Howard's camp, and drove off 200 horses. At least, they thought in the dark that they were leaving the cavalry without mounts, but the horses turned out to be mostly pack mules. Still, the mules were badly needed for carrying ammunition and other supplies, and the general would be greatly handicapped. The Eastern press covering the war thought that this incident was quite humorous, but General Howard saw nothing funny about it.

*The trek continued.*

Five years earlier, a vast land area dominated by spouting geysers had been designated as Yellowstone National Park by an Act of Congress. Still on the undeveloped side, it was not exactly crowded with tourists. But, in 1877, a party of nine from Radersburg, Montana, including Mr. and Mrs. George F.

Cowan, honeymooners, was camped near the West Entrance. They were startled to see Joseph's now bedraggled band starting through the park. The tourists had been warned about the bears, but not about Indians on the warpath. The Nez Perces, not wishing to leave any whites behind to report to General Howard, took the tourists along, and did not release them until several days later when they were well beyond the East Entrance of the park, now heading north.

Howard was not in a great hurry to catch up with the Indians, because he had set a trap. Guarding the Clark Fork River route ahead was Colonel Samuel D. Sturgis with 360 troopers. The Indians would be caught from in front and from behind. But, on September 13, when the Nez Perces and cavalrymen met at Canyon Creek, Colonel Sturgis made the mistake of having his men dismount so that they would be able to fire on the Indians from behind brush and rocks. He planned merely a holding action until Howard's forces could reach the scene. What Sturgis did not realize, however, was that Indians on top of bluffs were covering the Nez Perce advance, and they pretty well pinned down the troopers until the Indian cavalcade was far into the canyon.

*The trek continued.*

Nearing the Musselshell River, the Nez Perces knew treachery that was like "a knife twisted in the heart." While the Bannocks of Southern Idaho had good reason to hate them, the Crows of Western Montana had long been their allies. Yet, when the Crow scouts of Sturgis' contingent met the Bannocks of Howard's force, they agreed to help them in attacking the Nez Perces without waiting for the troopers of either command. For two days, both Crows and Bannocks harassed Joseph's band, killing three men and stealing many horses. The Nez Perces made them pay a high price in lives for the raids, but thereafter, whenever one of Joseph's band used the word "Crow," he spat.

*The trek continued.*

The pace of the march now speeded up, with Joseph assuring his charges that "you can do anything you have to do." In one 36-hour period, the Nez Perces covered 75 miles, leaving Howard farther behind.

On September 23, the Indians came to Cow Island Landing, head of steamboat navigation on the Missouri River. On the shore were great stacks of government and private supplies, guarded only by Army Sergeant William Moelehert and 10 privates. The Nez Perces wanted to buy supplies, but Moelehert said that this would be strictly against regulations. He gave them instead a side of bacon and a sack of hardtack from squadron rations—hardly enough to feed a hungry army of hundreds on the march.

That night the shooting started. The Indians could have wiped out Moelehert's outfit, but chose to keep it pinned down while women and children helped the men cart off sacks of flour, rice, beans, sugar—and ammunition. Consequently, as the band headed for the Bear Paw Mountains the next morning, its members had renewed strength. But their appetites were also growing greater.

Sighting a freight train pulled by oxen, they attacked it, killing three of the freighters and driving the rest off. They now had more supplies.

*The trek continued.*

The Eastern press, with long lapses of not knowing what was happening, kept asking the question:

"Will Joseph make it?"

In a way, this was a David and Goliath contest, and the journalists—and their readers—generally were rooting for Joseph, the Indian David.

Now it looked as if the long fighting retreat would be a success. (Joseph had zig-zagged for more than 1,600 miles and Howard had covered about 1,300 miles in chasing him.) Canada was near—but so was Colonel Nelson A. Miles, a son-in-law of General William Tecumseh Sherman, with 380 cavalrymen towing a 12-pound Napoleon cannon. Miles had been pushing hard from Fort Keogh on the Tongue River in response to a request for assistance from General Howard.

On September 30, Miles' force came upon Joseph's band camped on a creek below a bleak, open slope of the Bear Paws. The Nez Perces now had plenty of food and added supplies of ammunition, but they were miserably cold from a howling wind carrying with it snow flurries. Knowing that Howard was far behind, they had decided to take a much-needed rest. But they were sent into alarm and confusion when an Indian lookout on a high butte signaled with his waving blanket, "Enemy near."

Miles' first thrust was aimed at the Nez Perces' herd of horses, with the "hoorawing" cavalrymen running off more than 300 of them. Later, more horse were stampeded, leaving most of the Indians grounded. They scattered to coulee pockets, and for days and nights repeatedly beat back cavalry charges. Troop K lost 60 per cent of its strength. Other troops also suffered heavy losses.

Some of the Indians managed to fade into the mountains, but any mass escape with the women and children was out of the question. During the first night of battle, Joseph had sent couriers slipping through the enemy lines to seek help from the Sioux. But the help never came. The nights grew colder; no fires dared be lit. Children cried. Mothers whimpered as they tried to soothe them. Wounded braves lay on the cold ground, wrapped in a buffalo robe or blanket if one could be spared from the children. They just stared . . . and stared . . . at the darkness.

Colonel Miles moved up the Napoleon cannon, and started firing it like a howitzer into the Indians' position, but there were too many scattered islands of individual defense for it to be effective. No matter. The weather proved to be Weapon No. 1. It began to snow—hard.

On the fifth day, October 4, Miles was far from overjoyed when General Howard and his troopers finally reached the Bear Paws. Miles wanted the conquest of Joseph all to himself. But he was mollified when the understanding Howard told him:

"Any surrender by Joseph will be made to you—not to me. You are the one who caught the fox."

The surrender was not long in coming. Joseph knew that his warriors who were still on the fighting line could take bullets—many of them, including himself, had the marks of them on their bodies—but he also knew that the women and children and the old men could no longer take the weather.

*The trek had ended.*

At 2 p.m. on October 5, 1877, Joseph picked up his rifle. Before slipping it into its case of beaded buckskin, he fondly felt the heft of it. Then he mounted his horse, and, followed by five braves on foot, rode to meet the cavalry. He disdained the carrying of a white flag, but was not fired upon.

Before the waiting General Howard and Colonel Miles, he dismounted. Then, holding his rifle before him, he started to hand it to General Howard. The general smiled, and indicated that he was to present the weapon to Colonel Miles. Joseph complied, but, when he spoke through an interpreter, it was to General Howard. A chief dealt only with a chief.

117

Joseph's surrender speech has become an American classic:

"I am tired of fighting. Our chiefs are killed. Looking Glass is dead. Toohoolhoolzote is dead. The old men are all dead. It is the young men who say, 'Yes' or 'No.' He who led the young men (Joseph's brother, Alokut) is dead. It is cold, and we have no blankets. The little children are freezing to death. My people, some of them, have run away to the hills, and have no blankets, no food. No one knows where they are—perhaps freezing to death. I want to have time to look for my children, and see how many of them I can find. Maybe I shall find them among the dead. Hear me, my chiefs! I am tired. My heart is sick and sad. From where the sun now stands I will fight no more forever."

And so it was. The proud Nez Perces, who had welcomed the first white men to their land as brothers and equals, were now the wards of the white men. And their land was like the flow of a great river which had gradually dried up to a thin trickle. In the years to come there would be much lamenting of woes in tepee and at council fire, but there would also be this consoling fact:

They had gone down fighting.

In 1839, Alfred Jacob Miller, the artist, upon visiting the Nez Perces, had written:

"All these Indians seem to bear the impress of a doomed race."

Prophetic words, indeed! But the Nez Perces had made the prophecy come true the hard way.

Joseph died September 21, 1904, while staring broodingly at a campfire in front of his tepee on the reservation at Nespelem, Washington.

At times, after the Nez Perce War, he had known honors. In Washington, D.C., he was received by President Theodore Roosevelt. At Portland, he sat for a bas-relief plaque of his head by the noted sculptor, Olin L. Warner. Attending the commencement exercises at Carlisle Industrial School in Pennsylvania, he sat at the head table as a distinguished guest beside his old enemy, General Howard. He was even cheered at a University of Washington football game, and, in turn, cheered for the Huskies, sighing with relief each time the gridiron warriors got to their feet following a pile-up.

But, at other times, Joseph had known the scorn of his fellow tribesmen, because, even though he never ceased to fight—verbally now—for their rights, it was he who had surrendered at the Bear Paw Mountains. It would be only after his death that the Nez Perces would really start honoring him.

The agency doctor, who was called to the campfire where Joseph—Thunder in the Mountains—had toppled over in death, said:

"He died of a broken heart."

In Southern Idaho, the fighting was still not over for the Bannocks. Trouble was brewing at the Fort Hall Reservation. The Indians complained that the food rations supplied them were inadequate, causing them to go hungry three days out of the week. (An Indian agent was under indictment for sending some of the weekly rations to relatives in the East.) Frequently, the Indians got off the reservation, seeking game and camas roots, particularly on Camas Prairie. They claimed this area by the Fort Bridger Treaty of 1868, even though a Midwestern-born clerk had designated it in the treaty as Kansas Prairie. But, with or without the error, the whites were generally inclined to ignore the treaty's provision regarding the prairie. They were helping to back up Buffalo Bill Cody's famous observation:

"The Indians never broke a treaty; the whites never kept one."

The Bannocks' great fighting leader, Chief Pocatello, was dead. But a warrior named Buffalo Horn had ridden as a scout with Buffalo Bill, and then had added further to his stature by warring against the Nez Perces as a scout under General Howard's command. He became an important chief of the Bannocks.

While camped on Camas Prairie in the spring of 1878, Buffalo Horn talked of war against the whites. But another chief, Tendoy, who headed a mixed band of Lemhi Shoshones and Bannocks, opposed the idea. Tendoy was a warrior of strength, with gambling his only weakness. He would not hesitate to bet several hundred head of horses in an Indian "stick" game, but he was not about to bet on winning a war against the whites.

Buffalo Horn argued:

"I have learned much from Joseph's victories and defeat. I, too, will know victories, but defeat—never."

Snorting in derision, Chief Tendoy took off for his reservation on the Lemhi River.

The actual matter of the Bannocks (aided and abetted by some Shoshones) in going to war was decided, as in the case of the Nez Perces, by three young braves. Starting to guzzle some whiskey one morning, they became braver as they drank. Then, looking for trouble, they rode across Camas Prairie.

Near Soldier Mountain, they saw in a valley below them three cattle herders, Lou Kensler, George Nesby and William Silvey, squatting beside a campfire. Browsing cattle shifted in the background, trampling camas roots which the Fort Bridger Treaty said belonged to the Bannocks. Not only that, the Indians knew that hogs of cross-country drives had been tearing up the earth to get at the precious roots.

The well-liquored young braves started shooting. Although the whiskey in them impaired their aim, they hit Kensler and Nesby, wounding them slightly. Mounting their horses, they took off. Silvey, unhurt, also rode away—shooting.

The Bannock War of 1878 had started. Although of relatively short duration, the war would not only spread throughout Southern Idaho, but from the Columbia to the Platte.

Rounding up braves from various bands, Chief Buffalo Horn first initiated forays for food supplies and arms and ammunition. On the Snake River, near King Hill, the Bannocks attacked a freight wagon train, and got a lot of what they wanted. Cavalrymen from Fort Boise and volunteers from Silver City chased the hostiles, now numbering about 300, to the headwaters of the Owyhee River, with the Indians leaving behind a trail of dead settlers, some of them badly mutilated. (Some Indians believed that crippling of the bodies of their slain enemies prevented the foes from being dangerous to them in the spirit world.)

On June 8, a major battle was fought at South Mountain. The Silver City volunteers, under a Captain Harper, were in the forefront of this battle, and, when four of them were shot from their horses, the others bolted.

The Indians won this round, but lost their chief, Buffalo Horn. He was fatally shot from his horse by Pi-ute Joe, a Paiute scout for the volunteers. That a fellow red man should take Buffalo Horn forever from the saddle was in a sense retribution. After all, some Nez Perces were riding no more because of the rifle he had used in fighting with General Howard, although he always claimed that he fought on the side of the white men only to learn their war strategies.

With Buffalo Horn gone, there was no real leadership, and the war became largely a guerrilla affair, but vicious, nevertheless. In the Owyhee Country, some settlers, to avoid the sporadic and deadly raids, took to living in caves.

Women and children of settlers in the Boise Valley moved each day at sundown to the protection of the Boise Barracks, not knowing whether their homes and treasures would be gone the next day. A ball, long planned at the fort, was called off. This was no time for frivolity.

Word came of killings at ranches in the Steen's Mountain area, and cavalry troops, under a dashing young captain from Boise named R. F. Bernard, moved in. On June 23, they encountered a band of Bannocks near Silver Creek. Although outnumbered three to one, the cavalrymen attacked, and sent the Indians ducking for the protection of mountain crags. Repeated charges by Bernard's force failed to dislodge them. With three men killed and three wounded, and with ammunition running low, Bernard called for reinforcements.

General Howard, now serving out of Vancouver, again took a personal hand. He showed up with more troops, but, by that time, the Indians had slipped away, and were raiding and killing in Oregon's John Day Country.

With a plentiful supply of stolen horses, the Bannocks offered some Umatillas 2,000 of them if they would become allies. The Umatillas refused. So the Bannocks started shooting the Umatillas, killing several.

On July 8, General Howard, linking up with the troops of Captain Bernard, came upon the Indians on the north slope of the Blue Mountains. Outnumbered and outflanked, the Bannocks were again forced to flee to the higher ridges, leaving behind great piles of supplies and many horses. Keeping up the pressure, Howard drove the Bannocks higher and higher into the mountains, but finally had to give up the chase because both his men and horses were exhausted.

Other battles developed with other bands, but each succeeding one dwindled in significance. The final battle was fought on September 12, 1878, at Dry Creek in Wyoming Territory. Result: One Indian warrior killed; five women and 11 horses captured.

Chief Buffalo Horn's dream of succeeding where Chief Joseph had failed was only a dream. For the Bannocks, like the Nez Perces, it was back to the reservation.

Ever since white settlers had started coming in number to America, the odds for winning had been against the red men. Still, Idaho's most unlikely tribe of Indians, the Sheepeaters of the rugged Salmon River Country, took on the U.S. Cavalry in 1879—not exactly at their choosing.

The Sheepeaters, actually a blend formed from many tribes, were unlikely, not because they weren't brave and tough, but because there were so few of them—200 at the most. After the Bannock War, their strength was augmented by some Bannocks who preferred life in the Sheepeaters' high mountain country to that down on the reservation, but still they had a lot of nerve taking on the U.S. Army. Too, they had a lot to lose, because the government thus far had not taken the trouble to pry them off their mountain crags of freedom, and confine them to a reservation.

Traditionally, the inclination of the Sheepeaters was to bother nobody—

except for some petty thievery. And nobody, not even other Indians, bothered them—except for some petty thievery.

For most Indians, hunting the cliff-clinging mountain sheep and goats was difficult. For the Sheepeaters, it was relatively easy. The word "relatively" is important because hunting of big game with primitive weapons more often than not knew no rewards, resulting in lean days and weeks and months. Nevertheless, the Sheepeaters chose to go after the mountain game rather than to drift to the plains in quest of buffalo. In a couple of weeks, they might be able to kill enough buffalo to provide food for a year by simply driving them off a cliff, but they themselves might be killed by resentful Blackfeet or Sioux.

So what happened? Perhaps the Bannock refugees had a bad influence on the Sheepeaters. Or perhaps there was a dreamer like Buffalo Horn among them. Anyway, there was war—a very odd one, as it turned out—and this is the way it got started:

In February of 1879, five Chinese miners were robbed and killed on Loon Creek, 80 miles northeast of Boise. Sheepeaters were blamed for the crime. Then, in April, friends coming to visit Hugh Johnson and Peter Dorsey, ranchers on the South Fork of the Salmon River, found them slain and their stock run off. Indian signs were all around. Again Sheepeaters were blamed.

On May 1, General Howard received a telegram at Fort Vancouver from the Office of the Adjutant General, telling him to apprehend the killers. He hadn't expected Indian trouble in Idaho again so soon, but he took action—not too swiftly because he knew that a lot of winter's heavy snow still remained in the mountains.

Although considering the matter too insignificant for himself to climb into the saddle once more, he did take it seriously enough to dispatch more than one force to the mountains. On May 31, Captain R. F. Bernard, who had acquitted himself well in the Bannock War, rode out of Boise, headed north-east. He was accompanied by Lieutenant Jonathan Pitcher and 56 enlisted men. Moving southeast from Camp Howard, near Grangeville, at about the same time, were 48 men under Lieutenant Henry Catley. Then there was the "ace-in-the-hole" outfit formed later at Umatilla. This detachment, which did not start pushing eastward until July 7, was composed of two young second lieutenants, E. S. Farrow and W. C. Brown, seven enlisted men, and 20 Umatilla Indian scouts. All three units ran into trouble.

Bernard's force, scouting along Loon Creek, the Middle Fork of the Salmon and Camas Creek, found the swollen streams treacherous to cross. And the snow was still piled high in the mountains. Losing a string of ration-laden mules in a snowslide, the troopers went for three days without food until they could find game to replenish their larder. They encountered sheep, but no Sheepeaters. There were plenty of Indian signs, but always the red men kept just one mountain ahead of the cavalry.

Because of heavy snow packs, Catley's detachment, heading across the South Fork of the Salmon for the Big Creek area, had to turn back twice, on June 16 and June 26, and seek alternate routes. Then, on July 29, after weeks of fruitless searching for Sheepeaters, the troopers rode into a canyon am-buscade. Completely hidden by boulders and brush, the Indians (later esti-mated as numbering no more than 10) poured lead upon the cavalrymen and their mounts. Two troopers were seriously wounded, and many horses and mules went down. Catley ordered everyone to take cover.

Testing the wind, the Sheepeaters set the brush in the canyon on fire.

121

Flames and smoke swept down on the cavalrymen's position, sending them into coughing retreat.

Regrouping men and animals two miles down the canyon, Catley then made a decision that he was to regret. He decided to continue the retreat all the way back to Camp Howard where better treatment could be obtained for the wounded men. For this action, he was later courtmartialed, found guilty of misbehavior in the presence of the enemy, and sentenced to be dismissed from the service. Catley claimed that he had actually saved his men from annihilation. But not helping his case was the fact that the Sheepeaters followed him on the retreat, burning the James Rains' ranch, killing the owner, and wounding Albert Webber. On recommendation of the Judge Advocate General, however, the sentence was set aside by the President.

Meanwhile, Lieutenant Farrow, camped with part of the Umatilla detachment on Crooked River, had sent a message to Vancouver Barracks:

"Hostile Indians, over 100 strong, reported near the mouth of Crooked River."

This brought to Crooked River Lieutenant Brown with the rest of the Umatilla detachment. It also brought the force of Captain Bernard. Searching for the hundred hostiles, the troopers ran into a couple of white men, who replied to questioning:

"Sorry. Ain't seen an Injun 'round here in two months."

In early August, Sheepeaters were sighted way off at the Falls of the Payette—but not by the Army. Settlers in Indian Valley had had several horses stolen by the red men, and riding after the Indians were William Mundy, Jake Grosclose, Tom Healy, and "Three-Fingered" Smith—he who had found the fortune in gold at Florence and lost it in the saloons of Warren.

Scattered among boulders, the Sheepeaters started firing on the four-man posse. Only Smith escaped with his life. The mule he was riding stopped a bullet, and Smith was hit in both a leg and arm, but both man and mule managed to make it to Cal White's mail station on Little Salmon Meadows. The mule dropped dead on arrival.

Back at Fort Vancouver, General Howard was very unhappy with the reports he was getting from the field. He fired off a message to Captain Bernard, his field commander:

"Those Indians must be defeated."

The catch was to find them.

An advance party of Captain Bernard's main force made contact with some Sheepeaters on August 20 near Soldier Bar. In this skirmish, Private Harry Eagan was killed, and buried on the spot. When the Army erected a stone monument at the site in 1925, the headstone had to be hauled 70 miles from McCall by wagon, and then 40 miles by pack mule. It is still pretty rugged country.

For weeks after the Soldier Bar fight, the deadly game of hide and seek continued, with winter invading the mountains early, and the chase for both the hunted and the hunters becoming more difficult. Most dogged of the pursuers were the Umatillas under Lieutenants Farrow and Brown. These were the men who would wind up the war—in an anticlimactic manner.

Spotting the main camp of the Sheepeaters on the Salmon River on the night of September 20, the unit of Umatillas surrounded the camp as best they could with their small numbers, and prepared to attack at daybreak. When dawn came, however, the Sheepeaters were gone.

Splitting the detachment into two forces, Farrow started in pursuit with one unit, and Brown with the other. Came the night of September 25, 1879, with Farrow's men camped in Papoose Gulch. As they hunkered around a large campfire, trying to give the illusion of a major force, they heard a loud hooting in the woods. Moving to the darkness ringing the fire, they waited with guns ready.

Into the firelight stepped an Indian who said that he was Chief Tamanmo. Although part Bannock and part Nez Perce, he announced that he spoke for the Sheepeaters, and that they wanted to surrender.

"They are tired of running," he said.

Why didn't they hang tough just a little while longer—until winter locked them safely in the mountains behind high walls of snow? Because they knew that spring always follows winter. It was not a question of whether they would come to the end of the trail, but when.

In token of submission, Tamanmo laid his old Henry rifle on a log beside the fire. A search of his person revealed a new pistol tucked into his pants at the back, but it was not believed that he intended treachery with this weapon. He just hated to part with it.

And so the Sheepeaters taken prisoners in Papoose Gulch—they who had known the freedom of eagles in the mountains and who had never really been defeated in battle with the whites—came down to reservation confinement on the flats of Fort Hall. Adding to the irony was the fact that Idaho's final Indian war was actually won by Indians fighting Indians.

In a way, however, the Sheepeaters had the last laugh. A small band of them under Chief Eagle Eye stayed holed up in the mountains, avoiding reservation status until the dawn of the new century.

# Chapter X

# ROUGH AND RAGGED—BUT A ROAD

"Night after night, I have laid out in the unbeaten forests, or on the pathless prairies with no bed but a few pine boughs, with no pillow but my saddle, and in my imagination heard the whistle of the train engine . . . the paddle of the steamboat wheels . . . In my enthusiasm, I saw the country thickly populated, thousands pouring over the borders to make homes in this far western land."

> —Reflections of Captain John Mullan
> in building the wagon road from
> Walla Walla, Washington, to Fort
> Benton, Montana, 1859-1862

On a summer day in 1847, a thin, worn-looking man sat in an easy chair of his Washington, D.C., office, puffing his trademark—a long, homely clay pipe. He was President James K. Polk, and he had a lot on his mind. The Mexican War, which was supposed to have been taken care of quickly, had dragged on for more than a year now, and Polk was getting considerable heat from Northerners who believed that the war had been motivated by a Southern desire to expand the area of slavery.

Thoughts on the slow drive of General Winfield Scott to Mexico City were interrupted by an aide, who announced that a young man wanted to see the President. In those days, people just called at the White House when they had a hankering to confer with the nation's No. 1 man.

"What is the young man's business?"

"He doesn't say—just that it is urgent."

"Send him in."

So John Mullan, a Virginia born Irish youth of slight build, was ushered into the room.

"Well, my little man, what can I do for you?"

Young Mullan winced at the reference to his size.

"I am seeking an appointment to West Point."

"Don't you think you are rather small to want to be a soldier?"

"Can't a small man as well as a large one be a soldier?"

The President pondered the counter question. Although Mullan far from reflected the West Point image, he had a point. Also, Polk, as Commander in Chief of the Armed Forces, was anything but a big man, and this fact is believed to have had an effect on the President's decision—a decision that was to make the Irish youth one of the West's greatest road builders.

President Polk arranged Mullan's appointment to West Point, from which he was graduated in 1852 as an engineering officer. Before Mullan got around to his road building, however, he had some Indian fighting chores to perform —against the Seminoles in Florida and the Coeur d'Alenes and other tribes in Northern Idaho and Eastern Washington.

Then, in 1859, Mullan, sporting mutton-chop whiskers and several decorations for bravery, was assigned one of the toughest missions ever given a young first lieutenant—to build a 624-mile-long military wagon road from Walla Walla, Washington, to Fort Benton, Montana, with an appropriation by Congress of $30,000. Mullan would never have completed the road in 1862 and gotten his captaincy, if two things hadn't happened in the meantime. First, on September 30, 1860, the party of Captain Elias Davidson Pierce struck gold in Northern Idaho, and, second, on April 12, 1861, Confederate artillery in Charleston, S.C., opened fire on Fort Sumter, setting off the Civil War. To help finance its military operations, the Union badly needed gold, and figured that it might get some out of Idaho as well as Montana with a road across the area.

Eventually, Congress put out a total of $230,000 for the road. But that was dirt cheap considering all the earth which was moved.

Building the stretch through Idaho was the hardest part of the entire construction project. Damass, a Coeur d'Alene Indian, had warned Mullan:

"Ahead are steep mountains and deep canyons. If all the white men would work here a thousand years they could never make a road."

But the young lieutenant had only shrugged. With a crew of about 150, he had made good time in the spring of 1859 carving out the road, 25 to 30 feet wide, over Eastern Washington's prairie land and rolling hills. So, as he tackled Idaho in the summer, he was optimistic—for a while.

There were many problems to overcome, such as crossing the St. Joe and Coeur d'Alene Rivers. For traversing these waters, Mullan first had crude ferryboats constructed; later, bridges. Next came backwater swamps. Mullan's crew felled trees, and built stretches of corduroy highway over the soggy areas. But the worst was yet to come—the mountains and canyons about which Damass had warned.

There were irritating delays while wooden bridges were forged across streams and crevasses. Blasting of rocks and earth was kept to a minimum, but there were some 30 miles of it. The most arduous labor came with the cutting down of trees or removing of fallen ones. Altogether, the trail blazers axed their way through 125 miles of dense forest, with some of the trees more than 200 feet high. It was like hacking a path through a jungle, only the going was harder. Enroute, lightning-started forest fires were fought.

Snow started swirling down early in November. But Mullan kept his crew going, sending them to sub-camps with supplies and equipment loaded on hand-pulled sleds. Finally, on December 4, 1859, in the Montana canyon of the St. Regis Borgia River, he conceded that there could be no more road work until spring. Constructing Cantonment Jordan, the men wintered there.

Many mules and horses died during the winter, so when spring came, Mullan started the men off to lower-elevation construction sites with packs on their backs. Meanwhile, he went looking for mules and horses, preferably mules, because, as he wrote, "if you govern a mule as you would a woman, with kindness, affection and caresses, you will be repaid by docility and easy management." Mullan, however, got nary a mule—only 117 fractious Indian horses. Still, they generally served well, and again each sunset reflected on long stretches of new road . . . down to Hell Gate . . . up Hell Gate Canyon and Little Blackfoot River . . . across Mullan Pass to Prickly Pear Valley near the present site of Montana's capital, Helena . . . then to the Missouri River, and Fort Benton, the head of navigation on the river.

Mullan got to Fort Benton with an advance crew in August, 1860. He was well aware that his road was still in a very rough stage, but he had made a commitment, and he intended to keep it. He had sent a message to the War Department in Washington, D.C., advising that, if troops destined for Washington and Oregon garrisons would be sent by steamboat to Fort Benton, he would escort them to their stations over the new road.

A Major Blake, with 300 troops, was waiting at Fort Benton.

"If I can go ahead with some of my men, and clear out fallen trees and brush, I'll get your outfit over the mountains in jig time," Mullan told the major.

Blake agreed, and Mullan did just what he said he would do. It wasn't easy, but the troops and all their wagons of gear made it to Fort Walla Walla in 57 days. A wheel and axle or two were broken, and had to be repaired enroute, but it was estimated that use of the direct route saved the government $30,000. Mullan was ordered to keep working on the road so that it could be opened to general travel.

Whites in the area were happy with the idea, but the red men were not. Subdued by Colonel George F. Wright in the War of 1858, they watched broodingly as the road took shape through their domain—a road which they knew would bring more and more white men and take away more and more land. (It is puzzling to this writer why the Indians sold those 117 horses to Mullan.)

On the Fourth of July, 1861, Mullan and his crew encamped at a point in Idaho now marked by the Mullan Tree Monument. There they decided to knock off for the day and do some celebrating. They began by firing rifles, and, when that palled, they started setting off charges of dynamite. Mostly immigrants, they had a fine appreciation for the freedom they enjoyed in the new land, and did not stint in sounding off about it.

Indians who were observing the celebration from behind trees, however, were only confused and terrified. Racing to the Cataldo Mission, they reported to the Jesuit priests:

"The white road builders have gone *kultus*. They are shooting one another, and blowing up their camp."

127

It was too bad the Indians did not tarry to hear Mullan's patriotic speech. On the other hand, they would probably never have understood what it was all about. Even many tourists of today, traveling on U.S. Highway 10 and passing the site of the 1861 celebration, are puzzled by the odd name—Fourth of July Canyon.

(Some say that the celebration was the first in Idaho to mark America's Independence Day, but folk in Southeastern Idaho's Soda Springs claim the first celebration was held there in 1860 by George W. Goodheart and several other trappers, who were joined by Indians. Everybody danced around a campfire, with the beat of drums broken every now and then by the blasts of rifles. The Indians at Soda Springs thought that the whites had a good thing going with the Fourth of July.)

In 1862, the Mullan Road (officially, the Military Road, but rarely called that) was opened to general travel. Mullan was far from satisfied with the narrow and rough thoroughfare, but, years later, experts would refer to it as a "remarkable feat of engineering." Professors at West Point would capitalize on it as an example of what could be accomplished with training at the military school on the Hudson. And a town in Idaho and a pass in Montana would be named after Mullan to honor him for his achievement.

The first large party to travel over the road in the summer of 1862 was a covered wagon train of 300 emigrants, headed for Oregon. Later, the travelers compared notes with emigrants who had followed the Oregon Trail, and it was agreed that the Mullan Road was the better route to take—at least it was faster.

Then came the gold seekers, and the freight to serve their camps. By 1866, it was estimated that 20,000 persons, 300 wagons of assorted sizes, 6,000 pack mules and horses, 5,000 head of cattle, and more than a million dollars in gold dust had passed over the road. The estimate on people was probably a very generous one, but nevertheless, publicity in the early years drummed up considerable traffic for the road.

The Transportation Steamship Line of St. Louis advertised:
"Boats of the Line will leave St. Louis for Fort Benton. From that point we are prepared with wagons of our own to transport goods to all parts of the territories of Montana and Idaho. The service is excellent."

Even camel caravans moved over the road, but this method of mountain transportation was short lived. The camels, moth-eaten relics of an early military experiment in Texas, could carry 1,000 pounds, twice the load of a mule, and they ate forage at which a mule would wrinkle its nose. The trouble, however, was that camels did not mix with horses and mules on the road, causing stampedes among the latter. Too, it was hard to find camel herders among the equine-minded men of the period and place. The crowning blow was the shooting of a grazing camel by a young Kentuckian, who thought the animal was a Western moose.

With the coming of the railroads, the Mullan Road faded fast as a main wagon and pack train thoroughfare. Commenting on the road's demise, Father Joseph M. Cataldo, S.J., said that he missed the steady flow of traffic beside the Cataldo Mission, but then he added with a chuckle, "I think Mullan only built the road to get out of the country." What the road did do especially well was to serve as a basic path through the mountains to be followed by railroad tracks, and, eventually, by super highways. And, as a prize essayist on "Roads and Road Making" wrote in 1870, "Without roads we should never have emerged from barbarism."

As for Mullan, he was not finished as a pathfinder in the Far West. Resigning his commission in 1863 (he was by then a captain), he began laying out a mail and stage line between Chico, California, and Ruby City, Idaho. Having received a contract from the federal government and an appropriation from Congress of $75,000 to provide the new service, he figured that he would make his fortune off this route.

And things looked good—until Indians in Northeastern California began raiding and burning the newly-erected stage stations. Mullan called for military protection, and eventually got it. Contingents of troops were placed at stations along much of the line.

Then, on September 1, 1865, came a big day for the mining town of Ruby City in Southern Idaho. Six horses, pulling a rattling good Concord coach from Chico, galloped to the cracking of a whip down Ruby City's dusty main street. (The animals had been rested outside of town for the flourishing finish.)

First of several passengers to step off the stage was beaming John Mullan. "Just 11 days out of Chico," he announced.

The Boise press was laudatory:

"Whatever advantages Idaho and California may derive from expelling the Indian difficulties and opening this overland route are due in great measure to the energy and perseverance of Captain Mullan . . . The efforts of the proprietor of this enterprise are now in a fair way to realize the success that is due to the perseverance with which he has pushed ahead against difficulties that seemed insurmountable."

But the glory—and profits—soon vanished. Mullan did not have the political pull in Washington of Territorial Governor James W. Nye of Nevada, who, observing the Captain's success, had decided to establish a competing line. From the federal government, Nye received a contract and an appropriation double that granted to Mullan. For six months, the Battle of the Stagecoaches was fought, but, finally, Mullan went down in defeat—and $12,000 in debt.

Turning to law, the soldier-builder became a leading California authority on land conflicts. He was not forgotten, however, in the Pacific Northwest.

The Union Pacific and Central Pacific's golden spike driving ceremony at Promontory Summit, Utah, May 10, 1869, inspired the Northern Pacific to hold a similar celebration at Gold Creek, Montana, September 8, 1883, when the NP lines joined the Pacific Coast to Duluth, Minnesota. (A more pretentious preliminary ceremony was held September 3 at St. Paul, featuring 725 gaily decorated wagons, 100,000 American flags, and President Chester A. Arthur, and Generals Ulysses S. Grant and Philip H. Sheridan as guests. This caused the St. Paul Pioneer Press to comment: "The Northern Pacific now fastens its magic girdle about a smiling continent, and the struggle of years is ended and the guerdon won.")

At the frontier-style celebration held in Montana near the summit of the Rocky Mountains, Captain John Mullan was a guest of honor. A special invitation had also been extended to all the Indians in the area, and they turned out in force.

When President Henry Villard of the Northern Pacific stood up to make a speech, he was disconcerted because the beaded and be-feathered Indians, getting into the spirit of the affair, shouted, "Grant! Grant! Grant!" The railroad tycoon did not realize that this was the only name of an important white man familiar to the red men. Then, when Villard introduced "that great road builder, Captain John Mullan," the Indians again shouted, "Grant! Grant! Grant!"

Mullan was pleased. After all, a captain could ask no more than to be mistaken for a general.

130

# Chapter XI

# STEAMBOATS AND MOUNTAIN GOATS

"Nowhere in the Pacific coast area did steamboating assume the lasting importance that it did in the Pacific Northwest, which, before the coming of railroads, was dependent upon rivers, lakes, and coastal waters as avenues of trade, travel, and general communication."
—Oscar O. Winther in
*The Transportation Frontier*

When Robert Fulton, a painter turned inventor, started his steamboat, the *Clermont,* up the Hudson River to Albany, New York, on August 17, 1807, he had no idea that the historic voyage would establish a significant pattern for the winning of the West. But, early in the 19th Century, steamboats were churning for 3,100 winding miles on the Missouri River, known among rivermen as "The Big Muddy." When gold was discovered in California, steamboats began carrying eager prospectors up the Sacramento to various disembarking points for the camps and towns spawned without benefit of roads. The river boats plied the San Joaquin, too—even the unpredictable Colorado. And steamboat traffic on the Columbia was vital to early settlement in Oregon and Washington.

But steamboats in Idaho or, as Ruby El Hult intriguingly titled her book, "Steamboats in the Timber"? Indeed, there were. In fact, an early Idaho

Territorial Seal designed by Governor Caleb Lyon had on it a steamboat as well as an elk. Critics didn't object to the steamboat, but they contended that the elk looked "like a horse with antlers." Also, there was a canoe-shaped moon—shining in the daytime.

The Great Seal of the State of Idaho, which was adopted in 1890, has a stag that looks like one, but both the steamboat and the moon have been totally eclipsed. Designed by Emma Edwards Green (the only woman ever to create a state seal), Idaho's seal now has sketches depicting the State's highly-productive farms, tall timber, mighty rivers and majestic mountains, plus a miner and Justitia, the goddess of justice. The motto on the seal is "Esto Perpetua"—"It Is Forever."

Idaho is still favored with beautiful moonlight scenes—at night—but elimination of the steamboat was prophetic, because, although the colorful craft was of great significance in the early days, it gradually faded from Idaho waters. On the other hand, as this is written, there is a good chance of the steamboat again being a major means of transportation in Idaho—traveling up the Columbia and Snake to Lewiston.

The *Colonel Wright,* launched at the mouth of the Deschutes River on October 24, 1858, was the first steamboat to float above The Dalles, Oregon. Then, in May, 1861, with Captain Leonard White at her helm, she ventured where only much smaller craft had gone before—out of the Columbia River into the Snake. On one trip, the ship was loaded with passengers and supplies for Idaho's booming mining town of Pierce, and the captain, whose curly hair and beard gave him a constantly ruffled look, appeared more worried than usual. Steaming into the swirling, uncharted waters, he set his course "by guess and by God."

When he got to the Clearwater, he took on that river, too. But he was able to progress only to a bend near the site of the present town of Orofino. The current had become too swift for the heavily-loaded *Colonel Wright* to continue bucking it.

"Hey!" said a deck hand peering at a thrust of rocks in the distance. "Mountain goats! We don't belong here anyway."

All along the course, Captain White had been looking for a safe place to tie up and unload, but he had spotted none. So he maneuvered his ship back down the Clearwater to where it joined with the Snake, and, with a sigh, pulled the cord of the *Colonel Wright's* highly-polished steam whistle. When he had the attention of the passengers, he announced:

"This is where you get off."

"Where" was what is now Lewiston. And, with the docking of the *Colonel Wright* at that river valley site, Idaho had a seaport—of considerable significance, too. For years, before river dams frustrated steamer travel, big ships churned into the Lewiston Port, generating a steadily increasing flow of commerce.

In winter, when the river was low or ice-clogged, no ships came. But, along in March or April, a steam whistle would be heard echoing over the greening hills. Then, off in the distance, a rising feather of smoke would be seen, and someone would shout:

"Steamboat comin' 'round the bend!"

Still not too familiar with the lingering ways of winter along the route, Captain White tried taking the *Colonel Wright* to Lewiston early in the spring of 1862—too early. He had a rush cargo aboard: All the equipment necessary to set up an eagerly-awaited saloon and gambling hall, plus bartenders, card dealers, and about the best looking collection of dance hall girls ever rounded up in Portland.

Although under strict orders to proceed to Lewiston with all possible speed, the captain ran into more floating ice than he cared to dodge. So he decided to tie up for a few days at the Fort Walla Walla wharf, near the mouth of the Walla Walla River. That made ice floes seem a minor problem. Bachelor ranchers from miles around, with some of them claiming that they had merely smelled the perfume of the dance hall girls when the wind was right, stormed the decks of the *Colonel Wright*. Like eager pirates long at sea, they sought out the fair damsels aboard ship.

Alarmed, Captain White barked down to the engine room for steam, and moved the *Colonel Wright* to the isolated shelter of Ice Harbor. In canoes and rowboats, the bachelors followed. And, when the *Colonel Wright* finally departed for Lewiston, her passenger list was very short on females. In fact, it was so short that the steamboat, after unloading before dismayed Lewiston-ites, was speeded back down river to pick up a new supply of dance hall girls. However, it was reported that ranch life around the Walla Walla area had become much more tolerable for a good number of the male settlers.

The ships which plied the swift waters to Lewiston bore names no less colorful than those on Pullman cars—*Spray, Harvest Queen, Casadilla, Nez Perce Chief, Tenino, Okanogan, Owyhee, Yakima* . . . Of all these, the fastest was the *Yakima*, a handsome craft with 26 luxuriously appointed staterooms and a freight capacity of 200 tons. Travelers in the 1860s could take a ship at Portland on a Friday morning to Celilo Falls on the Columbia, portage around the falls by horse and wagon, catch the *Idaho* at Celilo in the evening, pass Umatilla at 6 a.m. Saturday, and reach Lewiston at noon on Sunday.

The *Harvest Queen* once made the fastest time for a short stretch on the route of the rivers. In 1890, she electrified watchers on the Columbia as she foamed past them through treacherous cascades over a four-mile course in four-minutes flat—60 miles an hour. Made a horse and buggy seem mighty slow.

Speed, however, was not always sought. Sometimes a steamship would leave her Lewiston mooring for a lazy, winding excursion trip to Spalding. There would be a makeshift, fiddle-dominated orchestra aboard, with dancing in both sunlight and moonlight. And, between dances, couples would dreamily watch the water unfolding before the ship's prow like earth before a plow.

Always, there was a crowd at the Lewiston dock to greet the incoming ships from Portland. Many persons made the ritualistic trek to the waterfront with each ship's arrival to get copies of Eastern and West Coast newspapers—to read about General Robert E. Lee's defeat of the Federals at the Second Battle of Bull Run (August 29-30, 1862) . . . or General George B. McClellan's victory over Lee at Antietam (September 17, 1862), which gave President Abraham Lincoln the opportunity to issue the Emancipation Proclamation, decreeing the freedom of all slaves in territory still in rebellion January 1, 1863.

The most important cargoes leaving Lewiston in the early days were in the form of gold dust. Richest of all the cargoes taken down the river during a single trip was on the *Nez Perce Chief* in October, 1863—$382,000 worth of gold.

Today, Lewiston sends out heavy shipments of grain, livestock and lumber —via train and truck. But, eventually, river improvements are expected once more to make Lewiston a seaport. In time, an alert resident will again be able to shout:

"Steamboat comin' 'round the bend!"

Probably Idaho's heaviest steamboat traffic in pioneer days was in its Panhandle—on Lake Coeur d'Alene. In fact, this 22-mile long lake, which is considered to be among the world's most beautiful inland bodies of water, at one time had more steamboat activity than any lake west of the Great Lakes. With more than 100 miles of Lake Coeur d'Alene's shoreline accessible by boat, and with two rivers which flow into it—the St. Joe and Coeur d'Alene— each navigable for more than 30 miles, it made sense to minimize travel by land and maximize it by water. Certainly, there was no cheaper way to move the area's great quantities of ore and lumber.

Dean of the lake's boat-builders and skippers was Captain Peter C. Sorrensen. A native of Krogo, Norway, he had been apprenticed to a stonecutter there, but, living in that water-minded country, he naturally had learned a lot about ships.

In 1879, he was engaged by Colonel Henry Clay Merriam of Fort Coeur d'Alene to supervise construction of the *Amelia Wheaton,* the first steamboat launched on Lake Coeur d'Alene. Later, he received the contract to build the lake steamers, the *Spokane,* and her sister ship, the *Colfax,* but his favorite was the trim little *Lottie* which he constructed for himself.

The amiable captain had never heard of Women's Liberation, of course, but on a warm summer day in 1888, he held the area's first Ladies Day, featuring a free steamer ride on the St. Joe. A week before the historic occasion, he had whistled up the St. Joe, stopping beside farmhouses on the way, and advising the ladies of the next trip which would provide a day away from chores and husbands and children.

When Ladies Day arrived, Sorrensen again maneuvered the *Lottie* up the St. Joe, and the women were waiting at their respective farmside docks— carrying heavily-loaded picnic baskets, and wearing best dresses and hats, carefully preserved for just such a day. Stopping at Ducommun Landing, Sorrensen blasted the steam whistle for Mrs. Ducommun. She sent word by one of her boys that she could not make the trip, because she was having trouble with setting hens, but would the captain please hold the *Lottie* until she could get down to the dock so she could say "hello" to everybody. What delayed her was her determination not to appear before all those other "gussied-up" women in her old calico work dress. When she finally came down to the dock, prettily proper, she was a match for any of them.

At the head of navigation, just beyond the Ferrell Ranch, Sorrensen docked the *Lottie,* and had lunch with the ladies beneath huge cottonwoods which spread their shade over the river bank. That was where he ran into a problem —how to partake sufficiently from the special-recipe delights in each woman's basket so he would not offend anyone. He always contended that he never ate for a week afterwards. And, for years, no man on the St. Joe dared say a word against the captain without a woman rising to his defense.

A year earlier, in 1887, another steamboat had a much less pleasant voyage on the Coeur d'Alene River. This was the *Spokane,* which was substituting

134

one day in April for the bigger *Coeur d'Alene*, regularly assigned to the Cataldo Mission run.

Because cargo and passengers had actually been booked for the *Coeur d'Alene*, the *Spokane* left port overloaded, but she made it all right to the mission. There, however, even more cargo and passengers were waiting to come down the river, swollen with the spring run-offs from the mountains.

As the *Spokane* steamed from port, the captain scratched his head, and the pilot loosened his collar. The pilot was particularly worried, because he had never gone down the river with the water so high and the current so strong.

The *Spokane* had not proceeded very far, when it became obvious to everybody that the steamer was in trouble. As some of the passengers had traveled the river before, they began giving advice to the pilot. But, not knowing port side from starboard, they only confused the nervous man with their directions.

Approaching an island which separated the Coeur d'Alene into two channels, the pilot hesitated. A passenger shouted to take one channel. Another cried, "Don't be a fool! Take the other."

About that time, the *Spokane* struck a pile of driftwood at the island's upper end, swerved sidewise into one of the channels, capsized, and sank. Five of the passengers drowned. Included among them was a mine operator. When his body was pulled out of the river, the pockets of his coat still contained $16,000 in gold dust and currency.

That was not the end for the steamboat, however. Nobody wanted to ride on the *Spokane* again. But, raised from the river, she successfully plied the area's waters for many years as the *Irene*.

In Southern Idaho, there was the steamship *Shoshone*, plagued with trouble from the start. Even construction of the 136-foot ship, completed by the Oregon Steam Navigation Company at Old Fort Boise in 1866, was a series of frustrating problems to be overcome.

As there was no foundry at the fort, iron had to be hauled in by pack mules over mountain trails, then beaten into shape on an anvil. With no mill handy, all the lumber which went into the ship's hull and superstructure was whipsawed by hand. Expensive? Three steamboats could have been built on the Columbia for the cost of the *Shoshone*.

But it was intended that she would be used on the Upper Snake, and the directors of the Oregon Steam Navigation Company could not see trying to take such a ship up Hells Canyon. Various attempts had been made in previous years to get steamboats up the Snake to Boise without success. In 1865, the *Colonel Wright* had managed to travel about a hundred miles up the river in eight days. Then, when her new captain, Thomas Stump, gave up, the ship roared back down to Lewiston in five hours. That was the end of steamboating from Lewiston up the Snake River.

So, meeting in their plush Portland office, the OSNC directors picked Fort Boise for the construction site of the *Shoshone*. They figured that, regardless of the cost of building her there, they could make a killing by monopolizing river traffic to and from the mines of the Boise Basin.

What they did not take into account was that the color of gold in the hills was beginning to fade, and that railroads, pushing into the Territory, were picking up the lion's share of remaining trade. The few runs made by the

*Shoshone* on the Upper Snake were highly unprofitable. Then, for more than three years, the *Shoshone* remained tied up at a Snake River dock.

Another meeting at the Portland office . . . The decision coming out of this one was "Hells Canyon be blowed!" The *Shoshone* would be brought down the precarious stretch of the Snake to the Columbia, and the man first engaged to produce the miracle was Captain Cy Smith.

A game skipper, Captain Smith started out with a game crew. He got as far as the swirling eddies at Lime Point before he gave up. Tying the ship to a tree, he sent a message to the directors of the Oregon Steam Navigation Company:

"Folly to take a ship the size of the *Shoshone* any further. I quit."

The directors held another meeting in their Portland office. As a result, in late March, 1870, Captain Sebastian Miller and Chief Engineer Daniel E. Buchanan were directed "to get that ship to the Columbia or wreck her."

Arriving at Lime Point on April 8 with five crewmen, Miller and Buchanan took a look at the *Shoshone*. She was really not in bad shape, but her engines needed a complete overhaul. Too, for safety's sake, it was decided to build extra bulkheads into the hulls.

All the while, Captain Miller kept an eye on the river. The water had to be at its highest, and it was rapidly peaking. The hull needed caulking, but there was not enough time.

"Man the deck pump, and wet the hull," the captain ordered.

Soon the planking began to swell. The seams closed.

Then, on the misty morning of April 20, the *Shoshone* began her historic —and hazardous—journey. At times, the river ride was akin to that on a bucking bronco. And there was no saddle horn for "grabbing leather."

At the first bend, the *Shoshone* was confronted by a mid-stream cluster of huge, jagged rocks, creating treacherous eddies on either side. Taking the wider of the two streams as the kinder, Captain Miller miscalculated its potency, and lost control of the *Shoshone.* Three times, she spun completely around, and was about to tip over when the straining and blanching captain managed once more to get her under control.

Next came a series of madly frothing rapids. The bow scraped gravel on the river bottom, and the stern raised so high the paddles fanned air. When the stern came down, it did so with a crash of shattering paddles. The *Shoshone* was now just flotsam on the water; but she kept going.

At Copper Ledge Falls, she crashed into rocks, ripping away eight feet of her bow, plus the jackstaff and flag. The weight was knocked off the safety valve, and all the steam departed with a long hiss and a short sigh. No paddles, no power . . . But somehow the crew pried the *Shoshone* free into the fast-running water, and, shortly thereafter, beached her for inspection of damage.

It could have been worse. The broken paddles were repairable; the damage to the bow was all above the water line, and the hull had received no rips which could not be mended by caulking.

"We sail again in the morning, so get busy tonight," Captain Miller told the crew.

Standing in hip-deep, ice-cold water, the crew worked all night by torch-light and with makeshift tools and materials. By 9 a.m. the next day, the *Shoshone* was once more defiantly going down the Snake. But the canyon became narrower, the rapids rougher, and the whirlpools more vicious.

"Awesome," Miller recalled later.

In the engine room, the strength and sanity of Engineer Buchanan were rapidly sapping away. Whenever the ship bounced hard, the pilot house would shiver convulsively, causing the engine room bell to clang. Confused, tired and angry, Buchanan finally quit asking up the speaking tube what the trouble was—just cursed the river, the ship and the captain.

On April 21, Miller jockeyed the *Shoshone* to shore for further repairs to the paddle wheel. These took two days. Off again on the morning of April 23, the captain had to pull to shore before noon, because the wind was whipping through the narrow canyon with such fury that a bearing could not be maintained.

Again, on April 24, the *Shoshone* bounced only a few miles before Miller ordered a stop to cut down trees for boiler fuel. The fuel was badly needed, but the captain soon wished that he had never stopped. As he walked on shore, a rolling log struck him. No bones were broken, but he was in such bad shape that he had to be carried aboard ship, and put to bed.

Still nursing painful bruises on April 26, he climbed to the wheelhouse, and again began guiding the *Shoshone* down river. The water now became less rough—even gentle at times—and the *Shoshone* made it to the mouth of the Grande Ronde before she was tied up for the night.

Starting off at 7 a.m. on April 28, the ship shot gracefully through Wild Goose Rapids. Then, at 9 a.m., she eased into Lewiston's port to be greeted by a cheering crowd of docksiders, who thought the crew had been drowned, because the *Shoshone's* jackstaff had been discovered earlier, floating down the river.

In the wheelhouse, Captain Miller yelled through the speaking tube to his engineer:

"I say, Buck, if the company ever wanted a couple of men to take a ship through hell, they would send for you and me."

Buchanan snorted back:

"Hell? We've already been through it."

For years, the *Shoshone,* operating on the Columbia and Lower Snake, made good money for the Oregon Steam Navigation Company, and the directors, meeting in the plush Portland office, were at last pleased. Both ups and downs . . . That was the way of early-day steamboating in the mountain country.

Inherent in man is the desire to travel at ever greater speeds, and the skies above offer the fewest "roadblocks."

For years, tall, lean and thoughtful Captain Stewart V. Winslow had been guiding on the Columbia and Snake rivers the *Spokane* (not to be confused with the steamboat of the same name on Lake Coeur d'Alene), and, on his voyages, he had a lot of time to think about the great potential of air travel. On the Columbia, he watched the graceful and swift soaring of seagulls, and, like the latter-day fictional Jonathan Livingston Seagull, he sought to free—and expedite—his own spirit in flight.

Then, on December 17, 1903, at Kitty Hawk, North Carolina, Wilbur and Orville Wright flew briefly through the sky in an airplane. That, according to the *Lewiston Tribune* of July 30, 1904, did it.

Captain Winslow would design his own flying machine, and it would be quite different from that of the Wright brothers. It would be modeled more after a seagull in flight, and would be powered for take-off by a bicycle, pedaled by the captain.

137

What sparked the bicycle idea was the fact that Wilbur and Orville Wright operated a bicycle shop in Dayton, Ohio. Captain Winslow figured that they had inadvertently passed up a good bet. To power their plane, the Wright brothers used a 12-horsepower engine, weighing 170 pounds. A bicycle was much lighter, and, keeping weight to a minimum, the captain believed, was vital.

Most important, however, he felt, was the shaping and positioning of the double wings. The lower wing—just above the bicycle—stretched out cross-wise, tilting slightly upward in front as a bird holds its wings in flight. The upper wing, placed in the opposite direction, took on the appearance of a bird's body.

With the aid of interested crewmen, Captain Winslow completed this unique flying device while the *Spokane* was docked at Lewiston between river trips. The day of the big test came in 1904, just about six months after the Wright brothers made their modestly successful flight. If his flight could be even more successful, Winslow believed, it would really put on the map the oddly-shaped new State of Idaho, which to some Easterners was still only "a figment of Congressional imagination."

Taking the aircraft atop a 700-foot bluff overlooking the Snake River near Lewiston, Captain Winslow began pedaling madly down a 300-foot plank track to the bluff's edge. The idea was to soar gloriously over the river, and, hopefully, much farther in the manner of a present-day glider. But little things have shattered many great hopes. In this case, it was a sharp pebble. The rock punctured one of the bicycle tires, caused the flying machine to twist off the track, flip over into sagebrush, and wind up in a heap of wreckage.

Picking up the pieces, the bruised and battered captain stored them in a Lewiston warehouse until he could get around to putting them together again for another try. But he never made that try—just stuck to steamboating.

In 1934, representatives of the U.S. Judge Advocate General's office showed up in Lewiston, looking for the broken plane parts. Captain Winslow had patented his design—basically sound—and there was a question of infringement on rights by new designs being brought to the War Department. The stored remains, however, had long since been thrown away.

Even more disappointed than the legal officials was the head of the Smithsonian Institution. He had reserved a spot for the bicycle-powered, forerunner of modern plane design near the present resting place of Charles A. Lindbergh's *Spirit of St. Louis,* which on May 21, 1927, became the first airplane to fly the Atlantic Ocean between New York City and Paris. (On September 4, 1927, the *Spirit of St. Louis* was flown to Boise by Lindbergh on a transcontinental exhibition flight.)

The aging Captain Winslow was pleased about all this, but what, he said, pleased him most was the Idaho "first" which had occurred on April 6, 1926. On that day, a plane of the Varney Air Transport Company took off from Boise for Elko, Nevada, with a load of airmail. The flight drew national attention, because, although the United States Government had earlier inaugurated transcontinental airmail service between New York and California, there were no feeder lines operated by private companies to serve the bulk of the nation. The Boise-Elko flight signaled the opening of such a network.

Among the thousands of airmail letters on that historic flight was a package addressed to President Calvin Coolidge at the White House. Significantly, it contained two choice Idaho potatoes.

Chapter XII

# AT THE CRACK OF THE WHIP

"Presently the Overland stage forded the now fast receding stream and started toward Carson . . . We seemed to be in a road, but that was no proof . . . We were cold and stiff and the horses were tired. We decided to build a sagebrush fire and camp out till morning. This was wise, because if we were wandering from the right road and the snowstorm continued another day our case would be the next thing to hopeless."

—Mark Twain in *Roughing It*

In the early days, the stagecoach was generally considered the fastest—and sometimes roughest—means of public transportation.

The Concord coach, manufactured by Abbot, Downing and Company in Concord, New Hampshire, and costing about $1,500, was considered to be the top of the class. With its gracefully-curved white oak body suspended on heavy leather straps, the Concord—a "cradle on wheels"—rolled where other stages jerked.

There were some Concords in Idaho, but not many. The problem: The Concord, being big enough to carry 12 passengers, including those on top, and requiring six horses to pull it, was difficult to weave around bends on mountain roads. Therefore, early Idaho travelers usually went the hard way in smaller stages. Just to watch a driver operate, however, was worth the price ($100 from Salt Lake City to Boise City).

In the West, the stage driver was a man apart. He carried much more prestige than a train conductor, because he was also the engineer—and protector against attacks by Indians or highwaymen.

Some shy and self-effacing drivers are known to have existed. But the typical driver was likely to consider himself king of whatever road he happened to be traveling, because he was not only carrying human cargo, but, more importantly, the U.S. mail. That mail, he figured, gave him the right of way over any freighter's ox or mule-drawn wagons. If the freighter didn't pull out of the way, the stage driver's bull whip started cracking, and the freighter's oxen or mules moved aside on their own—hurriedly.

With a whip, the driver was good. Some of the breed were said to be able to flick a blue-bottle fly off a lead horse's rump without touching the animal's hair.

Especially adept with a whip was Bill Delaney, who piloted the stagecoach which ran between Clarkia and St. Maries in Northern Idaho in the 1890s. Delaney just loved to crack out his whip even when the four horses he was driving didn't need stepping up. But every man—whether a golfing or whip-wielding expert—has a bad day, and Delaney had his with two ladies in the high seat beside him.

The ladies were Mrs. Sarah Renfro of Santa, widely known as "Grandma," and an Eastern woman who was visiting the Far West for the first time. So that the newcomer could get a better view of the rugged mountain country, Delaney had suggested that she ride top-side with him. Then Grandma, noting that the woman looked apprehensive, volunteered to sit beside her to keep her company—and to comfort her.

Once a year, Grandma, who ran a hotel and served as postmistress at Santa, used to go shopping in Spokane. But that meant a long and tiring trip —riding the stage to St. Maries, then boarding a steamboat for Coeur d'Alene, and finally taking a train to Spokane. So now Grandma just did her shopping in St. Maries, and she was thoroughly enjoying the ride as the stage swerved around sharp mountain bends, bouncing high over jutting boulders.

There was no joy in the eyes of the Eastern lady, however. She looked terrified. Grandma kept patting her hand, and assuring her that "Bill Delaney is the best driver in Idaho."

Delaney, of course, lapped this up, and began swirling his long black whip with greater and greater abandon. Then, at a bend in the road, it happened. Delaney could not see a fallen tree limb ahead, and, when the stage joggled over it, the whip went awry, catching Grandma's high-plumed hat, and sending it sailing in the path of the stage. Both a front and rear wheel rolled over the hat, crunching it thoroughly.

Doubled up with laughter, Grandma began to rock in the seat.

"Never did like that hat," she hooted. "Now I can get a new one in St. Maries."

The Eastern lady began to laugh, too. And from then on the trip to St. Maries was a gay one, except that Delaney at first had difficulty in joining in the hilarity. He was very embarassed.

At St. Maries, he paid for Grandma's new hat, and hoped that that was the end of the affair. But it never was. Thereafter, whenever Delaney would come charging into St. Maries or Clarkia with his stagecoach, someone was sure to grab his hat, and shout:

"Spare my hat, Bill! Spare my hat!"

Because towns in the early West were scarce, stage stations had to be built along the lines. According to present-day standards set by the American Automobile Association, the best of the stations would be rated as "poor." But, of necessity, these stations were often used by travelers on horseback or in wagons as well as by those riding the stages.

One station was called "Hotel de Starvation—one thousand miles from hay and grain, seventy miles from wood, fifteen miles from water, and only twelve inches from hell." When a traveler, stopping for the night at Hotel de Starvation, balked at putting his horses in the station's stable because "the flies have left no room," the landlady told him to forget it, and come to dinner.

"Just wait a few minutes," she said, "and the flies will all be in the dining room."

The man who ruled over more stage drivers and stations than any other individual in the early 1860s was Ben Holladay, a big fellow with more hair on his upper lip and chin than on his head. Known as "King of the Stage Coaches" to his friends and as "Napoleon of the West" to his enemies, he built, through his Holladay Overland Mail and Express Company, an empire extending from Kansas to California, then up into Idaho, with offshoots to The Dalles, Oregon, and Virginia City, Montana. To move several hundred stages over the 3,145 miles of the line, it took more than 2,000 horses, running up an annual feed bill of about a million dollars. And, on all of the rugged stretches, Holladay saw that the stages really rolled.

A typical Mark Twain tribute was paid to the stage tycoon by the famed humorist in his book, "Roughing It." Twain related the story of Jack, a young American visiting the Holy Land. There, an elderly pilgrim tried to impress upon the youth the greatness of Moses, who, "with unfailing sagacity guided the children of Israel for forty years across three hundred miles of fearful desert." Then, according to Twain, Jack replied:

"Forty years? Only three hundred miles? Hump! Ben Holladay would have fetched him through in thirty-six hours."

Of course, when Moses ran into trouble, he could not call on the U.S. Cavalry for help. Holladay could, and did.

In 1865, he got a report from Idaho on raids by Chief Pocatello's warriors:

"They have stolen several head of our mail stock, stripping the line completely of the stock at one time between Snake River station and Salmon Falls ferry. They have fired upon our employees and have driven others out of our stations."

Holladay roared for retaliatory action by the cavalry at Fort Boise. As a result, troops under Lieutenant James Curry established Camp Reed at Rock Creek on the overland stage line. Another camp, under Captain E. Palmer, was set up at the junction of the Salt Lake City-Virginia City-Boise City roads, three miles east of Fort Hall. From these camps and other points, the cavalry began patrolling the routes of the stages. On July 17, in an encounter with raiding Indians on Jordan Creek in Owyhee County, the soldiers killed four of the red men. A month later, during a 300-mile scouting trip to the headwaters of the Salmon, the cavalry killed three more Indians, and captured three. South of Boise, a large party of Indians was routed without count of dead.

These actions led to a council in 1866 at which Idaho's Territorial Governor, Caleb Lyon, made a treaty with the Shoshones. At the council, Chief Biting Bear asked "the Great White Father at Washington to take care of bad white men as well as bad red men."

141

Biting Bear had something. Actually, bad white men—highway robbers—gave the stage lines more trouble than bad red men.

Portneuf Canyon, southeast of present-day Pocatello, was considered to be one of the most dangerous pieces of freeway in the entire West. Gold from Montana was carried by stage over the route to Salt Lake City. And frequently highwaymen lurked behind boulders and brush, giving the area the name of Robbers' Roost.

On July 13, 1865, a southbound stage from Montana Territory—a big Concord—rocketed through the canyon, its leathers squeaking from too much dust and too little oil. A man by the name of Frank Williams, taking more than a casual interest in the scenery, was driving. He should have seen a half-dozen highwaymen stepping out of the brush in time to make a run for it, but he apparently did not.

Jerking the horses' reins—"ribbons," they were sometimes called—he slowed the Concord to a stop, and held up his hands. This gesture of surrender was not enough for the robbers, however. They started pouring lead into the stage. Several of the passengers returned the fire, but could not match that of the highwaymen. Four passengers were killed, and two wounded.

The robbers knew exactly what they were looking for—$70,000 in gold in the stage's boot. Taking this and more gold and valuables from the passengers, dead or alive, they raced to hidden horses, and rode off.

After burying the dead, Williams drove the bullet-riddled stage with the wounded passengers to Malad. Ten days later, he resigned from the Holladay Overland Mail and Express Company, and headed for Salt Lake City, where he began to spend money freely. Next, he went to Denver, tossing out more money as if he had an endless supply. At Denver, vigilante friends of the slain men, who suspected Williams of being a party to the Portneuf Canyon holdup, caught up with him, escorted him to the nearest tree, and hanged him. The actual robbers were never caught.

Stages out of the Boise Basin also carried a lot of gold, and were often subject to robbery.

On November 8, 1864, a stage headed south from Boise had not gotten far when it was held up by three masked men on horseback. Jake Easely, the driver, was ordered to unhitch the horses. When he remonstrated that this was not necessary, a bullet kicked up dust at his feet. He unhitched the horses.

Then, the passengers, W. R. Parks, B. F. Dursheill and John Harmer—were ordered to climb out of the stage. As they did so, Harmer drew a pistol—and accidentally shot Parks in the hip. Dismounting and disarming Harmer, the robbers proceeded to collect loot from all three of the men: Parks—$160 in currency and $100 in coin; Dursheill—$300 in currency and $300 in gold dust; and Harmer—$500 in currency and $50 in dust.

Finding no more treasure in the stage, the robbers walked over to Driver Easely, and thoroughly cursed him for "hauling so poor a crowd." With that off their minds, they mounted their horses, and galloped across the hills.

They were never caught. It was suspected that a bad man from Bitter Creek known as "Cross Roads Jack" was one of them, but he had a perfect alibi. On the morning of the holdup, he had been killed in a shooting match in the City Bakery Saloon in Idaho City. (As he died, he complained bitterly that his new suit had been shot full of holes.)

Most irritating of holdups for Holladay was the one in which he himself was the victim. He and his ailing wife were being driven from Denver to Salt Lake

City in the Ben Holladay Special—a plushly-fitted Concord which had been especially designed for the "king"—when two robbers stepped in front of the moving vehicle. One leveled a shotgun, and the other a pistol. The driver reined up, and, before Holladay could draw his always handy pistol, he was looking into the muzzle of the shotgun. His wife did not move. She was sleeping.

"Throw up your hands," the man behind the shotgun said. "We want all your money and valuables."

That was a large order, because Holladay was carrying $40,000 in his money belt, several hundred dollars more in coat pockets, an expensive key-wind watch, and an emerald tie pin valued at $8,000 (in a secret pocket).

"You can have everything I've got," Holladay declared. "Just don't go shooting off any guns. My wife is ill, and, if she awakens to a scene like this, I don't know what will happen."

After handing over the handsome gold watch, the stage magnate went through his pockets, coming up with a fistful of currency.

"Take it all, and go quietly."

But the robbers were in no hurry. Looking for more loot, they probed the stage, careful not to awaken Mrs. Holladay. Her distinguished husband, now standing outside, disarmed and with his hands in the air, turned to the robber with the pistol.

"My mustache—it's itching something terrible. Can I scratch it?"

"No . . . but I can."

With that, the highwayman scraped the pistol across Holladay's upper lip, taking some skin with it.

"Feel better?"

"Uh, yes. Thanks."

Shortly thereafter, the robbers departed, and Holladay, climbing back into the stage, signaled the driver to get going. When Mrs. Holladay awakened some miles down the road, she had a puzzled look on her face.

"Ben," she said, "I dreamed that there was some trouble. Was there?"

"No, dear—nothing to speak of."

And Holladay patted the hidden $40,000 in currency and the $8,000 emerald tie pin.

It is doubtful that the holdup had anything to do with it, but a short time afterwards Holladay began dickering with his biggest competitor—Wells, Fargo and Company. Probably the major factor involved in this move was the westward push of the railroads. Under any circumstances, on November 1, 1866, Holladay sold his stage lines to Wells, Fargo and Company for $1,500,000 in cash and $300,000 in stock, plus a directorship in the express firm.

Thus, by 1867, Wells, Fargo and Company was the dominant name on stages which rolled through Idaho as well as the rest of the West. That did not mean, however, there were no independent operators of significance.

Take Felix Warren, for instance. Running stages out of Lewiston to Genesee, Moscow, Troy, Kendrick, Colfax, Sprague, Dayton and Spokane, he had about 50 employees—drivers, hostlers, blacksmiths and agents. Daily, these men got his message:

"Don't abuse the horses, but don't be late."

With a Van Dyke beard, Warren looked enough like Buffalo Bill to be a first cousin. And, like the famous plainsman, he loved horses—loved them well enough to drive a stage himself.

Although a hearty man, he was a gentle exception to most drivers. His one gesture with a pronounced flourish was to stride into a saloon, clatter a $20 gold piece on the bar, and shout:

"Drinks for the house!"

While he was a stickler for keeping schedules, Warren did not hesitate to foul one up when necessary—as on a trip from Lewiston to Genesee. In his stage on that occasion, he had only two passengers, both female. One was a very thin old woman, and the other was a very pregnant young woman.

Nearing the summit of the Lewiston Hill, the old woman called up to Warren in the driver's seat:

"We'll have to stop. We're going to have a baby on our hands shortly."

"Whoa!" said Warren to the horses. Climbing down, he added to the old woman, "Can I be of any help?"

The old woman looked at him scornfully, so Warren unhitched the horses, and let them graze. Then he strolled over to the edge of the road, and, for a half hour, just gazed down at the valley where the Snake and Clearwater rivers meet—a scene which Margaret Bourke White, the world-traveled photographer, would later describe as "one of the most fantastic I have ever witnessed."

A baby's cry from the coach broke Warren's revery, and, after a bit, the old woman signaled him to come over and have a look.

"Well, I do declare! That's a handsome baby—so handsome, in fact, I'm not going to charge an extra fare."

And soon Warren and his three passengers were again rolling up the hill.

144

Chapter XIII

# RAILS REFLECTING THE PROMISE OF TOMORROW

"Clattering along beneath a billow of white steam and smoke from the Iron Horse . . . (was) the symbol of the end of the wilderness days. In a few short decades this rattling, snorting mechanism would span the entire West with shining ribbons of rail, driving the buffalo, covered wagons, and even the palatial river steamers into obscurity."

—George B. Abdill in *Rails West*

In 1859, the visionary New York newspaper editor, Horace Greeley, bounced across the continent to California in a stagecoach. Between bounces, he made notes for his book, "An Overland Journey"—notes which only he could decipher because his handwriting was notoriously atrocious. The notes referred to a "fearful dearth of water," but they also recorded that, despite the shortage of water in vast areas, the farmers' frontier was steadily creeping westward. Then, too, there was all that gold in the Far West. Greeley concluded that it would not only be smart for a young man to go west, but that a railroad should do likewise.

Editorially, he campaigned for ribbons of steel to bind the nation together. Tying of the knot, however, would have to wait until after the Civil War. But, once that war was ended, the people of the United States were more than ready to accept Greeley's advice. The only question was financing.

145

Private entrepreneurs were reluctant to take on the highly speculative project. So they got offers of aid from the government, including a gift of every other section of federal land on transcontinental right-of-ways. The argument was that, through the donations of land, the government was creating a new market for all its holdings, millions of acres which would otherwise remain unproductive and bring no taxes for years while "the prospective settler was loafing in the slums and grog shops of Eastern cities." Too, in return for the donation, the railroads would provide free transportation for livestock of all emigrants traveling westward.

(In the 1960s, Dr. William Fitzgerald of Mississippi dug up this old law when he moved west to accept the position of University Physician at the University of Idaho. He got a free ride for his horses and hound dogs. For the historically-minded physician and his family, the trip from the Deep South to the Far West was much more comfortable than for many of the pioneers. Early emigrant trains had no seat cushions, were warmed by flat-topped stoves on which the passengers could heat food or drinks, and had an arrangement by which boards could be laid out for bunks, with the passengers covering themselves with coats or shawls.)

Although the champagne-drenched knot, linking the Union Pacific and the Central Pacific, was tied at Promontory Summit, Utah, on May 10, 1869, and Idaho soon began deriving fringe benefits, the people of the Gem Territory were very unhappy. The *Idaho Statesman* argued that the Union Pacific should turn north—through Idaho—to tap the coastal trade, pointing out that "our gem of territories soon to be a state" was on a natural route to the Columbia River, to Portland and to Seattle. Too, there were Idaho's booming gold mines, plus the thriving ones in Montana. And, with the coming of the railroad, more rocks would be unlocked. Another line should reach out to Montana—through Idaho. One way or another, Idaho wanted a railroad.

In 1880, it finally got one of narrow gauge (changed to standard gauge in 1887) across the southeastern corner of the Territory—the Utah Northern (later, the Utah & Northern). Organized by 17 Mormons of Utah's Cache Valley with the blessing of Brigham Young, the Utah Northern Railroad Company began operations on August 23, 1871. Leader of the promoters was William B. Preston of Logan, Utah, who became known as "the father of Idaho's first railroad."

Construction of the railroad, destined to connect Ogden, Utah, with Butte, Montana (later, with Garrison), and to pass through Franklin, Preston, Pocatello, Blackfoot and Idaho Falls, was slow. Much of the work was done by farmers along the way who had to blend their railroad building with regular chores.

Still, there was no loss of time in fighting Indians as in the carving of the UP Trail across the Great Plains. (Union Pacific crews got no farther than 220 miles west of Omaha before they encountered the first of many attacks by Indians. Near Plum Creek in August, 1866, about 40 Sioux twisted newly-laid rails, wrecking a freight train. Then the Indians attacked the workers aboard the train, killing about a dozen of them, including the engineer and fireman, and looting and burning the cars. When heavily armed civilians approached the scene the next day, the Indians were still celebrating, some riding around with looted strips of calico tied to their horses' tails, and others stretched out beside two barrels of whiskey, also salvaged from the wreckage.)

Pay on the Utah Northern was in the form of railroad vouchers, which circulated as a medium of exchange. Wives of the farmers prepared the meals, and toted them on carts to the construction sites, but they got no pay. Even with this saving, however, the Utah Northern ran into financial trouble.

With flash floods washing away earth grades, maintenance costs ran high. Then there were snowstorms which called for considerable hand-shoveling on the tracks. In March, 1874, a storm blocked miles of track between Franklin and Ogden, requiring 200 men to shovel for seven days, and causing one of them to comment:

"If all the snow I've shoveled was grain, it would feed a hundred mules for a hundred years."

Matter of fact, there were some people who thought that it would be better to forget the railroad, and to continue to rely on mule-power. That appeared to be almost an economic necessity in 1876 when John W. Young, a son of Mormon Leader Brigham Young, appealed for help to Jay Gould. (In 1875, when Iowa farmers, building a railroad from the Mississippi to the Missouri, ran into financial trouble, they substituted wood for steel, forming rails out of hard maple. But there was no maple handy on the Idaho construction sites.)

New York Financier Gould, who, with his financial manipulations, was better known as a wrecker of railroads than as a builder, saw lucrative possibilities in the Utah Northern. He did not know much about Idaho at the time, but he had visited Montana, and was keenly interested in its gold bonanza. So he arranged the financing to buy the Utah Northern's stock at sacrifice prices. Later, in 1877, the line was reorganized under the name of Utah & Northern, which was felt to take in more territory, and the ownership and management were transferred to the Union Pacific.

While Gould was still in charge, he came out to look at construction in Idaho near Franklin. Walking along the tracks, he began picking up spikes and bolts dropped by workmen.

"You be a thrifty man," observed a farmer.

"And well I should be," replied Gould. "Thrift is the foundation of any great enterprise."

And thrift became a watchword on the Utah & Northern. Gould asked for exemption from taxes for 25 years, and didn't get it. But, with improved financing and management, the line moved more rapidly through Idaho—until it got to the Fort Hall Indian Reservation.

Long "pow-wows" were held with the Indians on the amount to be paid for the right-of-way through the reservation. The *Idaho World* of Boise, which boasted that it provided "more local reading matter than any paper of its size in the United States," extended its interests to call for "blotting out of the Fort Hall Reservation and removing of the gentle Bannocks to some better hunting grounds, and thus preparing the way for an influx of white population into the Snake River Valley."

This proved unnecessary. The Bannocks finally agreed to let the railroad through the reservation for 500 head of good cattle, plus free rides for the Indians on the railroad—on the outside of the cars, that is. But what greater thrill could there be for a red man than biting the wind on an iron horse? As for accidents and possible lawsuits, the railroads, at the time, didn't seem greatly worried about them. Neither was it worried about paying the 500 head of cattle to the Indians. Actual delivery was not made until several years later.

By May 9, 1880, the Utah and Northern line had wound 206.36 miles through Idaho to the Montana border. Idaho had a railroad. Settlers began to travel on it into the Territory. And posters in depots pointed out to potential

147

tourists that "the wonderful lava fissures of eastern Idaho . . . snowy peaks of the beautiful Salmon River Range, and glaciers of the Three Tetons are among features afforded from palace and parlor car windows on the Utah & Northern Railway."

But were Idahoans now happy? Not exactly.

Oh, there were some celebrations along the line, with the shooting of fire-crackers and shotguns and rifles, when the Utah & Northern reached the Montana border. Folk in Eagle Rock (Idaho Falls) were particularly jubilant because the main repair yards in Idaho had been established there. (Later, the yards would be relocated at Pocatello, and there would be strained relations between the two towns.)

But only one corner of big, sprawling Idaho was being served by rail. Actually, it appeared as if Montana would profit more than Idaho from the Utah & Northern. Certainly, Mayor Henry Jacobs of Butte thought that was the case when word was flashed to him by telegraph that the Montana border had been reached. The mayor made a speech to a crowd gathered at Owsley Hall in the copper city, declaring that the event was the most significant in Montana's history, because the railroad would not only bring "population, progress and prosperity to the Territory," but would quickly produce statehood for it. Some Idahoans groaned when they read that.

In 1881, things began looking up railwise for Idaho. Late that summer, the Union Pacific began construction of its Oregon Short Line. This line, taking off from the Union Pacific's main line at Granger, Wyoming, would run through Montpelier to Pocatello, then would go through Southern Idaho along and across the Snake River to Huntington, Oregon, where it would connect with the Oregon Railway and Navigation Company line reaching to Portland. (The latter line was eventually absorbed by the Union Pacific.)

Building of the Oregon Short Line across Idaho (434.06 miles) was hard and slow, and contractors were reported to have lost a total of $3,000,000. Most bitter of the contractors was Dallin & Company of Chicago, which ran advertisements in newspapers stating:

"Contractors and others who have been victimized on the Oregon Short Line are invited to send us a clear, succinct statement of their wrongs . . . We question whether a more dishonorable or reprehensible record can be found than that of the unscrupulous creatures who had the building of that badly located road. No act of duplicity or chicanery do we consider them incapable of, and honestly believe for fraud, imbecility, mismanagement, misrepresentation and general rascality, there is no parallel in railroad history."

Contractors today sometimes lose money, but rarely their tempers to such an extent. Still, it used to be good for a man to get off his mind what he actually thought, and not worry about libel laws.

Finally, on November 10, 1884, construction was finished on the Oregon Short Line, completing an 1,820-mile rail connection between Omaha and Portland. Just prior to completion of the line, a special train, with railroad and territorial dignitaries aboard, started across Idaho from Pocatello. It got as far as American Falls without any complications.

American Falls is now a center for the growing of such crops as wheat and potatoes, but in 1884 it was strictly a cow town, and all the ranch hands for miles around were on hand to greet the special train. Used to singing sad songs on the range without any musical accompaniment, the cowboys were

148

delighted to learn that the train had on board a top band from Salt Lake City. They called for music on the station platform, and got it.

When the bandsmen started to pick up their instruments at the urgent tooting of the train whistle, the cowboys called for more. The bandsmen kept on moving to the train, so a couple of the range riders pulled out their pistols, and began to place bullets around the feet of the leader. Result: The band played on and on until the cowboys finally decided that they had had enough.

The *Police Gazette,* which was very popular barbershop reading in those days, printed a lurid account "of a train trying to get through the wild cowboys of Idaho." Eastern newspapers also picked up—and enlarged upon—stories of the affair. As for the dignitaries on the train, they thought it was great sport.

Upon the final completion of the line, there was general rejoicing throughout Southern Idaho, although it was somewhat subdued in Boise, because that town was not on the main track. The late Thomas Donaldson, who held various governmental positions in early Boise, explained in his book, "Idaho of Yesterday":

"When it was practically assured that the Oregon Short Line was to be constructed, I did all within my power to impress upon Boise friends the importance of inducing the Union Pacific to run the line through Boise. The customary and infallible argument, money, was the sole requisite. One man urged the question, but no general subscriptions were made. For thirty thousand dollars Boise could have been located to great advantage. As it resulted, the capital of the territory was forced to be content with a branch railroad, extending twenty miles west to join the Oregon Short Line."

Referring to the new railroad as the "Oregon Crooked Line," the *Idaho Statesman* declared:

"It is evident that railroads are built not to accommodate the people, but to accommodate the builders. We do not believe, however, that the branch will make much difference with the growth and prosperity of Boise City."

Brave words indicating that Boise didn't give a hoot! But it did. For a long time—about 40 years—Boiseans regretted not putting up the $30,000 subsidy —until the Capital City finally got on the main line.

The Union Pacific had contended that to run the main track of the Oregon Short Line through Boise, which lay considerably below the cross-basin level, would have increased the grade so that helper engines would have been necessary. A branch line to Boise was much more feasible, according to the Union Pacific's engineers—something Boiseans really never did buy.

There was some consolation in the fact that the Union Pacific, in scurrying to Promontory Summit to join with the Central Pacific, had missed Salt Lake City, capital of Utah Territory. And down in New Mexico it was contended that "four railroads were built from border to border without really touching a town." But these crumbs of comfort did not lessen the train problems for Boise.

Limited to the branch line service, a Boise businessman who had to run over to Mountain Home, was forced to travel west for 20 miles, catch a train on the main line (after an annoying wait), and then journey southeast for 50 miles.

Still, Boiseans took some pride in the branch line which became known as the "Pony Express." The *Idaho Statesman* dutifully reported the acquiring of each new piece of equipment:

"The car (added in May, 1903) is equipped with electric lights, steam heat,

149

and all other modern conveniences. A new chair car and baggage car are expected to arrive in a few days. The wash room will be supplied with towels, etc., and everything kept in apple pie order."

Meanwhile, in the Eighties, each main line train which churned through Southern Idaho never failed to cause a stir of excitement. Probably the ultimate in this regard was reported by the *Caldwell Tribune* in 1886:
"One of the curiosities of the town this week was an old man probably 70 years old and a boy about 16 who caught their first view of a railroad while here. The boy, especially, was as wild as a deer and could not be induced to go into a restaurant to eat. He walked around town with his eyes sticking out like marbles and was prepared to jump at what was to him any unusual sound. The old gentleman was not much better and when the train came in they fortified themselves about a block away and gazed with evident terror and wonderment. We do not know where they hailed from, but evidently they had been holed up in some mountain retreat for many years past."

The fear of the mountain man and boy of a train, however, was nothing compared with that of Ah Moon and Ah Loy, two ancient Chinese at Pierce.
After living in the Northern Idaho mining town for 50 years, Ah Moon and Ah Loy decided in 1927 to return to China to die to be sure that they would be buried there. That year the remains of all Chinese buried at Pierce had been removed from their Idaho graves, and shipped back to China. That is, all the dead Chinese had been rendered this vital service except one. His remains are still at Pierce. The reason: He had neglected to pay dues to his tong.
This worried Ah Moon and Ah Loy, so with great trepidation they prepared to take their first train ride—a trip to Portland where a steamer could be boarded for China. The two got on the train all right, but as soon as it began to lurch into motion they began to scream, and tried to jump off. With the aid of husky male passengers, the conductor managed to hold the Chinese in their seats until they calmed down—after a fashion. All the way to Portland, Ah Moon and Ah Loy kept assuring fellow travelers that they would rather be riding a dragon.

While it had been a struggle to get a single railroad line across Southern Idaho, there was no problem in Northern Idaho. The railroad tycoons were battling one another in the race to join the Pacific Coast with the rest of the nation by northern routes, and, by 1910, three transcontinental railroads crossed Northern Idaho. The first, completed in 1882, was the Northern Pacific, linking Duluth, Minnesota, with Tacoma, Washington. Ten years later came the Great Northern under a head of steam generated by James J. Hill, most experienced railroader of all the early transporation giants. Then, in May, 1910, the main line of the Chicago, Milwaukee and St. Paul was finished between the Missouri River and Puget Sound.
Idaho never did get a main line running from its northern tip to southern border, but, to get out farm products, timber and ore, and to bring in people, branch lines sprouted all over the place. Moscow, for instance, boasted early in its history branch lines of the Northern Pacific, Great Northern and Union Pacific, providing quite a choice in the shipping of grain and livestock. Narrow Burke, where the rails had to be squeezed down the middle of Main Street and merchants had to raise their awnings when a train came through, was served by two branch lines. To accommodate Mormon settlers at Pocatello

150

Creek, a two-mile branch line was run from Pocatello. Naturally, it became known as the "Mormon Main Line." Between 1870 and 1910—the peak of rail building in Idaho—the population rose from 14,999 (an official but actually somewhat low figure) to 325,594.

How much did the railroad mean to a town—to the people in and around it?

The editor of the *Wood River Times* spoke for the women when the railroad was on its way to Hailey:

"To the women, the coming of the railroad will mean contact with the outer world. Whether they use it or not, it stands for progress, new neighbors, churches and activities to drive out the loneliness of the long winters. It means dress goods will be cheaper, and the telegraph will bring the latest news. Psychologically, it means everything."

Robert Strahorn, personable and optimistic publicity man for the Union Pacific, declared that, with heavy shipments of ore, "Hailey will become the Denver of Idaho." But he was accustomed to being generous with his predictions for small towns all the way between Omaha and Portland—towns, like Hailey, which were awaiting the magic touch of the rail lines. (Strahorn became very unpopular in Boise when he was accused of influencing the Union Pacific in routing the Oregon Short Line through Caldwell instead of Boise. Some Boise residents not only hung him in effigy, but, Strahorn said, threatened to "commit the act on me personally.")

From his philosophical reflections on the early railroad trains, Henry David Thoreau had this to say:

"They come and go with such regularity and precision, and their whistle can be heard so far, that farmers set their clocks by them, and thus one well regulated institution regulates the whole country. Have not men improved somewhat in punctuality since the railroad was invented? Do they not talk and think faster in the depot than they did in the stage office?"

Of all Idaho towns, Pocatello profited most by the coming of the railroads. When the shops of the Utah & Northern began moving there from Eagle Rock (Idaho Falls) on July 4, 1886 (there was a minimum of celebrating in Eagle Rock that year), Pocatello was a very small community—not much more than the Pacific Hotel and a depot. But moving of the shops brought to Pocatello about 500 workers, some with families.

Pocatello quickly became a roaring town, although Charley Nopper, manager of the bar at the Pacific Hotel, did his best to subdue the "rootin' and tootin'." Cooperating with railroad officials to keep the men in working shape, Nopper, operated for a while on a most unusual schedule of 15 minutes open and two hours closed. This frustrating practice encouraged the drinking of a shot of whiskey with a glass of beer for a chaser, the combination becoming locally and affectionately known as the "Pocatello Bomb." The bomb, which took only 15 minutes to explode in a man's stomach, dropped in popularity, however, when competition of newly arising saloons forced a change in the Pacific's schedule.

There was also change in the townsite. More space was needed, and 1,840 acres were purchased from the Bannocks and Shoshones at $8 an acre. If the price seems low, it should be remembered that New York's Manhattan Island was obtained from the Indians for little more than some strings of beads.

Wide-open gambling was a part of early Pocatello, and John ("Mizzoo") Townsend, who looked like a whiskered prospector minus a burro, was very much a part of the gambling. Drifting in from Missouri in 1889—that's why he

151

was known as Mizzoo—he announced that he was the best poker player in Idaho. And, from time to time at a game he ran in his second-hand store, he proved that he was indeed very good.

Mizzoo had a blackboard in front of his place on which he would write assorted messages such as:

"For rent—four-room house. Plenty of ventilation. Windows all out. No extra charge for bedbugs. I'll play any man from any land any game he can name for any amount."

When a notorious gambler from the Owyhee Country came to town and cleaned him, Mizzoo rushed out, and added another word to the sign:

"Once."

Not all of early Pocatello, however, was as rough as the surrounding lava beds. Culture began emerging in the town. Forming the Civic Club, a group of women petitioned the city council for a library. When they were turned down, they held a "book tea," with everyone attending it bringing at least one book. Following the successful tea, Pocatello's first library was opened in the front room of Mrs. Sam Winter's home.

Then there were home talent entertainments staged in makeshift auditoriums of railroad buildings. With the opening of the Auditorium Theatre, commercial troupes supplied top entertainment. On jumps between Salt Lake City and Portland, stage performers found that Pocatello was a natural and profitable stop.

Soon overshadowing the Auditorium was the Opera House, really plush with its red velvet seats, loges and boxes. It knew the acting of various Shakespearean companies and the singing of Schumann-Heink. For several years, the Opera House was the nation's only theatre in which the lights could be dimmed—a local invention.

Too, Pocatello early looked to better and higher education for its youth. In 1901, the State established the Academy of Idaho, providing for it a two-block long campus with two buildings. In time, the Academy became Idaho State University.

But part of the fame of early Pocatello was derived simply from some of the famous people who knew it "back when." Working as a young man in a Pocatello book shop was Edgar Rice Burroughs, who created the fictional Tarzan and men in outer space long before the first reported sighting of an "Unidentified Flying Object" was made on June 24, 1947, by Kenneth Arnold, an Idaho businessman flying his private plane near Mount Rainier in Washington. Walter P. Chrysler, automobile pioneer of distinction who was a founder and the first president of the Chrysler Corporation, got his mechanical start in Pocatello's railroad shops. And Judy Garland was cradled in a theatrical trunk at Pocatello as Frances Gumm, daughter of the vaudeville team of Frank and Ethel Gumm, billed at a Pocatello theatre as Jack and Virginia Lee, "Sweet Southern Singers." Judy would long linger in the memories of the many even if she had done no more than sing about the other side of the rainbow in "The Wizard of Oz" movie.

With Pocatello becoming known as the "Gateway City" by providing a main junction for both the Utah & Northern and the Oregon Short Line, Boise naturally began to press hard "to get on the main line." But accomplishment of the feat took a lot of doing, and it was not achieved until April 16, 1925—a big day for Boise.

The *Idaho Daily Statesman* referred to the marking of the event as "not a celebration, but a congeries of celebrations." Morning and afternoon programs were on the formal side, but the evening became one big carnival with flying confetti, tooting horns, beating drums and dancing feet as Boiseans strove mightily to carry out Mayor E. B. Sherman's dictum to "have one big time all day."

Setting off all this commotion was the coming in the morning of a special train, bearing Carl R. Gray, president of the Union Pacific. To greet him, many persons had arrived early at the beautiful new depot on the hillside overlooking Capitol Drive, the city and the State Capitol Building. For a while, the spectators were fascinated by an airplane flying overhead, little realizing that in years to come this mode of travel would overshadow that of trains, and Boise would once again be off the main line for rail passenger service.

On this glorious April day in 1925, there was not a dark cloud in the sky—just floating rings of white smoke puffing skyward off in the distance. A small boy shouted:

"Here she comes!"

The crowd cheered both the observant boy and the approaching train. A gun of the 148th Field Artillery, Battery D, boomed and continued to boom until the train whistled into the station at 10:27 a.m. Now the airplane swooped lower over the crowd, but little attention was paid to it. The train was the thing.

Dressed as a brakeman, Rose Regan ran down the tracks, waving a red flag and calling for President Gray. When he appeared, she announced:

"Mr. Gray, there is an obstruction ahead that only you can remove."

The "obstruction" consisted of 21 girls, representing the pulchritude of Boise and wearing hoopskirts and bonnets, decorated with apple blossoms. Escorted by "Brakeman Rose," Gray moved through the obstruction. As he did so, the girls released a flock of pigeons.

Besides presenting Gray with a key to the city, Mayor Sherman handed the Union Pacific president a loaf of bread and a salt cellar, which, the mayor said, followed an old Persian custom. Thomas J. Atkins, a Boise blacksmith, speaking as "one of the workers in the ranks of the toilers of Idaho," gave Gray an inkwell set in a horseshoe. The UP president responded by saying that "the railroad business seemed prosaic—until now."

In referring to the parade in the afternoon, he went further by calling it a "revelation." With pioneering the theme of the floats, aided and abetted by Indians and cowboys on horseback, the parade was both impressive and colorful. But what old-timers in Boise remember most was the donkey. It was carrying on its back a barrel of "whiskey," and, with each motion of hoofs, the barrel took on a churning motion. Someone shouted:

"There goes the original cocktail shaker!"

Indeed, it was an historic day, but more history was in the making with the advance of the automobile, the bus, and the airplane. Freight trains would continue to be an important factor in Idaho, but passenger trains would gradually fade from the scene.

As this is written, Idahoans were looking forward to the revival of intercontinental passenger train service through the southern part of the State via the National Railroad Passenger Corporation—Amtrak. This writer is all for the Amtrak renaissance if for no other reason than that it will again give travelers an opportunity to admire Boise's depot, with its Spanish-Italian decor gracefully capped by an 80-foot bell and clock tower. There is no more beautiful railroad station in the entire West.

154

Chapter XIV

# 'STRING 'EM OUT!'

"Punchin' cows in these mountains ain't like it is in a book I read, where all the cute waddie had ter do was ride slick fat horses, sleep on a geese-hair bed, set the boss' daughter en afterwards marry her, en she the prettiest girl in the West. I wonder why some sure-enough cowhand don't write the truth about it, heh?"

—Jess Hill, early cowboy, as quoted in *Pardner of the Wind* by Nathan Howard (Jack) Thorp

Down in Waco, Texas, on April 15, 1871, 1,500 head of longhorn cattle were bawling their way through branding chutes, getting the letter "T" singed on their hides. This herd now belonged to George R. Miller, with David L. Shirk, foreman of the 10-man drive crew, holding a share of 250 head, and another cowboy named Walters, also 250 head. The cattle had been purchased at $4.50 per four-year-old cow, and $5.75 per five-year-old.

Shirk, a lean and handsome young man with dark, curly hair and a triangular mustache, sat on a chute rail, breathing thick dust as if he enjoyed it. A little black boy, sitting beside him, asked:

"You goin' to Dodge?"

Shirk shook his head.

155

"That's the easy way. We're goin' after bigger money. Headin' for Idaho. The miners there are mighty hungry for good Texas beef."

"Where's Idaho?"

"Up north apiece."

"Will big you take little me along? I'm mighty handy doin' chores."

Shirk looked down at the eager youngster.

"You want to get scalped maybe by Indians?"

The boy rubbed his head.

"No, suh!"

"Then you better stay right here in Waco."

So the long drive north started—without the little black boy. On a good day, as many as 20 miles were covered. More often than not, the distance was much less. Relaxing in the saddle every now and then, the cowboys would merely keep a lazy eye on the cattle, letting them drift at their own pace. As one old-timer put it, "Anybody rarin' to git someplace in a hurry had no business on a cattle drive." And the life was as lonesome as it was slow. To meet one white man on a day's ride was considered a circumstance; to meet two was a happening.

The cattle lived entirely off the land, and their herders partially so from the wild game they were able to kill. At that time of year, the grass along stream banks was sometimes belly high to the cows. For the men, from time to time, there was fresh buffalo meat in the pot. Too, there were always a lot of reckless rabbits to be shot. And the cook could build a sturdy breakfast around rabbit meat. A steer was rarely butchered, because the idea was to keep the count of the herd at the end of the drive as near as possible to what it was at the beginning.

Liking the challenge of throwing a rope around a buffalo's big head, a cowboy would ride down one of the wild animals, loop it by the neck, and wait for another cowboy to ride up and toss his rope around a kicking leg. Then the buffalo would be quickly dispatched with bullets. Rifle shots, minus the roping, would have been much simpler. But, as Shirk pointed out in his journals, the roping livened up the day a bit. This was the spirit of rodeo rising on the plains.

And there was more spirit of rodeo when a horse, left in the remuda too long while a sore spot healed, had to be rebroken. (On a later cattle drive out of Texas, such a horse, called Brown Fox because of its coloring, threw its rider from the saddle, and joined a wild bunch of palominos. Found a year later, Brown Fox was still wearing the saddle. When the saddle was removed, a white back was revealed. The heat of the saddle had caused the brown hair to shed, with the new hair showing up like a blanket of snow. And that is what the horse's name was changed to—Snow Blanket.)

Then there were wild turkeys to be captured for food—with a little patience. Shirk related:

"As soon as it was light enough to see one morning, we (Shirk and another cowboy named Hickman) rode along the edge of the timber. The turkeys at that hour venture out of timber to feed upon the grass insects. We had gone but a short distance when we espied a big fellow about a quarter of a mile from the woods.

" 'Now,' said Hickman. 'Follow me, and do not speak a word.'

"The turkey saw us, and began to move along parallel with the timber, we keeping between him and the woods. We kept this up for nearly a mile, when the turkey turned about and started back. When he finally reached the starting point, he again turned back. Presently, his wings dropped to his side, and we rode up and picked him up without the least difficulty. He was the fattest fowl I ever saw, weighing fully thirty pounds."

On May 8, the trail herd reached Fort Worth, with a population estimated by Shirk at about 50, a hotel, saloon, blacksmith shop and store. Three times a day the trail cook had been serving cornbread, so the cowboys who were not minding the herd hurried into the store looking for wheat flour—the makings of sourdough Dutch-oven biscuits. The store had only cornmeal. Expressing very low opinions of Fort Worth, the cowboys ambled over to the saloon.

Ten days later, the herd crossed the Raccoon River, and entered the Chickasaw Nation. Fifteen Chickasaw and Osage Indians came galloping up. Their chief declared:

"White man must pay Indian for cows eating grass."

Miller, who, with Con Shea, had driven one of the first herds of Texas cattle to Idaho's Owyhee Country in 1869 and had paid tribute on the way, was off buffalo hunting. Shirk, in charge, shook his head.

"No pay."

"My men heap fight."

"My men heap fight, too."

And that was when the Indians decided to ride off.

There was no more Indian trouble until the moonless night of July 28, when the camp was aroused by the sound of about a hundred head of cattle being driven off by red men. Saddling up, all the cowboys in camp started in pursuit. Able to move much faster than the Indians with their newly-acquired herd of cattle, the cowboys soon caught up with them.

Shooting several cows so the night wouldn't be a complete waste of time, the Indians then abandoned their loot on the hoof, and headed for the hills. The cowboys, herding the live animals back to camp that night, returned in the morning to carve up the dead ones for beef.

Actually, the big headaches on the drive to Idaho came with lightning storms in the night. Usually, the cattle could be held bunched together or circled if they started running, but on occasions they scattered, and it took a lot of hard riding to round up the strays. Sometimes the cowboys missed a few animals. And sometimes they gained a few from somebody else's herd. Also, a "dogie" buffalo calf acquired a new mother among the cattle, and began tagging along with the herd.

Then there was the day that the cook drove the chuck wagon into a stream without first watering the oxen pulling it. Naturally, the oxen paused in midstream to drink and drink. And naturally, the wagon sank lower and lower, finally tipping over into the rushing water. All the provisions in the wagon washed away. Fortunately, there were some provisions, including coffee, in another wagon, but the cook suddenly became fresh out of cornmeal, and the cowboys missed getting cornbread three times a day.

The coffee—"get up an' get it while it's hot"—was always considered good, because it was strong. The cook of the Miller-Shirk-Walters outfit, in his own way, followed the classic cattleman's recipe:

"Take two pounds of Arbuckle's, put in 'nough water to wet it down, boil for two hours, and throw in a hoss shoe. If the hoss shoe sinks, she ain't ready."

On September 10, the herd finally moved into Idaho, arriving on the plains of the Raft River where Shirk reported finding "magnificent range, the bunch

157

grass waving like a wheat field, and with water abundant." But it was far from journey's end.

Reaching the Snake River, Shirk cut out his share of the herd. Shrewdly, he rounded up the first animals to reach water—the strongest. Miller wanted to buy him out at $24 a head, but Shirk had other ideas involving the hungry miners of Silver City.

With another cowboy to help him, Shirk moved his herd down the Snake, coming in late October to the confluence of Rabbit Creek. There the two men built a grass and dirt covered dugout just big enough to crawl into for the night. This was home for the winter of 1871-72, with the cattle feeding off the surrounding white sage and bunch grass.

In May of 1872, Shirk sold off some calves, but it was not until August that he made the big sale in Silver City of the cows at $35 a head. Since leaving Waco, a year and four months had passed, and Texas, Oklahoma, Kansas, Nebraska, Wyoming and Idaho had been traversed. But Shirk had a handsome profit, considering that he had paid only an average of $5 a head for the cattle. Both Miller and Walters also did right well, although they could not match Shirk who got top prices for the top cows he had cut out.

While gold mining in Idaho thrived, there were many other big cattle drives out of the south—from California as well as from Texas. Too, there were herds trailing in from Oregon—horses and sheep as well as cattle. Some herds traveled across Idaho via the northern route of the Mullan Road, but most followed the Oregon Trail in the South. Many of these herds were not destined for sale in Idaho, but in Eastern markets (to be carried usually by rail from Green River, Wyoming.)

Boise became a main stopping point for the herders to replenish their supplies and to pick up mail. At one time, the Boise postmaster was keeping track of mail for crews of more than a dozen herds moving across Idaho.

Like the cowboys who were disgruntled upon finding only cornmeal in Fort Worth, a group of wranglers, seeking new underwear in Boise, complained bitterly because they could buy nothing except red flannel "long johns." When they moved into the high country, however, they were pleased that they had them.

Jack Porter, a grizzled Texas hand who had spent a lot of years riding the old Chisholm Trail, had come north in 1881 wtih some longhorns. Then in 1882, he was hired at $30 a month to help take a herd of 3,100 steers from Baker City, Oregon, to the Pine Ridge Indian Agency in Dakota Territory.

The cry of "String 'em out!" came on July 24.

Porter began his account of the drive across Idaho by putting first things first—describing three horses he had purchased for the trail from Nez Perce Indians.

"They were very good animals; in fact, very superior Indian horses," he said in reminiscing with Writer-Cowman John K. Rollinson. "They were prettily built, had good endurance, good dispositions, and were generally 'showy,' as they were Appaloosas with coats of various colors and spots of different shades."

Before he got far across Idaho, Porter would be glad that he had as tough horses as he did. Not only did they prove to be good swimmers in crossing the Snake River, but they held up well under the heat waves which shimmered over and around the moving herd.

At Boise, the cowboys were unhappy because they had wanted to take turns going into town to slake their thirsts, but J. H. Ford, the trail boss, said "no."

"The trail herds have been heavy through here this year, and there are two days of short grass ahead," he explained. "We keep movin'."

The cook, however, who got permission to go through town to obtain fresh vegetables, also happened to pick up a keg of beer. When the cowboys got to it, the beer was as warm as a hot toddy. But who ever complained about a hot toddy?

Grass on the Camas Prairie was lush, so Trail Boss Ford decided to camp for two days near the headwaters of Canyon Creek and Camas Creek. Wagon wheels needed tightening by soaking in Camas Creek, and some of the horses could stand new shoes. When these chores were finished, the cowboys went fishing, and the cook did right well with the catches of trout. Topping off the fish supper were wild berries, obtained by trading tobacco with some Indians.

For supper the second night on the prairie, the cowboys feasted on grilled steaks. A herd of local cattle, which carried the Shoe Sole brand of Cattle Baron A. J. Harrell, was grazing nearby, and the herders proved to be most sociable. E. W. McGatlin, foreman of the Shoe Sole outfit, had spotted a stray with a brand he could not identify—well, at least not right off—so he ordered it killed for meat, and invited the herders from Oregon over for a steak fry.

When told about the trading with Indians for berries, McGatlin chomped down hard on a piece of steak.

"Watch out for them," he warned. "They've been sort of quiet since the War of 1878, but they still don't like the idea of white men grazing cattle on Camas Prairie, an' spoilin' their camas roots. Liable to go on the warpath any time."

His words proved to be prophetic before the night was over. Although Camas Prairie was claimed by the Bannocks, it was a party of Paiutes, moving from Utah to Montana to trade bundles of the intoxicating mescal root with the Blackfeet, which caused the trouble. Camped for two days near the Shoe Sole herd, they had been sampling their trading wares extensively. When thoroughly hopped up, they decided to do the Bannocks a favor.

While the Shoe Sole cowboys were sleeping off the big steak supper, the Paiutes, whooping and waving blankets, rode into the herd, stampeding it. Then, once they had the cattle on the run, the Indians began shooting them.

The Shoe Sole herd, numbering about 400 head, raced straight for the much bigger Oregon herd, and that started another stampede. The thunder of hoofs on Camas Prairie became literally earth shaking. Added to that were the shouts of the Indians and cowboys, the firing of their guns, and the howling of some frightened coyotes. It was a night to remember, and the days that followed were not soon forgotten either.

It took the better part of a week to round up all the cattle, and to cut out the Shoe Sole cows from the Oregon herd. The Paiutes, although no doubt well pleased with the havoc they had wrought, were rounded up by a troop of cavalry from Fort Boise, and had to pay the penalty of incarceration, never making it to Montana. The cowboys were happy about that.

Trail Boss Ford was most happy when he could once more cry, "String 'em out!"

Reaching the country of the Big and Little Wood Rivers, the herd began to move across ground "strewn for the most part with lava rocks." Many sore

159

hoofs developed. Then the herd came to a deathlike region which Porter called the "Giant Lava Beds."

Intrigued by the weird formations, the cowboys took turns riding far across this home of desolation. What they did not realize was that they were being typical tourists, and were pausing to view what in 1924 would become the Craters of the Moon National Monument, now reached from Arco on U.S. Highway 20.

The cowboys, who knew how to quickly cut out their own mounts from a corral full of milling horseflesh, or how to throw and brand a calf in seconds, knew little about the moon. If they had, they would have quickly recognized the resemblance of the area over which they were riding to the formations on that distant night light in the sky.

Scientists differ about the moon's origin, but they agree that there was once terrific heat with fireworks. On the earth in Idaho's Craters area, which extends for 80 square miles, the land also boiled—at 2,000 degree Fahrenheit. It shot rocks and chunks of lava into the air from myriad openings.

Strewn over the land are "bread-crust bombs"—pieces of lava which were blown into the air from volcanoes, and which expanded in flight and solidified with an effect like crusted loaves of bread. Other chunks of lava which had been shot into the sky came back to earth in the form of teardrops.

Hardened lava flows are even more impish: one looks like a neat coil of hawsers, another like a rope tied in a knot. As the moon is webbed with crevasses, so are Idaho's Craters. The largest of these, extending in a series of fissures, is called the Great Rift. From its cracks, lava once oozed, then was sucked downward into unknown caverns. (In 1973, this strange weaving by Nature, along with the Bruneau Sand Dunes, would provide background for the motion picture, "Idaho Transfer.")

An awesome sight, agreed the cowboys in 1882, but they were glad to get out of there, because the area offered only scant forage for their bawling charges. Still, for days, there was little improvement.

Trail Boss Ford knew that the grass would be better by going to Eagle Rock (Idaho Falls), and crossing the Snake River there. But at Eagle Rock a charge of 25 cents per head of cattle would be levied to cross the Taylor Toll Bridge. (The bridge had been built in 1866-67 by James Taylor and Robert Anderson, with timbers hauled from Beaver Canyon, 80 miles north, and iron salvaged from old freight wagons and a steamboat which had been wrecked on the Missouri River.)

At Blackfoot, the river could be forded free of charge. So to Blackfoot the herd moved.

"A blistering, dry, scorched wind blew out of the southeast," said Porter. "Our lead cattle stirred up clouds of hot dust which blew into the eyes, noses, and throats of both men and beasts . . . When the 'drag' drivers looked back, there was nothing to be seen but black billows of dust."

Eleven steers dropped dead on the trek between the Craters of the Moon and Blackfoot, but the rest of the herd made it to Blackfoot. There the cattle were watered and rested before crossing the Snake. The cowboys took turns going into Blackfoot, described as "lively."

"There were stores, saloons, hitch racks, and plank sidewalks, and the tinkle of a piano was a welcome sound," related Porter. "As the voices of women were heard when the dance music started, the long, hard hours on the dusty trail were forgotten."

And, in those few words, the man from Texas summed up the spirit of the early cattle drives across Idaho.

On August 22, 1870, the Surveyor-General of Idaho wrote:

"It has been discovered that the white sage, after the maturity of its seeds in the fall, is sought for by cattle in preference to grass. As more than one-half of the wild sage in the center and southern portions of the Territory is of this species, and the climate in winter generally mild, the prospects are that cattle will be raised here to supply the neighboring country."

He was so right, except that the weather tripped him up a bit.

Owyhee County cattlemen alone were soon supplying more beef than the regional miners could eat, even if they had steaks for breakfast. And it was better meat than that which came off the trail-toughened longhorns.

David L. Shirk, the trail-rider from Waco who had referred to "good Texas beef," settled in Oregon. Eventually, he put 50,000 acres "under fence" there, then spread out into Idaho's Owyhee County. And he had to admit that "a Texas longhorn is a mighty poor excuse for supplying beef compared with a Hereford fattened in this part of the country."

But Idaho's cattle industry almost died aborning—from freezing. There were two unusual winters—very severe—in 1876 and 1888.

During that first bad one, the Shoe Sole outfit was the big loser, counting more than 15,000 cows frozen to death. In 1888, Jack Burns, a big operator out of Bruneau, lost one-fourth of his herds. That was the year it got down to 29 degrees below zero in Boise. In the hills and on the plains, it was much colder.

The Snake River froze over throughout its winding Idaho course. Cattle, used to seeking water at the river's banks, drifted out onto the ice looking for openings. And, when enough of them stalked the frozen surface, it gave way. The Snake River gulped the cattle as if it were a huge python. (The same thing happened to some of the buffalo being collected for safe-keeping in Yellowstone Park.)

Still, in 1889, with Idaho approaching statehood, Governor George L. Shoup was able to proudly announce that the Territory had 350,225 head of cattle on its ranges, producing an annual income of $8,500,000. The stock was moving to Nevada, Wyoming, California, Oregon, Montana, the Dakotas . . . Even the big butchers of Chicago were coming out to have a look at Idaho beef.

Not all the cattle ranches in early Idaho were giants. Some homesteaders boasted no more than two beef cattle—one to butcher for meat, and one to sell for money needed to buy flour and sugar and other staples. But, in time, some of those small outfits grew into big ones.

In 1880, Charles A. Campbell drove an ox team into Council Valley near the site of the present town of Council. It was a pretty valley, with both the grass and timber running taller than in other valleys through which Campbell had passed. This, he decided, was where a roving man might sit a spell—figuratively speaking, that is.

Besides Campbell, who was then 27, had spotted living in the valley a 10-year-old girl, Caroline Osborne, who had a twinkle in her eyes which intrigued him. A patient man, he waited until she reached 18. Then he married her. From this marriage were born Anna, Rollie and Loyal.

Meanwhile, Campbell had built a two-room cabin on homestead land, and started raising cattle in a small way—seven calves of mixed stock. As the years passed, this "herd" grew. So did Campbell's land holdings—up to 20,000 acres known as the Circle-C Ranch, with grazing rights on many more thousands of acres.

Campbell died in 1932 after a long and good—although at times rugged—life. Unfortunately, he did not live five more years, because, in 1937, the Union Pacific made quite a to-do over a shipment of Circle-C cattle—4,500 Herefords, comprising the biggest single shipment in the railroad's history. To roll that many cattle east, it took a train of 108 cars.

And so, one way or another, the big cattle ranches in Southern Idaho developed, particularly in the counties of Owyhee, Idaho, Valley, Cassia, Bannock, Camas, Blaine, Butte, Lemhi and Custer.

The peak for the open-range cattle industry in Idaho was between the years 1880 and 1888. Those were the years when the cowboy was "king," even though a poor and unpolished one. His total assets or "plunder" might be no more than a horse and saddle, six-shooter, bedroll and gold watch. Yet he was a man in command of his destiny.

He might be a planless rover, but the point was that, if he didn't like things in one place, he could just climb into his saddle, and ride to another. And, when the barbed wire fences came and blocked his path, he had wire cutters in his saddle bag. There was no compunction about using the cutters, because, after all, a cut fence provided work for other wranglers.

A particularly positive view of the early cowboy was expressed in the autobiography of Theodore Roosevelt, who operated the Elkhorn Ranch in North Dakota in the 1880s. Roosevelt wrote:

"Life on a cattle ranch in those days taught a man self-reliance, hardihood, and the value of instant decision."

If the cowboy wanted to settle down on a ranch of his own, it did not take much money to start one. And, if he had no money, he sometimes was inclined to pick up some "strays" on the range, and slap his own brand on them. If he were caught in this nefarious practice, it could mean hanging. But that was the chance a rustler took.

The late Joe Elliott of Boise, who as a young man was a range detective for the Western South Dakota Stockgrowers Association, said that he did not know how many rustlers Idaho had in the early days, but that there "were more thieves between the Black Hills and Pierre than there were cattlemen."

Chasing rustlers made for excitement on the range, but generally the life of the cowboy was lonely—often monotonous. The cowboy sang sad songs about his lot. But he liked it, because with it came freedom. And there was no crowding.

In his book "The Humor of the American Cowboy," Stan Hoig tells the story of a cowboy who settled down on his own ranch, then decided to move because, the cowboy said:

"This country is gettin' entirely too crowded for me. I found out the other day that some *hombre* has moved in down the river not over ten miles from my place. An' derned if he ain't been there a whole year. I'm headin' out for some place where a man either don't have any neighbors at all or at least knows the ones he's got."

In Southern Idaho, the crowding on the range came because the climate, grass and water supply were so right for cattle, which grazed the plains until the hot and dry months of summer and then moved to the high country. And, if these conditions were right for cattle, they were also right for sheep. Perhaps even more so. So the sheep came—followed by feuding.

162

# Chapter XV

# MEETING OF THE TWAIN—SHEEP AND CATTLE

"Conflict is the first essential of drama. Thus invariably the most dramatic, most glamorous period in the history of any plains state is the era of the 'open range'."

—Joseph Kinsey Howard in *Montana—
High, Wide and Handsome*

The Reverend Henry H. Spalding, who was responsible for many "firsts," is generally credited with raising Idaho's first sheep at Lapwai in the late 1830s. He received a gift of several sheep from mission-minded residents of the Sandwich (Hawaiian) Islands. And, knowing that his wife, Eliza, badly needed wool for her spinning wheel, he carefully tended his little flock.

The missionary also tried to interest the Nez Perces in raising sheep. But wild sheep were fattening on their own in the mountains, and the Nez Perces figured that herding the domestic animals would be an unnecessary chore. They did not buy the idea.

The first big band of sheep in Idaho? Oddly enough, that was managed by the trappers at Fort Boise. They had about 2,000 head of sheep there, and, although the exact time when they were brought to the fort is not certain, the big band was contemporary with the Reverend Spalding's small flock.

When the first Mormon emigrants came to the Great Salt Lake in 1847, they brought with them bands of sheep. Under the tithing system of the Latter-Day Saints, every 10th lamb born belonged to the church. So the church was soon in a position, not only to provide meat and wool for the poor, but to "loan out" sheep to individuals to get them started in the business. When Mormon emigrants began moving up from Utah to settle in Southern Idaho in the 1850s and 1860s, some loaned sheep came the dusty miles with them.

Flocks were sometimes tended on a community basis, with an individual perhaps owning the odd number of 13 and 3/5 sheep. But odd numbers or not, they proved to be winning ones for the early Mormon settlers, who developed some of Idaho's big herds.

At Paris, in the Bear Lake Valley, Apostle C. C. Rich began encouraging the development of flocks by Mormon settlers in 1863. As the flocks began to expand, the settlers sold wool at a good profit throughout the Rocky Mountain area. But, in 1877, Rich passed a rule that no wool was to leave the valley. It all had to be spun into clothing in the homes. Soon, nowhere in Idaho were the settlers better dressed.

"King" of all Idaho's early sheepmen was a man from Scotland named Andrew J. Little. Born at Moffatt, Scotland, on December 19, 1870, he was a young man of 22 when he first landed in America at New York City in 1893.

The teeming metropolis held no lure for him. He was used to the hills of Scotland where sheep grazed that man might be nourished by their mutton and warmed by their wool. Having heard from a Scottish friend, Robert Aikman, that Idaho had similar hills, he promptly headed for them.

At Caldwell he asked for direction to Aikman's sheep ranch, and, when he was told that it was "about 15 miles thataway," he beamed. An easy walk!

Aikman knew Little as a good sheepman, and hired him as a herder. But Little did not tarry long with Aikman. By 1894, the newcomer from Scotland had started his own herd of sheep. (Eventually, he would buy out Aikman.)

Then, taking a liking to the Emmett Valley, Little acquired 40 acres of land there in 1895. That was the beginning of a sheep empire which was to include 27 irrigated ranches, with more than 6,000 acres in cultivation, and 60,000 to 100,000 sheep annually roaming the hills. One report said that Little owned 33 ranches, but this variance was not unusual, because no one except "Andy" Little really knew his total holdings.

"I don't talk about those things," he once told a probing reporter.

There was no question, however, about his annual wool clip (in the peak year of 1929, close to a million pounds) affecting the world market. And, if the price were not right, Little did not sell.

In the Depression Thirties, the price of wool, along with the price of everything else, went way down. Little's wool began stacking up in Boston warehouses—unsold. Banks in Nampa and Caldwell, holding Little notes for big loans, became worried. They told the sheep king that he would have to sell at least part of his wool.

"Not until the price is better," said Little stubbornly. "But, if you are worried, you can have my sheep. I will pass the word to my herders in the hills, and have the sheep delivered to your doors."

The bankers thought the husky, heavy-mustached Scotchman was bluffing. But he was not. Soon alarming reports came. Roads to Nampa and Caldwell were blocked with thousands of sheep trotting towards the cities. The bankers quickly changed their minds, and extended Little loans. When the price was right, Little sold his wool, and paid off.

In peak seasons Little employed as many as 400 men. Year 'round he also had quite a crew, arranging work so that there was a minimum of lay-offs. "A man has to eat every day," he said, feeling that it was his responsibility to provide a steady income. With many of his employees having served 20 or more years, he was ahead of his time.

Having had only a minimum of schooling in the old country, Little was determined that his five children should have good educations. One by one, he sent them off to college.

In the early 1930s at the University of Idaho, this writer was a fellow student of one of Little's three sons, Robert, and remembers well "Bobby" bemoaning the hardness of an examination in a forestry course.

"Why," Bobby was asked, "are you majoring in forestry?"

"Well," he replied with a grin, "my father said that I had to go to college, and I didn't know what to take, so I decided on forestry. You see, we've got a lot of different trees around our ranches, and visitors are forever asking what kind they are. I thought that if I took forestry I could tell them."

"But what are you really interested in?"

"Just one thing."

And Bobby tapped a golden sheep on his tie clasp. Like father, like son.

Whether or not Bobby was jesting about becoming an authority on trees of the Little ranches, he never got to learn all the names. He was killed in an accident during a summer vacation from the University of Idaho while driving a truck load of supplies to a mountain sheep camp.

The father followed the son in death on February 20, 1941—honored uniquely for a sheepman in the Far West. A portait of Andy Little was hung in the Saddle and Sirloin Club in Chicago.

Another sheepman who made quite a name for himself was Len Jordan. In the Depression Thirties, he ran sheep in mile-deep Hells Canyon. His wife, Grace, told about the Jordans' ranching experiences in her book, "Home Below Hell's Canyon."

They moved into the canyon to raise sheep, she said, "because good range is absolutely necessary, and you take it where you can get it." Too, it was a good place to be during the Depression.

"It was true we worked long hours," Mrs. Jordan wrote. "We had no luxuries, spent nothing on pleasure, and saw none of the people most dear to us. But we were confronted with none of the personal and economic tragedy that the Depression continued to produce. We had little upkeep and depreciation, and no social worries."

These came later, for Len Jordan went into business (at Grangeville), then into politics, becoming Governor of Idaho and a United States Senator.

In South-Central Idaho there is a valley which provided especially good grazing for sheep in the early days. In the 1930s, W. Averell Harriman, the youthful Chairman of the Board of the Union Pacific Railroad, took a liking to the place. He called it Sun Valley, and, to boost Union Pacific business, built in the valley what Frank J. Taylor described in a 1936 article in *Collier's* as "the most elaborate of all Rocky Mountain resorts."

In time, Sun Valley would be sold by the Union Pacific to the Janss Corporation. It would become a mecca—both in summer and winter—for the famous, the wealthy, and just plain ordinary tourists and recreation seekers.

Tragically, it would also become the last home of famed writer Ernest Hemingway, who loved so much to hunt in the surrounding hills. During early visits to Sun Valley, Hemingway wrote much of "For Whom the Bell Tolls," and when he finally chose the valley as his home he said that he never wanted to leave. The bell tolled for him there in 1961, and he now lies buried in the little town cemetery of Ketchum between two others who loved the great outdoors —a Sun Valley guide and a Basque sheepherder.

Back at its beginning, the Sun Valley resort intrigued James (Jim) Laidlaw, who had been successfully running sheep in the valley for many years. Not only had he made a lot of money out of sheep, he was the founder of the Panama breed, developed by crossing Lincoln ewes with Rambouillet rams. When Laidlaw exhibited these sheep in 1915 at the Panama-Pacific Exposition in San Francisco, they attracted so much favorable attention that he significantly called the new breed Panamas.

So, when he decided to pay a visit to the huge new Sun Valley Lodge shortly after its grand opening during Christmas Week of 1936, he was a man of both wealth and distinction. But he was in his working clothes. His hat was battered, his jacket and shirt and pants begrimed, and his boots scuffed and muddy.

Completely at ease, nevertheless, Laidlaw sat down in a plush chair, and gazed through a huge window at the valley where he had tended sheep before some of the passing movie starlets in ski clothes were born.

A bellhop came up to him.

"Are you a guest?"

"No. Just a visitor—just looking."

The bellhop called the manager. By this time, Laidlaw had taken a jack-knife from his pocket, and was idly sharpening a blade on the sole of one of his boots. Forcefully, the manager said:

"I'm sorry, but if you don't have money to register as a guest you will have to leave."

Folding up his knife, Laidlaw put it back into his pocket. Then, reaching into another pocket, he pulled out a roll of bills of a size usually seen only in motion pictures. Fanning of the roll revealed hundred dollar and fifty dollar bills as well as some measly twenties. (Laidlaw had just been paid at a sheep sale.)

"I'm offering to buy this place," the sheep baron told the eye-popping manager. "And, if you want to sell, you'd better take the money now, because I'm never coming in here again."

And Laidlaw never did. But the incident bore some fruit. The manager had a better understanding—and appreciation—of the sheepmen of Idaho.

The ones who did not appreciate the early sheepmen, however, were the early cattlemen. And the feeling was mutual.

The range wars, which developed throughout the Far West as competition for grass became keener, spawned many dramatic plots by writers such as Owen Wister and B. M. Bower, both of whom wrote in and about Idaho. But truth—at least some times—was stranger than fiction.

A courageous pioneer sheep raiser in Idaho was a woman—Lucy Morrison. But she had special problems, and let the cattlemen drive her out of the Territory.

Her husband, John, was an invalid, so Lucy had the full responsibility of caring for him as well as for three young daughters—and 2,000 head of sheep. What she didn't need was harassment from cattlemen, but she got it. Finally, in 1882, she decided to move to Wyoming. There she got tougher.

That winter all but 200 head of sheep froze to death, but Lucy determinedly began to build a home near South Pass—150 miles from the nearest settlement with a doctor. Suffering a bad attack of dysentery, she cured herself by living for a long period on ewe's milk. While she tended her small flock of sheep, she tied her children to sagebrush so they would not wander off. When Indians threatened her, she doused the home with strong-smelling camphor, telling the marauders, "My children—they all have smallpox." The Indians hastily took off. A lion started attacking her sheep, so she put ground glass in a lamb's carcass. The next day she found the lion dead by the carcass.

Then the cattlemen came, and she wished that she were back in Idaho where the cowboys, with a faint touch of chivalry, had really done little more than threaten her. The Wyoming riders put the torch to her wagons, and stampeded her sheep across the hills. But, on foot, she rounded them up.

In time, she owned 6,000 acres of land, and held grazing rights on many more thousands of acres. Her herds of sheep became among the biggest in Wyoming. When John Morrison died, she married Sheepman Curtis Moore, but continued to manage and expand her own operations, and thus the woman who had started raising sheep in Idaho became known as the "Sheep Queen of Wyoming."

In her last years, she acquired a fine home in California where she spent the winters. But she lived in the home just one winter. Renting it, she retained only the garage for herself. It was more like the early homes she had known in Idaho and Wyoming.

A woman sheep operator who could not be budged from Idaho was Mrs. Emma Yearian. And because of her determination she rose to the status of "Sheep Queen of Idaho." But first some background . . .

A band of sheep owned by a man named Porter had come into the Lemhi Valley in 1892, but the cattlemen ran both sheep and Porter out of the country. Then, a few years later, two more bands of sheep started grazing around old Fort Lemhi. The cattlemen drove one of the bands up Agency Creek and across the territorial border where they figured that Montana cowboys could carry on with the harassing. But getting rid of the second band of sheep proved to be more complicated. The owner said that the sheep would be moved "over my dead body." So the cattlemen dynamited his sheep sheds. (Sheds for commercial bands had recently been introduced in Idaho by A. J. Knollin at Soda Springs, and Frank and Fred Gooding near Shoshone.)

Quickly changing his mind after he saw his sheds in pieces, the pioneer Lemhi sheepman rode out of Idaho.

Well aware of these happenings, Mrs. Yearian came to the valley in 1908 with 1,200 lambs. Being a woman, she added a different dimension to the feuding in the area. The cattlemen told her politely to get out, and she replied —politely—that she was staying.

"So the cattlemen turned from guns to the law," she recalled years later. "I was arrested pretty often on charges of violating the Two-Mile-Limit Law and that old law passed in 1883 whereby no sheep might graze on range where cattle and horses had grazed before. I was the most unpopular belle of the range brawl, but I stayed to face the music."

Because this determined woman did, she encouraged other sheep opera-

167

tors—men—to come to the valley, and eventually there were many more sheep there than cattle.

In 1895, a young cowboy, who was proudly named Jackson Lee Davis by his Dixie-dedicated mother in Virginia but who later was known by the brand of "Diamondfield Jack," started riding the ranges of Southern Idaho as a gun-slinging harasser of sheepmen. He worked for the Sparks & Harrell Cattle Company (Sparks & Tinnen until A. J. Harrell bought out John Tinnen). John Sparks, who later became Governor of Wyoming, was the *major domo* of the outfit, and he had a reputation for backing his riders all the way if they got into trouble.

Thus, with Cattle Baron Sparks four-square behind him, Diamondfield Jack, although only 5 feet 7, rode tall in the saddle. He had a large head with black hair that kept flopping over his forehead. A mustache failed to hide thick lips, which, especially when he was threatening a sheepherder, formed a peculiar smile—a slow, sidewise effect. But his dark eyes beneath beetling black brows were his most dominant feature—said to "flash like a bullseye lantern." (The physical description of Diamondfield Jack is largely courtesy of Arizona State Prison, where he spent some time.)

Characteristically, Diamondfield Jack was a braggart. That's what got him his name. He claimed that he had hunted for diamonds while with Cecil Rhodes in Africa. Too, he joined in the Owyhee Country's false diamond rush in 1892. And when he wasn't hunting diamonds, he was likely to be talking about them.

Now, however, out to keep sheepherders on their side of the range in Idaho's Cassia County, he was, like Rhodes, a man of destiny—destined to become the central figure in the West's most famous and complicated range-feud trial, which would have far-reaching results. It started this way . . .

For some months, Diamondfield Jack had been "hoorawing" sheepmen, although the only shooting he did was target practice in their vicinity. Then, on November 15, 1895, Sheepherder Bill Tolman dared to maneuver his band across a ridge in Shoshone Basin, between Deep Creek and Goose Creek. This was taboo, so Diamondfield Jack rode up to Tolman, who pointed a rifle his way.

A violent argument developed, and Tolman became careless for two seconds, lowering his rifle. That was all the time Diamondfield Jack needed. Whipping out his Colt .45, he shot Tolman in the shoulder, signaled for a couple of other sheepmen on a nearby hill to come and take care of the wounded man, and rode off.

Then, on February 1, 1896, Diamondfield Jack and Jack Gleason, another outside man of Sparks & Harrell, were riding in the night northeast of the Brown Ranch near the Nevada border. Hearing the sound of sheep, Diamond-field Jack drew his Winchester rifle from its saddle scabbard. About that time, his horse "spooked," and the gun fired.

Joseph and Loren Wilson, brothers who were tending the sheep, grabbed their rifles, and started blasting away in the darkness. Gleason galloped off, but Diamondfield Jack wanted some action first. He returned the fire, emptying his rifle before he too rode off in the night. The next day at the Brown Ranch (owned by Sparks & Harrell) he learned that he had killed one of the Wilsons' horses.

That peculiar grin came to his lips.

"Not bad for shootin' in total darkness," he said.

Around the pot-bellied stove of the general mercantile store in Oakley, sheepmen did quite a bit of talking about what they were going to do to cattlemen, Diamondfield Jack in particular. But on the open range things were again generally quiet—for a brief spell.

On February 16, 1896, Sheepherder Edgar Severe noticed a band of sheep on the hills near Shoshone Creek—scattered and untended. Beside the creek was a canvas-covered wagon, so Severe decided to check at the wagon to learn who wasn't minding the sheep.

Two men—Daniel Cummings and John Wilson—were in the wagon, but their sheep tending days were over. Both had been dead for some days—shot to death. Severe quickly spread the news of the killings, and sheriff's deputies began an investigation.

Blood around the wagon tongue indicated that at least one of the slain men had been shot outside the wagon. Near the tongue of the wagon an expended .44 caliber cartridge was found. The mark of the hammer was off to one side as if it had been fired from a .45 revolver. It was known that Diamondfield Jack was not averse in a pinch to using .44's in his .45.

Also found beside the wagon tongue was a corncob pipe. Both Cummings and Wilson were Mormons, and had never smoked in their lives. Diamondfield Jack? He usually rolled cigarettes with one hand, in or out of the saddle, but occasionally he smoked a corncob.

Governor William J. McConnell of Idaho promptly posted a reward of $1,000 for the "arrest and conviction of the killer or killers." No names were mentioned, but it was perfectly clear—to the sheepmen—that Diamondfield Jack or both he and Gleason were wanted. The Idaho Wool Growers, Cassia County Wool Growers, and private individuals added $3,800 more to bring the total reward to $4,800—a lot of money in those days.


Both Diamondfield Jack and Gleason had disappeared. It was known that they had spent some time with a woman named Alice Woods at Wells, Nevada, shortly after February 4, the presumed date of the killings. And Diamondfield Jack, according to Alice, had bragged about "shooting up" an Idaho sheep camp.

As the hunt for the wanted men continued over various parts of the West, tension ran high in Idaho. In Blaine County, cattlemen met at Soldier on April 17, 1896, and formed the Farmers Protective Association. A resolution was passed stating that the attention of sheepmen should be forcefully called to the "statutes of Idaho which prohibit the grazing of sheep on the land or possessory claims of others or their herding or grazing same within two miles of the owner or owners of such possessory claims."

To assure the attention of sheepmen when the resolution was read to them, the cattlemen carried Winchesters. The sheepmen listened all right—as they leaned on *their* rifles. And so it went for almost a year—dynamite ready to explode on the range.

Then Frank Smith, a cowboy who had been fired from the Sparks & Harrell outfit, talked. He said that he knew where both Diamondfield Jack and Gleason could be found. Diamondfield Jack was in prison in Yuma, Arizona, under another name, and Gleason was riding range in Montana.

It seems that the two had split in Nevada, heading in opposite directions. In a town in Arizona, Diamondfield Jack became annoyed by a boy's dog nipping at his horse's heels. So he shot and killed the dog. The boy ran for a policeman. When the policeman tried to arrest Diamondfield Jack, the cowboy beat him to the draw, and took his pistol away. Another policeman came running up, and Diamondfield Jack disarmed him, too. But, as he was riding off, a citizen who had been watching the affray and who happened to be carrying a shotgun, knocked Diamondfield Jack from his horse with a charge of bird shot. For the assorted counts against him, Diamondfield Jack got a year in the Arizona State Prison.

He was not exactly an exemplary prisoner, and, when Idaho authorities requested that he be turned over to them, compliance was quick. Gleason was readily picked up in Montana.

On April 5, 1897, the trial of Diamondfield Jack began at Albion, which in its glory days flourished as a county seat and the home of Albion State Normal School (no longer operating, with the area now being served by the College of Southern Idaho at Twin Falls). The trial of Gleason at Albion was to follow Diamondfield Jack's.

With plenty of money available on both sides, top legal counsel was brought to bear on the case. Defending Diamondfield Jack were James H. Hawley of Boise, who was often described as "the greatest criminal lawyer in the West," and who later became Governor of Idaho (1911-1913); Hawley's sharp young law partner, Will Puckett, and Kirtland I. Perky, a former law partner of William Jennings Bryan in Nebraska, but now a Cassia County attorney. For the prosecution there were John C. Rogers, Cassia County Prosecutor; William E. Borah of Boise, who was destined for greatness as a United States Senator, and Orlando W. Powers of Salt Lake City, rated No. 1 criminal lawyer in Utah.

The evidence against Diamondfield Jack was all circumstantial, but it was plentiful. And sheepherders stood in line to testify about threats he had made to them.

Alice Woods had vanished from Wells, Nevada, so she did not testify as to exactly what Diamondfield Jack had said about shooting sheepherders. The defense claimed that he could have been bragging about the firing in the night at the Wilson brothers' camp—not about the killing of the two herders on Shoshone Creek.

The big issue became how fast a horse can travel. Diamondfield Jack had an alibi establishing him at the Brown Ranch on the night of the slayings, but the prosecution contended that he could have committed the crime and still made it to the ranch in plenty of time. Sheepmen, who had never before found anything good about cattlemen, testified that Sparks & Harrell had the finest horseflesh in the country, fleet of foot, and enduring beyond belief.

On April 16, 1897, Diamondfield Jack was found guilty, and Judge C. O. Stockslager sentenced him to be hanged. Hawley was reported in a state of shock, but the big disappointment among the trial spectators, according to an *Idaho Daily Statesman* reporter covering the case, was "the fact that Mr. Borah did not make a concluding address. His reputation as a pleader had preceded him, and those attending the trial had looked forward with a great deal of pleasure to hearing him plead."

In Gleason's trial, which followed, he was acquitted. As a "local boy," he had quite a bit going for him.

Hawley tried all sorts of legal maneuvers to save Diamondfield Jack, but they all failed. The hanging date at Albion was set for October 21, 1898.

On October 13, however, there came a sensational development. James E. Bower, a ranch superintendent for Sparks & Harrell, signed an affidavit stating that he and a cowboy named Jeff Gray had ridden into the sheep camp of

Cummings and Wilson on February 4, 1896, to question them about their grazing activities. A fight developed, and, declared Bower, the sheepmen were shot in self-defense. To avoid trouble, nothing had been said previously, but now Bower did not want to see an innocent man hanged. Gray backed up the statement.

Diamondfield Jack, however, was far from a free man. Bower was highly respected in Cassia County, but feeling was strong that this was just a ploy to save the gun-slinger. Diamondfield Jack was granted two temporary reprieves by the State Board of Pardons, but, finally, on January 23, 1899, the board denied a pardon, and he was resentenced to hang on February 1. Construction started on the gallows at Albion.

In Boise, Hawley did not quit. Early on January 31—one day before the scheduled hanging—he obtained a stay of execution from the U.S. Circuit Court of Appeals in San Francisco.

How to get word to the sheriff at Albion in time to save Diamondfield Jack's life? Albion had no telegraph service—only a telephone line, which was not working.

Bearing three copies of the reprieve, Will Puckett was dispatched by train to Minidoka, the nearest station to Albion, but still 25 miles away. At Minidoka, Puckett borrowed a horse, engaged two other riders, and gave each a copy of the reprieve. Then the three men started galloping over different routes to Albion—just in case there had been a leak somewhere, and sheepmen would try to prevent the reprieve reaching the sheriff. But all three horsemen got to the sheriff in time. There was no hanging.

On February 21, 1899, a hearing was held for Gray, and he was found not guilty because of self-defense. That fall the same thing happened at a hearing for Bower.

But did Diamondfield Jack go free? Strangely, he did not. There was still wide belief that Bower and Davis had never been anywhere near the scene of the killings. Diamondfield Jack's case got to the United States Supreme Court, and, in December of 1900, that body refused to issue a writ because of legal foul-ups down the line.

Then, at long last, on December 17, 1902, the State Board of Pardons, headed by Governor Frank W. Hunt, granted Diamondfield Jack a pardon. This decision was based on some experiments which showed that Diamondfield Jack's gun could not have fired the fatal bullets. The action, however, was not generally popular. The *Idaho Daily Statesman* blasted:

"When a board of pardons will thus overthrow the decrees of the courts without any reasonable excuse, releasing a murderer solely because wealthy friends have conjured up a flimsy explanation as an excuse for pardoning the convict, the very foundations of the temple of justice are threatened."

Nevertheless, on December 18, Diamondfield Jack, who had most recently been sojourning in the State Penitentiary at Boise, got his first taste of freedom in more than six years. It was in the form of a drink at the bar of Boise's Natatorium. Treating Diamondfield Jack to the drink was Attorney Hawley, who at 6 feet 4 inches had to stoop to clink glasses with the 5-foot-7-inch cowboy.

Then Diamondfield Jack faded forever from the Idaho scene—a scene that he left significantly changed. As a result of all the furor raised by his case, cattlemen and sheepmen—throughout other parts of the West as well as in Idaho—decided to try working out peaceable arrangements. The range wars did not cease entirely, but they started to taper off. In brief, the calf began to lie down with the lamb.

And what happened to Diamondfield Jack? He became a mining promoter in Nevada, courted "Diamond Tooth Lil," the Goldfield dancehall queen, and died in Las Vegas on January 2, 1949—after being hit by a taxicab.

# Chapter XVI

# MONARCHS OF THE RANGE—THE BASQUES

"Far nobler on our mountains is he that yokes the ox,
And equal to a monarch, the shepherd of the flocks."

—From an old Basque song

On a warm summer day in 1949, Jack Lane, president of the Sawtooth Graziers Association, and this writer sat on the tongue of a sheep wagon sagging beside the East Fork of the Salmon River in Custer County. Lane nodded toward a herder with storm-colored hair, dark eyes and blending olive complexion, who was minding a band of about 1,500 sheep.

"Again the Basques are giving us hope after the long dry spell in obtaining herders during World War II," the lean and weathered Lane said. "Just the other day 10 new Basques showed up in Idaho. A hundred more are expected to come to the West shortly. These Basques are hopefully being hand-picked for their herding experience in the old country. Herders don't come any better than Basques—if the Basques are herders.

"Several years ago a big group of Basques was brought over from Europe to herd sheep. There were college professors, merchants, politicians. Only about 25 per cent worked out as herders. Still, that 25 per cent was important."

If the Basques were important in the 1940s, they were doubly so in the early days of Idaho when the big bands of sheep roamed the open ranges. While it is true that many of the first Basques who came to Idaho were actually seafaring men, a good number had had some experience tending small flocks of sheep on the slopes of the Pyrenees.

A hardy and determined people, they were not to be pushed around—as the cattlemen learned. Most important, however, were their characteristics of energy, honesty and fidelity—good qualities to have in men who had to be trusted with a couple of thousand head of sheep far out on the range.

Homeland for the Basques—Euzkadi—consists of seven provinces. Four are in Spain—Navarre (Navarra), Guipuzcoa, Alava and Biscay (Viscaya or Vizcaya), and three in France—Basse-Navarre, Labourd and Soule. These provinces start at the ever-restless waters of the Bay of Biscay, and work their way up foothills to the towering Pyrenees Mountains.

How the Basques, a people with their own language (Euzkera) came to be in this part of Europe long before the birth of Christ is anybody's conjecture. And there is much conjecturing by baffled ethnologists. Some say that the Basques came from Phoenician stock, others that they are kin of the original Iberians. One belief has it that the Basques were once part of the lost continent of Atlantis. And another that the Basques originated in Asia, between the Euxine and Caspian seas, a part of modern Georgia. But the assumptions are all just theories. And the Basques have their own.

A Frenchman was once bragging on how far back he could trace his ancestors when a Basque smiled, and said:

"I have no beginning."

The language of the Basques is equally mystifying. Euzkera means "clearly speaking," but the language is complicated. In fact, it is so complicated that it caused Scallinger, a writer of the Middle Ages, to comment:

"They say that the Basques understand each other, but I don't believe it."

Another writer, Henri Gavel, had a kinder observation to make on the Basque language. He said that "in softness and sonority its pronunciation nearly equals that of Italian or Spanish." Primarily the difficulty in coping with the language comes not from the sounds but from the inordinate length of many words, making such English words as "irretrievableness" or "macrocosmology" seem puny.

But not only have the Basques kept their strange language intact in both Spain and France throughout many centuries, they have maintained their customs and traditions. This was done by successfully resisting attempts to subdue them by such invaders as the Celts, Romans, Visigoths and Moors.

Always the Basques have commanded a healthy respect. For one thing, the *irrintzi*, the battle cry of the ancient Basques—combination of a "derisive laugh, a shriek and a horse's neigh"—struck terror in the hearts of the enemy. For another thing, the Basques were very adept in following up with the sword. And with this heritage to back them up, the Basques even today in both Spain and France retain a degree (small though it may be) of autonomy.

The Basque poet Zalduby describes the solidarity this way:

"A mighty oak tree in our mountains
Spreads aloft its seven branches
In France and in Spain, on the two sides,
Here three and there four; seven in one."

So it was a proud and independent people who became famous in America's Far West as herders of sheep. The fame was not entirely of the Basques' choosing. More often than not, it was thrust upon them. Many who started new lives in the United States as sheep herders got into other occupations as soon as possible. Still, a surprising number developed flocks of their own, and were ranked among the West's leading sheep ranchers. By 1900, two-thirds of the members of the California Wool Growers' Association were Basques. (During the period 1792 to 1822, all the governors of California were native Basques.)

The first authenticated record of Basques in Idaho is dated 1873. It shows that three men from Vizcaya Province in Spain applied for citizenship papers in Boise City. Their occupations in Idaho? Herding sheep.

The three probably started it all. Word got back to the old country that a good way to climb the mountains of success in the new country was to begin by herding sheep in the hills of Idaho. So it was that most of the Basques who came to Idaho in the early days were from Spain, primarily from Vizcaya Province. (French Basques settled generally in California, Nevada, Wyoming and Montana, with the Spanish Basques looking primarily to Oregon, Idaho and parts of Nevada.) And the Basques who trekked to the Pacific Northwest were herders of sheep. Or so they said.

A question is raised, particularly on the Vizcayan Basques, because their homeland is a sea coast province, with the economy based on fishing, shipping, mining and farming. Actually, the Vizcayan Basques have always been particularly skilled at shipbuilding. (The *Mayflower* is thought by some to have been built by the Basques.)

Sheep? There were many small flocks of them in Vizcaya Province all right, but rarely did a flock have more than 50 sheep including lambs. And this is no doubt one of the reasons which made the Basques such good herders. Each sheep was considered a jewel of rare price. The spindly-legged lamb was placed on the richest grass; the orphan was fed from a bottle.

Then there is the Basque way with an unwanted twin lamb. The herder seeks out a mother sheep that has just lost a lamb. He fastens the hide of her dead lamb on the unwanted twin, and leads the twin back and forth in front of the bereaved mother. Scenting her lost one and seeing the new lamb, the mother thinks her own has come back, and takes the unwanted one unto herself.

Grass for grazing was often sparse in the Pyrenees, and the Basques had learned to take advantage of any break in a barren landscape. The story is told of one Idaho Basque herder who took the bells off his sheep at night, and hustled the animals onto the lush grass of the Territorial Penitentiary. Apparently prison guards at the time were counting imaginary sheep—not watching for real ones.

Too, the Basques were particularly adept in working the sheep with their dogs. After all, there is an old Basque proverb which states:

"I command the dog, and the dog commands his tail."

As for the early Scotch and English and Scandinavian sheep operators in Idaho, they took a liking to the ancient Basque sheep herding songs, especially the one which goes like this:

"Only two days did he stay shepherd.
When he became a shepherd, out of carelessness
They left the provision sacks with him.
He ate so much, so full was his belly,
That he could not follow his sheep.
That night fifty of his sheep were missing."

The song was a scowl for any herder who would think more of his stomach than his sheep. And to the Idaho sheep operators, it was like sweet grass among the sage. They couldn't get enough Basque herders. By 1900, Basques were being brought directly to Idaho for the express purpose of herding sheep.

Very bewildered young men, many of whom had never before been more than 10 miles from home, got off the boat in New York City, and they were still bewildered when they arrived in Idaho. Three Basque youths stayed in the Boise depot of the Oregon Short Line for three days before venturing out into the new environment.

The difference in languages was the big barrier to hurdle. Domingo Aldecoa of Boise, when new in this country at Mountain Home, dutifully listened to the conversation of waiters in a restaurant in the hope that he would learn some English. He was dismayed when he discovered that he was acquiring a smattering of Chinese.

Back in the old country, the old folks worried. This prompted one young man to write reassuringly to his *ama*:

"Mother, you do not need to worry. On the train ride to Idaho, I noticed many people reciting the rosary to themselves."

What they were actually doing was chewing gum.

Once out on the range, the Basque did not have to be concerned about a strange language or strange customs. Here he was indeed a "monarch," and his sheep wagon was his "castle."

One way to start a good argument is to state that the sheep wagon was originally designed in Idaho, Utah, Wyoming, Colorado or Washington. There are well-staked claims for this honor in all of these states. (Perhaps one of the best authenticated claims is that for James Candlish of Rawlins, Wyoming, who designed and built a "house on wheels" for a sheep herder in his blacksmith shop in 1884.) But the Basques didn't care who had produced the first sheep wagon. For them, it was sheer delight for efficiency and comfort.

Inside the canvas-covered conveyance was a stove, dish cupboard, bed which could be converted into a bench during the day, and a hinged table to be lowered at meal times. Trap doors in the floor of the wagon opened to a bountiful supply of food. This was living—living out where a man could "think free."

In his book "Thirty-five years of Sheep Herding," George Raich wrote that "herding sheep was sure a lonesome life for any young man to follow, and I often wondered if this kind of work wouldn't land me in an early grave." But this was not the feeling generally of Basque herders.

For centuries in their homeland, the Basques had been intrigued by the variations of nature—the zigzagging of a rocky coast line, the dotting of rugged mountains by gentle valleys, the carpeting of rolling hills with golden gorse and the decorating of them with forests of oak and chestnut and pine, the scrawling of a meadow brook punctuated by leaping trout . . . And in Idaho there were more variations—sagebrush dryly whispering beside rivers and creeks, shrubs blushing with the bewitching colors of fall, evergreens becoming even greener in settings of snow, a tree growing tenaciously in a rocky mountain crag where a mere man would say none could ever grow . . .

So much to gaze upon! So much to reflect upon!

Archer B. Gilfillan wrote in "Sheep" that "the herder, as the official chaperon for fifteen hundred strong-minded, but misguided, females, has a perfectly valid excuse (if he wishes) for going crazy at any moment he may elect." But Gilfillan quickly added that "there is really little monotony in it." Certainly, the Basques found that so.

One day the sheep were inclined to run, and the next day just to lounge around as if it were Sunday on a Tuesday. If the wind was strong and cold, they moved with it; if gentle and warm, against it. There were sheep which strayed, and had to be tracked down. Then there was the marauding cougar or coyote which tested the aiming of a rifle.

Sometimes, of course, things got too exciting. Take the experience of Martin Ascequinolasa with the bear.

Ascequinolasa had left a drowsing village in Spain to herd sheep in Idaho for Carl Nicholson out of Kuna. And generally on the range it was every bit as peaceful as in the Spanish countryside.

Then one day Ascequinolasa spotted a big black bear playfully batting her two cubs around on a tree-shaded knoll. Intrigued, Ascequinolasa kept one eye on the bears. His dog, however, had both eyes on the bears, particularly the cubs. They were about his size, and he decided to take them on.

Tearing over to the knoll, the dog began yapping and nipping at the cubs as he was used to doing with the sheep to make them move. The cubs moved all right, but perpendicularly—not horizontally.

Shinnying up a tree, they gazed down contemptuously at the dog, now raising a ruckus at the bottom of the tree. The mother bear moved toward the dog, a growl accompanying each step.

Fearing for the life of the dog, Ascequinolasa ran toward it, shouting in Basque to leave the cubs alone. The dog understood Basque very well— when he wanted to. But he was presently too preoccupied with the cubs to listen.

About that time, the mother bear, apparently convinced that her young ones were safe, decided to attack Ascequinolasa. Like a bull of the pampas, she charged.

Ascequinolasa ran to the left, to the right, in a circle. The bear gained on him. Then, racing up the knoll, Ascequinolasa came to a tree not far from the one in which the cubs were perched. What was good for the cubs was good for him, thought Ascequinolasa, and up the second tree he went.

His fanged and clawed pursuer tried to climb the tree after him, but it was too small for the bear to cling to. Still, the angry animal took a swipe at the ascending herder, ripping off the heel of his left boot as if it had only been pasted on instead of nailed.

Like a scared squirrel, Ascequinolasa shot two feet higher up the tree. And there he clung for ten minutes . . . twenty . . . thirty . . . Growling, the bear slashed at the trunk from time to time, ripping off chunks of bark. Ascequinolasa felt as if each chunk was a part of him.

Again he yelled at his dog to leave the cubs alone and to get back to the sheep, but again the dog was not listening. So it became a stalemate—a man and two cubs up two trees, and a bear and a dog keeping them that way.

On Ascequinolasa's tree, there was not a branch strong enough to hold him, so he had to support most of his weight. This could not go on forever. Ascequinolasa prayed. And it was to his prayers that he attributed his thinking about the wooden matches he had in his shirt pocket.

At the bottom of the tree was very thick and dry grass, and on this Ascequinolasa began dropping burning matches. One by one, the matches flared and flickered out without igniting the grass. Finally, Ascequinolasa was down to one match. Carefully, he lit it, and held it until it was at high flame before dropping it. This one had to do it. And it did.

The grass around the tree started to smoke, then flame. As the fire spread, the bear backed off, turned, and rushed to the tree where the cubs were besieged by the dog. With one paw flick, the bear sent the dog yipping down the knoll.

That was the signal for the cubs to slide down from their tree. This they did, and the last Ascequinolasa saw of them they were galloping over the knoll, with their mother close behind, swatting all the way.

With such goings on, one would have thought that other Basques would have hesitated in coming to Idaho to herd sheep. But, regardless of the number of bears around, the Basques figured that they were better off in the hills of Idaho than in a Stoughton, Wisconsin, wagon factory, or later in a Detroit, Michigan, automobile plant. So many of them started flocks of their own, went back to Euzkadi, married a hometown girl, and returned with her as quickly as possible.

Of course, some Basques, after saving enough money to live handsomely in their homeland, went back to Euzkadi. Significantly today in the Spanish towns of Bilbao and Guernica are taverns called the Boise Bar.

The Basque women probably had more difficulty adjusting to Idaho than the men. In an article in *Travel Magazine* for September, 1942, Sax Bradford quoted Widow Belaustegui of Boise:

"You cannot know what it is to come still eager and happy to the disappointment of a lonely land. Each night I prayed that somehow we would find the money to buy our passage back to Spain . . . back to Vizcaya where there were roses; there was laughter; there were friends in the dooryard; there were bubbling kettles on the hearth.

"But now it seems our life is here always . . . and that other land, the homeland, it is almost unreal. Its remembrance drifts away. Sometimes I could wonder if there was a Spain."

At last, Widow Belaustegui felt at home. She may have believed as some do that the name for Basqueland in Europe—Euzkadi—comes from the Basque word for "sun," but she did not realize that the word "Idaho" also refers to the sun. There was a link.

The Basques, women as well as men, kept coming. In fact, special immigration quotas were approved by Congress from time to time to see that they did. (Getting more Basques to Idaho was a continuing pet project of U.S. Senator Henry C. Dworshak.)

Idaho centers for the Basques sprang up wherever sheep were a dominant factor. At Mountain Home, for instance, the Basques rapidly became an important part of the town's economic and social structure.

Many of the Basques who headquartered in Mountain Home worked for Jose Totorica, a fellow Basque, who ran big herds of sheep over vast stretches of Owyhee County. For some reason buried in the past, the Totorica herders and other Basques chose a grove of aspens at the foot of Juniper Mountain southwest of Mountain Home to leave their mark.

To wander through the grove today is to see the names of dozens of Basques carved in the bark of the aspens. The Basques in the strange new land had a tendency to cling together, and perhaps the clustering of names in the grove brought them closer to one another in the wide open spaces.

Boise was (and still is) the Basque "capital." In Boise, the early Basques crowded homogeneously into the area between the Church of the Good Shepherd on Idaho Street and the Delamar Hotel at Eighth and Front Streets. Most of the men were bachelors, and the married ones had left their wives behind. To be able to transport the women from the old country, the men first had to earn enough money in the new. Consequently, there were Basque boarding houses all over the place. And there was no greater delight for a Basque new in Boise than strolling past Anduiza's *fronton,* and hearing in progress the sounds of a *pelota* (or *jai alai*) contest, called by some the world's fastest game. The thumping of the ball and the cheering of the crowd were like echoes from Spain.

"My muscles need limbering up," the newcomer would promptly decide.

And the *fronton* had another steady customer.

Too, in various places, *muz* was being played. An ancient card game, *muz* makes a women's afternoon bridge game, colored with conversations on baby or husband problems, seem very tame. Signals to partners in *muz* are not only permitted but vital. They involve eye movements including full-fledged winks, body twitches, hand flicks. And the shouting! When a key card is played, a stranger would think a last-second touchdown had just been made at a high school football game.

But preserving the old ways with *pelota* and *muz* was not enough, especially when more women came, and they began having something to say. One day Juanita Uberuaga Aldrich of Boise announced:

"The old customs must not die. I will keep them alive by teaching the dances and songs to the Basque boys and girls."

Interesting a group of about 50 young Basque couples, she formed an organization called *Euzkaldunak.* On Sunday after mass at the Church of the Good Shepherd, the *Euzkaldunak* began holding meetings with dancing and singing to the music of accordion, guitar, flute, tambourine and drum.

A dancing group was also started in Emmett by Juan Bilbao, the noted Basque scholar who came to the Boise Valley in 1939 to do research on the Basques. Fearing that the Idaho Basques were becoming too Americanized, Bilbao revived many of the ancient dances. For these, he beat the drum himself.

Then there developed the Sheepherders' Ball held between Christmas and New Year's Day, and the picnic staged whenever practicable on the Sunday following July 31, feast day of St. Ignatius Loyola, a native Basque who became the patron saint of his people. Both events annually drew Basques from various Western states.

Credit for inaugurating the Sheepherders' Ball goes to John Archabal. In a way his story is typical and in a way it isn't, because in his youth he had a little more trouble than usual in making the trip to Idaho.

The ship on which Archabal sailed from Spain was wrecked, and he had to be fished out of Atlantic waters by sailors on a freighter, eventually landing at Galveston, Texas, instead of New York City. By cleaning his pockets of everything except a jack-knife and a handkerchief, he was able to buy passage on a train as far north as San Francisco. There he wrote of his plight to friends in Idaho, and lived off hand-outs in the Bay City until money came to get him to Boise.

On November 8, 1893, Archabal went to work for "Uncle Billy" Howell. Then he moved to the W. C. Cleveland ranch. Saving his money (out-of-pocket living expenses amounted to about $50 a year), he became a partner of Cleveland. And, before he was through, in 1916, he bought out Cleveland.

To help other Basques get started in the sheep business, Archabal parcelled out flocks on shares. In some years, he had as many as a dozen partners. And, like Archabal, they prospered.

Archabal became a leader of the Boise Valley Basques, and when two factions got to feuding he took action. It seems that when a member of the colony would become ill and needed financial help, the two factions would decide to hold benefit dances. Choosing the same night, the factions would start cutting prices until one or both would sometimes admit the dancers free.

"This," said Archabal, "is fine for the dancers, but not for the sick person."

He got the feuding ones together, and it was decreed that there would be one big charity dance a year. And so the annual Sheepherders' Ball came into existence, with donated sheep auctioned to the highest bidders, then turned back and auctioned again and again. And a new tradition developed—that all the funds should go to non-Basque charities.

Although the Basques became synonymous with sheep raising in Idaho, they also emerged in such various fields as insurance, banking, food service, barbering and dairying. Some even went into beef cattle raising.

Particularly notable for his success in the latter field was Antonio Azcuenaga, son of a basket weaver in Bilbao, Spain. Young Azcuenaga seemed to be all thumbs when he too tried to weave baskets. So, in 1887 at the age of 19, he immigrated to the United States.

Herding sheep from the Winnemucca area in Nevada to the Jordan Valley in Oregon to the Boise Valley in Idaho, Azcuenaga decided that the wool and mutton business was not for him either. He switched to blacksmithing for a while, then finally settled on cattle raising, founding the Azcuenaga Livestock and Land Company. With the money he made in this endeavor, he built the famous old Oregon Hotel in Boise.

Then there was Jesus Urquides, Boise Valley's best known packer (and also the founder of the "Spanish Village," an early Basque community on Boise's Main Street). In California where he was born, Urquides had never had anything to do with sheep, but he had packed supplies to mines. A man should do what he knows best wherever he is, Urquides figured, so he became a packer out of Boise for Idaho's mines.

When Colonel William H. Dewey got interested in developing the Thunder Mountain gold strike about the turn of the century, he decided to erect a stamp mill at the site. Someone told him, however, that "only Jesus Christ" could get a stamp mill over the hundred or more miles of treacherous trails from Boise to Thunder Mountain. So naturally Dewey thought of Jesus Urquides, and engaged him to perform the miracle with the aid of 40 mules. Urquides and the mules came through all right, but it wasn't easy.

The steel stems of the stamp mill weighed almost a ton each, and were slung between two mules (a normal load for a mule is 400 pounds). But Urquides was getting 10 cents a pound for the freighting, and the mules extra rations of hay.

On trail switchbacks—of which there were many—it was impossible for the mules to make a turn. After some deep thought on a trailside boulder, Urquides came up with a solution. At each switchback, he brought up more mules, carrying supports. The supports were placed under the load, then a pair of mules, headed in the opposite direction, were hitched to the load, toting it to the next switchback where the procedure was repeated.

When Urquides finally got the stamp mill to Thunder Mountain, he was very modest about the whole thing.

"I thank God," he said, "that He gave us mules."

Today the Basques in Idaho are thoroughly integrated in the American way of life, including the running for political office. (As this is written, Basque Pete T. Cenarrusa is Secretary of State.) The motto of the Basques in the old country is "Gu Euzkadirentzat eta Euzkadi, Jaungeikoarentzat"—"We are for Euzkadi, and Euzkadi is for God." But the Idaho Basques have now changed that to "Gu Amerikarentzat eta America, Jaungeikoarentzat"—"We are for America, and America is for God." Still, that doesn't mean that the Basque culture and customs have been obliterated.

True, the *pelota* courts are gone in Boise except for a faded one on Grove Street—the younger generation prefers tennis or golf—but *muz* games are still going strong beside bridge foursomes at the big Basque Center in the capital city. Basque dances, dinners and weddings are also staged at the center. In addition, the center sponsors the Oinkari (Fast With the Foot) Dancers, young men and women of college and high school age, who have given demonstrations of native dances throughout this country and in Canada.

The Oinkari Dancers—they are something special, because they demonstrate that dancing is truly a universal language.

When the Oinkari troupe went to Reno, Nevada, in 1966 to perform in a show with Singer Pat Boone, the members—particularly Director Al Erquiaga —had some misgivings. They knew that there would be many fellow Basques in the audience—but mostly French Basques.

Before the show, Erquiaga was asked:

"The Spanish and French Basques have a friendly rivalry perhaps? Like Democrats versus Republicans?"

"Oh, lots more friendly than that," grinned Erquiaga.

"Then why are you concerned?"

"The language. Spanish and French Basques speak the same language, but the dialects are different. I have difficulty understanding a French Basque."

By the same token, a French Basque puzzles over the language of a Spanish Basque. So, when the Oinkari group broke into song, there was little response from the French Basques. But then came the dancing, and, before it was over, the French Basques were leaving their seats to join in. A Basque is a Basque is a Basque—when dancing.

And are the annual Sheepherders' Ball and picnic still held at Boise? Indeed, they continue to be a part of the life of Basques from other states as well as from Idaho.

Ah, the picnics which have been held . . .

Some years ago this writer had the good fortune to be invited to one, and it was a never-to-be-forgotten experience. That year the picnic was staged in a hill setting near Boise, and as it progressed it seemed as if the pages of a picture book on another land were being turned.

Over there, under the shade of a big wind-woven tree, stood three old Basques talking in their strange language. A nondescript sheep dog lay at their feet with one eye and ear alert as if *he* understood. One of the old men had strapped to his side a *bota*—a goatskin wine bag—with a tube running from the *bota* to his mouth. Also in his mouth was a well-caked pipe. And, with years of practice to guide him, the old-timer would simultaneously and effectively maintain conversation, smoke and drink wine by pressing the *bota* with his elbow.

While the men idled, the women—some dressed for the occasion in native garb of white blouses, red skirts and black satin aprons—heaped tables with food. The meats were in variety—at least eight different kinds, including the Basque favorite, *chorizos,* highly spiced, freshly barbecued sausages. Coffee by the gallon.

Then this writer heard for the first time the national Basque anthem. *Guerni-kako Arbola.* Lilting but forceful, this song!

Dances followed on a specially erected wooden platform. There were the *Jota, Aurresku* and *Porrusalda.* Differently paced, but all vigorous. Of the three, the *Jota,* a dance of young hearts in bodies of all ages, was most popular. And most amazing were the grace and dexterity of the elderly men and women, many with the plumpness that comes from irresistable Basque food. Both sexes of the Basques are born to dance, and they do not seem to lose the spirit of youth.

Rhythmically, couples moved in and out in patterns that changed like those in a shimmering pool. The dancers circled, swung, clung, broke. Fingers snapped the cadence. Heads tossed, feet flicked in and out faster, faster until the accordions squeezed into silence, the tambourines gave final clangs. Then a wave of happy, breathless chatter.

"Mama," said a dark-eyed, teen-aged girl, "you and papa should not dance so lively."

But there was pride in her eyes.

The Basques are good people to know.

And break it to ride.

To feed the many miners in the 1860s and 1870s, big herds of cattle moved into Idaho.

If a cowboy didn't have a horse, he could find a wild one.

—U.S. Bureau of Reclamation

Then cattle raising became a major industry of the Territory.

Competition for the free grass developed with the coming to Idaho of bands of sheep such as this one on the fringes of the Sawtooths.

To keep the bands intact, sheepmen imported Basques, who considered each sheep a "jewel of rare price."

And to run sheepherders and their charges off the range, cattlemen imported hired guns.

But after the famous "Diamondfield Jack" incident, peace came to the land, and cattle began to graze beside sheep.

—Bureau of Reclamation

Horsepower was vital in early Idaho, pulling a creaking stagecoach along a
mountain road or . . .
—University of Idaho Historical Archives

Propelling a clanking combine over the rolling hills of the Palouse Country.
—University of Idaho Historical Archives

At first, oxen were the moving force in the woods. They were slow, but they could get the biggest of logs down the old "skid road." —University of Idaho Historical Archives

Manpower came from all over, but mostly from Scandinavia via Wisconsin and Michigan.

In Idaho agriculture, the two most important breakthroughs were in the early development of irrigation on vast stretches of desert land, and the later establishment of potato processing plants.

Utilizing all of all potatoes grown made the man in overalls a gentleman of distinction.

Today, Idaho is a place where modern man, just like his pioneer ancestors, can reflect upon the great force of nature which carved out mile-deep Hells Canyon.

Or a mother can show her children the prankishness of nature in holding rivers captive beneath the earth, then releasing them through the Thousand Springs.

For an artist, there are many beautiful scenes to paint—hundreds on Lake Coeur d'Alene alone.

For the fisherman, lines tighten on the Lochsa and a wealth of other waters.

Idaho is a lot of things. It is a big-game hunter venturing into the Primitive Area . . .

Young men riding a raft over the tumbling waters of the Little Salmon out of McCall . . .

An old man practicing beside a placid stretch of the Snake River for the annual fiddlers' hoedown at Weiser . . .

Or just a tree in the Owyhee desert country, past its prime but stubbornly reaching out to the dawn of a new day.

Indeed, Idaho is a very special and thoroughly fascinating state. On the Craters of the Moon, people can look to the past ages.

And they can be proud of the two flags—of America and of Idaho—which fly over the majestic capitol building at Boise.

Chapter XVII

# MOUNTAIN WITH A SILVER LINING

"I came for gold, but I have no objections to getting rich on silver."

—Musing of a prospector in a Wallace
saloon, 1889.

A jackass named Old Bill brought fame and fortune to the Coeur d'Alenes of Northern Idaho in 1885 by being involved in a rich silver find. Well, that's the unvarnished story as backed up by official court records. But there are assorted reports as to just *how* the jackass was involved.

One version of the story has it that the smart Spanish burro kicked up a choice chunk of galena after its master, Noah S. Kellogg, had done poorly prospecting himself. Another version has Old Bill stubbornly not moving a muscle, but pointing like a bird dog at a mountain of silver until Kellogg did something about it.

The latter version is Kellogg's own. But it should be remembered that the whiskered, fumbling and kindly old prospector was not noted for his veracity. He just naturally liked to dress up a story, even though adornment was entirely unnecessary.

After his—or Old Bill's—big discovery in Milo Gulch which became the fabulous Bunker Hill and Sullivan Mine, Kellogg dictated his account of the epochal event to John R. McBride, a former Chief Justice of the Idaho Su-

183

preme Court. The good judge must have raised his eyebrows from time to time as he scratched away with a pen, but, nevertheless, he carefully preserved for posterity what the whimsical old man told him:

". . . I started up a narrow, rough gorge with the burro followin' along like a dog. Suddenly it stopped and refused to budge. All my persuasion wouldn't move it, as it stood and stared up the side of the mountain. I took hold of the halter rope and tried to drag it forward. It wouldn't budge. I cut a switch and lashed it. It stepped a few paces and stopped again, gazin' at the mountainside. Further forced leadin' got it a few yards further . . .

"Then the burro turned his head so's to point directly at the high peak, brayin' long and loud. I was amazed. The thought came to me of the protest made by Balaam's ass, as related in the Bible, against the false prophet's treatment, and might this not be another example of his information?

". . . Men may say what they choose, but for that dumb beast the Bunker Hill mine wouldn't have been discovered by me. I knowed the rich mine was there, right where the burro was pointin'. I led it back to the base of the hill, stripped the load from it, and turned my 'minin' prophet' loose to wander at its will as I proceeded to complete my journey alone, without the slightest doubt that I'd made my great discovery. And there it was, the rich, almost pure silver and lead ore stickin' up out of the mountainside, glistenin' bright in the sunshine . . ."

Before Kellogg would have any spending money from the discovery, however, he would go through a very involved lawsuit.

It seems that the mooching old fellow was originally grubstaked at Murray by Origin O. Peck, a building contractor, and Dr. John T. Cooper, a former surgeon in the British Navy. On August 1, 1885, they gave Kellogg $18.50 worth of food and tools—and Old Bill. The backers had no hope that the meager grubstake would pay off (with the usual fifty-fifty sharing of a find), but they did hope that Kellogg would quit pestering them for handouts.

Happily, they watched him and Old Bill fade into the mountain scenery. But, on August 27, they were dismayed to see man and beast back in town, with Kellogg wheezing that he needed more provisions.

"Found some encouraging prospects, but can't follow up on them on an empty stomach," he said.

After giving Kellogg the brush-off for a couple of days, Peck and Cooper again provided him with food—at least enough to start him and Old Bill trudging back up a mountain trail. But what goes up must come down, and Kellogg and his four-footed friend were no exceptions. On September 13, the two were again spotted by Peck and Cooper on Murray's main street. Sadly shaking his head, Kellogg turned over tools and Old Bill to his backers. The agreement on the grubstake, which Kellogg had considered "mighty puny," was at an end.

"Now, if you good gentlemen could spare enough to buy an old man a drink . . ."

A few days later the mountains came alive with activity. Stampedes started for Milo Gulch when it was learned that, on and shortly after September 10, two lode claims had been staked in the names of four Murrayites—Phil O'Rourke, genial part-time prospector and part-time gambler; Jacob (Dutch Jake) Goetz and Harry Baer, saloon operators, and Cornelius (Con) Sullivan, who, like O'Rourke, had left the green of Ireland early in life to seek the gold of America (silver would do). The two claims of these four—for the Bunker Hill and Sullivan mines (whether the second property was named after Con Sullivan or Prize Fighter John L. Sullivan is still argued)—were based on samples of galena whose richness boggled the mind. But what really boggled the minds of Peck and Cooper, the "former" backers of Kellogg, was the name of the witness on the location notice for the Bunker Hill claim—Noah S. Kellogg.

Peck and Cooper charged that they had been swindled. They contended that when Kellogg had headed back to Milo Gulch for the second time, just before the dawn of August 29, he had been accompanied by O'Rourke. And perhaps by others. More important, there was a four-footed member of the party—Old Bill, the grubstake jackass. Peck and Cooper wanted their cut, and went to court to get it.

The court sessions were held at Murray in June, 1886. Peck and Cooper were not the jolly mixers in Murray that the defendants were, and the jury decided against them. The presiding judge, Norman Buck, however, was not obligated to follow the jury's decision in an equity case, and ruled in favor of the grubstakers. The judge declared:

"From the evidence of the witnesses, this court is of the opinion that the Bunker Hill Mine was discovered by the jackass, Phil O'Rourke and N. S. Kellogg, and the plaintiffs. The latter are entitled to half interest."

This ruling was appealed to the Supreme Court of the Territory of Idaho, which upheld Judge Buck. At the time of the territorial court's decision, Kellogg's cut of the pie was estimated at about $100,000, but the value of his share went up. At one time, it was figured that he was worth $600,000—but not for long.

Meanwhile, the discovery story had greatly intrigued Eastern editors. They had become a bit jaded with reports of rich ore strikes in the Far West, but one that featured a jackass was something else again.

The editor of *Outlook,* a popular national magazine of the time, sent Writer F. G. Morehead to Murray to do an article. After conducting interviews in various saloons, which are always good sources of imaginative information, Morehead wrote:

"The burro did it. That's the God's truth . . .

"Kellogg was getting back to the settlement where there was always whiskey, women, and something doing even if the grubstaking had not panned out. So, he made his last camp in the Coeur d'Alenes, tied the burro, Old Bill, to a rock and hunted around for another slice of bacon that would make him think of home and mother.

"Bill smelt the bacon and thought of his own appetite. He gnawed on the rope that held him but gave it up in disgust. He wanted something to eat just as Kellogg did. Finally he got so blooming mad that he snorted and rared around and pawed up all the loose gravel and boulders, then let out with his heels as though he'd kicked the lining out of the sky. Kellogg gulped down his bacon and wandered over to see what ailed Bill. I guess Kellogg never did think to give that burro anything that night. He even forgot his own hunger, for Bill had uncovered a ledge of galena ore that certainly looked good to Kellogg. There it was, plenty of it, riches for everybody, but Bill the burro was just as hungry as ever . . ."

So the stories went. And so Milo Gulch boomed, with new mines popping up all around.

In 1887, Jim Wardner (after whom the town of Wardner was named) came along. Even while a teen-ager in Milwaukee, Wisconsin, he had been promoting deals, and now, in Idaho, he put together a big one. He packaged several mines, including the Bunker Hill, and sold them to Simeon G. Reed, Portland financier and founder of Reed College. With Reed's millions for backing, the Coeur d'Alenes area was really on its way.

The Coeur d'Alenes not only produced great amounts of ore, but great figures in the mining industry. There was, for instance, young Frederick W. Bradley, whose intuition—and stubbornness—saved the Bunker Hill from extinction in the Nineties. When the mine seemed to be running out of ore, Manager Bradley went to San Francisco to make a report on the sorry situation. But, before he left for the Coast, he gave instructions to William McDougall, operating superintendent, to start the men digging in a different direction.

Helping McDougall chart the new course was a sharp young engineer, Stanly A. Easton. Actually, Easton had been brought to the mine to help close it, but that wasn't the way it worked out. While Bradley was still in San Francisco, he received a telegram from McDougall reading:

"JUST BROKE INTO LARGE VEIN OF RICH GALENA."

And the Bunker Hill has been going strong ever since.

Then there were the sons of Henry Loren Day, pioneer general store operator in Wardner—Harry, Eugene and Jerome—who became millionaires along with August Paulsen and L. W. (Lou) Hutton when a claim in Burke Canyon known only as "The Hole" evolved into the rich Hercules Mine. As this is written, Harry's son, Henry, carries on the Day legend of "knowing where to find it."

Then there was James F. McCarthy, who took over the financial administration of the Hecla Mining Company in Burke Canyon when it was a successful operation, and made it many times more successful until it became the talk of mining magnates all the way to Johannesburg, South Africa.

Synonymous also with successful mining operations in the early days was the name Sweeney. Charles Sweeney, at a very young age, had fought in both the Civil and Mexican wars. Then, footloose, he took an interest in mining camps, first in Nevada. When he landed in the Coeur d'Alenes, he was nearly broke, but he made a fast and sizable stake by buying up building lots cheap around new mines, and selling them at a handsome profit. The depression year of 1893 wiped him out financially, but he recouped his losses by buying and selling mining options at Rossland, British Columbia.

Then, back in the Coeur d'Alenes, Sweeney invested heavily in the Last Chance Mine near Wardner. The mine proved to be a lucky chance. Selling out to the American Smelting and Refining Company in 1905 for $2,660,000, Sweeney bought the Morning Mine at Mullan for $3,000,000 and proceeded to become, some say, America's richest mining operator.

Noah Kellogg, who inspired the visions of the great developers, did not do so well. True, he became quite a celebrity—and a "good fellow." When he met a friend on the street, or even if a stranger merely nodded to him, he would tell the individual to go into a saloon, order a drink, and "Charge it to Noah!"

Then three attractive young ladies came from Dayton, Washington, to Wardner where Kellogg was living at the time. They were Kellogg's stepdaughters by his long forgotten and deceased wife. They had tried suing Kellogg for half his wealth on behalf of their departed mother, but, failing to collect in court, they just moved in on Kellogg.

Delighted with the attentions the fair damsels showered upon him, Kellogg, in turn, showered them with gifts of money. But, finally, he began to tighten the purse strings, and that was the signal for the step-daughters to leave. By this time, they were comfortably well off, anyway.

Feeling lonesome, Kellogg got married again in 1888 to Mamie M. Reed, a widow from Billings, Montana Territory. Moving to the newer town of Milo (Kellogg), he built a fine home there for his bride, and lavished money on her. But, as the funds faded, so did the romance. In 1893, Noah and Mamie Kellogg were divorced.

During the next 10 years Kellogg became a lonely old man, shuffling down the street, and chuckling with delight when someone would invite him to go into a saloon, order a drink, and charge it to . . . Well, not to Noah! For him, the big money had run out. Finally, time did, too. He died March 17, 1903, and was buried in Kellogg, the city on U.S. Highway 10 which bears his name.

Today a 10-foot tall obelisk of white marble, erected by admirers, rises above his grave. And off in the distant background is another beautifully-sculptured monument, this one—Kellogg Peak—provided by nature.

What happened to Old Bill, the jackass? There are various stories. But this writer, who has a North Carolina heritage and whose grandfather once hid an aging jackass in the woods so the troops of General Sherman would "keep their cotton pickin' fingers off it," hopes that this story is the true one:

While Kellogg was still very solvent, he bought Old Bill, and paid a man in Forest Grove, Oregon, $50 a month to look after him until he died at the ripe old burro age of 21. Jackass Ski Bowl, south of the city of Kellogg, was originally named in Old Bill's honor. (The city of Kellogg was first known as Jackass and later as Milo before the name of Kellogg was finally adopted.)

About once a year Noah Kellogg and Old Bill live again. No major parade in the city of Kellogg would be complete unless someone with whiskers and a jackass were leading it.

Neither Kellogg nor Old Bill, however, were responsible for the opening of the Coeur d'Alenes to mining. This honor is generally accorded to Andrew J. Prichard, a scholarly Civil War veteran, after whom Prichard Creek and the town of Prichard are named. Some say that a grizzled old prospector by the name of Gelatt, who at one time was a partner of Prichard, actually swished out the first pan of good-paying gold on Prichard Creek in 1882. But Gelatt did not stick with the diggings. Prichard did.

Prichard's story, like Kellogg's, gets a bit tangled with the threads of legend. One version has him spilling samples of his find on the polished surface of a bar in Spokane in the winter of 1882-83. The word spread rapidly through that town, then with a population of about a thousand. Eighty tough characters insisted that Prichard lead them to the strike. He said that it wouldn't do them any good until spring when the snow had melted and the earth thawed.

The eager eighty, however, were opposed to any delay. They threatened to hang Prichard unless he took them to the gold site immediately. So Prichard did. And he was right. Nobody could dig down deep enough to tap the placer gold. Most of the disillusioned eighty headed back for the saloons of Spokane. A few stayed with Prichard until spring, and started staking claims as new strikes were made all around the original one.

187

The Northern Pacific Railroad, now rolling into Spokane, ran advertisements in the East telling of the wealth that could be found easily in the Coeur d'Alenes. The tent city of Eagle sprang up—soon had a population of 2,000. Then came Murray with more permanent structures, attaining at one time a population of 10,000 when canyon environs were included.

In 1884, Colonel William R. Wallace, a cousin of General Lew Wallace who authored "Ben Hur" and a nephew of Idaho's first governor, William H. Wallace, built a store and cabin in a cedar grove on the Coeur d'Alene River, and named the settlement Placer Center. Wallace began to sell lots. Four years later, even then struggling for space in the narrow canyon site, the city that was to become known as Wallace began to emerge. Then there were the booming mining towns of Gem, Burke, Osburn, Mullan, Kellogg, Wardner . . .

For quite a while Murray was the metropolis, swinging enough weight to garner the county seat. And there was enough money floating around Murray to attract to it in 1884 Molly b'Dam', a madam who shall forever be unmatched among the madams of the roaring mining camps of the early Far West.

This spirited and shapely, blue-eyed blond was born Maggie Hall in Dublin, Ireland, on December 26, 1853. Unusually well-educated for a female of the time, she could quote the Bible more readily than a Southern U.S. politician, or recite Shakespeare or Milton better than the average college English professor. But there was then little place for women as politicians or scholars.

At 20, Maggie immigrated to America, and, like many another Irish lass of the time, got a job as a maid in a wealthy New York City home. Marrying and divorcing the worthless son of the owner, she again began supporting herself —but not as a maid of virtue. She became a prostitute and madam.

As such, she moved to Virginia City, Nevada, San Francisco, Portland, Chicago. It may have been a Northern Pacific advertisement which she read in Chicago in 1884, telling of the rich pickings in the Coeur d'Alenes, that caused her to return to the Far West where the women were then very scarce. But, whatever the reason, early that year Maggie rode a horse into Murray—a beautiful sight for the sore eyes of the sidewalk loiterers.

One of them, Phil O'Rourke, who would later play a leading and disputed role in the discovery of the Bunker Hill and Sullivan mines, grinned widely.

"And what be your name, Ma'am?" he asked as he gave her a hand down.

"Molly," replied the dazzler, who had never liked the name of Maggie.

"Molly b'Dam'!" exclaimed O'Rourke. And that became her name.

O'Rourke's heart, turning flip-flops, was no doubt jolted hard against the walls of his chest when Molly's sparkling eyes turned to the row of little cabins on Gold Street with their unmistakable purpose.

"Which is Cabin No. 1?" she asked.

O'Rourke gulped as he pointed.

"But that's the cabin which is always reserved for the madam."

"I know," smiled Molly. "Occupied or not, that cabin is the one I'm taking over."

And so she did. Until her death in 1888, she kept her eye on the "girls" from Cabin No. 1.

Molly did things with a flair and a flourish. Once, while visiting with friends in a saloon, she got her Irish temper up when a starving prospector in from the hills began gulping food from the "free" tray on the bar, and the operator started to throw him out. Drawing a derringer pistol, Molly pointed it at the saloon owner's fat stomach, and announced:

"Drinks and food are on the house for everybody until I put this gun away."

The object of Molly's attention did not move a muscle as the patrons proceeded to clean him out. He did make a major move several weeks later—out of town—when he found that his place had been officially ruled off limits by the miners.

Molly could be as tender—and kind—as she was tough. There was, for instance, the time a prospector known only as Lightnin' came down with typhoid fever in his shack up in the mountains. He had no money to buy medicine, because he had blown much of what he had in his poke in Murray saloons, and then one of Molly's girls had "appropriated" the poke and what remained in it. An equally broke friend came to town seeking help for Lightnin', and, when Molly heard about it, she acted swiftly.

She had a particular interest in Lightnin', because he had threatened to tear her cabin apart after the missing poke incident. Molly, speaking over her derringer, had sent him on his way.

But now she looked up Lightnin's friend, and told him that she would accompany him back to the sick man with two burro loads of food and medicines. When she arrived at the cabin, Lightnin' squinted at her with feverish and puzzled eyes.

"What you doin' here, Molly?"

"Just happened to be ridin' past, and thought I'd return your poke," she replied. "I put out a call for it one night, and the next day there it was—on my table—with a little more in it, I suspect, than when it disappeared."

For the next two weeks, Molly proceeded to successfully nurse Lightnin' back to health.

Molly's biggest claim to fame as the "woman in silver country with a heart of gold" came, however, with the smallpox epidemic that swept Murray in the spring of 1886. Like the victims of the medieval black plague, people were dying in droves in cabins and tents, generally unattended. Few persons wanted to go near the ill, few wanted to bury the dead.

Murray's population was made up mostly of men, and their attitude finally got to Molly. Their inclination was to bemoan the situation—over a stiff drink in a saloon—and do nothing. Well, if it took a woman to jar them into action, Molly was the woman.

Calling a mass street meeting, she proceeded to shame the men into action. What was needed, she said, was to turn every public building and every hotel into a hospital. If that didn't take care of the situation, she knew of some saloons which had quite a bit of space. And then there would have to be volunteers to help with the care of the sick.

The first to volunteer? It was Phil O'Rourke, who never could get out of his mind how beautiful Molly looked when she first rode into Murray. Others quickly followed in offering their services. But the one who worked the hardest —and longest—in the makeshift hospitals was Molly.

Little wonder then that when she died of "consumption" on January 17, 1888, the procession for her funeral—led by three ministers—was the longest ever known in Murray. All businesses and public buildings respectfully closed their doors. The front page of the Murray newspaper was bordered in black, and the editor said:

"She has drawn more public attention than any other woman in this part of the country for her many generous deeds towards others. We will never forget her."

The Methodist minister, who gave the eulogy, declared:

"She was a ministering angel to the sick and suffering when exposure of illness laid men low . . . and these kind acts have been recorded in the Book of Books to her credit, far overbalancing the debit side . . . She will live forever in our hearts, a woman so strong, so forthright that only her good deeds will be remembered."

True, indeed, Molly's grave, carefully tended by the women of Murray, is today the best kept in the cemetery.

Down in Tombstone, Arizona, at 2 p.m. on October 26, 1881, pistols started roaring at the O.K. Corral. Thirty seconds later the firing ceased. When the dust, kicked up in the corral by frightened horses, settled, two of four cowboys involved—Tom and Frank McLowery—lay dead, and a third—Billy Clanton—was dying. The fourth—Ike Clanton—was uninjured.

Viewing the results of the Far West's most infamous gunfight were the Earp brothers—Wyatt, Virgil and Morgan—and Doc Holliday. Virgil and Morgan Earp were wounded, but not seriously.

"Somebody pull off my boots," begged 19-year-old Billy Clanton. "I always told my mother I'd never die with my boots on."

The Earp brothers and Holliday were all technically deputy marshals, whose guns had been hired to bring peace to Tombstone. They claimed that the cowboys were threatening trouble, and had refused to throw up their hands when ordered to do so. But two of the cowboys were unarmed, so, after considerable delay, the Earps and Holliday landed in the court of Justice of the Peace Wells Spicer—fortunately. Spicer, who was a friend of the Earps, ruled that the marshals had killed the cowboys in the line of duty. A lot of folk thought otherwise.

It was time for the Earps and Holliday to get out of town. So the Earps drifted to Idaho, landing in the Coeur d'Alenes tent city of Eagle. (Doc Holliday settled down in Leadville, Colorado, where he died of tuberculosis at 36 in 1887.)

Wyatt Earp brought with him to Idaho his six-shooters, handlebar mustache and Josie Marcus, 26-year-old daughter of a wealthy San Francisco merchant. Earp couldn't marry her at the time, because his first wife, Mattie, was still living. But that never seemed to bother the one-time deacon of the Union Church in Dodge City.

As might be expected, Wyatt, fastest of the three gun-slinging brothers, got involved in a shooting fracas—over a real estate deal—in Eagle. But his lead-throwing ability was no longer up to what it had been in Tombstone, and earlier in Dodge City, Kansas. He didn't even ruffle his opponent, William Buzzard of Spokane.

In Eagle, the Earps ran a saloon called the White Elephant. Housed in a white tent as big as a dozen elephants, the saloon did a rip-roaring business. But nobody got out of hand. Wyatt Earp might not have been able to hit Buzzard with one shot, but no one wanted to test him on a second.

The Earp brothers poured what money they made from the White Elephant —some from fast shuffling of cards—into mining ventures and town properties. Several of the deals were well-shaded in the Earps' favor, but the brothers never really made much on any of them. In fact, Wyatt Earp, who died broke in California at 80 on January 3, 1929, still owes an Idaho tax bill. Not only that, many of the Coeur d'Alenes' early mining folk probably do some grave-gyrating every time there is a television rerun of the series showing Earp as

190

Dodge City's marshal of sterling character.

With men like the Earp brothers around Eagle, what the Idaho mining camp needed, figured Warren Hussey of Virginia City, Montana, was a bank. In February-March of 1884, Hussey moved to Eagle all his banking equipment, including safe, gold scales and counters. It was easy to set up a new bank then, but hard to move one, especially in the winter.

Hussey had his equipment hauled over the mountains by horse-drawn sleds or toboggans. It took almost as much pushing as pulling to get the sleds through the snow drifts, 10 to 20 feet high. In his diary for March 4, Hussey wrote:

"Awful hard pull up Baldy Mountain, but got through with it, and easy going down. Eagle Creek at 2 p.m., Eagle Town at 3 p.m."

While Hussey was shoveling snow to clear space for the board floor of his new tent bank, a man came up to him and asked:

"Are you the banker?"

"I am."

"Well, my name is Yomans—H. A. Yomans. I've got a six-hundred dollar draft from St. Paul I'd like to deposit."

So Hussey, with tent still on the sled, was in business—just like that. Money was handled lightly in those days, although Hussey had a special security force in the form of a big white bulldog, which slept with him in the tent bank.

Some years later, when Hussey stepped off a train to get lunch at a depot counter, he gave a small boy on the train 50 cents to watch his briefcase. In it, was $30,000 in cash.

Excerpts from 1884 issues of the *Murray Nugget,* a weekly newspaper published by C. F. McGlashan and W. F. Edwards, convey the spirit—and flavor—of the times:

"This metropolis (Murray) of the Coeur d'Alenes needs no word of praise. Beautifully located, peopled with men of energy and enterprise, and offering superior inducements to capital, she has burst into a city in a day . . . New signs painted on canvas peep up—'Tin Shop,' 'Jeweller,' 'Hardware,' 'Dance House,' 'Theatre,' and the like . . . Buildings that will be no disgrace when brick and lumber have superseded logs are being put up in all quarters of the town. The advent of a sawmill would greatly accelerate the growth of the city . . ."

\*　　\*　　\*

"Frank Reed's house 20'x35' in the clear, 2 stories high, cost $1,200 and rents for $300 per month on a 6 month lease."

\*　　\*　　\*

"Mrs. M. Chandler of Osburn was the only white woman who wintered in the Coeur d'Alenes. She and her children, two in number, came over the Evolution Trail in October, and located about 2 miles above Eagle. Until the trails become impassable, the boys of Eagle used to send their clothes up to Mrs. Chandler to be washed."

\*　　\*　　\*

"The death of Oregon John, a well known prospector, occurred recently. He had been supported by the camp in his illness. He died in sleep. Doc Sanborn bro't out a table and placed it in front of his saloon. From this table, Rev. W. C. Skipper delivered the first sermon ever preached in the new mines."

191

On the afternoon of April 29, 1899, Lou Hutton, a reluctant engineer (who later would make millions out of the Hercules Mine), piloted a train on the single track winding beside the Coeur d'Alene River between Wallace and Wardner. With some 1,200 miners of the Western Union Federation riding the two coaches and a half-dozen box cars, both inside and on top, the train looked somewhat as if it were toting refugees to Calcutta. The difference was that virtually every man was armed with a rifle or pistol or both. Many of the weapons and much of the ammunition had been stolen from a federal armory. The mission of the miners was to do as much damage as possible to mining properties at Wardner because of long-standing wage disputes, and Hutton had been told that he would provide the transportation to Wardner "or else."

Previously, the union had not been too successful in its moves against the mine operators, largely due to a Pinkerton detective named Charles Siringo, who had been hired by the operators to infiltrate the union ranks. Playing the role of a jovial boomer, Siringo became highly popular with the miners, and was made secretary of the union local at Gem. As such, he reported every move planned by the union to the mine operators.

On the day when his duplicity was finally discovered, furious miners stalked sidewalks to kill him, but Siringo was hiding under one of the sidewalks. In the darkness of night, he escaped, dirty, but otherwise unblemished.

Now, as the train on its mission of destruction rumbled to Wardner, there was no Siringo around. At every curve and trestle, Engineer Hutton yanked hard on the cord of the steam whistle. He was careening along with a hijacked Northern Pacific train on a Union Pacific track without the blessing of a dispatcher of either railroad. And besides the armed passengers, there were 40 cases of dynamite aboard—enough to blow up a mountain or turn an engineer's stomach.

Only Hutton, however, seemed worried. The passengers were in a gay, picnic mood. They passed bottles and sang, with the favorite number being "There'll Be a Hot Time in the Old Town Tonight." Then, as the liquor made them more sentimental, they gave several renditions of "Break the News to Mother."

At the Wardner depot, the engineer, very pale beneath the soot on his face, slowed the train to a stop. Everybody piled off. Included among those disembarking were Sheriff Jim Young and Deputy Tom Heney, who had come along for the ride and "to preserve law and order." In sympathy with the union cause of higher wages—which had provided the impetus for the expedition—the officers drew their pistols, and ordered the mob to disperse. Everybody, including Young and Heney, laughed.

With the formalities over, W. F. Davis, the head of the Gem local who was in command of the loosely-organized "army," ordered 10 scouts to proceed up the hill to the huge concentrator of the Bunker Hill and Sullivan operations. Finding the concentrator without armed guards, the scouting contingent fired a single, agreed-upon shot, and began loping back down the hill.

With the distance by train between Wallace and Wardner being about 15 miles, a lot of liquor had naturally been consumed on the trip, and naturally some confusion resulted. Several men, thinking the returning scouts were attacking company guards, started firing at them. Scout Jack Smith pitched into some brush—dead.

Too bad . . . He was a good hard-rock man; in fact, had won several drilling contests. But, as General Sherman had once indicated, war is no picnic, and the earlier picnic overtones of the expedition began to moderate.

With Smith's body laid out in the depot, miners began as soberly—and as carefully—as possible to carry the dynamite up to the concentrator. While placing the explosive charges in and around the concentrator, other miners were interrupted by Jim Cheyne, a young, unarmed watchman who had been foolhardy enough to stick around the place. He was shot and killed. Another company man, J. J. Rogers, listed as a stenographer, was slightly wounded as he fled.

The men who planted the dynamite in the boiler room and lit the fuses found themselves locked in, but broke a window and managed to get out before the first big blast went off, rattling windows in Wallace. When the smoke cleared, the concentrator, valued at more than $250,000, looked pretty much like another slag pile.

But the "scorched-earth" mission was not complete. Kerosene was poured throughout the big boarding house which served the men at the concentrator when they were working. The boarding house "burned like hot pitch."

Then someone shouted, "Get the boss' house!" So the vacant home of the superintendent went, too.

Now there was jubilation—shouting and tossing of hats—at all the damage which had been wrought in such a short time. But Commander Davis figured he had to get his army out of there fast. He had Engineer Hutton blow warning blasts on the train whistle, and passed the word that anybody who didn't get aboard in five minutes would be left behind.

On the ride back, one mild-mannered, blue-eyed little fellow (about 5'6"), was very thoughtful. A Canadian, he had been moderately successful as a cheesemaker in Ontario, but short-weighting practices made it necessary for him to leave for distant parts. Before he did, he set fire to his factory to collect the insurance.

In April of 1897, he arrived in Wallace, and went to delivering milk. Later that year, he bought a wood and coal business at Burke, and an interest in "The Hole," which became the fabulous Hercules Mine. If he had not had an addiction to gambling and been forced to sell his interest in The Hole when that was all it was, he would have become a millionaire capitalist. But even the wood and coal business went to pay gambling debts, and now, on that eventful day in 1899, he was just another disgruntled miner—a member of the night shift at the Tiger-Poorman.

Although he had never handled dynamite before, he had volunteered to help with the placing of it in the boiler room of the concentrator. And this was what he was thinking about as the train rolled on. He could, he figured, do better as a professional hatchet man than as a pick-and-shovel man. His real name was Albert E. Horsley, but, before coming to the Coeur d'Alenes, he had adopted the alias of Harry Orchard.

Down in Boise, Governor Frank Steunenberg was irate. Sympathetic to labor, he had generally stayed clear of the strife which had been building up for some time in the Coeur d'Alenes. But what had happened at Wardner was too much. Steunenberg called it "out and out anarchy."

Idaho's National Guard was in the distant Philippines, doing its bit in the Spanish-American War. So Steunenberg appealed to President William McKinley for federal troops, and the President promptly responded. On May 2, 1899, soldiers from Spokane, Walla Walla and Boise began pitching tents in Wallace and Wardner.

193

Martial law was declared, and all members of the Western Federation Union were accused of guilt in the Wardner crimes. Hundreds of miners were rounded up at bayonet point, and marched into a giant "bull pen," formed with barbed wire around a warehouse and a string of box cars. (Later, barracks were added.) Reports on sanitary conditions in the bull pen vary widely, but, viewed in the perspective of today, they were no doubt far from good.

Those who would renounce their allegiance to the Western Federation—and pledge themselves to law and order—were released, and allowed to return to work in the mines. Some, upon release, high-tailed it out of the Coeur d'Alenes. Others, who had managed to escape the net of the federal troops, did likewise. One of those in the latter group was Harry Orchard, who agreed with the Western Federation that some day Governor Steunenberg would have to pay with his life for bringing martial law to the Coeur d'Alenes.

Only one man, Paul Corcoran, secretary of the Burke local, was actually convicted and sentenced in the Wardner dynamiting and killing. He got 17 years in the state penitentiary, but was pardoned by Frank W. Hunt, who succeeded Steunenberg as Governor in 1901. Steunenberg, who had retired to private life in Caldwell, remained a marked man.

After doing fairly well as a "high-grader" in mines at Cripple Creek, Colorado—stealing choice bits of gold which he mined—Harry Orchard got on the secret payroll of the Western Federation to perform secret chores. There followed such successful operations as the setting off of a bomb at the Vindicator Mine in the Cripple Creek area, which cost the lives of the superintendent and shift boss. Then there was the bombing of a depot at Independence, Colorado, which killed 14 miners and badly injured many others—all non-union men.

Also, there were the failures—attempts on the lives of Frederick Bradley, former manager of the Bunker Hill and Sullivan; William H. Gabbert, Chief Justice of the Colorado Supreme Court, and James H. Peabody, Governor of Colorado. Orchard, however, drew some consolation from the Bradley affair. He had first tried killing Bradley by placing strychnine in bottles of milk left at his San Francisco doorstep, but the maid did not like the taste of the milk and never served it to the Bradley family. Then Orchard planted a bomb on the same doorstep, and, when it exploded, Bradley was left deaf and a cripple. Also, Lyle Gregory, a detective, was slain in the unsuccessful attempt on the life of Governor Peabody.

But the job in 1905 which Orchard was determined should be completely successful was the assignment to "get" Steunenberg—even though there was now peace with the unions in the Coeur d'Alenes.

In September that year, Orchard registered at the Saratoga Hotel in Caldwell as Thomas Hogan, calling himself a lamb buyer and looking as meek as what he was allegedly buying. In fact, neatly and conservatively dressed, he gave the appearance of an early-day "man in a grey flannel suit." In his briefcase, however, were a pistol and explosives. More armaments were in his trunk.

Orchard hoped to get his mission over quickly, but there were a series of frustrations. A bomb he had rigged to go off in Steunenberg's yard failed to explode, and he had the tricky job of dismantling it in his hotel room. Then, when he spotted Steunenberg walking home, he got his broken-down shotgun assembled too late to shoot him. He was making good progress with a maid in the hotel, but, otherwise, time was wasting.

194

Steunenberg took a trip out of town, so Orchard decided to do the same —to Salt Lake City to discuss matters with friends there. Back in Caldwell at the Saratoga, Orchard learned that Steunenberg was again taking off on a train, and he tried to plant a time bomb under the former Governor's seat. But this did not work out, and Orchard returned a very discouraged man to his lonesome hotel room. The maid, noticing his downcast look, tried to cheer him up, but Orchard told her to forget him—that he was no good for her.

Then, on the evening of December 30, 1905, Orchard spotted Steunenberg in the Saratoga lobby, talking to an insurance salesman—about renewing a policy on his life. Orchard hurried up to his room, wrapped a ready bomb in a newspaper, and walked quickly out of the hotel to the Steunenberg residence. Beside the gate, he planted the bomb, set to go off when someone opened the gate. It could be a neighbor boy, but Orchard hoped that it would be Steunenberg. An assassin, he figured, had to take some chances—with the lives of others.

Retracing his steps hurriedly to the hotel to establish an alibi at the bar, Orchard met Steunenberg happily returning to home and family. Neither man spoke.

Just before Orchard reached the hotel, he heard a terrific explosion. He went on to the hotel bar, and ordered a drink. By the time he was ready to sit down to a celebration dinner, the word was out. Steunenberg had been bombed, and was dying. He would become Idaho's martyr governor, and a statue honoring him as such would be erected on the capitol lawn in Boise.

Orchard was arrested for the murder. The maid had expressed suspicions about him, and a search of his room and trunk revealed damning evidence. Orchard had never really been pressed for answers by the law before, and, under grilling for the first time, he "sang" like Idaho's state bird—the mountain bluebird. He said that he got his orders from Charles H. Moyer, president of the Western Federation; William D. (Big Bill) Haywood, secretary-treasurer, and George A. Pettibone, a handy man in the miners' union.

At the trial, which became a *cause celebre,* Clarence Darrow, the famous criminal lawyer out of Chicago, headed the defense, and James H. Hawley, later to become Governor of Idaho, the prosecution. Assisting Hawley was the Boise attorney, William E. Borah.

During the trial, President Theodore Roosevelt got carried away, and wrote in a letter that whether or not Haywood, Moyer and Pettibone were guilty, they were "undesirable citizens." This got into the press, and unions throughout the nation held demonstrations of protest. Many members started wearing buttons stating that "I Am an Undesirable Citizen."

The decision of the court was a victory for both sides. Orchard was sentenced to life imprisonment in the state penitentiary, but Moyer, Haywood and Pettibone went free.

Newspaper reporters from all over the United States and from some foreign countries had covered the trial. Its sensational revelations and eloquent oratory made daily headlines, especially the summing-up address by Borah. If television had been there, Borah could have run for President of the United States. As it was, he had to settle for United States Senator. Still, as Senator for many years and as the vigorous Chairman of the Foreign Relations Committee, he became better known in some foreign countries than the President of the United States. In this country, his name was a household word.

When this writer first left Idaho in 1936 to become a newspaperman in

Milwaukee, Wisconsin, he was continually reminded: "Oh, you're from Idaho —where Borah and the potatoes come from." Later, after Borah's death on January 19, 1940, the comment was changed to ". . . Idaho—where Sun Valley and the potatoes are." But, in a sense, Borah will never really be topped in Idaho. The highest point in the State (12,662 feet), towering far above Sun Valley, was named Mount Borah.

As for Orchard, he died at 88 on April 13, 1954, in the state penitentiary after spending almost a half-century of his life as a prisoner. While in prison, he got religion, and wrote a book entitled "The Man That God Made Again." He might well have written another: "The Man Whose Trial Made Borah." As a result of the trial, Borah, who had arrived in Boise in 1890 with $15.75 in his pockets, moved up fast.

In time, Walter Lippman would call him "the Pacific Northwest's greatest citizen."

True, the early years in the Coeur d'Alenes were rough. For the most part, they carried the brand of a male society. But gradually women came—women who were not charges of Molly b'Dam'. And, although men are given credit for taming the West, it was the women who tamed the men. They did not yet have the vote, but they had minds of their own.

Take, for instance, Lucy, wife of Colonel W. B. Wallace, who founded the city of Wallace, which was first called Placer Center. On June 22, 1885, Lucy came to Placer Center to join her husband, bringing with her one dog, one bird, several cats, and about a dozen chickens. She became the first woman to spend the winter at Placer Center. She also became the town's first postmistress.

As postmistress, she had quite a bit of correspondence with Washington, D.C. The U.S. Postal Department objected to the name of Placer Center—said that it was too long, and wanted to change it to Wallace.

"Wallace is a good name," agreed the colonel. "But there are already too many towns in the United States called Wallace. Placer Center it stays."

Lucy, however, had already had enough correspondence on the matter. Ignoring her husband, she filled in forms declaring that Wallace was the name of the town. And so it is today. It is also known as the "Silver Capital of the World."

At the same time that Lucy was changing the name of Placer Center, Burke was getting its first women—Mrs. F. R. Culbertson and a French woman. Unfortunately, they could not speak each other's language, and the female social life was limited until more women came. But come they did. Also the railroad.

Burke, which lies in such a narrow canyon that it once made Robert L. Ripley's "Believe It or Not," had little space for mothers to push baby carriages during Sunday afternoon strolls. Consequently, mothers had a local blacksmith attach flanged wheels to the middle of the axles of the carriages so they could be pushed along a single railway track. Some of the carriages had bright-colored umbrellas attached to them to keep the sun off the precious contents. Altogether, it was a delightful sight.

Ripley missed this fact about Burke. What he dwelled on was the Tiger Hotel—trains ran through it, and the North Fork of the South Fork of the Coeur d'Alene River under it. (An average of three light bulbs went every time a train came.) The location was necessary because there was no place else with enough space to build the 150-room hostelry.

This writer will always be pleased that he was privileged to visit the Tiger Hotel in the 1940s before it was torn down . . . to watch the manager waking up miners for the next shift by slamming a plumber's helper against doors . . . to observe an engineer parking his train for lunch beneath the second floor of the hotel and stepping from his cab directly into the dining room.

Burke has never been the same since the passing of the Tiger Hotel, but it is still well worth a tourist's time to turn off U.S. Highway 10 at Wallace, and to drive the seven miles up State Highway 4 to this quaint, canyon-compressed town. There, even today, he will have the experience of parking his car on railroad tracks while he gets it filled with gas. (Ripley said that the station pumps have to lean to avoid being knocked over by a train, but this is not true.) The tourist himself will not have to worry about being hit by a train, because the engineer will patiently wait until the visitor's car moves off the tracks. Burke is the town where trainmen "stop, look and listen."

Mullan, in its borning period, took pride in the fact that it did not have a single house of prostitution. The Mullan correspondent reported in the Wallace newspaper:

"This is the one town in the Coeur d'Alenes which is not yet afflicted with those individuals of the feminine gender who build their houses on the way to hell, those beings who have been forsaken by the purity of angels and who flaunt their festering identity in the face of public decency . . ."

With family settlement, churches and schools came to the Coeur d'Alenes. The first public school in Wardner was started in December of 1887. Wallace got a school in 1888, and the cost of its first three-month session totaled $364.30. This included the teacher's salary, rent of a building, stove wood and supplies.

And something for which the Coeur d'Alenes area has never really been given due credit is the fact that its mines played a major role in obtaining for Moscow the University of Idaho. The Palouse Country, then boasting primarily scattered farms and limited lumbering, had relatively little political clout, but the Coeur d'Alenes, with its rich mines, had plenty. To appease the North as a whole, the Idaho Territorial Legislature established the University of Idaho at Moscow on January 29, 1889.

Too, the mines of the Coeur d'Alenes have been important to the growth of the cities of Coeur d'Alene and Spokane. The Washington metropolis today has the nation's largest exchange for the buying and selling of mining stocks. And most of the stocks traded are those of mining operations in the Coeur d'Alenes, which produce about half of all the nation's silver.

Prosperity of the mining area has fluctuated widely with the price of ores. Too, the placer gold deposits, which brought the first rush of prospectors to the Coeur d'Alenes in 1882, soon gave out. (Gold today makes up less than 1 per cent of Idaho's total mineral production.) But there is all that silver in the Coeur d'Alenes which has for many years made Idaho the nation's leading producer. Then there are significant quantities of lead and zinc.

More important, the ore deposits of the Coeur d'Alenes are in depth, with shafts of some producing mines fingering out a mile below the earth's surface. Formation of the uniquely-structured mineral wealth was started millions of years ago with the compacting of mud from an ancient sea, and the waters ran deep.

The pay-off today is big, with the Coeur d'Alenes being one of fewer than a dozen areas in the world to have produced more than $2 billion worth of metals. In the area are four of the five largest silver producing mines in the United States, four of the ten largest lead producers, and two of the ten leading zinc mines. And the prospects are favorable for making ever-richer strikes. As this was being written, a new ore body, averaging approximately 30 ounces of silver per ton, was discovered by diamond drilling at the 4,800-foot level of the Sunshine Mine east of Kellogg.

This writer has visited the Coeur d'Alenes in good times and bad, but always he has sensed in the people a feeling that before long "we'll really strike it rich." If darkness settles over the narrow, pine-covered canyons, that is not important, because there is always the dawn of the big tomorrow.

Chapter XVIII

# CRIES OF 'TIMBER-R-R!' AND 'WOOD 'EM UP!'

"Today it isn't a matter of timber. There is plenty of timber left. It isn't likely that Americans will ever know a timber famine. But the timber is being harvested, mostly, by a new and different breed of men—men . . . with families, who wear conventional clothing, vote in elections, and play tennis and golf. Few of them need to know how to handle ax or peavey, and few of them are given to kicking plate glass out of barroom windows. They roar no louder than their city brothers . . ."

—Stewart H. Holbrook in *Holy Old Mackinaw*

The early logging days of Idaho, when the crashing sounds of falling trees began echoing through one of the nation's greatest stands of virgin timber . . .

Ah, there were tough men in the woods then—men, as Historian Irving Stone would have said, "to match my mountains." And they included the bull (boss) as well as the faller (a man who cut down the trees) or the bucker (one who sawed them into logs) or the hair-pounder (a teamster).

No intimation is intended that the men of the woods today are not a hardy lot. But it is difficult to match such characters as those recalled by Ralph W. Andrews in his "Glory Days of Logging"—Step-and-a-Half Jack Phelps, who, when he fired a man, would ask if he had a partner, and, if he did, would

199

fire him, too, so neither would be lonely; Moonlight Joe, who would howl like a banshee for "Logs! More Logs!"; and Boomer Tod, the cook, who, when pranksters placed a bear in his kitchen, killed the bear with a cleaver, and served bear meat that night—to everybody except those who had planted the bear in his sacred domain.

As the legendary Paul Bunyan was supposed to have commented, "Etiquette, dainty speech, sweet scents, poetry and delicate clothes belong properly in the drawing room, the study and the sanctum—not in the bunkhouse."

Then, of course, in the Clarkia area of Northern Idaho, there was a big Swede known as Slow John. Always in his mouth, except when eating or sleeping, was a sizable wad of "Swedish condition powder," a potent brand of snuff, which had once stretched out the great prizefighter, John L. Sullivan, for a count of about a thousand.

Slow John was standing in front of a Clarkia saloon one day when three young men toting "bindles" or blanket rolls approached him.

"We've got jobs with the Rutledge Timber Company up on Marble Creek," one of them said. "How far to the camp?"

Squinting across the tall, timbered mountains, Slow John calculated:

"Couple of miles—maybe t'ree. Nuttin' to it."

This was a very rough calculation, because actually the distance to the Rutledge camp was about 19 miles over some very rugged terrain. But then Slow John became more helpful.

"You fellers stay here in Clarkia tonight. In the mornin', you foller me. I get you there pretty quick."

That night Slow John went into "training" for the hike with a steady diet of whiskey and beer. To liven up things, he started a fight in a pool hall, which wound up with him taking on four men at once. Finally, long after midnight, he went to bed, humming songs of the day.

At breakfast in a restaurant next morning, Slow John was in great shape and spirits, eating mush and hot cakes and eggs and bacon. Also joshing with a waitress and giving her a pat that was more like a swing with an axe at a tree.

"Hoh! I had a great time las' night," Slow John told the three newcomers. "One feller, he was give me a smack on the nose that was a jim dandy. Lots of fun, by golly. Maybe we walk so fast we get to camp in time for lunch, huh? But we take along sandwiches in case our bellies start yellin'."

On the hike over the mountains, the husky Swede set a pace that soon had the three younger fellows gasping. For three hours, it was almost a steady ascent. Then they slithered down into a canyon, and for another hour followed a creek, sometimes splashing through it to save time by avoiding twists in the trail. On a sandy bank of the creek, they sat down to eat the sandwiches they had brought along, although the "babes" being led through the woods by Slow John were so exhausted that they had to sit for a spell before starting to nibble.

Along in the middle of the afternoon, one of the three painfully squatted on a boulder, and observed:

"John, we covered those two or three miles a long time ago. How much farther do we have to go?"

"Oh, yust a little way—over a couple more hills—maybe four, five."

"Hills? God help us when we get to the mountains!"

It was dark when the four finally reached camp. The neophytes were so tired that they crawled immediately into bunks, but Slow John tucked away a big dinner—before he picked his way in the moonlight for five miles down Marble Creek to deliver a letter to a friend. For two days, the exhausted ones stayed in bed, but Slow John was out bright and early the first morning, chopping down trees and joshing with fellow loggers about "dat feller who was bust me a good won." That weekend, he hiked back to Clarkia "to kick up my heels—whee!" at a square dance.

Men of many ethnic heritages migrated to the Idaho woods, but probably the Scandinavians were in greatest number. They came from the timberlands of Wisconsin and Michigan and Minnesota because they had gotten the word that Idaho, particularly the northern part, would make them think of home. Indeed, the tall, rugged mountains, the deep, blue lakes, and the fast, cold streams did.

When the loggers from the Midwest—and from many other parts of the country—got to Idaho, they chewed and spat in amazement. They had never seen such big timber, and so much of it. They didn't know it, but, in 1898, a survey had indicated that there were 31 billion board feet of timber standing in the Coeur d'Alene area alone. White pine, considered the aristocrat of the world's softwoods (and the Idaho State Tree), was in abundance. There were also hemlock, western larch, Engelmann spruce, western red cedar, Douglas fir and western yellow pine. Why had Paul Bunyan stayed so long in the Midwest?

In a way, it was a sawmill—and sabotage—that got the beautiful lake city of Coeur d'Alene going.

In April, 1878, a detachment of cavalry from Fort Lapwai bivouacked on the shore of Lake Coeur d'Alene, a body of water whose grandeur is hard to match. The mission of the commander, Colonel Henry Clay Merriam, was to build Fort Coeur d'Alene. (The fort's name was changed to Sherman in 1891 to honor General William T. Sherman upon his death that year. The famed Civil War general had recommended the erection of the fort on the lake site after a tour of inspection there in 1877.)

Colonel Merriam had brought along all the equipment for a sawmill, including a circular saw and a steam power plant, but he had a problem as his troopers had not been trained in the operation of the mill. Nevertheless, after doing some fast recruiting of knowledgeable civilians from distant parts to serve as bosses, Colonel Merriam got the mill going before winter set in.

The soldiers, who made up the main work force, disliked the non-military labor, and from time to time there was sabotage. So the colonel hired more civilians to work in the mill, and, between 1880 and 1884, they largely made up Coeur d'Alene's non-military population of 20 to 30 persons.

From 1878 to 1898, the Army's little mill turned out all the lumber for the fort buildings, for the steamboat *Amelia Wheaton,* and for at least one school building.

What was good for the Army was good for private enterprise, figured Glassford T. Hawley, and, in 1883, he constructed Coeur d'Alene's first commercial sawmill. Then the town really began to grow. Soon it even had a Ladies' Aid Society with 13 charter members. Within five years, the population had passed the 1,000 mark, and, by 1910, it was nearing 8,000. (As this is written, Coeur d'Alene on Interstate 90 is now known as much as a resort and tourist center as a lumbering town, and has a population of 16,228. It is also the home of North Idaho College.)

In 1852, with little money but with enough food for survival on a two-month voyage, Frederick K. Weyerhaeuser set sail from Germany for America. By 1857, he was the owner of a small lumber mill at Rock Island, Illinois, which showed a profit of $3,000 in his first year of operation. Frequently quoting *Poor Richard's Almanac*—and following it—Weyerhaeuser was well on his way to becoming a legend in the lumber business.

Choosing the Upper Mississippi area in which to start the expansion of operations, and taking as a partner a brother-in-law, Frederick C. A. Denkmann, Weyerhaeuser began the buying and selling of timberlands. Logging, at first, was limited, but where it was practiced it was generally successful, due no doubt in good measure to Weyerhaeuser's "no liquor—no thermometer—no conversation" rules. By not allowing liquor in the camps, fighting was decreased, and timber output increased. With no thermometer around, the men worked uncomplainingly in sub-zero weather. The "no conversation" rule was enforced only at meal times. Although the food of these early days was nourishing, it was not always kept well, and its preparation was too often of the "catch-as-catch-can" school of cookery. Silence at the table prevented the cook from overhearing unflattering remarks which might cause him to quit. Cooks were harder to come by than 'jacks.

From the Midwest, Weyerhaeuser operations spread to the South, then to the Pacific Northwest, where the railroads were selling off grants of timberlands at $9 an acre. By 1900, the Weyerhaeuser organization was in Idaho.

Early that year, Weyerhaeuser showed up in person at Sandpoint, accompanied by another lumber tycoon, Edward Rutledge. Weyerhaeuser had had a particular interest in Idaho ever since 1893 when he went to the Chicago World's Fair, and studied in detail the State of Idaho exhibit, featuring a map which showed more timberland than anything else.

Arriving in Sandpoint late at night, however, Weyerhaeuser began to wonder. Sandpoint, not yet a tourist and skiing center with a wide choice of fine motels, had only a small frame hotel—filled. So Weyerhaeuser and Rutledge slept—and tossed and turned—on hard depot benches. During the night, they were awakened by a man clattering in to take over an adjacent bench.

"Got crowded out of my hotel bed by bugs," he muttered.

After that, the benches didn't seem nearly so hard to Weyerhaeuser and Rutledge.

A visit the next day to the Priest River Valley, with its towering stands of pine, larch, fir and cedar, convinced Weyerhaeuser that he had been right in believing that Idaho had a lot to offer. On December 6, 1900, the Humbird Lumber Company was organized at Sandpoint as a Weyerhaeuser enterprise. And that was only the beginning. Eventually, Weyerhaeuser interests were operating the huge Clearwater Timber Company plant at Lewiston, the Potlatch Lumber Company mill at Potlatch, and the Bonners Ferry Lumber Company mill at Bonners Ferry. Then, too, there was the Edward Rutledge Timber Company plant at Coeur d'Alene in which Weyerhaeuser had a major interest.

Locating of a mill on the Palouse River at a site which was later to become the town of Potlatch was a one-man decision. Business leaders of Moscow, who had been successfully persuasive in efforts to get the University of Idaho located in their town, had maneuvered to have the meeting on a mill site held in a Moscow lodge room. The Moscowites thought that they had the Weyerhaeuser officials pretty well sold on locating the plant in the university town, but they reckoned without William Deary, who had been too busy drying his socks before a lodge room stove to take part in the conversation. A tough Irish lumberjack (after whom the town of Deary is named), he had come up the hard way in the Weyerhaeuser organization, and his way had won for him quite a bit of respect. (Eventually, he would become the first general manager of the Potlatch Lumber Company.)

Now, barefooted, he suddenly bounced over to the conference table, and declared:

"Gintilmen, Moscow doesn't have enough water to be baptizin' a bastard. The mill will be here."

And he pointed on a map to what is now Potlatch.

Although Moscow has really never been short of baptismal water, it must depend on wells which have had to be sunk deeper and deeper as the population of the city on U.S. Highway 95 has grown to more than 14,000. Paradise Creek flows impressively through Moscow—only in the spring.

As for the people of Potlatch, they missed some of the cultural advantages of Moscow, but were quite happy with their new little company town. The Potlatch firm kept rents low, promoted a cracking-good baseball team, and, when war came, plowed and harrowed the victory gardens of the residents. Also, hunting and fishing were good.

Not all the Weyerhaeuser plants in Idaho prospered, and that brought to the State in the early 1920s a grandson of Frederick K. Weyerhaeuser. He was George Frederick (Fritz) Jewett, Sr., a mild-mannered man of considerable ability. His first mission was to dissolve the Bonners Ferry Lumber Company, which showed quite a bit of red ink on its ledgers.

Then, in 1928, Jewett became general manager of the unprofitable Edward Rutledge Timber Company at Coeur d'Alene. His next move was to merge this company with the Clearwater Timber Company at Lewiston and the Potlatch Lumber Company at Potlatch. From this merger, the highly successful Potlatch Forests, Inc., was born, with Jewett serving as president and chairman of the board from 1946 until his death in 1956.

With headquarters for many years at Lewiston and later at San Francisco, Potlatch Forests is today one of the nation's major diversified forest product enterprises. Its mill at Lewiston is the world's largest pine plant, and, flourishing near it, is a colossal Potlatch pulp and paper mill.

Jewett was a member of the Board of Regents of Washington State University and had extensive philanthropic interest in Spokane. Consequently, Professor Hall M. Macklin, head of the Music Department at the University of Idaho, was uncertain how the industrialist would receive him when he called on Jewett in the 1940s to ask him to donate a specially designed pipe organ for the university's new Music Building. Jewett said nothing as Macklin talked, and the professor held his breath when he concluded. Finally, Jewett spoke:

"I have just one question. Are you sure the organ you propose will be adequate?"

At Harvard University, Jewett also established the Donald Kirk David Fellowships, honoring the early University of Idaho graduate from Moscow, who became one of the nation's leading financiers, and, from 1942 to 1955, served as Dean of the Harvard Business School.

Potlatch Forests gained fame throughout the United States for carrying on river log drives after they had been abandoned in New England and the Midwest. This writer is particularly pleased that among the memories he has acquired in his time is sitting on a bank of the Clearwater River, and watching a log drive to the Lewiston mill pond.

Logs—thousands of them—careening and rumbling down the stream . . . Some logs jamming up in a rapids, and 'jacks skipping nimbly across them to find the key one causing the pile-up . . . A well-muscled man with a peavey freeing one log only to have it lodge tightly against another . . . Dynamite being called for . . . The booming of the explosive, with water and log splinters geysering upward . . . Then a great cacophony of crackling and screeching sounds as the jam gives way, with the logs once more rushing to an eventual meeting with whining saws . . . The "river rats" scrambling to get out of the way . . . One falling in the cold water, and another shouting helpfully, "Dry land is thataway!"

Little wonder then that, when Metro-Goldwyn-Mayer filmed "Come and Get It," Edna Ferber's story of lumbering in the Midwest, the logging scenes were shot in Northern Idaho. (Needing primeval forest scenes for "Northwest Passage," MGM made that motion picture at McCall. Twentieth-Century Fox also came there to shoot extensive footage for "Hudson Bay.")

In Southern Idaho, the largest logging organization was the Boise Payette Lumber Company, turning out about half the area's lumber. Boise Payette was formed on Christmas Eve in 1913 from a merger of the Payette Lumber and Manufacturing Company and the Barber Lumber Company. C. A. Barton, a Minnesotan, after whom the early Idaho logging town of Cabarton was named, became general manager. By 1923, Barton had upped the timber holdings of Boise Payette from 2,432 million board feet to 3,330 million. Then he developed an extensive system of retail yards, fanning out from Idaho into Oregon, Wyoming and Colorado.

In 1950, Boise Payette got as its president a native son of Idaho—John Aram. Big and rugged, Aram was raised on a cattle ranch in the Salmon River Country, but he thought punching cows was far from as exciting as portrayed in a William MacLeod Raine novel. He decided to study Business Administration at the University of Idaho.

This writer remembers Aram from the Thirties mostly as looking very uncomfortable while squeezed into a desk chair in one of Professor Erwin Graue's economics classes. But, uncomfortable or not, Aram learned well from the stern, unbending economist.

At Boise Payette, even before he had been boosted to president, Aram sold the idea of tree farming.

"Took a bit of doing," he said later. "I guess members of the board were just hesitant about committing themselves to something they didn't think they could live up to."

But, before long, Boise Payette had 12 tree farms, and shared ownership in two others. New timber was growing to replace the old which was cut down.

Then there was the matter of purchasing federal and state timber. Small mill owners thought that Boise Payette, with its bigger and more efficient plants, was able to enter the low bid on too many offerings. They protested. So Aram adopted the policy of buying large quantities of rough lumber from the small mills, and finishing it at Boise Payette's big Emmett plant. The protests faded like a 'jack's paycheck on a Saturday night.

When Aram left Idaho in 1956 to become a vice president of the Weyerhaeuser Timber Company, he was succeeded by a Harvard Business School graduate, Robert V. Hansberger, who engineered the development of a new company. Merging in 1957 with the Cascade Lumber Company, Boise Payette became Boise Cascade Corporation.

Although maintaining lumber as its base, the corporation greatly diversified its operations, and, by 1959, had become the 55th largest industrial corporation in the nation. Some of the diversification fell by the wayside as unprofitable. But, as this is written, Boise Cascade, with headquarters at Boise and with John Fery as president, was rapidly gaining new strength with 18 lumber mills, 25 plywood and veneer plants, 1 particleboard plant, 1 fiberboard plant, 1 wood beam plant, 1 pole and piling plant, 11 wholesale building material distribution branches, 29 builder service centers, 14 manufactured housing plants, 6 kitchen cabinet plants, 12 pulp and paper mills, 19 corrugated container plants, 19 composite can plants, 6 envelope plants, 24 office product distribution centers, and 16 retail office supply stores. In addition, Boise Cascade owns 2,000,000 acres of forest land, operates 300 tree farms varying in size from 500 to 100,000 acres, and has an unique geothermal-heated nursery for rapid growth of seedling trees. Literally, Boise Cascade was a case of a big oak growing in the Idaho woods from a little acorn.

But independents made timber history in Idaho, too.

One day in Idaho's early logging period, the captain of the steamboat *Bonnie Doone,* which had been docked at Coeur d'Alene, yanked at the whistle, and the high-decked craft of the Red Collar Line began churning into the open water of Lake Coeur d'Alene. Beside the rail stood a tall, firm-jawed, clean-shaven man with his hair swirled slightly to hide an expanding forehead. Next to him was another man, short and bearded. Obviously, by his first question, the second passenger was a newcomer to the area.

Pointing to the Coeur d'Alene Mill Company plant sprawling on the fading shore, he asked:

"Who owns that sawmill?"

"Fellow by the name of Fred Herrick," replied the tall man.

Again, with night falling, the two were together as the steamboat reached the docks of Harrison. The stranger was impressed by the size of the Export Lumber Company whose lights cast an orange glow far out on the water.

"Who owns that one?"

"Herrick."

Now, the stranger was beginning to get really interested, so, when the boat passed the lights of the St. Maries Mill Company plant on the south bank of the St. Joe River, he hurried up to the knowledgeable traveler.

"Uh, that mill—it wouldn't be owned by—"

"Yep! Herrick."

Soon the boat approached the docks of St. Maries where there was still another big mill—that of the Milwaukee Lumber Company.

"Herrick?"

"Herrick."

This was too much.

"I suppose Herrick even owns this boat on which we're riding."

"Correct! Belongs to Herrick."

"And the river, too?"

"Wrong! It belongs to the government."

"The government! How did the government get it away from Herrick? Uh, by the way, what's your name?"

"Herrick."

The story, often told in St. Maries, was vouched for by Howard Drake and Andy Porterfield, old friends of Herrick, who were also on the boat that day. But, actually, the Coeur d'Alenes lumber tycoon didn't need anybody vouching for the color associated with him. He dripped with it.

One of the things the stranger on the steamboat never learned was that on the walls of Herrick's St. Maries office were the mounted heads of many big game animals he had bagged. When Eastern dignitaries visited him, he introduced the trophies as "my board of directors."

In his day, Herrick *was* St. Maries. He didn't initiate lumbering there. The Fisher brothers, Hogue, John and Jesse, did that, building in 1887 the first sawmill on the picturesque site of the shadowy St. Joe—the world's highest navigable river (more than 2,000 feet above sea level). But, in 1909, Herrick came to town with a wad of money, and things began to happen fast in lumbering—in a big way—throughout the whole area.

In Wisconsin, Herrick owned and operated the Flambeau Lumber Company, and, in Alabama, the Scotch Lumber Company, but the lumbering potential in those states was on the decline. In Idaho, Herrick could stand on a mountain top, viewing nothing, as far as he could see, except timber . . . timber . . . Now, here was something for a man to really sink an axe into.

First off, Herrick bought up great stretches of timberland in the Big Creek area, east of St. Maries. (There would be many more acquisitions of forested acreages.) Then, on the edge of St. Maries, he constructed a company town of 50 frame houses and a general store. Overlooking this new town, called Mill Town, he built his own home, sparing no expense to be sure that it was big enough.

In March, 1910, he started construction of a railroad line up Big Creek. Forest fires in August of that year wiped out much of the spring and summer's work, but, with ashes still hot, Herrick put rail crews back on the job.

It was said that the fire had left him financially shaky, but one would never have known it by talking with him. Oh, he got perturbed on occasion, and would roar like a treed cougar, but nothing seemed to stop him.

Deciding to build a flume along Benewah Creek, he started buying right-of-way easements from homesteaders. Some sold; some didn't. Herrick tried to get the courts to give him the authority for condemnation of needed property. When the courts refused, he agreed to make the flume a common carrier, and began condemnation proceedings. From time to time, disgruntled homesteaders felled trees across the flume, smashing it. But, in the end, Herrick made the flume work, keeping his word and letting anybody who wanted to float logs down it do so.

When Herrick got into a financial argument with someone, he usually ended it with:

"Sue me!"

On one occasion, he was taken at his word.

One day in a St. Maries barbershop, according to Logger Arthur Victor, who was getting lathered in a chair at the time, Herrick encountered a gyppo operator.

"How come you're suing me?" Herrick wanted to know.

"You owe me money. Pay up, and I'll drop the suit."

"I'll drop you."

And Herrick swung. But the gyppo operator was not only younger and bigger than the tycoon. He was faster. Dodging the blow, he began to give Herrick a brief lesson in "bunkhouse ballet." Quickly stretched out on the barbershop floor, Herrick said, "All right. I've had enough—I'll pay." Then, getting up and dusting himself off, he started for the door, paused with his hand on the knob, and added:

"I'm getting too old to fight."

In his seventies, however, Herrick didn't figure that he was getting too old to continue to expand his lumbering operations. Not satisfied with his mills up and down Lake Coeur d'Alene, he decided, in the 1920s, to bid on a big block of government timber in Oregon's Malheur National Forest. His high bid made him perhaps the biggest independent timber operator in the Pacific Northwest, but it would prove to be a mistake that would dwarf the one in the barbershop.

Under the contract, Herrick not only had to build 30 miles of common carrier railroad from Crane to Burns, but 60 miles of logging railroad extending out of Burns. He was short on cash when a lot of other people found themselves in the same position—with the Stock Market crash in October, 1929.

Herrick tried desperately to weather the Great Depression of the Thirties which followed, but did not make it. His vast empire crumbled, but he was too hardy to do that himself, living on until he was 98. He died January 20, 1953. Today his name is little known, because he left it on no maps—only on an abandoned Milwaukee Railroad station at the mouth of Big Creek.

As well known as Herrick in early St. Maries were the three O'Gara sisters —Margaret and Anna, with buns of raven-black hair, and Mary, with sunset-red tresses. Fair Irish colleens all, only Margaret ever married. Then quickly deciding that the bargain was a poor one, she returned to single life with her sisters.

Running a rooming house and two restaurants, the O'Gara charmers did right well; in fact, they amassed a small fortune. 'Jacks deluged the sisters with gifts, and that was fine with them.

Margaret also had a very profitable sideline. She was a bootlegger. The time was before the Prohibition Era, but Margaret was not inclined to pay the taxes involved with legal liquor. Obtaining whiskey from a mountain supplier who had learned his rapid distilling process deep in the Ozarks of Arkansas, she sold it at about 500 per cent profit.

Generally, the law officers tolerated Margaret's extracurricular activities— after all, she was a right pert and pretty piece—but every now and then they figured that they had to do their duty by raiding the O'Gara establishments. Usually, they found nothing more in potent liquid form than that which filled teapots, but Margaret hurried them along before they could get a whiff of the pots' contents.

Then there was the time that Margaret appeared particularly furious at a raid, refusing to move an inch as the officers stalked through a restaurant kitchen. With arms akimbo and feet planted wide apart, she stood glaring at the violators of her domain.

"We know you just got a fresh supply of booze, Margaret," a deputy advised her. "We'll find it."

But they never did. After their departure, Margaret hoisted her long skirt, and there, between her feet, was a keg of Arkansas-style white lightning.

To McCall came Carl Brown. A lean native of New Hampshire, Brown arrived with his family at the mile-high community beside Payette Lakes in 1910. He had been ranching at the bottom of the South Fork Canyon, where,

207

to eke out a living, he also packed mining supplies and carried the mail—sometimes by horseback and sometimes by dog sled—from Warren to Edwardsburg for $75 a month. Losing the mail route on a bid, he traded the ranch for a two-room house and six lots in McCall, plus $500.

At McCall, Brown got a new mail contract, and plenty of opportunities to do freighting. In 1914, he also got the long-awaited opportunity to go into the lumber business on a big scale by forming a partnership with a husky Minnesotan, Theodore Hoff. This partnership lasted for 14 years. When it was dissolved, Hoff kept a planer the company ran at Horseshoe Bend, eventually expanding this into complete mill operations. Thus, Brown became "Mr. Lumberman" of McCall, and Hoff of Horseshoe Bend.

In bad times as well as good, Brown bought timberland. More important, he became a working boss, because he believed that you couldn't roll out the logs sitting at an office desk. He loved to show up in the tall timber, to take a hand at "wooding 'em up," to sit behind a team of big Percherons pulling a sleigh of logs that God and man could be proud of. Horses, he understood and appreciated. But mules and the mechanical "cats" which came later—well, they were mysteries to be tolerated only as necessary evils.

Most of all, Brown loved people—his people—the people of McCall. Just south of the town lay 40 acres of state-owned land with some scattered yellow pines—and grave markers. The tract was an early cemetery of sorts, long neglected. When a crying woman came to Brown and explained that a tree had fallen across her daughter's grave, Brown told her that he would see what he could do. Sending out a crew to move the tree would be no trick at all. Certainly, the State would have no objections. But would that be doing enough for all the people who were buried there? Buying the tract, Brown then deeded it to the village of McCall so that it could be permanently cared for as a cemetery should be.

As McCall became modernized, Brown learned that an old-time lumberjack with arthritis had only an outdoor privy at his home. So one day he showed up with a crew of carpenters and plumbers, and a modern bathroom quickly emerged.

Then, in 1937, with skiers struggling to "make do" on various slopes, Brown gave to McCall 80 acres of mountainside land so that it could build a first-class ski area. Today, skiing is about as important to McCall as lumbering.

Brown also got into politics, becoming a State Legislator. Not one for introducing bills, he figured there were enough laws—just needed enforcing.

In 1940, after the lean Depression years, things were picking up at the Brown Tie and Lumber Company, with railroad ties in big demand at $40 a thousand. Then, on July 16, Carl and his wife, Ida, were in Chicago, where Carl was a delegate at the National Democratic Convention (the one at which Franklin D. Roosevelt was nominated to run for an unprecedented third term). And that was the day that fire struck in McCall.

Brown's mill on the shore of Payette Lakes seemed to explode into flame. Whipped by strong, swirling winds, the fire leaped to the planer shed, then to the roof of the Payette Lakes Star newspaper building, Ding's Club, Dewey's Barbershop, Lowe's Cabinet Shop, nearby homes . . . Firefighting efforts were futile. But suddenly the wind stopped, and so did the spreading of the flames. The town was saved, but the mill—the mainstay of McCall's economy—was a smoldering ruin.

In Chicago, when he heard the news, Brown began to add up the insurance. It would cover half—maybe only a third—of the loss. But somehow the mill must rise again. There were all those employees and their families who were dependent upon it.

Delaying his return to McCall just long enough to cast his vote for Roosevelt, Carl drove into the town, expecting to find great sadness. Instead, he found a joking crew of men working under the direction of his son, Warren (who would later follow his father into the State Legislature), clearing debris and hewing timbers with axes.

"Thought you'd want to start construction of a temporary mill," explained Warren. "There are a million feet of logs in the pond, and more coming in. With the temporary mill, we can fulfill our present contracts. With the income from them—and what can be borrowed—we can build a new mill."

Warren, who as a State Senator in the 1970s would refer to himself as "a dumb old lumberjack legislator," hadn't been born a Brown for nothing. The father nodded. He was greatly pleased, but demonstration of family pride was limited to the home.

As this is written, the rebuilt mill at McCall is still going strong. And, although Carl Brown is no longer around to josh with the workers, the spirit of "wood 'em up" which he brought to the town continues to pervade it.

Probably the most colorful and best liked among the early parsons of the pines was the Reverend Dick Ferrell, Presbyterian missionary. Dick—he blushed when this writer once called him "Reverend"—was originally a blacksmith, who had become a welterweight fighter of note in the Midwest. Then, one night while attending a Presbyterian church service in Chicago, he became greatly moved by the sermon. He tarried to shake hands with the pastor, Dr. John Timothy Stone, who noted his crushing grip.

"What are you?" asked Reverend Stone. "A blacksmith or a prizefighter?"
"Both."

"The Lord could use a man like you as a missionary in the lumber camps of the Pacific Northwest. The lumberjacks ran the last two missionaries sent there out of the camps."

The challenge appealed to Dick, who promptly began studying for the ministry. He made his entry into the Idaho woods as a missionary in 1914—a somewhat unusual entry for a parson.

Two 'jacks, with murder in their fists, were fighting in a camp upcreek from Prichard. Now, ordinarily 'jacks love a good fight, but this one was no longer good. It had become primitively brutal—the kind any one of the hundred men watching would try to stop, providing he cared to risk a cracked jaw.

Then, pushing through the crowd came a stranger—a little man standing no more than five feet eight and weighing perhaps 155. The stranger rushed between the big fighters, grabbed a man in each hand, raised both off the ground, and shook them like apple-loaded tree limbs.

"Fight's over," he said.

Released, each man ran in opposite directions—one down the trail leading out of camp, and the other for a bunkhouse, crying:

"I'll get my rifle. I'll kill him."

The stranger raced after the bunkhouse-bound 'jack, and met him coming out the door with the gun. Twisting the rifle away, the little man knocked the 'jack sprawling back into the bunkhouse.

"Now don't come out till you're cleaned up and cooled off," he said.

Then, closing the door, the stranger walked calmly down to the circle of admiring lumberjacks, laid the rifle aside, and announced:

"I'm Dick Ferrell, the new missionary. As long as you men are all assembled, we'll hold services right here under the pines. Let us pray."

The woods grapevine carried the news of the new parson's great physical strength, and it became a sword of Damocles hanging from the pines—even for the I.W.W.'s.

The Industrial Workers of the World was a radical organization of the period. Its members, sometimes called Wobblies, were not without some justifiable grievances regarding working conditions for the common man. But their tactics were far from justifiable. Through Zane Grey's novel, "Desert of Wheat," they were best known in the Pacific Northwest for setting fire to wheat fields, but they carried their incendiary activities to the woods, too—and raised general havoc there. For them, Karl Marx's book was the gospel, and they were not inclined to listen to anything from the book which Dick Ferrell carried.

At a camp near Bovill, the I.W.W.'s were particularly strong. So, when Dick strode into the camp on a Sunday afternoon and announced that he would hold services, an I.W.W. leader suddenly decided that it was time for an organizational meeting.

"Get out of camp," he ordered Dick.

The missionary tossed his hat into a circle of men lounging in the shade of sun-curtaining evergreens.

"My hat's in the ring," he said, doubling up his fists. "Any man who wants to throw it out will fight me first."

But the I.W.W.'s, tipped off about Dick, were not inclined to back up their leader. No one took up the challenge. Dick preached his sermon.

For more than 40 years before his death, Dick annually traveled 20,000 miles throughout Northern Idaho, Eastern Washington and Western Montana to hold services in some 200 camps. With his main mission in life to get the loggers to thinking about their Maker, he never wore his Presbyterianism as a badge. He read to a Christian Scientist; he heard the confession of a dying Catholic. ("If it will ease you, go ahead," he told Pat. "God will be listening, too.")

Dick Ferrell, in brief, was a two-fisted pioneer in the Ecumenical Movement.

Long before the white man came to Idaho, its woods knew terrible fires. But the oldest Indian could not remember anything like the fires of 1910. They reached out into Washington and Montana, too, but, in Northern Idaho, they wreaked the greatest havoc.

Virtually no rain fell that summer. The humidity? It dropped almost to nothing. To start flames leaping from tree to tree, it didn't take much—lightning flashing earthward from a "dry" storm, sparks wafting skyward from a train engine, hot ashes dropping from a hiker's pipe, glowing embers reaching out from a deserted campfire, a burning match being flicked from the hand of an incendiary . . .

By August 1, almost 2,000 forest fires, big and small, were burning in the three-state area, with more than 10,000 men fighting them. They included rangers, loggers, miners, ranchers and anybody else who could be induced or ordered into battle against the red menace. In addition, at the direction of President William Howard Taft, three companies of soldiers were rushed to the fire fronts.

Then came August 20—so hot and dry it just made a man want to curl up beneath the cool shade of trees. But the trees' brittle branches gave off no coolness. They themselves exuded heat. And rivers and creeks which had traversed burning areas ran warm like bath water.

"Makes Death Valley seem like an oasis," said one ranger, up from California.

But the worst was yet to come. A hot "devil wind," emerging from the southwest, sent flames racing through the forests at speeds up to 70 miles an hour. Little fires linked with big ones, making mountains and valleys one great roaring furnace. The smoke-clouded sky turned yellow, then orange, and finally purple, real dark purple, except where darting red tongues of flame licked at the tree tops.

In Billings, Montana, 750 miles from the fires, people grew fearful and prayerful as the smoke shut out the sun. On the Missoula to Billings run, a train conductor had to use a lantern to read tickets at midday. At Denver, still farther away, eyes smarted from the smoke, throats became rasping dry. Even across the prairies of the Dakotas and Kansas and Nebraska, residents looked at the darkened skies and wondered, "What is happening to the people of Northern Idaho?"

They were living in hell on earth.


On a ridge between Big Creek of the Coeur d'Alene River and Big Creek of the St. Joe River, about 10 miles from Wallace, Ranger Edward C. Pulaski, a husky fellow who was once a plumber at Burke, was bossing a crew of 150 fire-fighters. Cut off by the flames with 40 of his men from the rest of the crew, Pulaski ordered a retreat to Wallace.

Leading two frightened horses, the men had covered about five miles, when a mountain of flame blocked their path. Panicking, they started to flee back to the certain death of more fire. Pulaski roared at them to halt, then added in a soothing tone:

"We can make it easy to the old War Eagle Mine. Just follow me."

And the men and horses did. All arrived safely at the mine's 100-foot tunnel except for one man, who died after being knocked down and set afire by a flaming branch.

Inside the tunnel, Pulaski ordered the men to lie down, faces to the earth made wet by a trickling stream. Then he yanked blankets from back packs, wet them in the water, and hung them over the mouth of the tunnel. One by one, the blankets burned away. Flames licked inside the entranceway. Smoke drifted throughout the entire tunnel.

"I'm getting out of here!" shouted one of the men, staggering to his feet.

But Ranger Pulaski, who happened to be a great-grandson of General Casimir Pulaski of Revolutionary War fame, had been steeped in the tradition of obedience to orders. Whipping out a pistol, he leveled it at the man, and said:

"Go any farther, and I'll drill you."

The rank-breaker returned to the prone position.

As the darkness of day merged into the darkness of night, all the men lost consciousness—except for one. When he noticed early in the morning that the fire was abating, he scrambled over what he thought were corpses, and made it to Wallace. A rescue crew found all but five men alive—just barely. The two horses were also alive, but were in such bad shape that they had to be shot.

Most of the men were moved from the tunnel to Wallace on stretchers. Determined to walk into town on his own two feet, Pulaski, almost sightless with heat-puffed eyelids, did so with the help of two other men.

Years later, F. B. Foltz, the cook for the Pulaski crew, recalled:

"When I checked in for my pay, Supervisor Weigle told me that the rate was only twenty-five cents an hour, but that he would allow me twenty-four hours a day so that I could receive a larger sum."

Wallace was far from a safe haven. By August 21, the fire had destroyed a third of the town, and was threatening more of it. The heat was so great that it caused frame structures to sway.

Up to noon on August 20, with the flames getting near, Wallace insurance men had grudgingly continued to sell fire insurance. Finally, they said, "No more." There were angry protests.

"Would anybody sell life insurance to passengers on a sinking ship?" retorted an insurance agent.

Five special trains of Pullmans, baggage cars and boxcars, brought to Wallace in fear of the worst, pulled out with their human cargoes for the safety of Spokane or Missoula. A pregnant woman, trying to get aboard one of the trains, was shoved aside by a burly man who figured that he had a priority on life. Several other men yanked him from the steps of a Pullman, and beat him until he cried for mercy. Then they helped the mother-to-be aboard as a black porter grinned approvingly.

Seven-year-old Willie Graffenberger, who had become separated from his parents in the depot turmoil, rode on a train without them to Spokane. When he arrived there, he strode into the Spokane Hotel lobby, and told the startled room clerk:

"Wallace got too hot for me. I want a room with a bed."

Back in Wallace, a man was offering big money to anybody who would help him tote a grand piano to a mine tunnel. He found no takers.

Providence Hospital was filled to its corridors with badly burned fire-fighters. Some begged to be put out of their misery. Others feared that the hospital would burn, and that they would die in bed after escaping death on the trail.

A husky lumberjack told a Providence nun:

"This hospital will go as sure as I'm a no-good sinner."

The nun smiled:

"You forget that we pray as we work. We have promised God that, if the hospital is spared, we will erect a statue of Christ in front of it. The hospital will be spared. The statue will be erected."

She was right on both counts. All the buildings and trees and shrubs immediately surrounding the hospital were destroyed by flames, but the hospital was not touched. Standing in front of it today is a large statue of Christ in all His serenity—a memorial to answered prayers.

At a lonely homestead on Fisher Creek, Mrs. William Boll was milking a cow in the barn when she heard the crackling of fire. Setting down her pail, she hurried out into the barnyard. The fire was leaping down Elk Creek Canyon, straight for the homestead.

Mr. Boll had taken a lumbering job that summer, leaving Mrs. Boll alone with two children, Wallace, 9, and Naomi, 4. She knew terror, but not the terror of Wallace, who came running out of the house with a .22 rifle.

"Shoot me, mother!" he screamed. "We're going to burn."

"Young man, put that rifle away," replied Mrs. Boll, "and help me saddle up the horses. We're riding, not shooting."

With Naomi clutched in the mother's arms on one horse and Wallace mounted on another, the Bolls raced the flames for three hours, finally reaching safety at Elk River.

212

From Avery, on August 23, U.S. Forest Supervisor W. C. Weigle at Wallace received a telegram:

TWENTY-TWO BODIES FOUND ON SETSER CREEK. WILL GIVE MILITARY BURIAL AT PLACE MEN FELL . . .

DEBITT

Another telegram followed on August 25:

KOTTKEY AND HIS CREW ARE SAFE. DEBITT'S TWO BIRD CREEK CREWS WITH ALLEN SAFE. ONE DEAD, ROCK'S CREW. BALANCE SAFE. FERN AND CREW IN WOODS, BUT WITH CHANCES OF ESCAPE. HOLLINGSHEAD SAFE. HAD SIXTY MEN ON BIG CREEK. FOURTEEN BODIES FOUND. NO RELIABLE INFORMATION REGARDING BALANCE YET EXCEPT MANY MEN IN ST. JOE HOSPITAL . . .

FISHER

When fire threatened to engulf Avery (and it did), the entire town was evacuated via a special train sizzling over burning ties and bridges. Residents of Mullan, Burke and Murray thought that their towns were doomed. While the men fought fires on the edges of the towns, the women began burying prized possessions. To help at Mullan, all prisoners were released from the jail. But the big assist in saving the towns came from the shifting winds. They detoured the main fires around the towns, saving them from destruction.

The fires were fought for weeks. When the toll was counted, the dead numbered 85—77 of them in Idaho, five in Montana, and three in Washington. More than 3,000,000 acres of forest land were burned, destroying a half-billion feet of timber. Losses to property in towns and on ranches and farms ran into millions of dollars, with Wallace the hardest hit.

Although Forest Service officials tramped through hot ashes spotting timber to be salvaged, and commercial cutting crews followed on their heels, these actions were too little and too late. Less than 10 per cent of the burned timber was saved. Much of it, particularly the spruce, quickly started to check and blue-stain, making it worthless. Then there were the invading hordes of bark beetles. Not only did they thrive on the burned-over timber, but they quickly fanned out into areas beyond the fire's path, destroying millions of feet of additional timber.

The Forest Service learned that man cannot move too swiftly into a fire-ravaged area, and this lesson paid off in Oregon's great Tillamook fire of 1933. But the big contribution of Idaho to the nation as a result of the 1910 fire was in improved forest protection. In 1911, Congress passed the Weeks Act, providing federal aid to state and private forest owners for the maintenance of forest protective organizations. Progress had come—the hard and hot way.

More progress was to be spawned in Idaho—selective logging.

For centuries, this type of logging had been practiced in Europe. This writer can remember his grandmother telling how, as a girl, she went into a national forest in Germany with a basket to gather sawdust and chips and twigs from a tree cut down by foresters. And, where the tree had been removed after careful study, two new ones were planted.

But America was the land of plenty, or so it seemed. Cutting of trees in the forest was indiscriminately done. And the ravaged land was left to heal its own wounds.

Then, in 1931, E. C. Rettig, chief forester for Potlatch Forests, Inc., Clearwater Unit, read a paper of tremendous significance before the Pacific Logging

213

Congress in Spokane. He said:

"Selective logging has never before been practiced in America on a definite rotation plan, and so to the Potlatch Company goes the distinction of being the first among the big timber operators in this country to put such a plan in actual operation. It is making the experiment alone—an experiment of colossal proportions, with a $9,000,000 investment at stake. It is a courageous undertaking in that it contemplates century periods rather than usual annual periods of industrial plant operation, and in that it is a gamble with the forces of nature in which man's ingenuity and scientific forestry will be exercised to the limit in growing and farming timber as a 30-35 year crop in three-crop rotation . . .

"In general, the Potlatch selective logging plan is based on limiting cutting of trees of specific girth; cutting only such species as can be profitably marketed; clean cutting of mature stands; fostering young growth by exercising care in cutting; keeping the forest floor clean by brush disposal; replanting; and destroying weed and insect life responsible for tree disease, such as white pine blister rust, and spruce budworm . . ."

Today, selective logging is common practice throughout the United States. It is not all done as well as it might be—perhaps "man's ingenuity and scientific forestry" are still not being exercised to the limit—but it is being done. And it is paying off, proving that nature is ready and willing to cooperate with man—if he just meets it halfway.

Ralph Waldo Emerson once remarked that "steam is no stronger today than it was 100 years ago, but it is put to better use." And so, too, our forests, thus assuring for generations to come the cries of "Timber-r-r!" and "Wood 'em up!'"

Chapter XIX

# BORN OF VOLCANOES—THE GOOD EARTH

"Millions of years ago Idaho was one of the hottest spots on earth, with violent volcanic eruptions. This has had much to do with making the State a present-day leader in agriculture."

*—Encyclopedia International*

Within two hours after the first party of Mormon emigrants, fleeing from persecution in Illinois, arrived in the Salt Lake Valley in 1847, they were plowing. The hard earth broke two plows, so, within four hours after arrival, the Mormons had dug irrigation ditches, flooding the land to soften it. Sowers followed the plowmen, and, within 48 hours, the first crop of potatoes and corn had been planted. With continued irrigation and with what was known as "Mormon capital"—sweat, bone and sinew—the crop thrived.

Thus, the pattern was set for the first Mormon missionary-colonists who came to Idaho in 1855, settling in the Lemhi Valley and establishing Fort Lemhi. The earth was too parched for dry land farming, so the Mormons promptly channeled irrigation water to it.

Minor irrigation projects had been engineered at Old Fort Boise to provide fresh vegetables for the resident factors of the Hudson's Bay Company (historians debate whether Fort Hall had similar irrigated gardens). And the Reverend Spalding, hoping that irrigation would seep into the way of life for

215

the Nez Perces, introduced it at Lapwai. But the Mormons really brought irrigation to Idaho on a broad farming scale.

At Fort Lemhi an early frost destroyed most of the late-planted first crop. More supplies and seed were brought from Salt Lake City. The next year grasshoppers gleaned the fields ahead of the missionaries, but still the Saints persevered. In May, 1857, with potatoes, peas, turnips and corn looking good (and the harvest did turn out well), President Brigham Young of the Church of Jesus Christ of Latter-Day Saints paid a five-day visit to the valley, and was pleased with the fertility of the land and the industry of the missionaries. Gold had been discovered in California, but Young had trumpeted from the pulpit that seeking the gleaming ore was not the way of life for the Mormons.

"Instead of hunting gold," he cried, "we ought to pray the Lord to hide it up. Gold is not wealth. Wealth consists in the multiplication of the necessities and comforts of life. Instead of hunting gold, go and raise wheat, barley, oats. Get your bread, and make gardens and orchards."

Aging Luis Peralta, a Spaniard who had been given a vast grant of land in California comprising the present cities of Berkeley, Oakland and Alameda, put it another way. He told his sons who were anxious to take off for the gold fields:

"My sons, God has given this gold to the Americans. Had he desired us to have it, He would have given it to us ere now. Therefore, go not after it, but let others go. Plant your lands, and reap: these be your best gold fields, for all must eat while they live."

But the word of Young alone was sufficient for the early Mormon missionaries at Fort Lemhi. They took his advice, and were well on their way to prospering in the Lemhi Valley when the Indians ran them out in 1858.

Coming back to Idaho in greater strength two years later, the Mormons established at Franklin, just across the Utah border, a new and permanent settlement. And, although some irrigation of significance had been accomplished in the Lemhi Valley, the Mormons went much further at Franklin. They constructed an intricate irrigation system totaling 3½ miles in length, bringing water from Maple Creek to the new and productive farms where the sagebrush had been arduously grubbed off.

The farming was done on a communal basis, but each family had its own tract of land. When the colonists first reached the valley, the acreage to be settled was marked out by those with some surveying knowledge. Then Bishop Preston Thomas held a drawing, awarding farmsteads by lot.

According to Byron Defenbach in his "Idaho—The Place and Its People," there was some muttering because Lot No. 2 was drawn by Peter Lowe, a young bachelor (at first, bachelors had been ruled out of the drawing). But Peter's choice acreage in the center of the settlement was not his alone for very long.

A log meeting house called the Bowery was built at Franklin. Even before branches could be placed across the top to form a thatched roof, a dance was held there, and to it came Peter Lowe and Mary Hull, daughter of William Hull, who had Lot No. 1, adjoining Peter's place.

Some of the girls wore beaded moccasins acquired in trade from the Indians for bread, butter or homemade lace. Several young ladies even had dressy, high-topped shoes. But a goodly number of the females—and males —were barefooted.

Mary was among the latter. She was not concerned, however, because Peter, on whom she had her eye, was also barefooted. (Donning shoes only when winter's snows came, he could step on a cockleburr without wincing.) Too, Mary was confident that her linsey-woolsey dress set her off well. It had cost $14 in Salt Lake City—money she had earned by working as a hired girl for 14 weeks at a dollar a week.

There was a charge for the dance—a squash, some wheat or potatoes. The caller, John Corbridge, came free, but the fiddlers, Dab Keele and Ike Vail, figured it was unprofessional to play without pay. Also considered part of their due was an extra share of the refreshments—hand-pulled sorghum taffy flavored and colored with service berries and seeded black haws.

For three hours, barefoot Peter and barefoot Mary skipped through square dances on the Bowery's dirt floor (it was sprinkled from time to time to hold down the dust). Then Peter whispered in Mary's ear:

"Let's really skip, and see Bishop Thomas on some official business."

At the bishop's home, a man with twinkling eyes and flowing beard greeted the two, one of whom—Mary—was blushing like a desert sunset.

"And what can I do for you?" asked Thomas.

"We'd like to be married," replied Peter.

"Well," said the bishop, his mind flashing back to Brigham Young's arrival in the Salt Lake Valley, "this is the place."

As the Mormons began to spread to other areas in Southern Idaho, they increased their efforts at bringing irrigation water to the land. To provide an adequate flow of water at the right times around the new settlement of Weston, established in 1865, the Mormons constructed a dam—with the help of some neighborly beavers.

Lars Fredrickson, one of the first settlers of Weston, wrote in his diary (the early Mormons kept detailed records, because they believed that "what is written on earth is also written in heaven"):

"The men started to put in willows, dig sods, and carry them onto the dam. They had to carry all the dirt because they had no other way. They made a rack with two poles and wove it in with small willows so it would hold dirt, load that up, then a man to each end to carry the load over on the dam and unload, then repeat.

"The creek was full of beavers, so as soon as the beavers understood that there was going to be a dam built, they would work at night. They would cut willows into three or four-foot lengths, sometimes longer, weave these together in the water where the dam was to be, and plaster the whole thing up with mud. The beavers run the night shift . . ."

With help like that, the pioneering Idaho farmers couldn't lose.

Although irrigation was not necessary for all areas of Idaho, it was primarily what made the land into one of the nation's great agricultural states. Most important of all was the fact that, although Idaho had known some glacial action, its earth was largely composed of rich lava soil, formed from tremendous volcanic activity in prehistoric times. The vast Snake River Valley, which was so born, has been called "Idaho's Valley of the Nile," but crops raised along the Nile are pretty puny compared with those sprouting on the sides of the Snake, a magnificent, 1,038-mile-long river which deserves a better name. (The Indians first called the river the Sho-sho-nee, which in their language means "Snake in the Grass.")

217

In 1864, an enterprising young man of Boise took a covetous look at all the gold that was being dug out of the hills around Idaho City and Placerville. He wanted some of it, and decided that the best way to get it was to sell fresh vegetables to the affluent miners.

So, with a partner, he went over to Jerusalem Valley on the Payette River, and started a farm. The year before, he had observed the success of Tom and Frank Davis in raising a bountiful crop of hay on a Boise farm with sub-irrigation from a slough. He would also utilize irrigation.

Before long he was turning the gold of carrots into the gold of the placer mines. Chinese peddled his garden products for him, carrying them in large baskets attached to a pole. Later, as business increased, the Chinese utilized horse-drawn carts from which they would continually enumerate in a singsong manner what they had to sell. At a regular customer's home which was complete with a housewife, the Chinese would disembark, rap at the door, and call, "Missy! Missy!"

With this kind of hard-sell merchandising, the young farmer had to expand his acreage considerably. In agriculture he saw the future of Idaho, and in Idaho he saw his own future as a farmer, merchant (at Moscow) and politician. He was William J. McConnell, who became the third Governor of the State (1893-1897).

But McConnell and the Davises weren't the only ones pioneering irrigation in Southeastern Idaho. By June 30, 1864, settlers had formed a webwork of eight irrigation canals, totaling 50 miles and extending from the canyon above Boise to the Parma area.

Across the mountains and plains, the people of Missouri were caught in the crossfire of the Civil War (1861-1865). Missouri had many Southern sympathizers, and had been recognized as a slave state upon its admission to the Union, but during the war it remained predominantly with the North. A total of 109,000 Missourians fought in blue uniforms, and 30,000 in grey. Not only that, 11 per cent of the war's engagements took place in Missouri. The bitterness in the State was great, although it could not always be expressed. After the Union victory at the Battle of Pea Ridge, Arkansas, on March 6-8, 1862, the Northern forces were pretty much in control in Missouri, and many Southern sympathizers began to migrate to the West. They had heard that it was still untamed. But what could be worse than living among neighbors who thought General Robert E. Lee was a scoundrel?

Figuring thus, a party of Missourians left Independence in a wagon train early in 1864, headed for Oregon. By fall the weary emigrants got as far as a meadow just west of present-day Caldwell. There they found water, grass, wood and wild game in abundance. Deciding that there was no necessity of going any further, the Confederate-minded Missourians established the community of Dixie, where they could discuss Yankee scoundrels freely. (An early Northern Idaho mining town south of Elk City was also named Dixie by a prospector from Dixie, Georgia. This town lives on today with a population of 10, but the Dixie down south in Idaho has faded as a post office address.)

At the Southern Idaho Dixie, the Missourians built log cabins (including a church and school) near two waterways, the Boise River and a slough . . . so that the streams could be tapped for irrigation water. The raising of good crops in the area proved no problem, but the Indians did, and iron bars (flattened wagon wheel rims) were placed across all doors at night. The settlers were used to raids by Union forces, and knew how to handle the situation.

"But what this country needs most," said Reuben Cox, "is a mowing machine."

And what may have been the first mowing machine in Idaho was brought to Dixie by Cox. It cost him $500 shipped to The Dalles from Portland, and brought to Dixie by ox team. Then, to run the new-fangled thing, Cox had to pay a man $60 a month. Virtually everybody in the community used it during the years that followed, with the farmers gradually getting the hang of how to operate it.

They hauled their wheat to Middleton to the Pacard and Stevenson flour mill to have it ground into flour. In 1863, M. B. Palmer had settled a couple of miles east of where Star is now located. The following year he began to irrigate his land. He built a dam, dug a ditch, and took water out of the slough. It was Palmer's ditch which the Middleton mill took over. In 1899, however, S. S. Foote, who had become owner and operator of the mill, decided that the new town of Caldwell would become the trading center of the area. So he tore down the mill, and moved it to Caldwell.

Foote was indeed right. Although Middleton today is a bustling community of 739, Caldwell has a population of 14,219. Caldwell, too, has long been a cultural center. The College of Idaho, linked to the United Presbyterian Church, was founded there in 1891 by William Judson Boone. (The college boasts among its distinguished graduates Robert E. Smylie, who served as Governor of Idaho, 1955 to 1967.) Also founded at Caldwell in 1903 was the firm of The Caxton Printers, Ltd., one of the few successful regional book publishing establishments in the nation.

Meanwhile, west of Caldwell, John Mammem had started another community called Roswell. There Mammem and other settlers had trouble getting water on the land. The Dixie Ditch, nicknamed the Methodist Ditch because of the religious persuasion of many of the builders, was constructed in 1884. The problem was that the ditch wouldn't stay put.

Breaks continually occurred all along the line, messing things up generally. When a farmer would come riding like Paul Revere, shouting to the neighbors that there was a break in the ditch, everybody would rush out, and grab whatever was at hand to dam the break. Usually this was sagebrush and earth, but once in desperation the farmers plugged a leak in the dike with a dead horse. Finally, they sold their ditch to the Boise Land and Water Company, and, by 1893, were getting all the water they needed without difficulty. Settlement began in earnest.

Irrigation developments came a little slower to Southeastern Idaho, although as early as 1862 a ditch was dug from Willow Creek to water a garden located on land which now forms the City Park of Idaho Falls. Later, in 1880, farmers got together and organized a major irrigation operation near Idaho Falls called the Anderson Canal Company. This was typical of irrigation developments in Idaho until 1894 when Congress passed the Carey Act.

Under the Carey Act (named after sponsor Joseph M. Carey, pioneer Wyoming cattleman, judge, opera-house builder and United States Senator), the federal government gave the arid Western states 1,000,000-acre units of land. The states were responsible for seeing that dams, reservoirs and canals were built for irrigation. It took two amendments (the last one in 1901) to make the law efficiently operable, but, by 1902, it was a highly potent force in the opening of the West to settlement.

When water was wanted in an area, the settlers petitioned the State Board of Land Commissioners for construction of an irrigation works. If the project was approved, bond issues were authorized, and construction carried out by development companies under state supervision. By paying off the water liens, the settlers gained clear title to the land.

There was some defaulting on payments. Traditionally, many of the first generation had difficulties making a go of it on new land. But there was always a second generation to follow. And important was the fact that the gray of sagebrush was being replaced by the gold of grain and the red of apples.

Of all the Western states, Idaho had the most Carey Act projects—a total of 19. Many towns such as Twin Falls, Buhl, Filer, Wendell, Gooding and Jerome, owe their development to Carey Act projects. (Gooding was destined to render special service to the people of the State, becoming the home of both the Idaho State School for the Deaf and Blind and the Idaho State Tuberculosis Hospital.)

But the Carey Act was not enough. The West needed—and, in 1902, got—the Reclamation Act, providing for the advancing of money by the federal government to build big dams and other facilities vital to major irrigation projects. Among the early Reclamation Act accomplishments which were so important to Idaho were the Minidoka Project, completed in 1909, and the Boise Project, completed in 1915.

Created by the construction of Minidoka Dam was Lake Walcott Reservoir with a storage capacity of 95,000 acre-feet to serve 120,000 acres with irrigation. Then, expanding on this project in 1927, came mile-wide American Falls Dam and 26 mile-long American Falls Reservoir with a storage capacity of 1,700,000 acre-feet. Directly or by exchange, the combined resources of the Minidoka Project eventually brought water to 700,000 acres extending from the Wyoming border to the lower end of Hagerman Valley.

When the Boise Project, to divert water of the Boise River to 223,866 thirsty acres of the valley, was getting under way in 1911 with the lining of the New York Canal, Frank T. Crowe visited the construction site with James Munn, project superintendent. Crowe, who was about to start supervising the building of Arrowrock Dam and who would become one of the world's greatest dam builders, commented to Munn:

"I drove up on the ditch bank to the concreting operations bossed by a long, slim kid without a hat. I wanted to talk to that kid, but, before I could get to him, he took off, hell-bent on a saddle horse. What about him? Is he as good close-up as he looks at a distance?"

Munn grinned.

"That's some lad, all right. He wants to line the whole ditch in one day. It will take several months, but it won't hurt him to try. His name is Harry W. Morrison."

Crowe did not let the matter drop there. Arrowrock Dam, a project of the Bureau of Reclamation on the Boise River 24 miles from Boise, was to be when completed in 1915 the highest dam then constructed in the world. It would rise 348.5 feet above bedrock, with a waterfall twice as high as that of Niagara (165 feet on the American side). Crowe was looking for the best man he could find to work on the project. He wanted Morrison.

But the young man had other ideas. The American West—indeed, the whole world—needed a lot of construction, particularly in the taming of rivers, and Morrison wanted to capitalize on that fact. He poured his enthusiasm into the ears of Morris H. Knudsen, an employee of the Reclamation Service, and on March 1, 1912, a partnership which was to become known as Morrison-Knudsen Company, Inc., was formed with a handclasp.

Morrison-Knudsen Company, Inc., now one of the world's largest contracting firms, started in Boise with small assets—$600 in cash, a dozen wheelbarrows, three dozen shovels, one dozen picks and a few odd tools. The first job was also small—a $14,000 subcontract to build a pumping station near Grand View, then linked to Mountain Home only by a dusty trail. The pumping station site was on a mound, and concrete had to be hauled up to it in a wheelbarrow, with one man pushing and another pulling. But, when the job was completed, there was a profit of $1,400. Morrison-Knudsen Company, Inc., was on its way.

The first dam building job for M-K was the Three-Mile Falls project on the Umatilla River near Hermiston, Oregon. Morrison was particularly pleased about that job, because he got it by underbidding the next lowest competitor by $200.

But then came the big Western dams such as Boulder (now Hoover), Bonneville, Parker and Grand Coulee, with the latter requiring three times as much masonry as had ever been placed in a single structure in the history of man. These jobs were large orders for any single contractor, so Morrison persuaded leading builders of the West to pool their working capital and varied skills as the Six Companies (actually seven). The results made history in construction—and in irrigation and power and recreation development.

Meanwhile, M-K was building smaller dams on its own. There were, for instance, the Idaho Power Company's Twin Falls dams built on the Snake River in 1935-1936. At cliff's edge, above the powerhouse, a small concrete dam was constructed to provide power diversion. Then, across the north channel, a flexible-arch dam—the only one of its kind in the nation—was built. The dam can and does "flex its muscles." More than 500 feet long; it is separated from its foundation base by a thin but tough sheet of tar paper so that the concrete arch is left free to adjust itself to load and temperature changes.

Regardless of the construction problems (not just dam ones), M-K engineers were ready to tackle them—any place in the world. Soon the firm began to have offices in such far-flung corners of the earth as Rio de Janeiro, Shanghai and Kabul. But, even after the deaths of Morrison and Knudsen, M-K maintained its headquarters in Boise. It helped build the West, and was sticking with it.

Not all Idaho's irrigation water was to come from the damming of its rivers. The Indians of Southeastern Idaho were wrong when they told the first white men who came to their dryly forbidding land:

"Evil spirits deep in ground. They hold captive waters that have disappeared. They will never return them to let the desert bloom."

The red men were referring to four major streams which tumble out of Idaho's mountains with much promise, then gradually vanish among the sands. But disappearing Big Lost River, Little Lost River, Beaver Creek and Birch Creek—collectively known as the Lost Rivers—would eventually be released from their underground prisons through the ingenuity of the white man. Particularly in a huge project north of Rupert, wells would be sunk to tap the water of the Lost Rivers, bringing it back to the surface of the earth to nourish the soil.

The story of the Lost Rivers goes back many years—perhaps a million. During those long-ago yesteryears, the Snake River Valley was a very hot place. Molten lava spewed from huge volcanoes, crept across the land and shoved rivers aside. Even the mighty Snake was moved many miles to the south. Puckishly, the lava twisted Big Lost River, flowing south, so that it reversed its course, and started flowing back north.

"That sort of thing," explained Raymond L. Nace of the United States Geological Survey, "continued for thousands of years. Lava piled up in some areas maybe 20,000 feet high. As the lava rose, the earth sank. Net result was the formation of a sort of shallow bowl. Outside the rim of this bowl flows the Snake River. Inside are the Lost Rivers, all dressed up with good water and no place to go except down."

Big Lost River, Little Lost River, Beaver Creek and Birch Creek formerly found their way to the sea via the Snake. But the lava barriers trapped them. Meanwhile, as the lava cooled, cracks formed. And the Lost Rivers, fed by melting glaciers, carried down from the mountains great deposits of sand and gravel. Then into the lava cracks, into the sand and gravel, the Lost Rivers began to disappear.

The Indians thought that there was no outlet at all for the Lost Rivers, but, said Nace, geologists of recent times found that some of the waters from the vanished streams were actually getting to the Snake by gushing out with other waters in the Thousand Springs of the Hagerman Valley near Twin Falls—a major attraction today for tourists traveling across Idaho on U.S. Highway 30. The Indians, however, are not to be discredited entirely, for a large share of the water that sinks into the earth each year stays sunk.

"Many people today have the idea that big rivers are flowing underground," added Nace. "This is not true. There is a lot of water, but it is in a vast web-work of small channels formed by cracks and extinct volcanoes."

Pioneers suffered from thirst while rocking along in covered wagons over the interwoven reservoirs of water. The crackling-dry sagebrush gave no indication of water below.

Then, in 1947, Julian Clawson, owner of several thousand acres of sage-brush and jackrabbits, got to wondering about the Lost Rivers. Would wells gush forth great enough flows of water to irrigate the land? The lava-based soil itself was good, so very good.

Clawson sank a well. The drill went down 200 feet . . . 300 . . . 400 . . . Then there was water—more water than Clawson had dared to dream there would be, the flow reaching 4,000 gallons a minute. Sinking the hole cost about $5,600, and the pump and 300-horsepower motor $12,000. But the gamble paid off for Clawson—and for many others in the area. Today, the Lost Rivers continue to add handsomely to the dividends provided by Idaho's streams which are tapped for irrigation above ground.

When irrigation water, or even the prospects of it, first came to Southern Idaho, it drew settlers by the hundreds, the thousands. Many were lured to the then somewhat hostile land by a brochure gotten out in 1881 by Robert E. Strahorn under the direction of Idaho's Territorial Legislature. The brochure, titled "The Resources and Attractions of Idaho Territory" and aimed at "the homeseeker, capitalist and tourist," pointed out:

"In the southern half of Idaho, irrigation is generally necessary to insure the ripening of crops. This the Idaho farmer considers an advantage. He is entirely free from solicitude in regard to drouth or flood while his grain is ripening, and is sure of pleasant weather during harvest time. Irrigation enables him to keep his pastures green in autumn, or start them early in the spring; it enables him to produce heavier crops and to secure a larger growth of fruit trees, shrubbery, etc., in one season than can be obtained by any unaided process in nature. The same stream that beautifies and fertilizes his soil can be led by his door and be made to furnish power for his churn, grindstone, saw, fanning-mill, etc. Better than all these, it carries to his land just such qualities of mineral and gaseous matter as is needed to keep it productive for years. In New Mexico lands have been regularly cultivated in this way, without any other fertilizer, for 200 years; in the valley of the Nile it has been the principal fertilizer on lands cultivated continuously for over three thousand years . . .

"Rough lumber costs $22.50 per 1,000 feet . . . Beef in quantity sells at five cents per pound; venison, six to seven cents . . . Rents of cottages, four to six rooms, $10 to $25 per month. Board and lodging at hotels, $9 to $14 per week; at boarding houses, $6 to $10 per week. Livery, single seated rig per day, $4 to $6; double seated, $6 to $8; saddle horses, per day, $3 to $4."

Under such circumstances, who would want to turn down government land offered free as homesteads?

Some young men could not even wait until they were of age to go homesteading, either on dry or irrigated land. C. T. Stranahan, one of the early settlers in the Palouse Country, wrote:

"It was on September 3, 1878, that I crossed the territorial line into Idaho. I went unshaven so that I looked older, and could pretend I was of age. Squatting on 160 acres of land on American Ridge just above the present town of Juliaetta, I began to realize my early ambition—a home of my own. Immediately upon becoming of age, I filed on the land, making it legal."

The lure of free land in America had been great since Revolutionary days when, to step up enlistments in the Continental Army, a bounty of land was offered, with the acreage depending on rank—1,100 acres for a general, 500 for a colonel, 100 for a private. In 1947 and 1948, when 75 farm units on federal reclamation projects in the Pacific Northwest were made available for homesteads, 30,000 persons from all over the United States submitted applications for the drawing. But the Bureau of Reclamation had learned a lot by then, and ruled out all except about 4,000 applicants (each had to have assets of farm experience and $3,000 in cash or equipment).

Of the 75 available homestead units, 43 were on the Hunt unit of the Minidoka Project in Southern Idaho, site of a Japanese evacuee camp during World War II. Barracks of the abandoned camp were thrown in free with the land, and the new generation of homesteaders did some interesting things with them such as forming U-shaped, ranch-style houses. The homes were quite an improvement over the 10 by 14-foot, one-room shacks of many of the earlier homesteaders.

"It was no land of milk and honey when we moved on it," cowboy-hatted young Eugene Kenner told this writer on a visit to the project in 1949. "Most of the land was covered by sagebrush, with two jackrabbits fighting for shade under each bush. The Japanese had grubbed off some of the land for farming, but brush and weeds had snuck back in. Still, the land was ours, and there's something special about land that's free. 'Course we were assessed about $100 an acre for irrigation-construction charges, but the land itself was free.

"I was one of the extra lucky ones. I won a surplus truck on a drawing. My grandfather homesteaded 80 acres over by Rupert in 1906. When he came onto the land, all he had was a wagon, a slab of bacon, some flour and beans. But we still have to get in and dig just like Grandpa."

And, in that last sentence, young Kenner summed up the story of the early settlers who made a go of homesteading in the West.

Crops successfully tried by the early settlers in Southern Idaho were varied —beans, onions, sugar beets, hay, clover, wheat, hops, assorted fruits . . . But the key to the land's rewarding virtues, particularly in Southeastern Idaho, eventually proved to be the potato.

The big Idaho baked potato became famous early in the Twentieth Century. Remember when meals on transcontinental trains, even though turned out in quarters as cramped as a telephone booth, rivaled those at Delmonico's? If you do, you also remember that the Idaho potato was featured, especially in the dining cars of the Union Pacific with their white linen tablecloths and waiters who demonstrated the grace of ballet dancers as they moved through the swaying cars.

But what really put Idaho ahead of Maine as the No. 1 potato state was the advent of processing.

Way back on October 27, 1881—almost a century ago—a writer on Boise's *Idaho Statesman* suggested that "evaporation" be used to reduce the weight and bulk of potatoes with a view to lowering shipping costs. But at the time it was thought that the newspaperman was merely dreaming on a dull news day.

Then, at the start of World War II, J. R. (Jack) Simplot, a potato broker from Burley, who had never read any 1881 issues of the *Statesman,* came to Caldwell with the same idea—evaporation for potatoes. He figured that the U.S. Armed Forces, fighting in distant parts, would need potatoes in condensed or dried form—lots of them. In a machine shop, he sketched on the oily floor with chalk his conception of a drying apparatus.

"Now, build me that," he said.

The mechanics got to work on the drying equipment, but they were not up to fashioning a boiler. And, with steel rationed, boilers were hard to come by. Simplot, however, was as lucky as a nearby lumber mill operator was unlucky. The mill burned down, and Simplot acquired its boiler.

Originally, he planned the Caldwell plant for about 50 employees. But he did not figure on the war getting so big or lasting so long. Eventually, more than 10 million GI's overseas ate dehydrated potatoes. The Caldwell plant grew until it needed 2,000 employees. Other big processing plants sprang up, but of all the dehydrated potatoes used in the war Simplot supplied about a third. (This gave the J. R. Simplot Company a firm financial foundation for its expansion into such other varied operations as phosphate and clay mines and hotels and motels. Although Simplot now has his headquarters in Boise, he has never forgotten where he got started, and has been a major benefactor of the College of Idaho in Caldwell.)

This writer remembered the dehydrated potatoes he ate in the Air Force during World War II as being gluey. When he mentioned this on a visit to Simplot's Caldwell plant, he was given the blindfold test. With a cloth covering his eyes, he was served fresh mashed potatoes and dehydrated mashed potatoes. He couldn't tell which was which.

Scientists had discovered what caused the gluelike formation, and licked the problem. Free starch was the stickler. The processing has now been controlled so that the starch cells are not broken up, but remain in their natural state.

Then came the emergence into the frozen food market—from French fries to hash browns. And it was discovered that Idaho potatoes were "naturals" for processing in any form. The State's volcanic-ash soil, high elevation, abundant cold water for irrigation, warm days and cool nights made them so. Also deserving some credit is Luther Burbank, the plant wizard who kept about 3,000 experiments going at one time, with one of the successful experiments in the 1870s giving rise to the Russet Burbank potato, which proved particularly adaptable to Idaho's soil, and to good eating in whole-baked or processed form.

The advent of processed potatoes brought much greater stabilization of prices. Prior to the processing period, the price of potatoes in some years hardly made the tubers worth growing.

Back in 1914, which was a bad year for potato prices, a farm family near Oakley did more than its share in trying to get rid of the surplus of potatoes by eating them three times a day. A seven-year-old boy in the family said that he ate so many potatoes that he "felt like a sack of them." His name was George Romney. Later, he became president of American Motors Corporation, Governor of Michigan, United States Secretary of Housing and Urban Development, and a front-runner for the 1968 Republican presidential nomination.

Today, about one-third of all the farms in Idaho grow potatoes, producing about 32 billion pounds annually—25 per cent of all the potatoes consumed in America and more than double the amount grown in the second largest potato producing state. In processing, Idaho is also No. 1. Sixteen processing firms with plants in various towns throughout the southern part of the State— from Simplot in Caldwell to Ore-Ida in Burley to R. T. French in Shelley— provide about 35 per cent of the nation's processed potatoes.

Comedian Bob Hope summed it all up this way:

"Idaho—that's the place where even the village bells peal potatoes."

While early settlers in Southern Idaho were sweating out irrigation projects, those in Northern Idaho simply waited for moisture to drop from the sky. On the great Camas Prairie in the north, the native bunch grass first lured cattlemen, then sheepmen (accompanied by feuding), then farmers. The latter figured that there was no reason why they couldn't produce abundant farm crops on the land where the wild grass grew so lush. And they were right.

Loyal P. Brown, who came to the area in 1862, wrote in 1888:

"In the spring of 1863 . . . grain was sowed, and I think the first timothy ever grown in Idaho was planted; gardens were made, and it became a settled fact that this fair land would produce far better than had been anticipated. Settlers continued to come, and we find today, nearly all the public lands taken up and occupied for homes. The first trees were brought from Walla Walla in the spring of 1864 and set out here at Mount Idaho. Small fruits were also cultivated, which have done exceedingly well. This beginning soon extended, and we find good orchards all over the Prairie; we can boast of good apples, pears, plums, cherries and smaller fruits in abundance. We can also boast of well cultivated farms, producing grain and vegetables, all that the country requires. It is generally conceded that no section of the northwest produces better than our Camas Prairie. Oats and barley often exceed one hundred bushels per acre, with wheat from thirty to sixty bushels. Truly, this is the land of homes, a good climate, rich and productive soil, fine pasturage for the stock grower. What more should we ask?"

So the settlers came, and established such towns as Grangeville, Cotton-wood, Nezperce, Craigmont, Winchester . . .

Farther north in Idaho's Panhandle lay the Palouse Country, representing a particularly rich heritage of the Glacial Age. Silt, blown from the Tri-Cities area of Washington, sifted down upon the land. Too, there was lava dust from vol-canic action to the south. When the dust finally settled down in the form of soil, it lay in gently rolling hills. And the soil ran deep—with no rocks.

As a young man, this writer drove six head of horses, pulling a plow on his father's farm northeast of Moscow. In the middle of a hot afternoon, the horses would annoyingly slow their plodding steps just short of a halt. But nowhere on the farm could a pebble be found to toss at the lead team. So back to the farmyard this writer would go, and, obtaining a sack of cull applies, he would toss them as inspiration at the horses.

Earlier settlers who came from the Dakotas or Ohio or Pennsylvania could not believe what they found in the Palouse Country. The hills seemed every bit as fertile as the valleys. To raise good crops on most of the area, it was just a matter of putting a plow to it. Of course, there were some less-productive fringe areas . . .

Frank C. Robertson, who was born at Moscow in 1890 and eventually au-thored about a hundred Western novels, lived as a child on a farm in one of those fringe areas. In his biographical book, "A Ram in the Thicket," he wrote:

"The land adjoined some timber. Ground squirrels swept through the wheat in hordes, cutting off the stalks at the joint and leaving them to wither and die. Mother and the boys (the father was off looking for a job to obtain some cash) fought the pests with every means at their command. Win Matthews brought some strychnine to mix with flour. He suggested that it might be a little more efficacious if the stuff was mixed with ground glass, but this Mother couldn't consider; poisoning was cruel enough . . . Almost equally troublesome were the weeds on the summer fallow, which had grown so thickly that the ground was a brown mat sucking all moisture from the soil . . .

"That summer we lived mostly on bread and milk and the products of the little garden which Mother and the boys tended carefully. There, they could keep the weeds down. What staples we had Win Matthews brought out from Moscow where he 'stood good' for them at the store."

At first, the people of the Palouse Country were not certain what they should plant, because everything seemed to grow well. Many farmers set out or-chards, and got abundant crops of fruit—in the good years. In the bad ones, early frost in that high area beat the farmers to the harvest.

Most impressed by the fruit trees were the Indians, because the trees bore delicacies of which they had never dreamed. Particularly addicted to cherries was Peopeo Moxmox (Yellow Bird), originally of the Walla Wallas, who once paid 10 cents to Cecil Roberts, young son of an early Palouse Country settler, to fill him and his squaw with the fruit. While Cecil climbed up one of his father's cherry trees, the warrior and wife lay on the ground beneath the tree's shade. Then, as Cecil dropped cherries, the two Indians ate them, seeds and all.

Before long, however, the farmers began digging out the trees, and the Palouse Country became primarily a rolling sea of wheat. Small separators, powered by a dozen horses moving in a circle of monotony, were brought into the area. Then came the steam-powered threshing machine, which could keep a crew of about 20 men busy—some forking bundles into wagons and some driving the wagons, one or two jigging and sewing sacks of grain which had poured out of the separator, another serving as "clean-up man" at the machine, a teamster hauling water for the steamer and sweating harvesters, a mechanically-minded fellow trying to keep the whole cantankerous outfit going.

With some harvesting crews, a cook-wagon rolled along on wheels, but generally the wife of the farmer whose grain was being threshed was responsible for providing the food. The meals for supper and "lunch" were marvels of both quantity and quality. A typical spread beneath the shade of trees at a farmhouse: Pot roast, mashed potatoes and gravy, carrots, cabbage, squash, pickles, bread fresh out of the oven and butter just spooned from the churn, two kinds of pie, both "dark" and "light" cake, and gallons of milk and gallons of coffee. Some of the farmers' wives provided pitchers of pudding-thick cream, even though selling the cream was the way they got money their husbands "didn't count." Each wife tried to outdo the others. One woman drew cries of "foul" by passing out new-fangled chewing gum at the end of the meal.

Eventually, moving combines replaced the binders and stationary threshing machines, and that ended the bundling and shocking of the grain. Horses and mules—as many as 32—pulled the first combines over the rolling hills, but were soon replaced by tractors. And something went out of harvesting, especially foodwise. There was no more dining at groaning tables in the front yard during threshing time.

Who introduced the raising of peas on a big scale in the Palouse Country will probably long be debated. Certainly one of the early pioneers in this regard, however, was Nathaniel Williamson, who operated a general mercantile store at Moscow as well as several farms. Being basically a merchant, he believed in maximum utilization of space. If the leguminous peas could put back into the soil what the wheat took out, he reasoned, alternate-year summer fallowing of the land would not be necessary.

So peas were tried by Williamson and others on acreage which had produced wheat the year before. And the peas not only revitalized the land, but in some years brought a better return than wheat. To encourage more and more farmers to grow peas, Williamson ran advertisements in the Moscow newspaper urging farmers to "plant peas—peas will save the Palouse Country."

Of course, to keep the land from becoming too weedy, summer fallowing could not be completely abandoned. But peas were a great boon to the Palouse Country—indeed, as Williamson predicted, they were the saving of the area, particularly in years of low wheat prices. And, in time, Moscow became known as the "Dried Pea Capital of the Nation."

As for the State as a whole, it has emerged as one of the nation's greatest "bread baskets," especially when potatoes are included in the Idaho basket.

# Chapter XX

## GOVERNMENT IN THE ROUGH

"American democracy was born of no theorist's dream; it was not carried in the *Susan Constant* to Virginia nor in the *Mayflower* to Plymouth. It came stark and strong and full of life out of the American forest, and it gained strength each time it touched a new frontier."

> —Frederick Jackson Turner in "The West and American Ideal," *Washington Historical Quarterly,* V, October, 1914

On a warm summer day in 1890 in Washington, D.C. (before air conditioning), U.S. Senators eased into congressional committee seats to listen to an address. They figured the speech would be at least tolerable, because it would be given by Fred T. Dubois, Idaho Territorial Delegate, who had done well as a student orator at Yale University, and had been improving ever since.

In the period, glowing words were greatly admired. And, on this occasion when Dubois was seeking statehood for Idaho, he definitely did not let his listeners down. He declared:

"These people (of Idaho), who have subdued the desert and the forest, who have wrenched untold millions from the solemn and reluctant hills, thus aiding struggling humanity everywhere, who have borne the hardships which have opened up an empire for thousands of homes, are the worthy descendants of their fathers of the revolution, and seek now by petition what these fathers gained one hundred years ago by arms and blood, the right of self-government.

"Idaho, in its material embodiment, is large enough and prolific enough to serve as a theatre for the activities of a great American community for more centuries than mortal beings are warranted to think or dream about. Partly by her common inheritance in the beneficial forces of nature and partly by a bountiful endowment, all her own, she is able to tender the custodians of the national welfare every reasonable guaranty and prospect that she will be no laggard in the never-ceasing onward race . . ."

Before he finished, Dubois was perspiring freely. Although the statehood bill had passed the House on April 3 that year, Dubois was worried as to how it would fare in the Senate—for three reasons.

First, there was the matter of population. Territorial Governor George L. Shoup had done some generous estimating, but had managed to come up with a total population of only 113,777 (it actually was 88,548). Then there was Idaho's Test Oath, forbidding anyone to vote if he belonged to an organization allowing the practice of polygamy. That disfranchised about a fourth of the people of Idaho—members of the Church of Jesus Christ of Latter-Day Saints, which had not yet formally rejected polygamy. Particularly concerned about this were the Democrats in Congress, who contended that most Mormons belonged to their party. Also, it was argued that Idaho's constitutional convention had not been legally convened. (At that time in the West, governmental affairs were sometimes handled as casually as a calf on a rope.)

Nevertheless, when the showdown came on the afternoon of July 1, 1890, the act adding a forty-third star to the American flag for Idaho breezed through the Senate by voice vote. After all, who would have wanted to be counted among the dissenters when Idaho's two new senators took their seats?

When the vote was taken, Dubois was in a corridor talking with a friend. As senators leaving the chamber came up to him, they began shaking his hand and slapping his back.

"Is it—?"

"Yes, Idaho is a state."

Later Dubois commented in his memoirs:

"It came so quickly at the close that I hardly knew the child was born."

On the afternoon of July 3, 1890, Dubois strode to the White House, accompanied by the statehood bill and the enrolling and engrossing clerk of Congress. The weather was typically and miserably humid, but Dubois thought it was a beautiful day.

President Benjamin Harrison was in his upstairs office with Secretary of State James G. Blaine. Both were cordial in their congratulations.

"Mr. President," said Dubois, "I wish you would put off signing this bill until tomorrow. Our people almost unanimously wish to become a state on the Fourth of July."

The President hesitated, then replied:

"Very well, I will do as you wish. But let me call your attention to this fact —the star of a new state goes on the flag of the United States on the Fourth of July following the date of admission to the Union. If I wait until tomorrow to sign the bill, the star of Idaho will not be on the flag for another year. If I sign the bill today, your star goes on the flag tomorrow."

Now it was Dubois' turn to hesitate before he replied:

"Mr. President, this is a rather momentous question. I am the sole representative here of Idaho, and my constituents have wired me what they desire. I am quite sure, however, that they do not know any more about the star than I did. So, taking full responsibility, I will ask you to sign the bill now. I want the star of Idaho on the flag tomorrow."

"I think you have chosen well," said President Harrison. Secretary Blaine nodded.

Thus, Idaho became a state on July 3, 1890. And Dubois would long be remembered with a town in the new state named for him—the seat of Clark County. (His grandfather had a whole county in Indiana named for him.)

In years to come, Idahoans would favor Democrats as well as Republicans, but, at the time, the creation of the new state looked like a definite coup for the Republicans. It did not set well with Democratic newspapers in the East. The *New York Post* declared:

"Another 'mining camp' becomes a state . . . The Republicans in Congress thus add two more votes in the Senate for free silver coinage and against sound money."

But Idaho was not without press support. Perhaps most vigorous in this regard was the *Salt Lake Tribune,* which flared back at the *New York Post:*

"The West does not care a cent for New York, or the opinion of the men of New York City. They are a set of slaves that wait for some English or German banker to take snuff before they sneeze . . . New York be blowed."

As for Idahoans, they were ecstatic. There was some celebrating on the night of July 3, but it was just a prelude to that on the Fourth of July.

The parade on the Fourth at Boise proved to be the city's finest hour to date. Leading the floats, both patriotic and industrial, was Colonel Orlando (Rube) Robbins, noted Idaho Indian fighter and lawman. West Point-straight, he sat astride the aged but celebrated cavalry horse ridden by General Thomas J. (Stonewall) Jackson when he was shot down May 2, 1863, at Chancellorsville by his own men who thought he was a reconnoitering enemy.

Following Colonel Robbins came the "Liberty Wagon," with "Kid" McMullen driving six milk white horses, whose harness was wrapped in red, white and blue bunting. On the center of the wagon stood golden-haired Hattie Hart, Goddess of Liberty, surrounded by a court well chosen for its beauty. Also, of course, there was a "Ship of State," escorted by small boys in Navy suits, standard Sunday dress in the period.

At the capitol grounds, Mabel Sheehey read the Declaration of Independence, and Governor Shoup, President of the Day, spoke at some length on the past, present and future of Idaho. Then W. H. Weir, Speaker of the Day, orated at still greater length—in fact, for more than an hour. At 8 p.m., fireworks ($5,000 worth) began exploding and scattering their dazzling colors, and men stood around with buckets of water—just in case.

For the parade at Moscow, the entire length of Main Street was decorated with pine boughs, and red, white and blue bunting. The smallest float drew the most applause. It was a red coaster wagon, ably pulled by 12 boys. As it passed W. J. McConnell, who would later become a United States Senator and Governor of Idaho, he beamed broadly, because in the wagon sat his little daughter, holding a banner which read "Idaho, Gem of the Mountains." The daughter was destined to become Mrs. William Edgar Borah, wife of the famed United States Senator from Idaho.

Press coverage of the Moscow parade was not all that had been planned, because the float of the *North Idaho Star* newspaper met with disaster. It consisted of a printing press mounted on a flatbed wagon, and, midway during the parade, the press toppled off the wagon, shattering into pieces.

Hailey celebrated with something special—a horse race down its Main Street. Here the trouble which developed was more serious. One of the horses swerved too wide, seriously injuring seven sidewalk spectators. Two of the seven, Bertie Butler and James Murdock, were at first thought to be dead, but doctors brought them around.

At Silver City, the new state citizens were faced with a Fourth of July dilemma. A baseball game had been scheduled with DeLamar on Silver City's sagebrush-studded field, and the question was whether the game should be played or a parade staged to mark Idaho's statehood. The miners of the town, who had been doing preliminary celebrating in their favorite saloons, and who outnumbered all other factions, insisted on the baseball game. So it was played—to the town's chagrin. DeLamar won, 14 to 4.


In view of the fact that in the new State of Montana, Helena, Virginia City, Butte, Anaconda, Missoula, Bozeman and Deer Lodge were still fighting over which would be the permanent capital, Idahoans were particularly pleased that their capital had already been definitely determined. That is, everybody was pleased except the people of Lewiston, where the capital had originally been located.

When the Territory of Idaho was created on March 4, 1863, William H. Wallace, a native of Ohio who had fought against the Yakima Indians as the captain of a company of volunteers, was named the first Governor by President Abraham Lincoln. Given authority to select a temporary capital, Wallace picked Lewiston, where a two-story structure became the first capitol building. An adjoining log cabin was used as the Governor's "mansion."

Opening for a 60-day session on December 7, 1863, the First Territorial Legislature passed 612 pages of handwritten bills, but two important bills got sidetracked. The first bill to run amuck was on education, and the second on the permanent capital.

On December 9, William B. Daniels, Secretary of the Territory, made a speech which was rather remarkable, considering the frontier setting in which it was given:

"I congratulate you upon the bright prospects of our young community, and upon those indications of rapid and permanent growth with which we are surrounded . . . The child is born who shall see railroads and telegraphs connecting our great centers of trade with the Atlantic and Pacific oceans . . . He shall see the states of the Pacific rival those of the Atlantic seaboard in population and wealth; shall see a city located on the western side of the continent, by the Pacific ocean, surpassing in trade and magnificence ancient Tyre when she sat as a queen and her merchants were princes, and cities in the interior surpassing Palmyra and Persepolis in the days of their glory— splendid, not with heathen temples and palaces decorated with barbaric pomp and pride, but with churches dedicated to the worship of the God of our fathers, and institutions of learning devoted to the education of our youth in arts and science, morals and religion . . .

"It cannot be necessary to argue the necessity of education to the preservation of our free institutions. 'We must educate,' said a great American orator, 'or we must perish by our own prosperity;' and all history attests the

232

truth of that proposition. Prosperity, wealth, luxury, vice and ruin are the successive steps in the career of every nation that does not rely upon the virtue and intelligence of the people. All the gold in these mountains will not save us from the fate of free nations that have gone before us if we do not educate our children, but rather make our decline more swift and sure. Who does not know that it is to the ignorance of the many, operated upon by the ambition of the few, that our insurrectionary states are indebted for the desolation which is laying them waste and making their palaces the abodes of owls. Let us establish schools and churches, encourage teachers, patronize the arts and sciences, teach our children to seek knowledge rather than wealth, and labor to perpetuate our institutions by a union of intelligence and virtue, liberty and law.''

Daniels' eloquent appeal for public-supported education caused Legislator E. B. Waterbury on January 6, 1864, to introduce in the Council a bill ''establishing a common school system for the Territory of Idaho.'' The bill swept through the Council without a dissenting vote on January 12, 1864. Ten days later it also received unanimous backing in the House, but some amendments were added, and these irked the Council. The records are not clear as to just what the amendments were, but definitely they were enough to leave the bill in limbo when the session ended.

The oratory of Daniels thus created only a hollow echo—for a year. At the second Territorial Legislature in Lewiston, Joseph Miller introduced another bill calling for a common school system, and it was quickly passed by both the Council and House. On December 17, 1864, Governor Caleb Lyon signed it into law.

The bill for establishing a permanent capital in Idaho followed a similar but rockier road. Boise had the best arguments for being the capital. It was the center of a big and booming mining area, it was located on the Oregon Trail not far from the Utah tracks of the new transcontinental railroad, and it had an Army garrison for protection. But Boise needed some northern support, and got it in the first session of the Territorial Legislature from Virginia City.

Then a part of Idaho Territory, Virginia City was hoping for the formation of a new territory in which it would be the capital. The case for the new territory would be greatly strengthened if the capital of Idaho Territory was way off in Boise. But Alonzo Leland, a Lewiston attorney and newspaperman with an unlimited supply of words, staged a one-man filibuster, talking in the darkness of the Legislative hall long after lamps had been blown out, and all other legislators had departed. Because of his vocal persistence no action was taken on the permanent capital during the first legislative session.

A Lewiston partisan commented:

"The wheels of the capital refused to roll, and thus as corrupt a scheme as ever was connected with a legislative body was thwarted, and a set of swindlers have learned that fortune sometimes favors those who act honestly.''

At the time of the second session of the Legislature, Virginia City was no longer in Idaho, but Boise didn't need its support anyway. Owyhee, Alturas and Oneida counties had been formed in the southern part of the Territory, and their representatives were all for Boise as the capital. The bill making this a fact was passed in December, 1864, strictly on geographical lines.

Again Lewistonites cried ''foul.'' Attorney T. M. Pomeroy of Lewiston argued that the bill and all other actions of the Legislature were null and void, because

233

the session had been convened six weeks before the terms of the Legislators were supposed to begin. The contention was scorned by the backers of Boise as the site for the capital, so Probate Judge John C. Berry of Lewiston promptly issued an injunction against the removal of the Territorial Seal and archives from Lewiston.

Ordered to appear in court and answer charges including one which alleged he was not Governor, Lyon passed the word that he and Sol Hasbrouch of Owyhee County were going duck hunting on John Silcott's ranch across the Clearwater. The two men scrambled into a frail duck hunting boat all right, but shot past the ranch at the highest speed that oars could generate.

At White's Ferry, a carriage with horses and driver was waiting. Climbing into the carriage with Hasbrouch, Lyon instructed the driver:

"Lay on the whip!"

And Lyon's bouncing body in the carriage on the way to Portland was the last view of the Governor north of the Salmon River.

With Lyon sojourning in Portland while waiting to go to Washington, D.C., to discuss the matter, Silas D. Cochran, Acting Secretary of Idaho Territory without appointment, became the sole remaining federal representative of the Territory. He was handed a writ which said in effect:

"Go to jail or put up a $20,000 security bond that you won't leave Lewiston."

Ignoring the writ, Cochran stuck around—for a while.

Becoming suspicious, the Lewiston sheriff posted an around-the-clock guard of six men to see that the Territorial Seal and archives were not stolen. Such an attempt, believed to have been master-minded by Governor Lyon in Portland, was made by several men at 2 a.m. on December 21, 1864, but was foiled by the guards.

This inspired Lewistonites to ask Congress to fire Lyon as Governor, to expel the offending Southern Idaho counties, and to establish a new territory linking Washington and the Idaho Panhandle. Congress did do the latter, but President Grover Cleveland pocket-vetoed the bill creating the new territory.

Meanwhile, Governor Lyon was pleased to see Clinton DeWitt Smith, the duly appointed Secretary of Idaho Territory, come strolling into his Portland hotel. Smith had been a long time getting there—eight months, in fact. He had tried coming to Idaho by the overland route, but the Indians were objecting strenuously to such travel that year, and he was forced to return East, where he took a ship the long way around to Portland.

After being well briefed by Lyon on what he was up against in Idaho, Smith proceeded to Lewiston. A pleasant and friendly sort of fellow who was not adverse to bending his elbow on a saloon bar, he quickly became popular in the town. What didn't hurt was the fact that he had brought with him sufficient money to pay off Lewiston's share of the territorial debt. This was the first federal money provided for territorial operations.

Still, there was one thing about Smith which bothered Lewiston folk, who continued to have Governor Lyon's "duck hunting" trip strongly in mind. Smith had a habit of taking long horseback rides. For his health, he said.

On the afternoon of March 29, 1865, Smith took an especially long ride— to Fort Lapwai. Worried, Judge Berry picked up a pen, and quickly scratched out another injunction forbidding removal of the Territorial Seal and archives. Then he appointed J. K. Vincent as a special deputy to enforce the order.

About that time, a Lewiston patriot who had been at Fort Lapwai, galloped a lathered horse into town. Smith, he said, had requested and been granted a detachment of cavalry to get him out of Lewiston with seal and archives. And, added the Lewiston-loyal messenger:

"The soldiers have orders to burn the town if necessary."

The cavalrymen did come, ominous in their rifle-bearing saddles as they rode down Lewiston's muddy Main Street. Stares and glares followed them, but there was no trouble. Some men fingered guns. Marshal Vincent restrained them. Then quickly the soldiers picked up the Territorial Seal and archives, and rode off to join another unit of cavalrymen guarding Secretary Smith at the Clearwater ferry.

Waving Judge Berry's injunction, Marshal Vincent ran after the departing troops. But the mounted men just sat stiffly in their saddles, never looking back.

On the night of April 2, Lewiston held an indignation meeting which brought out most of the town. Both Smith and the cavalry were roundly condemned—especially Smith. Among other things, it was decided that he was "too dishonorable for an officer, and too great a drunkard and liar to command respect as a man."

But the Territorial Seal and archives were gone forever from Lewiston. And, when Smith rode into Boise with them on the night of April 14, 1865, he got all the respect and cheers any man could want. All over Boise there was general chuckling and backslapping, because the happy residents had not yet received word that President Abraham Lincoln had been shot that night in another capital city.

Just as Lincoln did not live long after his achievement in keeping the United States one nation, neither did Smith after his success in obtaining the "key" which locked in Boise as Idaho's permanent capital. On August 19, 1865, Smith, who had taken to drinking more than usual, toppled over dead after playing chess with a miner at Rocky Bar—and losing.

Smith was not the kind of person who won in the early West. He never adjusted to its frontier conditions. Shortly before his death, he had written to his sister, Ada, in the East, complaining about the "rough" food:

"No fruit, no fresh vegetables, but onions, onions, and popcorn and potatoes."

Caleb Lyon? Unquestionably the most colorful governor Idaho ever had, this suave man with a very pointed beard continued to run to color—not always bright.

Born in Lyonsdale, New York, and graduated from Norwich University in Vermont, Lyon at an early age got himself appointed as U.S. Consul at Shanghai, then decided to join the gold rush in California instead. While in California he wedged his way into the Constitutional Convention for that state as part of the clerical staff. (He claimed that he designed the California State Seal, a contention which was later proven to be untrue.) Then, after showing up in assorted parts of South America and Europe, where he lived off his wits and charm, he served in both branches of the New York Legislature, not only managing to switch branches midway during a session, but to get himself elected as a United States Congressman in the same year.

Also, according to press reports Lyon brought with him to Idaho, he had served heroically in both the Mexican and Civil wars. It should be noted, however, that the heroic feats were all mentioned in quoted statements made by Lyon. In addition, Lyon claimed to be a close friend of such greats as Daniel Webster, Henry Clay and John C. Calhoun, just to drop a few names. And perhaps he was, because he traveled in high circles. (When he had his photograph taken, he posed between a painting of George Washington and a sculptured bust of Abraham Lincoln.)

Besides being a poet of some distinction, Lyon was a collector of art of still greater distinction. (Following his death at Rossville, Staten Island, September 17, 1875, his art collection was sold at auction, and buyers picked up many rare works, including some by Rembrandt and Corot. When a purchaser of one art item asked if it came with a certificate of authenticity, the auctioneer wryly replied, "No, but, if Caleb were still alive, he would be pleased to write one for you.")

When Lyon held his first dinner party at the Overland Hotel in Boise, he insisted on the finest foods and wines brought up the Columbia from Portland, believing that there should be no stinting with United States government funds in encouraging friendly territorial relations. The dinner may well have been the first eight-course affair held in Idaho. Not only that, Lyon presided over it in a swallow-tail coat.

Most of all, however, Lyon was noted for his speaking ability—a deluge of flowery eloquence. His address to Idaho's Territorial Legislature following the end of the Civil War was typical:

"The temple of war is closed. No more shall its iron-mouthed and brazen-throated cannon peal forth dread miseries over half a thousand battlefields, where sleep their last sleep the victor and the vanquished. No more shall the ear of night be pierced with the echoes of fierce assault and stubborn defense from encompassed and beleaguered cities . . .

"The Constitution of our common country has been vindicated, and the Union gallantly sustained. The destroyers have become restorers, and those who were the last in war have been the first to hail the glorious advent of peace."

Idahoans, like others of the period, appreciated gilded words in a formal address, but not in casual conversation. And Lyon never ceased to use them. He fit in the Far West like a saddle on a cow. More significantly, he was not trusted. Usually, he signed his name with a flourish as "Caleb Lyon of Lyonsdale," but the people converted this to "Cale of the Dale." A newspaper story referred to him as a "revolving light upon the coast of scampdom," which may have been a more apt observation than the writer figured when he wrote it.

On April 27, 1866, Lyon hurriedly departed forever from Idaho for New York State, and $46,418.40 in federal funds not yet distributed to Idaho Indian tribes disappeared when he did. Later, Lyon disclosed that he took the money with him for safekeeping, but he claimed that it was stolen while he was riding on a train. His bondsman eventually had to reimburse the federal government, but it is not clear how the Idaho Indians finally came out.

At the time, Idaho was losing money fast. H. C. Gilson, an ex-bartender who succeeded Smith as Secretary of the Territory, had been in Idaho only a short while when he stripped it of all its operating funds, fleeing to Hong Kong with $41,062. Eventually caught, he was freed without trial when it was discovered that the grand jury had neglected to indict him.

In 1870-71, General Ulysses S. Grant was in strange—and hot—waters as President of the United States. In those uncertain post-Civil War years, Grant's cabinet was largely made up of inept—and, in some cases, corrupt—men; Northern adventurers, known as "carpetbaggers," were fouling up reconstruction efforts in the South by trying to get rich quick in governmental positions, and generally the nation was heading for a severe depression. But along with all this, Grant was having difficulty in finding someone who would accept the governorship of far-off Idaho Territory.

Samuel Bard, a "carpetbagger" turned newspaper publisher in Atlanta, Georgia, agreed to take the job. But he never got to Boise, deciding instead to stay in Atlanta where he wangled an appointment as postmaster.

Looking north next, Grant gave the nod to Attorney Gilman Marston of New Hampshire. That astute lawyer, who would later be awarded an honorary Doctor of Laws degree by Dartmouth, was willing, but not at the salary—$2,500 a year.

Grant's third try was made in the Midwest. There he selected Alexander H. Conner, a prominent Indiana attorney. Another rejection slip.

Next Grant picked Ebenezer Dumont, also of Indiana. But Dumont died before his commission could be carried out.

With these failures rankling him, Grant began thinking of old soldiers who knew how to take an order from the Commander in Chief—and stay alive. Out in Arkansas was Thomas M. Bowen, a former brigadier general, who was now a judge.

"Yes, sir," said Bowen, and headed for Idaho with his wife. After spending a few days in Boise, the couple headed back.

Thomas Donaldson in "Idaho of Yesterday" quoted Bowen as commenting to him:

"As soon as the country north of Salt Lake burst on our gaze, my wife and I determined to return East. I never saw so much land to the acre in all my born days. I counted my subjects as I came in, and there were 130 people in 250 miles."

All of this prompted a newspaper advertisement which offered a cash reward to anyone who could name the Governor of Idaho—and prove that he was.

Back in Washington, President Grant went looking again, and came up with Thomas W. Bennett, who had been mayor of Richmond, Indiana. Bennett, who served as Idaho's Territorial Governor from 1871 to 1875, has been described as "the most jovial, reckless gentleman who ever sat in a gubernatorial chair." In 1874, Bennett ran for Congress, and, although he did not get the most votes, as chairman of the Board of Canvassers he declared himself elected. He served as a Delegate to Congress from 1875 to 1877 when he was thrown out and replaced by Stephen S. Fenn of Mount Idaho.

D. P. Thompson, a Westerner from Portland who replaced Bennett as Governor, did much for the commercial development of the Pacific Northwest in general, but nothing for the Territory of Idaho in particular. During his term as Territorial Governor, he was credited with spending only 19 days in Idaho. He resigned on a conflict of interest problem, and Grant again began looking over the field for an Idaho governor. Meanwhile, Thompson stayed in the Northwest to become Mayor of Portland, and, in his later years, had a major role in building up the public school system of Oregon.

Idaho's territorial governors ran from bad to mediocre to good. Overall, they were perhaps a cut above the governors of most Western territories. As Maude Cosho of Boise explained in her thesis for a master's degree:

237

"The 'spoils system' as first practiced by Andrew Jackson appeared in its worst forms in territorial government. Non-resident men were sent to new territories to occupy the most important offices. These men, in many instances, knew little and cared less about the needs and problems of the local citizens. Some meritorious selections were made in Washington, but not too often . . . Harassed presidents often appointed 'misfits,' in order to remove them from the political sphere in eastern areas . . . Men of mediocre ability sought and were frequently appointed to territorial positions of responsibility because of outstanding political service in some distant state."

It should be added that the governors who left the plushness of the established East for the roughness of the wild West frequently were more interested in what they could get out of the territories than what they could give to them.

Significantly, Idaho's two most outstanding territorial governors were Idahoans—Edward A. Stevenson, 1885-89, and George L. Shoup, 1889-90. (Shoup also served as the first State Governor.)

Born in the East (some reports say in Pennsylvania, and some, in New York) Stevenson came to California as a young man. Serving in the Army, he had attained the rank of colonel, and, with this background, he was appointed agent of a California Indian reservation. While Stevenson was away from the reservation on business one day, rebelling Indians murdered and mutilated his wife and children, and burned down the agency building. Leader of the attack was a young Indian who had been befriended by the Stevensons and given a place in their home.

All the participants in the massacre had fled the reservation, but Stevenson went after them with a mounted posse. Catching up with the killers, the posse shot all of them to death—except for their young leader. Stevenson personally saw to his hanging.

In 1864, with too many memories haunting him in California, Stevenson left for Idaho. Settling first in Boise County and later in Ada County, he went into business and politics. Serving many terms in Idaho's Council, he represented both counties well, and was frequently speaker of the Council.

Then, in 1885, President Grover Cleveland appointed Stevenson Territorial Governor. At the same time, his brother, Charles, served as Governor of Nevada. Their reunion in Boise in 1887 was the big social event for Idaho that year.

Edward A. Stevenson worked hard for the development of Idaho, but his biggest job was simply holding together the Territory, which was caught in a tug of war between the territories of Washington and Nevada. Washington wanted to annex Northern Idaho, and Nevada sought Southern Idaho. The people of Northern Idaho were generally ready and willing to go with the more populous and affluent Washington Territory, but those of Southern Idaho could see no advantage in becoming a part of Nevada Territory.

Nevada did not get far with its expansion ideas, but, on March 1, 1887, House Bill No. 2889 passed Congress, making Northern Idaho a part of Washington Territory. Then Governor Stevenson, who had long been opposed to any dismembering of Idaho, played his last card. He sent a strong telegram of protest to President Cleveland. The telegram pointed out that Idaho could no more afford to lose its northern area than the United States could have afforded to lose the Southern states. Cleveland pocket-vetoed the bill.

This caused the *Lewiston Teller* to lament:

"During the week, last past, the people of North Idaho have been living in the mazes of a most poetic and captivating dream—our utopian visions of happiness were, indeed, but the transitory and flitting images of joy born only to the imagination. The thrilling news was sped to us over the wires that Congress had annexed us to Washington Territory, and the seal, necessary to make permanent the union was the simple John Hancock of the President . . . But our dream is at an end . . . We have returned from our phantom pilgrimage . . . We can continue to do the sneezing for the snuff takers at the capital."

The *Moscow Mirror* turned to poetry—of a sort:
"Cleveland, chosen of the nation,
Went and vetoed annexation.
The reason given by President Cleve
Was based on wire from Governor Steve.
It's all right, Cleveland, you just wait:
We'll veto you in eighty-eight."

Bitterness? Indeed, there was! But the fact remains that Idaho would not be nearly as strong a state as it is today if Governor Stevenson had not been on the job in 1887, and sent that telegram.

Besides, the bitterness did not last long. Idaho's last Territorial Legislature in 1889 poured balm on the wounds. Northern Idaho was provided generous funding for building a major link of the North-South Highway, and the University of Idaho was established in Moscow. Even C. B. Reynolds, editor of the *Moscow Mirror,* decided that the idea of annexing Northern Idaho to Washington was a lot of nonsense.

Colonel George Laird Shoup, the last Territorial Governor and the first State Governor, was an Idaho pioneer (from Pennsylvania) and statesman of distinction. A handsome man whose eyebrows remained determinedly black when his hair and mustache had turned white, Shoup brought considerable stability to the gubernatorial office. Popular throughout the Territory and State, he was elected grand master of the Idaho Masons three times. And he was the only Idaho Governor to have his statue placed in Statuary Hall of the National Capitol.

What did he do for Idaho? He was, of course, Governor when Idaho's Constitution was drafted—a document which was approved by a seven to one majority of the people on November 5, 1889. He fought hard for statehood—after having worked diligently to build up the Territory so that it might merit the star. Primarily, however, Shoup gave to the people of Idaho faith in the future by passing on to them his own faith, which called for the support of honest toil.

On July 20, 1881, Shoup wrote from his home in Salmon City to Robert E. Strahorn in Boise City:

"No other Territory has as bright prospects for its future, or can offer as great encouragement to the farmer, home-seeker, prospector or capitalist . . . I have watched Idaho's growth and development with more than usual care and interest, and will anticipate a question that will be asked you quite often. 'If Idaho presents such promising inducements, why has her advancement not been more rapid?' This can be easily explained. Idaho has, until recently, been isolated from railroad communication, was only accessible by long and tiresome journeys by team or stagecoach, while all around us were wide and open fields, easy of access, aided by railroads and emigration societies, inviting the capitalist, home-seeker and prospector. Idaho had no such

239

advantages, and it was only the most venturesome and daring that were willing to leave civilization so far behind . . .

"I know of no field so inviting and promising for a speedy fortune to the industrious prospector, as is now open in Idaho. All prospectors are not successful. Some are indolent and spend most of their time lounging about the small towns, waiting for the more enterprising and industrious to make a discovery, when they expect to drop in and secure a claim; others go out, find a pleasant and shady camp by a mountain stream, walk over the ground for a mile or two around camp, prospect the adjacent mountain sides with the eye, and if they do not see a vein or lode standing up in open sight, will say, there is nothing here. They will then fish (mountain streams are full of trout), and lounge about camp until their supplies are about exhausted, return to some camp or village and report that they have prospected such a range of mountains thoroughly, when the fact is, they have done no prospecting at all. The prize or fortune is left for the prospector who will . . . climb to the top of the loftiest and most rugged mountain, and when indications are favorable, will dig and work for weeks until he succeeds in finding the treasure . . .

"It is not alone in gold and silver that Idaho possesses great wealth; her rich and fertile valleys are not excelled in any State or Territory . . . The dairyman finds a ready market for his butter and cheese . . . And the stock grower is rewarded with a handsome income from his herds of cattle, sheep and horses . . . A few stockmen have been disappointed in not realizing their expectations . . . Their stock was permitted to run at will, many of the increases went unbranded, and much of the old stock wandered off to neighboring ranges . . . Those taking care of their stock, however, will in all cases do well."

This was the faith of Shoup, and he never lost it.


Although Shoup did much in a short time, it was a man familiarly known as "Ned" who gave most of the polish to Idaho's government in the rough during territorial years. He was Edward J. Curtis, who was never Governor, but who as Acting Governor spent more time in the gubernatorial office than any appointed Governor.

Curtis was named Secretary of Idaho Territory in 1869, and served in that position a good share of the time until 1890. When an appointed Governor failed to show up in the Territory, or took off after a quick look at it, Curtis was there to step in as Governor. And praise be that he was!

With a well-trimmed goatee adorning a firm and forceful jaw, Curtis managed to look like a man of dash and integrity at the same time. And indeed he was both. He swung through Boise in a buggy with a fast-stepping, matched team, but when he climbed down to discuss a territorial problem he paused in solid reflection before he spoke.

A native of Massachusetts, Curtis was admitted to the bar in that state. Taking off for California in the gold rush of '49, he didn't pan for ore, but did well as an attorney in claim disputes. After being twice elected to the Legislature in California, he was made a judge there (Trinity County). Then, in 1865, he migrated to Idaho's Silver City, where he practiced law for a while before moving to Boise City. In 1869, he accepted the appointment of Territorial Secretary because he figured that it was "high time somebody with a real interest in Idaho took the job."

In 1877, Curtis was maneuvered from the position by Territorial Governor Mason Brayman (1876-1880), last of the series of governors appointed by President Grant. Brayman wanted to have a son-in-law named Secretary in place of Curtis. But at the time Brayman, a Civil War general of some repute from Ripon, Wisconsin, was looking very silly.

The Nez Perce Indian War had started, and Brayman figured that Chief Joseph would move through the Weiser and Payette country, so he ordered the Idaho militia there instead of to the Clearwater. It was right peaceful in the Weiser and Payette country, and the militiamen enjoyed the ride.

President Rutherford B. Hayes decided that Brayman's judgment wasn't so good. Curtis was removed as Secretary, but Brayman's son-in-law didn't get the job. The replacement was R. A. Sidebotham of Rocky Bar. Then later, by popular demand, Curtis came back as Secretary.

The *Idaho Statesman,* which had been highly critical of some of the Territory's leaders (for good reason), said of Curtis:

"He brought order and system out of the confusion of the Governor's office in Idaho, and labored hard and successfully to build up a State Law Library."

In his book "Idaho of Yesterday," Thomas Donaldson wrote that Curtis "deserves a prominent place in Idaho history." And certainly this writer intends to give him due recognition by ending the last chapter of this book on a Curtis note.

The too often forgotten man deserves this place, because his service to Idaho points up the fact that always in the history of our government—both national and state—leaders of integrity have been able to pull it through troubled times. And Curtis, probably more than any early Idahoan, helped to bear out Historian Frederick Jackson Turner's words:

"American democracy . . . came stark and strong and full of life out of the American forest, and it gained strength each time it touched a new frontier."

# EPILOGUE

Idaho is different. Even more significant, it is grand. And some of its panoramas—like the view from the summit of Whitebird "Hill"—are downright stupendous.

Walt Disney designers are very good. Yet they still haven't come up with anything in California or Florida that is bigger and better—or boasts more variety—than nature produced in Idaho.

But perhaps Idaho's greatest treasure lies in her good, deeply loyal people. Idahoans appreciate what they have, and they intend to keep it basically that way. Make no mistake, however. The people have a forward outlook on life. They are just not seeking change for change's sake.

Consequently, those persons who are striving to recapture something of America's past should come to Idaho. There is still quite a bit of the past around.

Reference is not made so much to a broken wagon wheel weathering beside a rail fence near Nezperce, or to a cowboy in a high-crowned hat and high-heeled boots checking his saddle as baggage at the Boise Airport, or to a grizzled prospector once again heading up the mountains from Riggins with his grub-laden burro. No, the past is reflected mostly in the adherence of Idahoans to those personal qualities admired for generations—honesty, stability and independence. Most important, all these characteristics are blended with a spirit of friendliness—friendliness that is as wide open as the spaces in which the people live.

Thus, it is the combination of the people and the land which makes Idaho so special today.

With a population of about 800,000, Idaho lags behind 41 other states in number of people. But those 800,000 persons, scattered over 83,557 square miles so that there are only nine humans per square mile, are like their pioneer ancestors. They are proud and happy to get up in the morning to face the challenges of the big, sprawling land—without the tenseness of those on the other side of the continent as they prepare to tackle the traffic tangles of the New Jersey Turnpike.

While an Idahoan is generally on the conservative side—just like his ancestors, who were inclined to be as solid as they were bold—he will vote for any candidate whom he thinks is basically good for country, state or community. Does the candidate walk tall? That is the question.

In Idaho, a man or woman is presumed to be honest until proven to be otherwise. This writer, who has spent some time in large Midwestern and Eastern cities, is still startled when he cashes a check in an Idaho supermarket without being asked for identification. Or when he fills up at a self-service gasoline station, and the attendant asks, "How much gas did you get?"— without checking.

That was the way business used to be done in Idaho, and that is the way it is still generally done today. It must be remembered that most of the scoundrels, gun-slingers and assorted sinners mentioned in this book left few heirs. And there were really not so many bad eggs in the frontier basket. The disreputable character simply stood out like a coyote howling on a hillside. Certainly there were relatively few horse thieves. (Galloping off on thy neighbor's horse was a quick-hanging offense.)

In New York City today, a man walking down the street with grimy hat and shirt and dusty boots is likely to be wondering how he will buy his next meal. In an Idaho town, he might be a well-to-do rancher or farmer—about to step into his new car, a sleek vehicle up to and including that of the Cadillac class. More important to him than dress is the fatness of his cattle or the fullness of his potato hills.

This writer can recall an overalled farmer making a $74.50 purchase of pipe and fittings in a Moscow plumbing shop.

"Give me a blank check on the First Security Bank," the farmer told the woman cashier.

"I'm sorry, but we're out of First Security blanks."

"Oh, well," said the farmer, "then give me a blank on the Idaho First National. It makes no difference which bank I write the check on."

Alarmed, the woman glanced at the shop's manager, seated at a desk. He nodded for her to take the check.

New York City is supposed to be America's greatest "melting pot." Perhaps so. But the whole State of Idaho forms a very special melting pot. It would be difficult to find a state with more varied interests, but somehow the people manage to pull together—well, most of the time.

Then there is the matter of tolerance. Always there are exceptions, but generally the people get along with their neighbors regardless of race, creed or color.

J. Leslie Rollins, Assistant Dean of the Harvard Business School for graduate students, once commented to this writer:

"We like to get students from Idaho, because they are likely to come without preconceived 'isms.' Learning for them is thus a continuing adventure."

Although Idahoans started on the road to settlement toting gold pans, they soon turned to the plow to provide their main source of income. And agriculture today is still dominant, producing annually more than a billion dollars worth of food for the tables of the nation and the world. Of the 25 leading crops of the United States, Idaho in recent years had 6 in the top 10—potatoes, sugar beets, barley, sheep and lambs, hay and wheat.

For about a half-century wheat, grown in every one of Idaho's 44 counties, was the No. 1 crop in the State. But no more. Today Idaho is most famous for its potatoes—in fact, is the leading producer in the nation—although cattle rank first among the State's agricultural commodities in cash receipts. Following in order behind cattle are potatoes, dairy products, wheat and sugar beets.

Idaho is not thought of as a manufacturing state, yet manufacturing is next to agriculture in income—mostly from processed potatoes, and dairy and wood products. Altogether, manufacturing annually accounts for about three-quarters of a billion dollars in cash receipts. Next come tourism (estimated at about $200,000,000 annually), forest products and mining.

Each year Idaho, with the fifth largest saw-timber reserve in the nation (16 million acres), harvests about 18 per cent of the West's wood products. Leading lumber manufacturers include such widely known firms as Potlatch Forests, Boise Cascade, Diamond National, Atlas-Tie, Hoff, Pack River and Idaho-Pine Mills, which not only turn out lumber but railroad ties, poles, veneer, beams, paper, boxes, tissue, pulp, plywood, furniture and gun stocks. The annual payroll for some 13,000 lumber workers in Idaho totals more than $90,000,000, accounting for 30 per cent of the manufacturing wage outlay in the State.

In mining, the Coeur d'Alenes area alone yields 50 per cent of the nation's silver, 30 per cent of its lead, and 17 per cent of its zinc. At Kellogg, the Sunshine Mining Company operates the world's largest mining complex.

True, the State can do with more development. But Idahoans are just naturally cautious in how they accomplish it. Governor Cecil Andrus explained:

"Lately, Idaho has emerged as one of the few remaining livable places in the nation. In the past, Idaho's uncluttered lands, clear skies and clean air have been mimicked as symbols of economic depression. Because we haven't had a massive industrial surge, Idaho has been two decades behind—but only by economic standards.

"Whether by chance or design, Idaho's refusal to 'develop at any cost' has made her one of the few states in a position to apply preventive medicine. As we grow, we can do so in an orderly and well-planned fashion. In a sense, by being 20 years behind, we are 20 years ahead."

That does not mean that Idaho today is not without problems of pollution. But the brook that defaces and destroys has not yet become a river. And, if Idahoans continue to give attention to the problems of pollution as they have in recent years, they can avoid the flood.

Idahoans are particularly proud of the fact that more than six million tourists now come annually to their state. Or perhaps it should be said that they are particularly proud of the attractions that draw the tourists.

Beckoning to about a half-million visitors yearly is the Craters of the Moon National Monument. Then, of course, there is Yellowstone National Park, that giant of geological caprice, which is the nation's single most popular park, and which is partly in Idaho, Wyoming and Montana. Too, tourists are lured in good numbers to Nez Perce National Historic Park in North-Central Idaho where the Nez Perce Indians successfully fought their running battles with the U.S. Cavalry; to the Ice Caves near Grace in Southeastern Idaho that reach back into the earth for a half-mile; to the Lolo Indian or Lewis and Clark Trail (Highway 12), which traverses the route of the early explorers along the meandering Lochsa River . . .

In Idaho, there are 29 ski areas from Schweitzer Basin (Sandpoint) in the Bitterroots to Brundage Mountain at McCall to Boise's Bogus Basin to Sun Valley (Ketchum) in the Sawtooths to Grand Targhee in Eastern Idaho (out of Driggs). Rodeos are held all over the place, with three of the West's largest being staged at Lewiston, Nampa and Caldwell. Then there are the many special events from the national Old Fiddlers' Contest at Weiser, where "Turkey in the Straw" is still a hit tune, to Lumberjack Days at Orofino, where men—and women—make the chips fly and the logs roll.

The attractions that are the biggest draw are those which were on the Idaho stage long before the first tourists—Lewis and Clark—came in 1805. What Idaho has by right of natural heritage caused A. B. Guthrie, Jr., of "Big Sky" fame to write in *Holiday Magazine* for July, 1954:

"Idaho, they will tell you, means sunrise; and the sun, they will agree, must be astonished each time he lifts his bright face on the place. No state can surpass, if any can equal, its contrasts, its extremes, its huge natural fancies that exist as if to stun wonder."

An observant man, Guthrie . . .

Mount Borah in the Challis National Forest (one of 16 such forests in the State) brushes the clouds at 12,662 feet; Hells Canyon in the Seven Devils Scenic Area cuts a mile deep into the earth. In the north are the great subalpine lakes—Priest, Pend Oreille and Coeur d'Alene—bordered by vast stands of evergreens; in the south are the broad deserts of the Owyhee Country with the Bruneau Sand Dunes which look as if a sheik on a white horse might come riding over them any time. The Palouse Country has its rich black soil, and the Craters of the Moon National Monument its solid black rock; yet both substances came from the same source—volcanoes (the difference in time of eruptions accounting for the differences in the land). Then in Central Idaho is the huge Primitive Area which would look virtually unchanged to Idaho's earliest Indians if they wandered back today. And oddly enough, near Arco within hiking distance of the Primitive Area—well, if you are a good hiker—is the National Reactor Testing Station, where the first atomic submarine was spawned.

Idaho is indeed a land of contrasts. Not only that, the hunting and fishing are good. (The Kamloops trout in Lake Pend Oreille run up to about 40 pounds.)

For this writer, Idaho will always have many special memories . . . rippling seas of golden wheat in the Palouse Country—ah, the smell of it on a dew-freshened morning! . . . the fragrance, too, of a syringa bush—Idaho's State Flower—emerging each spring on Moscow's Cherry Street . . . or the aroma of freshly-caught trout from the cold, clear waters of Priest Lake simmering in a pan . . . silent shadows on silent stretches of the beautiful St. Joe River . . . a rustic cabin beside Twin Lakes to which the family came eagerly each summer . . . the autumn colors of the shrubs and trees beside Highway 95 changing with the miles between Moscow and New Meadows, and the quixotic loop in the highway circumnavigating a rancher's corral . . . gorgeous wild flowers, so fragile but so brave as they push upward in the harsh desert lands of the Owyhee Country . . . Riverman Kyle McGrady looking completely relaxed as he piloted his boat through the tortuous rapids of awesome Hells Canyon . . . aged Indians at Fort Hall staring stoically at the blazing sun as they shuffled through the motions of the sundance—with some younger dancers wisely wearing sunglasses . . . the view from a sage-covered plateau of the deep, green valley which provides a just-right setting for the unhurried pace of life in the town of Fairfield . . . or the view out of Victor of the spiraling magnificence of the Grand Tetons that causes the driver of many a car to put on the brakes, to look, and to become for precious moments one with the wonders of nature.

Most important of all are the memories of the people . . . such friendly people . . . people who make this writer hope that Idaho's motto really means what it says . . . "Esto Perpetua"—"It Is Forever."

# BIBLIOGRAPHY

Books

Abdill, George B., *Pails West,* New York.

————————, *This was Railroading,* Seattle, 1958.

American Heritage Editors, *The Great West,* New York.

Andrews, Ralph W., *Glory Days of Logging,* New York, 1956.

Athearn, Robert G., *Union Pacific Country,* New York, 1971.

Bailey, Robert G., *River of No Return,* Lewiston, 1947.

Bankson, Russell A., and Harrison, Lester S., *Beneath These Mountains,* New York, 1966.

Barber, Floyd R., and Martin, Dan W., *Idaho in the Pacific Northwest,* Caldwell, 1961.

Barsness, Larry, *Gold Camp,* New York, 1962.

Beal, Merrill D., *Intermountain Railroads—Standard and Narrow Gauge,* Caldwell, 1962.

————————, and Wells, Merle William, *History of Idaho,* Vols. I, II and III, New York, 1959.

Becher, Edmund T., *History, Government and Resources of the Spokane Area,* Spokane, 1965.

Bird, Annie Laurie, *Boise—The Peace Valley,* Caldwell, 1934.

Bond, Towland, *The Original Northwesterner, David Thompson, and the Native Tribes of North America,* Spokane, 1970.

Brooks, Juanita, *The History of Jews in Utah and Idaho,* Salt Lake City, 1973.

Brosnan, C. J., *History of the State of Idaho,* New York, 1918.

Cenarrusa, Pete T., Editor, *Idaho Blue Book,* 1973.

Chittenden, Hiram Martin, *History of the American Fur Trade of the Far West,* Vols. I and II, Stanford, California, 1954.

d'Easum, Dick, *Fragments of Villainy,* Boise, 1959.

Defenbach, Byron, *Idaho—The Place and Its People, Vol. I,* New York, 1933.

————————, *Red Heroines of the Northwest,* Caldwell, 1929.

DeVoto, Bernard, *The Journals of Lewis and Clark,* Boston, 1953.

Dimsdale, Thomas J., *The Vigilantes of Montana,* Butte, 1945.

Donaldson, Thomas, *Idaho of Yesterday,* Caldwell, 1941.

Drago, Harry Sinclair, *Lost Bonanzas,* New York, 1966.

Driggs, Howard R., *The Old West Speaks,* Englewood Cliffs, N.J., 1956.

Driscoll, Ann Nilsson, *They Came to a Ridge,* Moscow, 1970.

Dryden, Cecil, *The Clearwater of Idaho,* New York, 1972.

Eide, Ingvard Henry, *Oregon Trail,* New York, 1973.

Elsensohn, Sister M. Alfreda, *Idaho Chinese Lore,* Caldwell, 1970.

————————, *Pioneer Days in Idaho Country, Volume One,* Caldwell, 1947.

Federal Writers Project, American Guide Series, *Arizona,* New York, 1940.

_____, *Idaho,* New York, 1937.

_____, *Montana,* New York, 1939.

_____, *Washington,* Portland, 1939.

_____, *Wyoming,* New York, 1941.

_____, *Idaho Lore,* Caldwell, 1939.

Fisher, Vardis and Holmes, Opal Laurel, *Gold Rushes and Mining Camps of the Early American West,* Caldwell, 1968.

Frederick, J. V., *Ben Holladay—The Stagecoach King,* Glendale, California, 1940.

Gallop, Rodney, *A Book of the Basques,* Reno.

Greever, William S., *The Bonanza West,* Norman, Oklahoma, 1963.

Grodinsky, Julius, *Transcontinental Railway Strategy—1869-1893,* Philadelphia, 1962.

Grover, David H., *Debaters and Dynamiters,* Corvallis, 1964.

_____, *Diamondfield Jack,* Reno, 1968.

Hafen, LeRoy R., *The Mountain Men and the Fur Trade of the Far West,* Vols. II, IV and V, Glendale, California, 1968.

_____, *The Overland Mail,* Cleveland, 1926.

Hailey, John, *The History of Idaho,* Boise, 1910.

Hanley, Mike, with Lucia, Ellis, *Owyhee Trails,* Caldwell, 1973.

Hawgood, John A., *America's Western Frontiers,* New York, 1967.

Hedges, James Blaine, *Henry Villard and the Railways of the Northwest,* New Haven, Connecticut, 1930.

Hidy, Ralph W., Hill, Frank Ernest, and Nevins, Allan, *Timber and Men,* New York, 1963.

Holbrook, Stewart H., *Burning an Empire,* New York, 1943.

_____, *Holy Old Mackinaw,* New York, 1938.

_____, *The Rocky Mountain Revolution,* New York, 1956.

_____, *The Story of American Railroads,* New York, 1947.

_____, *The Wonderful West,* New York, 1963.

Howard, Helen Addison, *Northwest Trail Blazers,* Caldwell, 1963.

Howard, Helen Addison, and McGrath, Dan L., *War Chief Joseph,* Caldwell, 1958.

Howard, Joseph Kinsey, *Montana—High, Wide, and Handsome,* New Haven, Connecticut, 1945.

Howard, Robert West, *The Great Iron Trail,* New York, 1962.

Hult, Ruby El, *Steamboats in the Timber,* Caldwell, 1953.

Idaho Department of Commerce and Development, *The Idaho Alamanac,* 1963.

Irving, Washington, *The Adventures of Captain Bonneville,* Portland.

Johansen, Dorothy O., and Gates, Charles M., *Empire of the Columbia,* New York, 1957.

Johnson, Jalmar, *Builders of the Northwest,* New York, 1963.

Jordan, Grace Edgington, Editor, *Idaho Reader,* Boise, 1963.

—————————————, *Home Below Hell's Canyon,* New York, 1954.

—————————————, *The King's Pines of Idaho,* Portland, 1961.

Josephy, Alvin M., Jr., *The Nez Perce Indians and the Opening of the Northwest,* New Haven, Connecticut, 1965.

Karolevitz, Robert F., *Doctors of the Old West,* Seattle, 1967.

Lavender, David, *Land of Giants,* New York, 1958.

—————————————, *The Big Divide,* New York, 1948.

—————————————, *The Rockies,* New York, 1968.

—————————————, *Westward Vision,* New York, 1963.

Lucia, Ellis, Editor, *This Land Around Us,* New York, 1969.

Madsen, Brigham D., *The Bannock of Idaho,* Caldwell, 1958.

Magnuson, Richard G., *Coeur d'Alene Diary,* Portland, 1968.

Mahoney, Tom, *The Story of George Romney,* New York, 1960.

Miller, John B., *The Trees Grew Tall.*

Morrison, Ann, *Those Were the Days,* Boise, 1951.

Nations, Paul D., *River Tamers,* Boise, 1947.

Oliphant, J. Orin, *On the Cattle Ranges of the Oregon Country,* Seattle, 1968.

Payette, B. C., *The Mullan Road,* Montreal, Canada, 1968.

Phillips, Paul Chrisler, *The Fur Trade,* Vols. I and II, Norman, Oklahoma, 1961.

Potomac Corral of the Westerners, *Great Western Indian Fights,* Lincoln, Nebraska, 1960.

Poulsen, Ezra J., *Joseph C. Rich—Versatile Pioneer on the Mormon Frontier,* Salt Lake City, 1958.

Pyle, Ernie, *Home Country,* New York, 1947.

Riach, George, *Thirty-five Years of Sheepherding,* New York, 1964.

Ricks, Joel E., Editor, *The History of a Valley,* Logan, Utah, 1956.

Robertson, Frank C., *A Ram in the Thicket,* New York, 1950.

—————————————, *Fort Hall,* New York, 1963.

Rollinson, John K., *Wyoming Cattle Trails,* Caldwell, 1948.

Ross, Alexander, *The Fur Hunters of the Far West,* Edited by Kenneth A. Spaulding, Norman, Oklahoma, 1956.

Salisbury, Albert and Jane, *Here Rolled the Covered Wagons,* Seattle, 1948.

Scott, Orland A., *Pioneer Days on the Shadowy St. Joe,* Coeur d'Alene.

Shirk, David L., as edited by Martin F. Schmitt, *The Cattle Drives of David Shirk,* Portland, 1956.

Spencer, Betty Goodwin, *The Big Blowup,* Caldwell, 1956.

Stone, Irving, *Men to Match My Mountains,* New York, 1956.

Strong, Clarence C., and Webb, Clyde S., *King of Many Waters,* Missoula, Montana, 1970.

Thorp, Jack, as told to Neil McCullough Clark, *Pardner of the Wind,* Caldwell, 1945.

Timmen, Fritz, *Blow for the Landing,* Caldwell, 1973.

Tobie, Harvey E., *No Man Like Joe,* Portland, 1949.

Twain, Mark, *The Complete Travel Books of Mark Twain,* New York, 1966.

Waters, Frank, *The Earp Brothers of Tombstone,* New York, 1960.

Wentworth, Edward Norris, *America's Sheep Trails,* Ames, Iowa, 1948.

Winther, Oscar O., *The Transportation Frontier,* New York, 1964.

Wolle, Muriel Sibell, *The Bonanza Trail,* Bloomington, Indiana, 1958.

Yarber, Esther, *Land of the Yankee Fork,* Denver, 1963.

Documents

Annals of Wyoming, Vol. 45, No. 2, Fall, 1973, published by the Wyoming State Archives and Historical Department.

Brown, Colonel W. C., *The Sheepeater Campaign,* Idaho County Free Press, Grangeville.

Cosho, Maude, *Idaho Territory: Its Origin, Its Governors and Its Problems,* Master's Thesis, University of Idaho, 1951.

Day, Henry L., *Mining Highlights of the Coeur d'Alene District,* speech given on July 18, 1963.

Dubois, Fred T., *The Making of a State,* document in the possession of Maude Cosho, Boise.

Eiguren, Joe V., *The Basque History,* Boise.

Fereday, Lynne, *The Basques,* Boise.

Flamm, George R., *History of Fort Boise,* Boise.

Gray, Margery P., *A Population and Family Study of Basques Living in Shoshone and Boise, Idaho,* Doctoral Thesis, University of Oregon, 1955.

Idaho Historical Society, *A Short History of Idaho,* Boise, 1974.

_____, *Idaho Yesterdays,* Vols. I, II, III and IV, Boise, 1957-60.

Idaho State University, *The Idaho Heritage,* Pocatello, 1974.

Idaho Statistical Reporting Service, *1973 Idaho Agricultural Statistics,* Boise.

Kester, Frank J., *Beginnings of Masonry in Idaho,* speech given on September 14, 1953.

MacDonald, Eileen Hubbell, *A Study of Chinese Migrants in Certain Idaho Settlements and of Selected Families in Transition,* Master's Thesis, University of Idaho, 1966.

Masonic Report, *Idaho Grand Lodge of 1885,* Davenport, Iowa, 1885.

Mullan, Capt. John, *Report on the Construction of a Military Road from Walla Walla to Fort Benton,* Washington, D.C., 1863.

Pierce, E. D., *Reminiscences,* Edited by Ralph Burcham, Jr., Washington State University, 1957.

Robison, Kenneth Leonard, *Idaho Territorial Newspapers,* Master's Thesis, University of Oregon, 1966.

Spokane Corral of the Westerners, *The Pacific Northwesterner,* Vols. 16 and 17, 1972-73.

Strahorn, Robert E., *The Resources and Attractions of Idaho Territory,* Boise, 1881.

Trull, Fern Cable, *The History of the Chinese in Idaho from 1864 to 1910,* Master's Thesis, University of Oregon, 1946.

*Washington Historical Quarterly,* V, October, 1914.

Wells, Merle W., *Gold Camps and Silver Cities,* Bulletin 22, Idaho Bureau of Mines and Geology, Moscow.

*Western Folklore,* Vol. XXIV, No. 4, October, 1965, University of California Press, Berkeley.

Encyclopedias

*Collier's Encyclopedia,* New York, 1972.

*Compton's Encyclopedia,* Chicago, 1971.

*Encyclopaedia Britannica,* Chicago, 1969.

*Encyclopedia International,* Chicago, 1968.

*The World Book Encyclopedia,* Chicago, 1971.

Newspapers

*Albion Times*

*Boise Capital News*

*Caldwell Tribune*

*Chicago Weekly Drovers Journal*

*Fort Benton* (Montana) *Record*

*Idaho County Free Press,* Grangeville

*Idaho Daily Statesman*

*Idaho Falls Post-Register*

*Idahonian,* Moscow

*Idaho State Journal,* Pocatello

*Idaho World,* Boise

*Ketchum Keystone*

*Lewiston Morning Tribune*

*Murray Nugget*

*Owyhee Avalanche*

*Portland Oregonian*

*Sandpoint News-Bulletin*

*Spokesman-Review,* Spokane

*St. Paul* (Minnesota) *Pioneer Press*

*Wood River Times,* Hailey

Magazines

*Collier's*

*Ford Times*

*Holiday*

*Outlook*

*Popular Mechanics*

*Saturday Evening Post*

*Travel*

# APPENDIX

## IDAHO HISTORY IN BRIEF THROUGH THE YEARS

1805   Lewis and Clark discovered Idaho at Lemhi Pass and crossed North Idaho over the Lolo trail.

1806   Lewis and Clark spent more than six weeks with the Nez Perce Indians around Kamiah before returning eastward across the Lolo trail.

1808   David Thompson commenced the Idaho fur trade near Bonner's Ferry.

1809   David Thompson built Idaho's earliest fur trading post—Kullyspell House—on Lake Pend Oreille for the North West Company.

1810   Andrew Henry built a winter fur trading post near later Saint Anthony. This was the earliest American fort in the Pacific Northwest.

1811   A Pacific Fur Company expedition—the Astorians—explored the Valley of the Snake on their way west to the Columbia.

1812   Donald Mackenzie established a winter fur trading post at Lewiston for the Astorians.

1813   John Reid started a fur trading post on the lower Boise, but some Bannock Indians wiped it out early in 1814.

1818   Donald Mackenzie explored southern Idaho with his Snake expedition of trappers who continued to hunt beaver in the Snake country for 24 years.

1824   Alexander Ross led the Snake expedition in exploring much of the upper Salmon country, where Jedediah Smith joined him with a band of American trappers. Rivalry between British and American fur hunters continued in Idaho for 14 years.

1832   The great Rocky mountain fur trade rendezvous was held at Pierre's Hole (now known as Teton valley) in July.

1834   Fort Hall and Fort Boise were established as Snake River fur trading centers, but they became important as outposts on the Oregon trail.

1836   Henry Harmon Spalding founded his Nez Perce Indian mission at Lapwai.

1839   Spalding started publishing the Bible in Nez Perce on the earliest printing press in the Pacific Northwest.

1842   The Jesuit Coeur d'Alene Mission of the Sacred Heart was started near Saint Maries. Moved to a site near what now is Cataldo in 1846 (where the old mission church still stands), it now continues at Desmet, where the mission was transferred in 1877.

1846   Idaho, which later became a territory, became part of the United States by a treaty dividing the old Oregon Country with Great Britain.

1849   Over 20,000 emigrants who joined the gold rush came through southeastern Idaho on the California Trail. Heavy traffic on the trail continued for many years.

1854   The Ward Massacre in Boise Valley on the Oregon Trail led to the closing of Fort Boise the next summer and Fort Hall in 1856.

1855   Mormons from Utah established an Indian mission at Fort Lemhi southeast of Salmon, but they had to abandon the site in 1858.

1860    Idaho's oldest town, Franklin, was founded just north of the Utah border, April 14. Gold discoveries at Pierce, September 30, led to the founding of Pierce early in December and to the gold rush in 1861 and 1862.

1861    Lewiston was established as a service community for the Idaho mines, May 13.

1862    Idaho's earliest newspaper, the *Golden Age,* was started at Lewiston, August 2. Boise Basin gold discoveries, August 2, led to the founding of Idaho City and other important mining camps in the basin, October 7.

1863    Idaho territory was established by an act of Congress signed by President Abraham Lincoln on March 4. Idaho was organized at Lewiston by Governor William H. Wallace, July 10.

1864    Boise became permanent capital of Idaho, December 24.

1866    Telegraph service commenced through southeastern Idaho.

1869    Completion of the transcontinental railway at Promontory Summit, Utah, May 10, brought greatly improved transportation to Idaho.

1874    Rail service reached Idaho with completion of the Utah Northern to Franklin, May 30. The line was extended north to Montana by 1880. On October 11, Idaho's first daily newspaper—the *Owyhee Daily Avalanche*—was issued at Silver City.

1877    The Nez Perce War broke out in north Idaho in June, with fighting continuing into October in Montana during Chief Joseph's famous retreat.

1878    The Bannock War was started in southern Idaho and moved on into Oregon and back in a summer-long campaign.

1880    With discovery of lead-silver lodes around Ketchum, Bellevue, and Hailey, the rush to Wood River transformed south-central Idaho.

1882    Construction of the Northern Pacific across North Idaho; commencement of the Oregon Short Line across southern Idaho brought rail service to all parts of the territory.

1883    Telephone service in Idaho commenced at Hailey.

1884    The Coeur d'Alene stampede, followed by important lead-silver discoveries later in the year, got Idaho's major mining district going in a big way.

1886    Construction of the Idaho territorial capitol was completed.

1887    Hailey's electric light plant went into operation, May 19.

1889    In its last session, the territorial legislature located the University of Idaho at Moscow, where it opened in 1892.

1890    Idaho was admitted to the union as a state, July 3.

1891    Boise's electric street railway commenced operation, August 22. The College of Idaho opened in Caldwell, October 9.

1892    All of the important Coeur d'Alene mines shut down because of freight rates and low silver prices, January 16. The Farmers Alliance and the Knights of Labor organized the Idaho Populist Party in Boise, May 26. Martial law commenced in the Coeur d'Alene mines July 14, after the dynamiting of an abandoned mill at Gem. The University of Idaho opened in Moscow, October 3.

1893    The office of state mine inspector was established March 6. The Idaho

State Medical Society organized in Boise, September 12. The state wool growers association started at Mountain Home, September 25.

1894    Albion Normal School opened January 8.

1895    The Idaho Irrigation district act was approved, March 9.

1896    Lewiston Normal was dedicated, June 3.

1897    President Cleveland established the Bitterroot Forest Reserve, including much of North Idaho, February 22.

1898    Idaho Spanish-American War Volunteers left for the Philippines, May 19.

1899    The Coeur d'Alene mine labor war erupted again with the dynamiting of the Bunker Hill & Sullivan concentrator at Wardner, April 29.

1900    The Idaho State Dairymen's Association organized, March 6. The new York Canal, completed June 22, expanded irrigation greatly in Boise valley.

1901    The Academy of Idaho (now Idaho State University) was established in Pocatello. The Idaho State Library was established.

1902    After concluding that Diamondfield Jack Davis had been convicted by mistake, in a case growing out of the most notable incident in the Idaho sheep and cattle wars, the State Board of Pardons turned him loose.

1903    Idaho's hunting and fishing licensing system began.

1904    With the beginning of irrigation in the Twin Falls country, the city of Twin Falls was started.

1905    Former Governor Frank Steunenberg was assassinated, December 30.

1906    One of the nation's large sawmills was built at Potlatch.

1907    William E. Borah was elected to the United States Senate, where he gained an international reputation during thirty-three years of service. William D. Haywood, charged with conspiracy and the assassination of Frank Steunenberg, was found not guilty at the end of an internationally celebrated trial.

1908    The Idaho revised code was published.

1909    Idaho adopted the direct primary and local option. Minidoka Dam was completed.

1910    Idaho's worst forest fire burned over a large tract in the northern part of the state.

1912    Constitutional amendments were adopted authorizing the initiative, referendum, and recall, and the establishing of a state board of education to supervise all levels of education.

1913    The Idaho State Public Utilities Commission was established. Northwest Nazarene College in Nampa and Gooding College were both established.

1915    Arrowrock Dam was completed. Columbia and Snake River improvements for navigation to Lewiston were completed.

1916    Prohibition went into effect statewide in Idaho. A state highway program began as part of the national good roads movement.

1917    Workman's compensation system and the state insurance fund were established. Ricks Academy became a college and was accredited by the state board of education.

1918 Because of the success of the Non-partisan League taking over the Idaho Democratic primary, September 3, Idaho's primary nomination system for state offices was abandoned for twelve years.

1919 State administrative consolidation was enacted by the legislature. Boise's Music Week began.

1920 Whitebird hill grade, connecting north and south Idaho was opened. The State Capitol was completed. A constitutional amendment providing for five justices of the Supreme Court was adopted.

1922 A state budget system was established. Radio broadcasting began in Idaho.

1924 Craters of the Moon National Monument was established. Black Canyon Dam was completed.

1925 The State Forestry Board was established.

1926 Commercially contracted airmail service began in Idaho. The state chamber of commerce organized.

1927 American Falls Dam was completed.

1928 Commercial radio broadcasting began in Idaho.

1931 The direct primary was restored for state offices, and a state income tax was imposed. A large primitive area was established in the mountains of central Idaho.

1932 Idaho judges were elected on a non-partisan ticket. The annotated Idaho code was published. Boise Junior College was established.

1933 The state school equalization law was adopted. North Idaho Junior College was established in Coeur d'Alene.

1935 Statewide prohibition was repealed, and a state liquor dispensary system was adopted. A state employment service was established. A sales tax was established, but failed in a referendum in 1936.

1936 Sun Valley was established as a ski resort by the Union Pacific.

1937 An open primary election system was adopted.

1938 Paving of the north and south highway finally was completed. A state fish and game commission was established by initiative of the voters.

1939 A state junior college district law was enacted.

1940 Senator William E. Borah died, January 19.

1941 Gowen Field was completed and became a military air base.

1942 Farragut Naval training station was established on Lake Pend Oreille, a Pocatello army air base and a Pocatello gun relining plant were established, and a Japanese relocation center was built at Hunt.

1943 Mountain Home Airbase was opened.

1945 The State Tax commission was established.

1946 The most recent Idaho code was published. A teachers retirement system was established, and a report on public education in Idaho was prepared. Election of Idaho's governor and other state officers for four-year terms began.

1947 A state school reorganization plan was enacted, and Idaho State College at Pocatello became a four-year institution. The Idaho State Archives were established.

| 1948 | Columbia river floods, which followed heavy flooding in Idaho's rivers, led to a Bureau of Reclamation plan to construct a high Hell's Canyon dam in Snake river for flood control. |
|---|---|
| 1949 | The National Reactor Testing Station near Arco was established. |
| 1950 | The State Highway Department was established, with provision for non-political administration. |
| 1951 | Nuclear Electric Power generation was developed at the National Reactor Testing station. |
| 1952 | Anderson Ranch Dam and Cabinet Gorge Dam were completed. |
| 1953 | Television broadcasting commenced in Idaho. |
| 1954 | A submarine reactor was perfected and tested at the National Reactor Testing Station. |
| 1955 | The State Department of Commerce and Development was established. |
| 1956 | Construction of Palisades dam was completed. Construction in Idaho of the national interstate highway system was commenced. |
| 1958 | The Boise Stanley Highway Association was organized. |
| 1959 | Brownlee Dam was completed on Snake River. |
| 1960 | A state employee group insurance system was established. |
| 1961 | Oxbow Dam was completed on Snake River. W. A. Harriman and E. Rolland Harriman provided that their holdings at Railroad Ranch eventually would become a state park, providing that the state established a professionally managed park system. |
| 1962 | The Lewis and Clark highway up Lochsa canyon was completed. |
| 1963 | The legislative council was established. |
| 1964 | A combined convention and primary system was tried. State parties assemblies restricted the number of state primary candidates who could appear on the ballot. |
| 1965 | A state sales tax was adopted. A state parks department and a state water resource board and a state personnel system were created. Nez Perce National Historic Park was established in North Idaho. |
| 1966 | Jet scheduled air service began. |
| 1967 | The legislative compensation commission was established. An international Boy Scouts Jamboree was held at Farragut State Park. |
| 1968 | Hell's Canyon Dam was completed on Snake River. |
| 1969 | Annual legislative sessions commenced. |
| 1970 | A complete revision of the Idaho constitution was rejected by the voters. |
| 1971 | Idaho returned to the open primary system, and the major political parties were released from previous provisions in the primary and convention laws regulating their systems for choosing delegates to the national conventions. |
| 1972 | A new Idaho uniform criminal code went into effect. |

Source: *Idaho Blue Book,* 1973-1974.

# INDEX

264

## ABOUT THE AUTHOR

Rafe Gibbs knows Idaho—has lived in it and has written about it for 34 years.

His writing career began at the age of 13 when his first short story was published in *Action Stories* magazine. Since then he has produced three books, and hundreds of articles and fiction stories for such varied publications as *Family Weekly, Esquire, Nation's Business, International Encyclopedia,* and *Houghton Mifflin Readers.*

Gibbs was graduated from the University of Idaho in 1934 with highest honors and a Phi Beta Kappa key. Later, he served for 25 years as Director of Information and Publications at the university, and wrote its history, *Beacon for Mountain and Plain.* He has also served on the editorial staff of *The Milwaukee Journal* in Wisconsin, in the Air Force during World War II, rising to the rank of colonel, and at Florida International University in Miami where he was Assistant Dean of University Relations and Development. With the recent publication of his book on the Florida institution, *Visibility Unlimited,* he became the only author of the histories of two state universities. He now does full-time, free-lance writing at Cape Canaveral, Florida—and some spare-time fishing.